Contents

Le Chevalier d'Eon

Volume 2

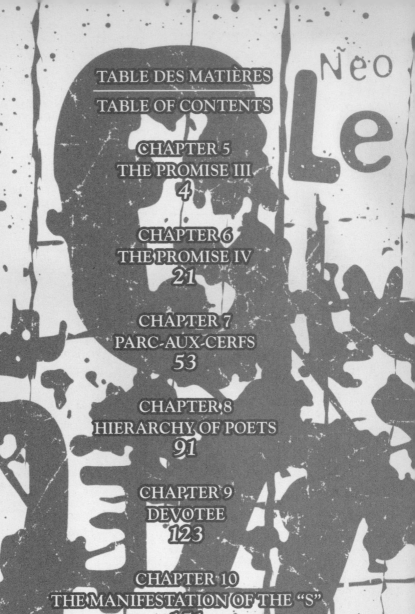

TABLE DES MATIÈRES
TABLE OF CONTENTS

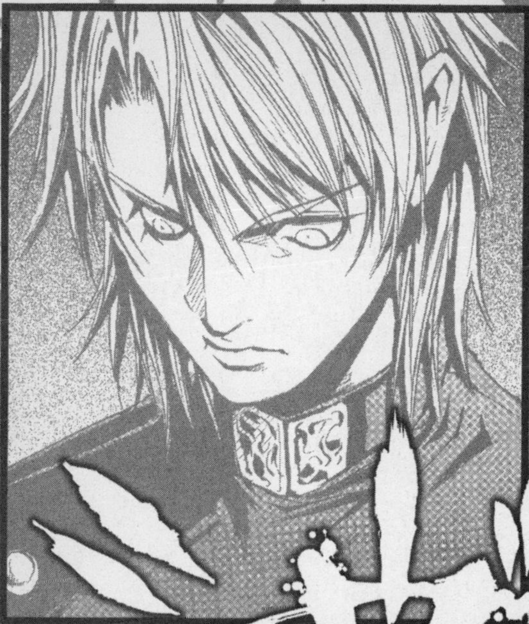

SUMMARY OF VOLUME 1

ON THE BANK OF THE FALAILLE RIVER, A BODY IS DISCOVERED, WITH THE WORDS "PLEASE FORGIVE ME" SEARED ON ITS FACE. THE CHEVALIER SPHINX SETS OUT TO DESTROY THE NEW POET RESPONSIBLE FOR THIS MURDER, ONLY TO FIND PAUL, A BAKER'S APPRENTICE. PAUL HAS NOT FULLY AWAKENED TO HIS POWERS AS A DEADLY "POET," SO THE SPHINX SPARES HIM. D'EON IS NOT CERTAIN HE AGREES WITH THE SPHINX'S ACTIONS BUT STEELS HIMSELF FOR ACTION AFTER KING LOUIS TELLS HIM, "THE CELLS OF BASTILLE WILL ANSWER FOR YOU, D'EON."

Le Chevalier d'Eon

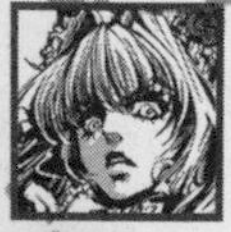

SPHINX (LIA)

WHEN LIA DESCENDS INTO HER BROTHER'S BODY, SHE BECOMES THE SPHINX, HUNTER OF MURDEROUS POETS.

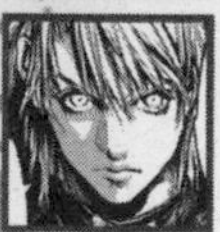

D'EON

HE IS A MEMBER OF KING LOUIS'S SECRET POLICE (KNOWN AS LE SECRET DU ROI), AS WELL AS AN OFFICER FOR THE PARIS POLICE.

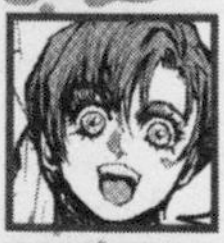

ROBIN

HE IS D'EON'S LOYAL ATTENDANT. ROBIN IS VERY BLUNT AND SHOWERS HIS MASTER WITH TOUGH WORDS AND LOVE.

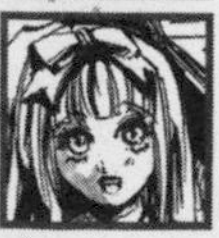

SOPHIE

THE DAUGHTER OF KING LOUIS XV. THE VERSES OF THE POETS' DEADLY PSALMS MYSTERIOUSLY APPEAR ON HER BODY, AND HER VOCABULARY HAS BEEN REDUCED TO A SINGLE WORD, "PALM."

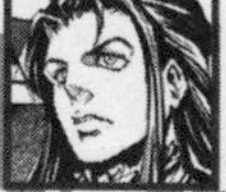

LOUIS XV

GRANDSON OF LOUIS XIV, WHO WAS ALSO KNOWN AS THE SUN KING. LOUIS XIV BELIEVED IN ABSOLUTE MONARCHY AND RULED ACCORDINGLY DURING HIS REIGN.

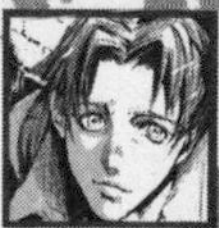

PAUL

A BAKER'S APPRENTICE. HE VERY SUDDENLY LEARNED TO READ AND WRITE.

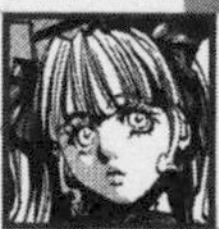

CÉCILE

SHE LIVES IN THE FALAILLE DISTRICT AND SELLS FLOWERS. PAUL IS SECRETLY IN LOVE WITH HER.

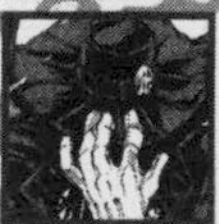

ROBLE

A MYSTERIOUS FIGURE WHO SERVES AS THE SHADOW AND MENTOR OF POETS.

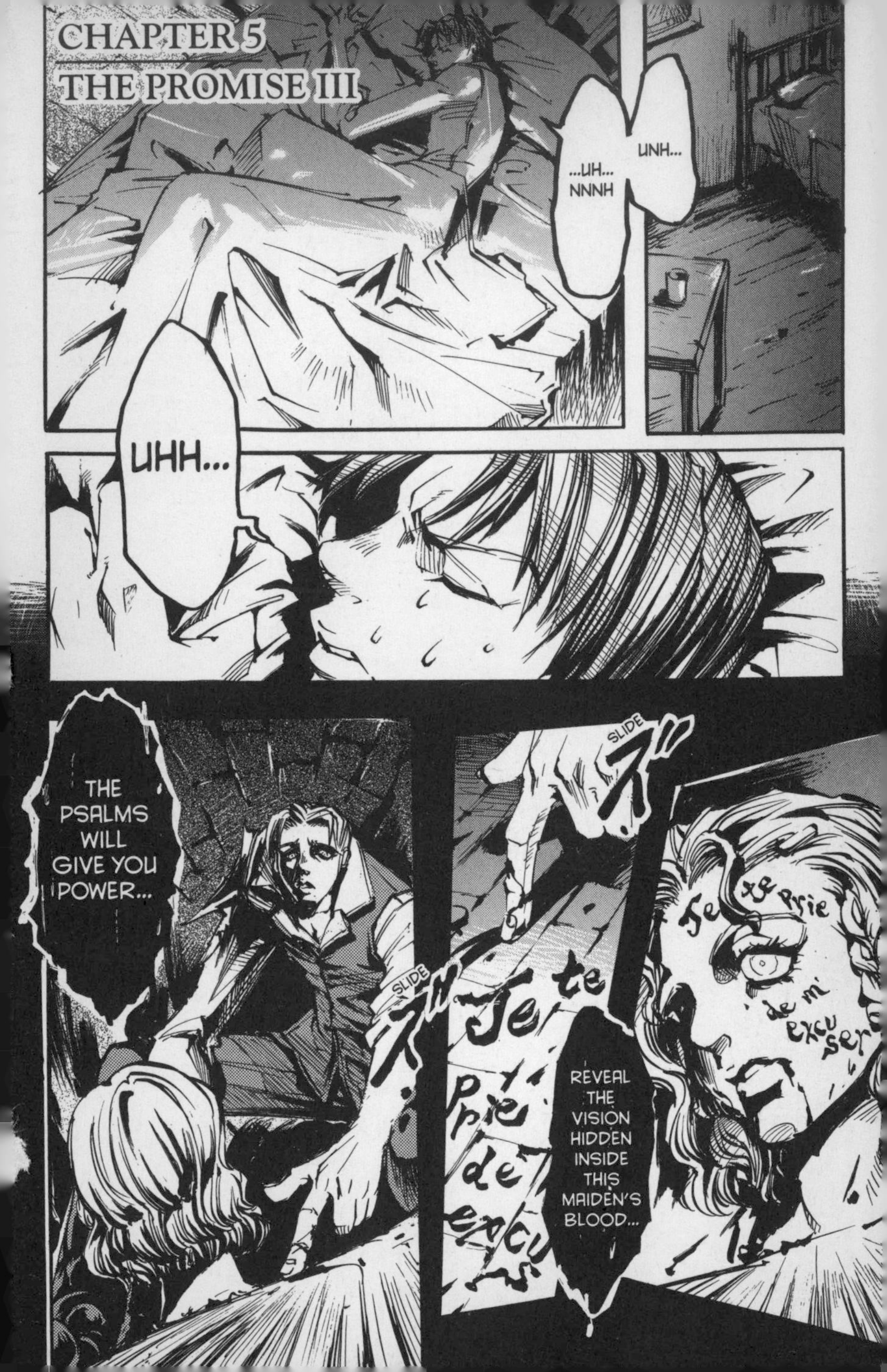
CHAPTER 5
THE PROMISE III
UNH...
...UH... NNNH
UHH...
SLIDE
Je te prie de m'excuser
SLIDE
REVEAL THE VISION HIDDEN INSIDE THIS MAIDEN'S BLOOD...
THE PSALMS WILL GIVE YOU POWER...

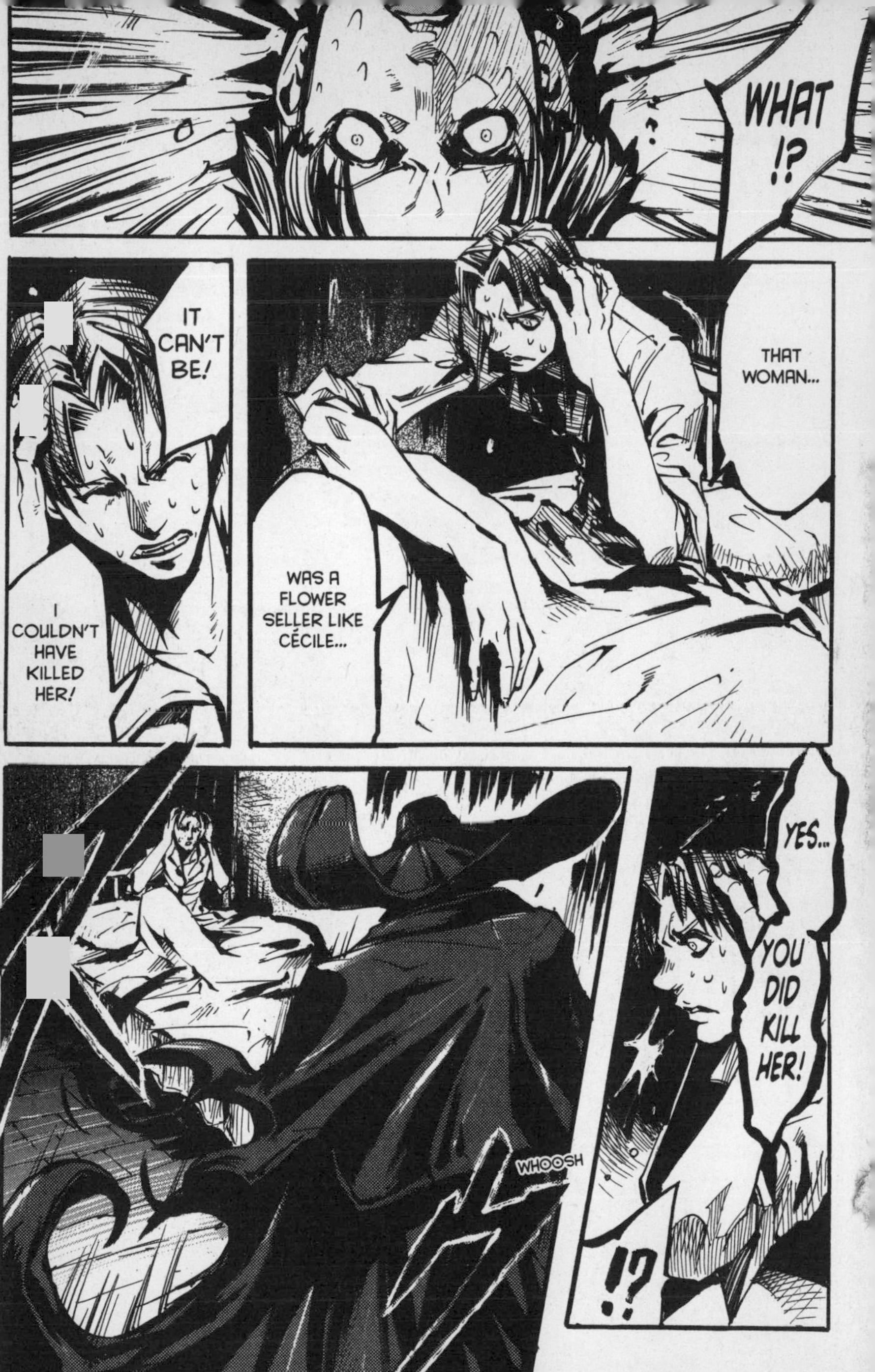
WHAT!?
THAT WOMAN...
WAS A FLOWER SELLER LIKE CÉCILE...
IT CAN'T BE!
I COULDN'T HAVE KILLED HER!
YES...
YOU DID KILL HER!
!?
WHOOSH

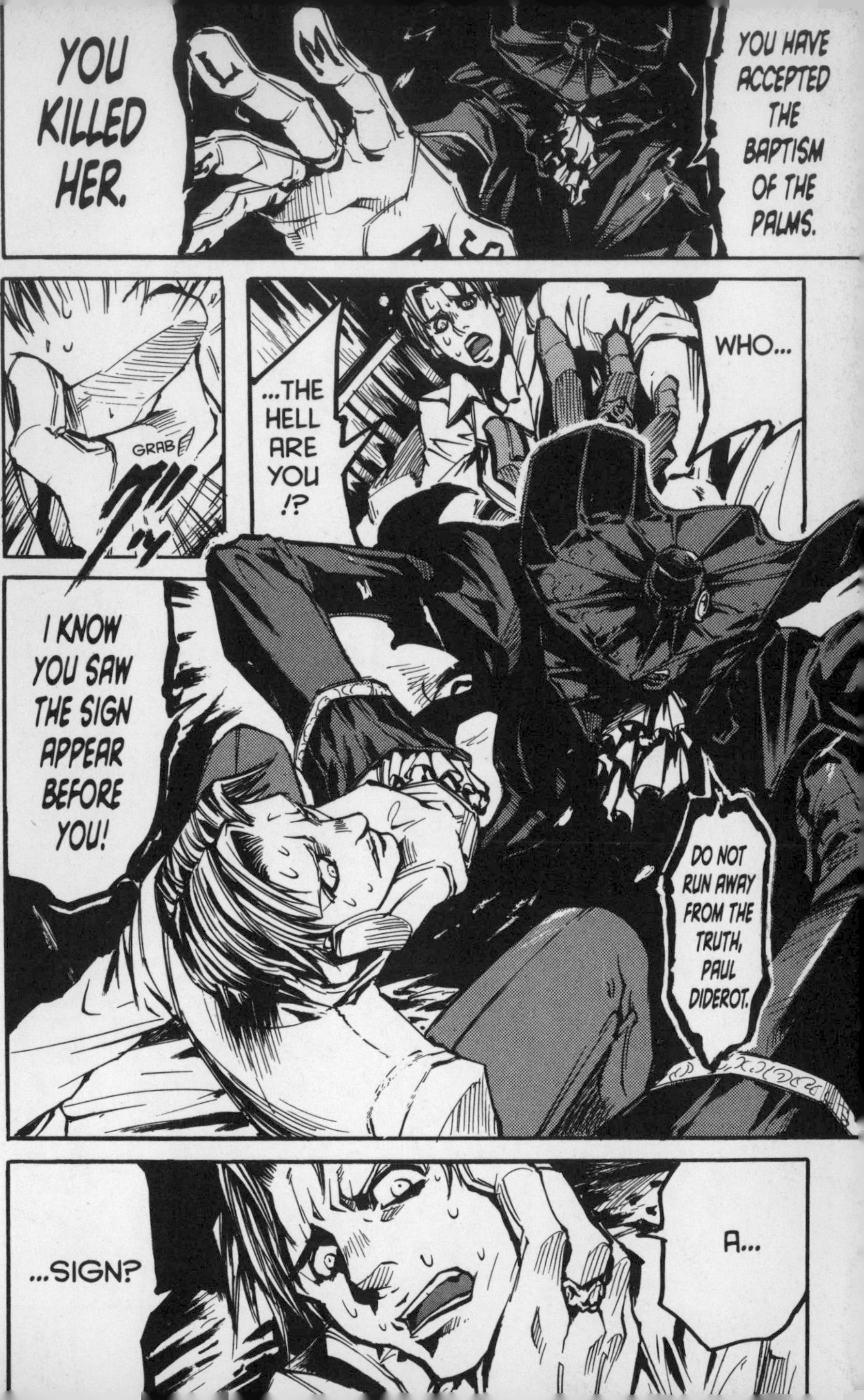
YOU HAVE ACCEPTED THE BAPTISM OF THE PALMS.
YOU KILLED HER.
WHO...
...THE HELL ARE YOU !?
GRAB
DO NOT RUN AWAY FROM THE TRUTH, PAUL DIDEROT.
I KNOW YOU SAW THE SIGN APPEAR BEFORE YOU!
A...
...SIGN?

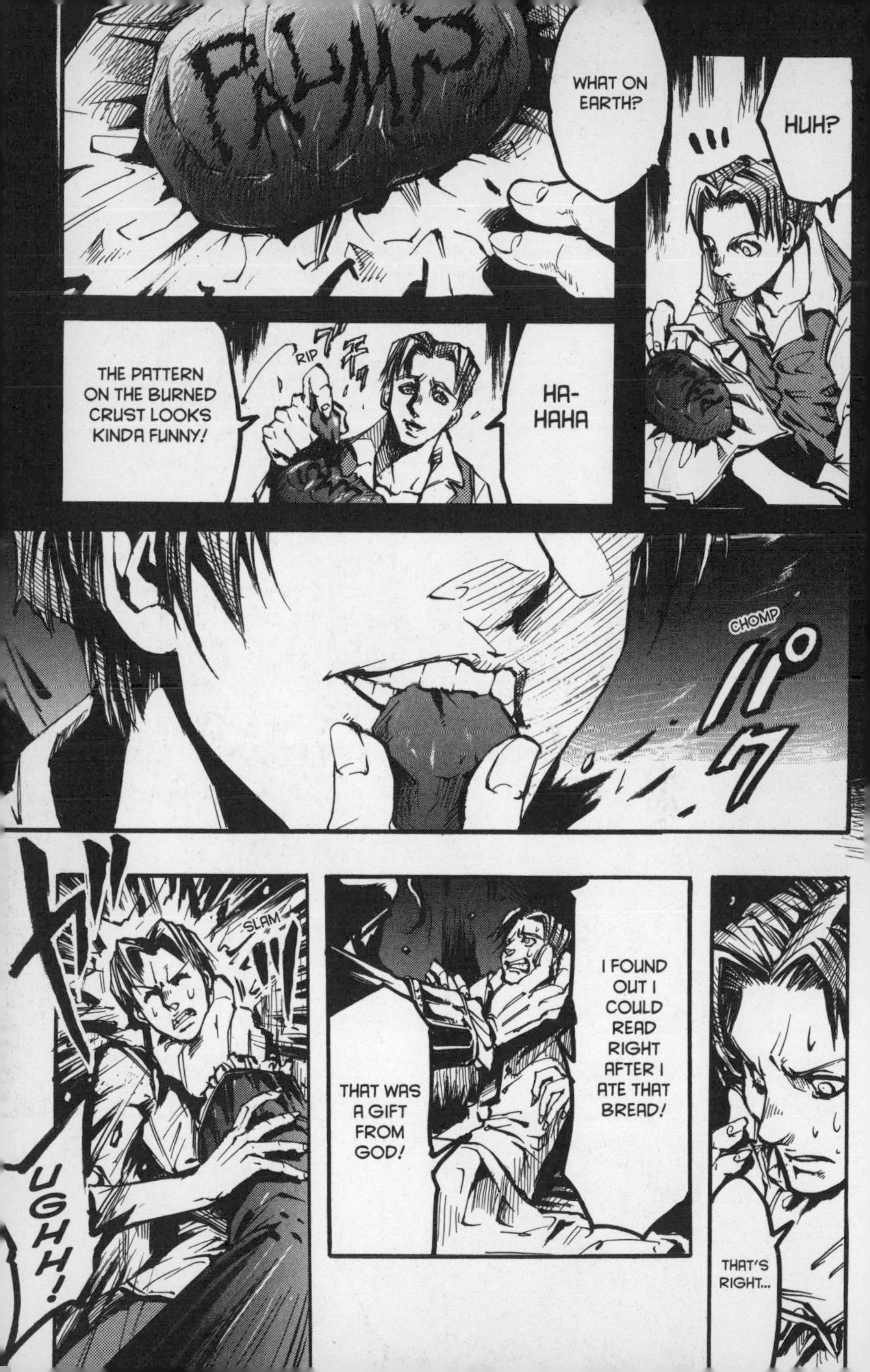
HUH?
WHAT ON EARTH?
PALMP
HA-HAHA
RIP
THE PATTERN ON THE BURNED CRUST LOOKS KINDA FUNNY!
CHOMP
THAT'S RIGHT...
I FOUND OUT I COULD READ RIGHT AFTER I ATE THAT BREAD!
THAT WAS A GIFT FROM GOD!
SLAM
UGHH!

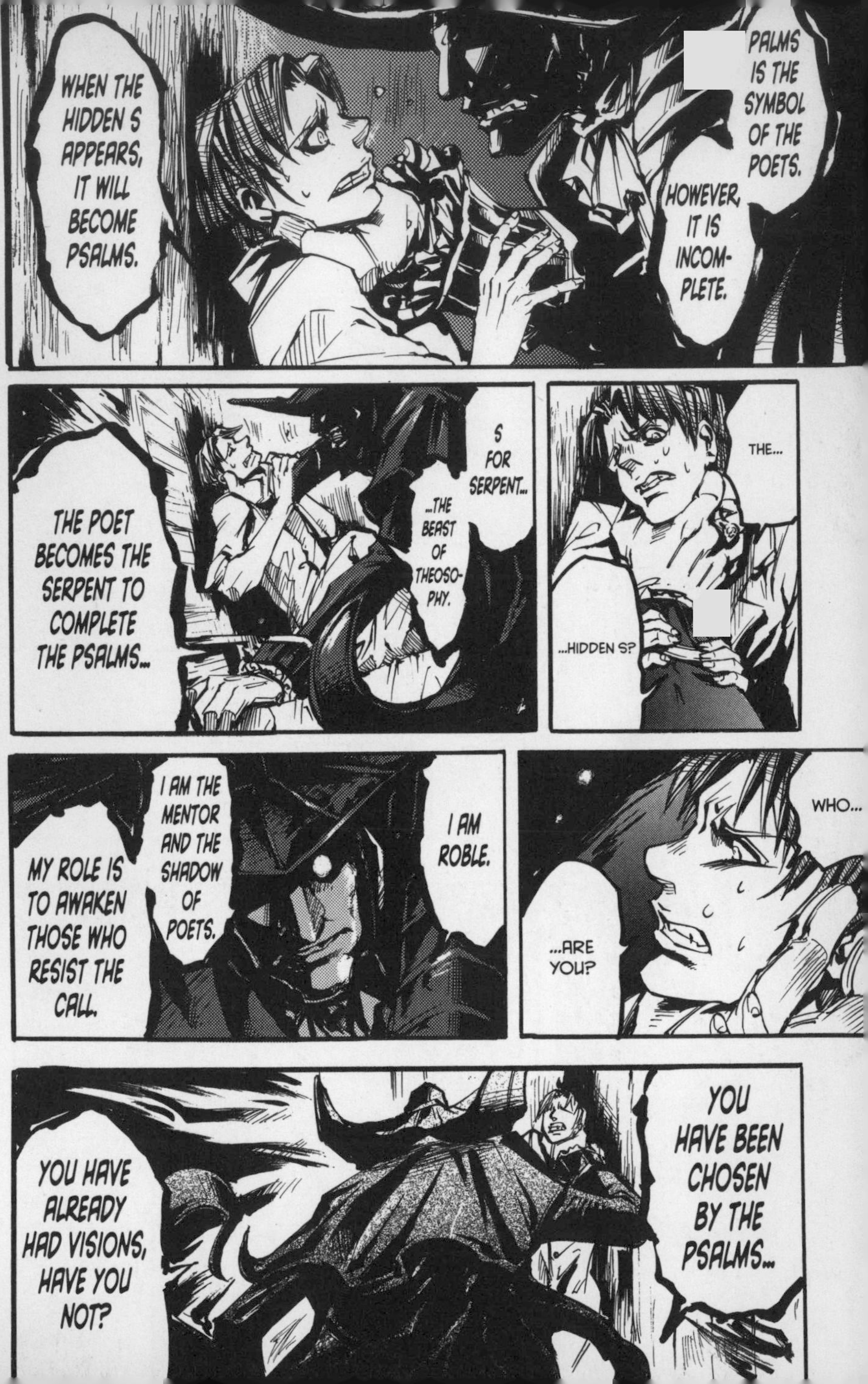
PALMS IS THE SYMBOL OF THE POETS.
HOWEVER, IT IS INCOMPLETE.
WHEN THE HIDDEN S APPEARS, IT WILL BECOME PSALMS.
THE...
...HIDDEN S?
S FOR SERPENT...
...THE BEAST OF THEOSOPHY.
THE POET BECOMES THE SERPENT TO COMPLETE THE PSALMS...
WHO...
...ARE YOU?
I AM ROBLE.
I AM THE MENTOR AND THE SHADOW OF POETS.
MY ROLE IS TO AWAKEN THOSE WHO RESIST THE CALL.
YOU HAVE BEEN CHOSEN BY THE PSALMS...
YOU HAVE ALREADY HAD VISIONS, HAVE YOU NOT?

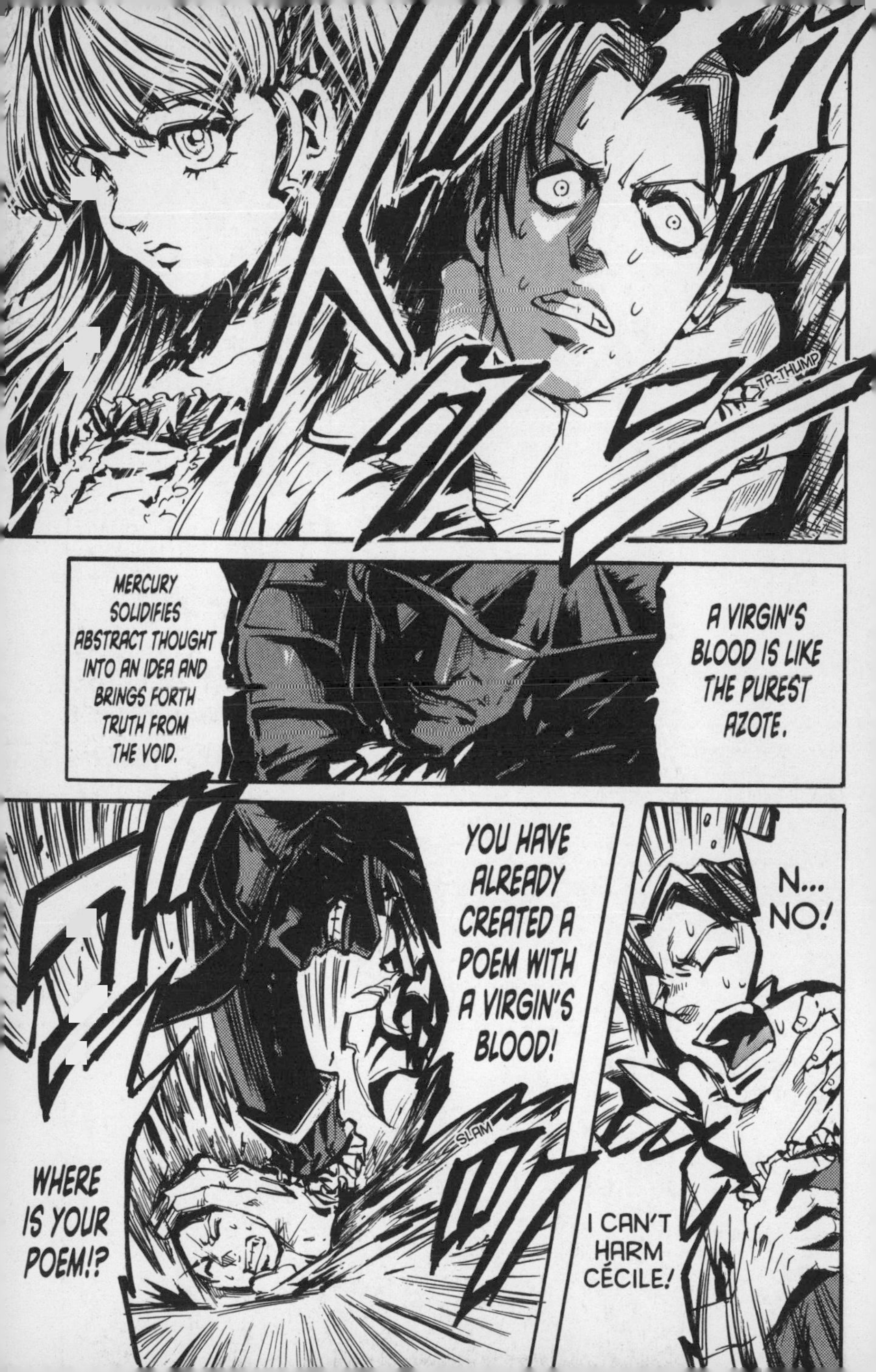
TA-THUMP
A VIRGIN'S BLOOD IS LIKE THE PUREST AZOTE.
MERCURY SOLIDIFIES ABSTRACT THOUGHT INTO AN IDEA AND BRINGS FORTH TRUTH FROM THE VOID.
N... NO!
I CAN'T HARM CÉCILE!
YOU HAVE ALREADY CREATED A POEM WITH A VIRGIN'S BLOOD!
SLAM
WHERE IS YOUR POEM!?

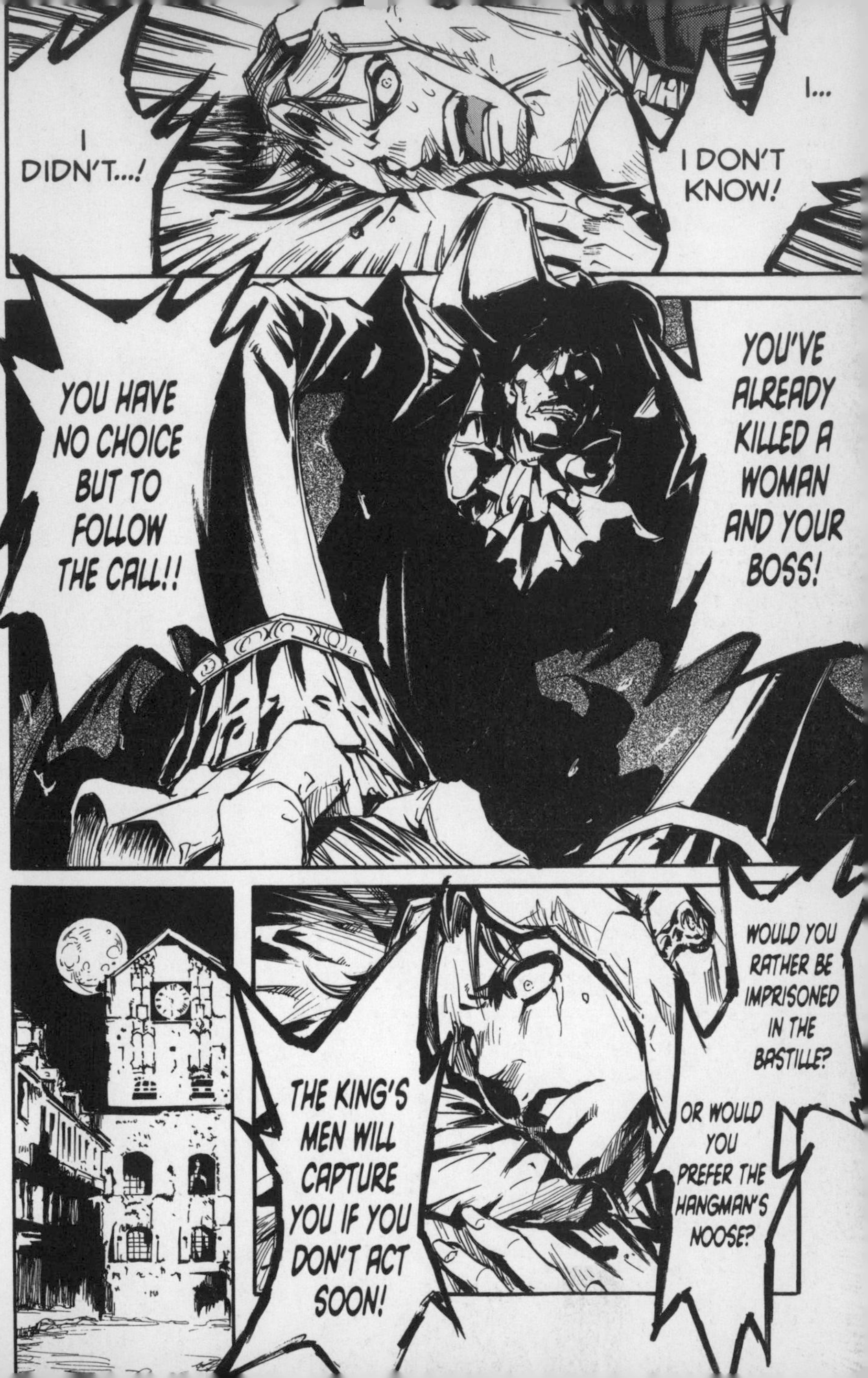
I...
I DON'T KNOW!
I DIDN'T...!
YOU'VE ALREADY KILLED A WOMAN AND YOUR BOSS!
YOU HAVE NO CHOICE BUT TO FOLLOW THE CALL!!
WOULD YOU RATHER BE IMPRISONED IN THE BASTILLE?
OR WOULD YOU PREFER THE HANGMAN'S NOOSE?
THE KING'S MEN WILL CAPTURE YOU IF YOU DON'T ACT SOON!

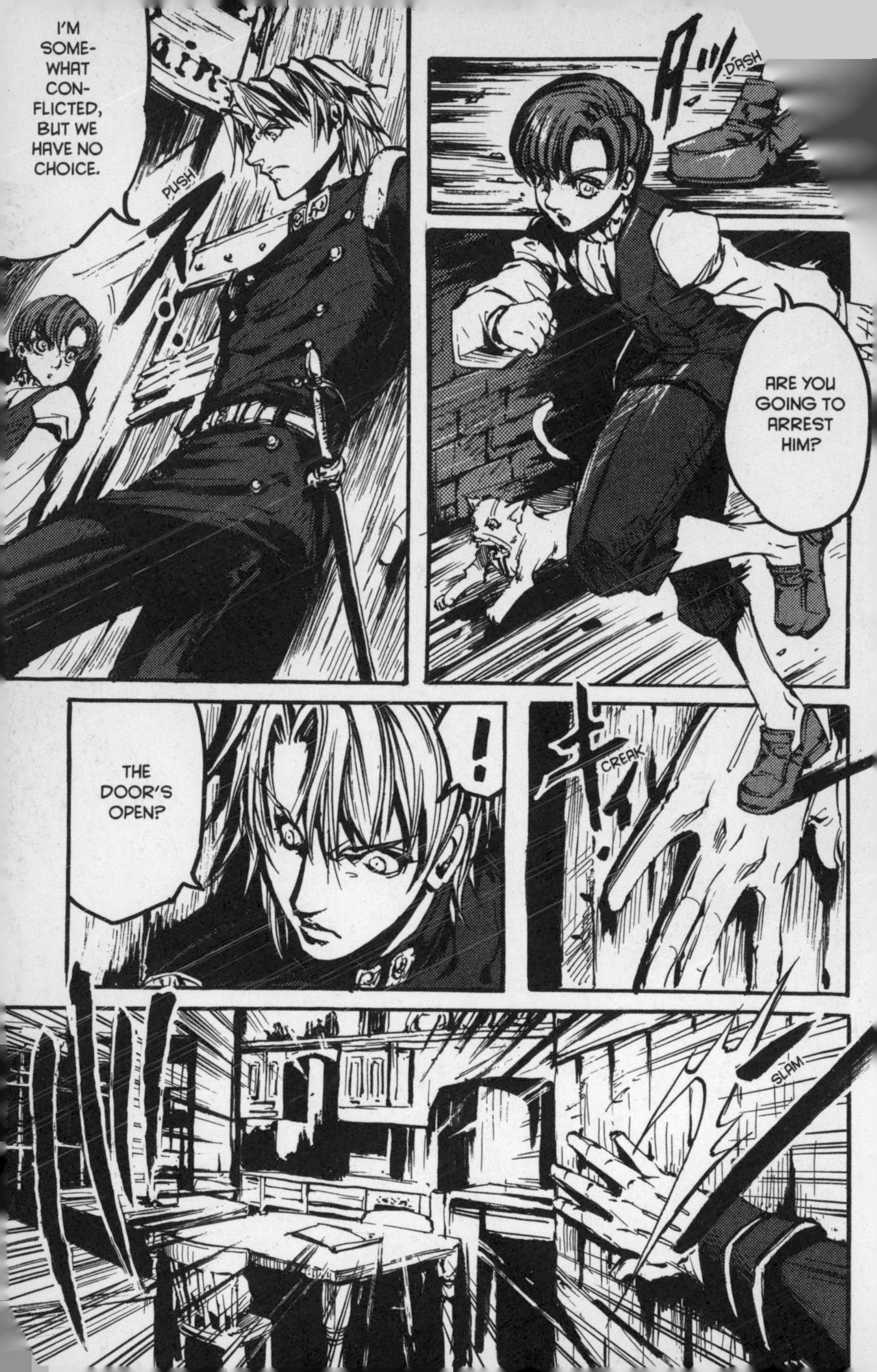
DASH
ARE YOU GOING TO ARREST HIM?
I'M SOMEWHAT CONFLICTED, BUT WE HAVE NO CHOICE.
PUSH
CREAK
!
THE DOOR'S OPEN?
SLAM

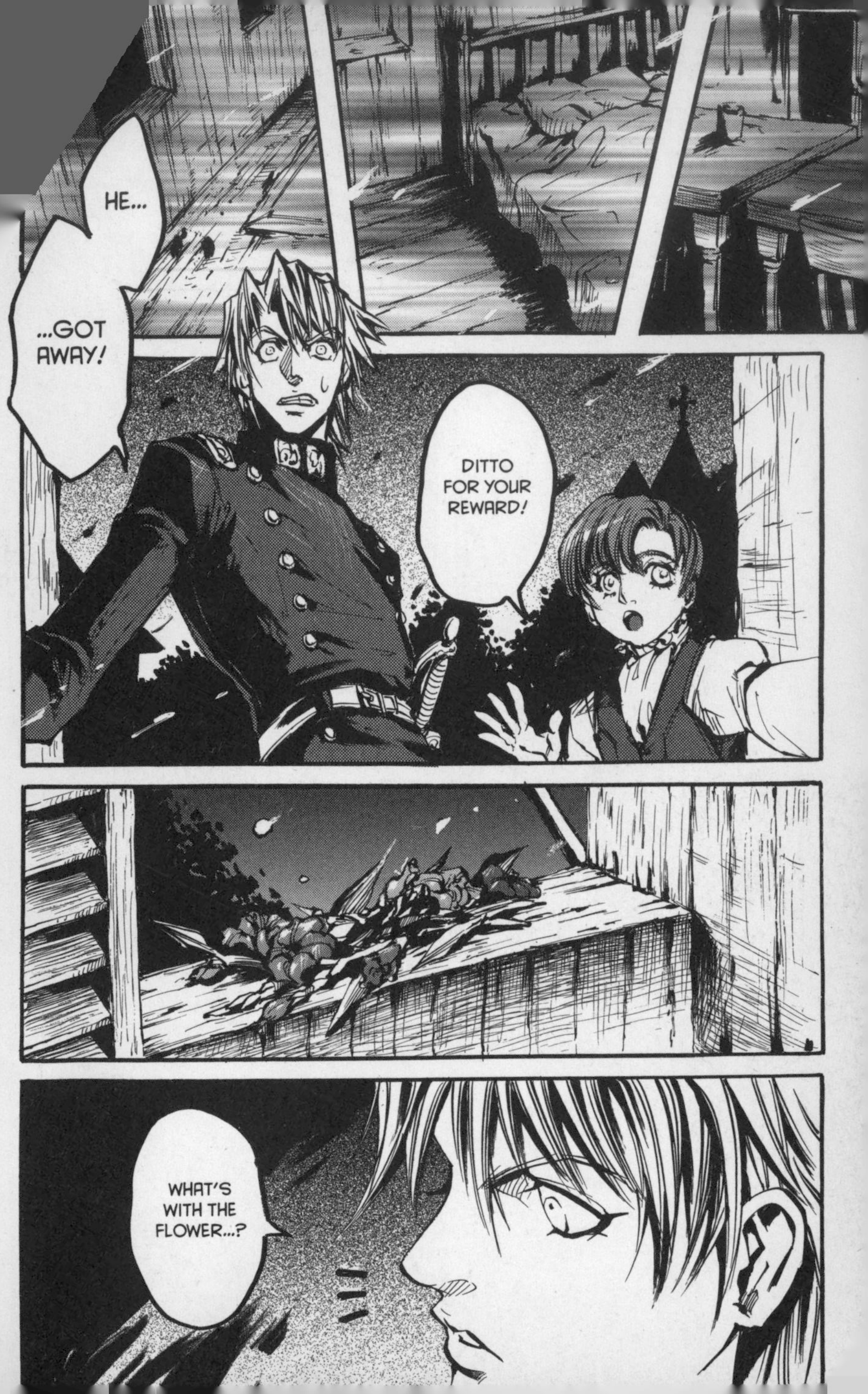
HE...
...GOT AWAY!
DITTO FOR YOUR REWARD!
WHAT'S WITH THE FLOWER...?

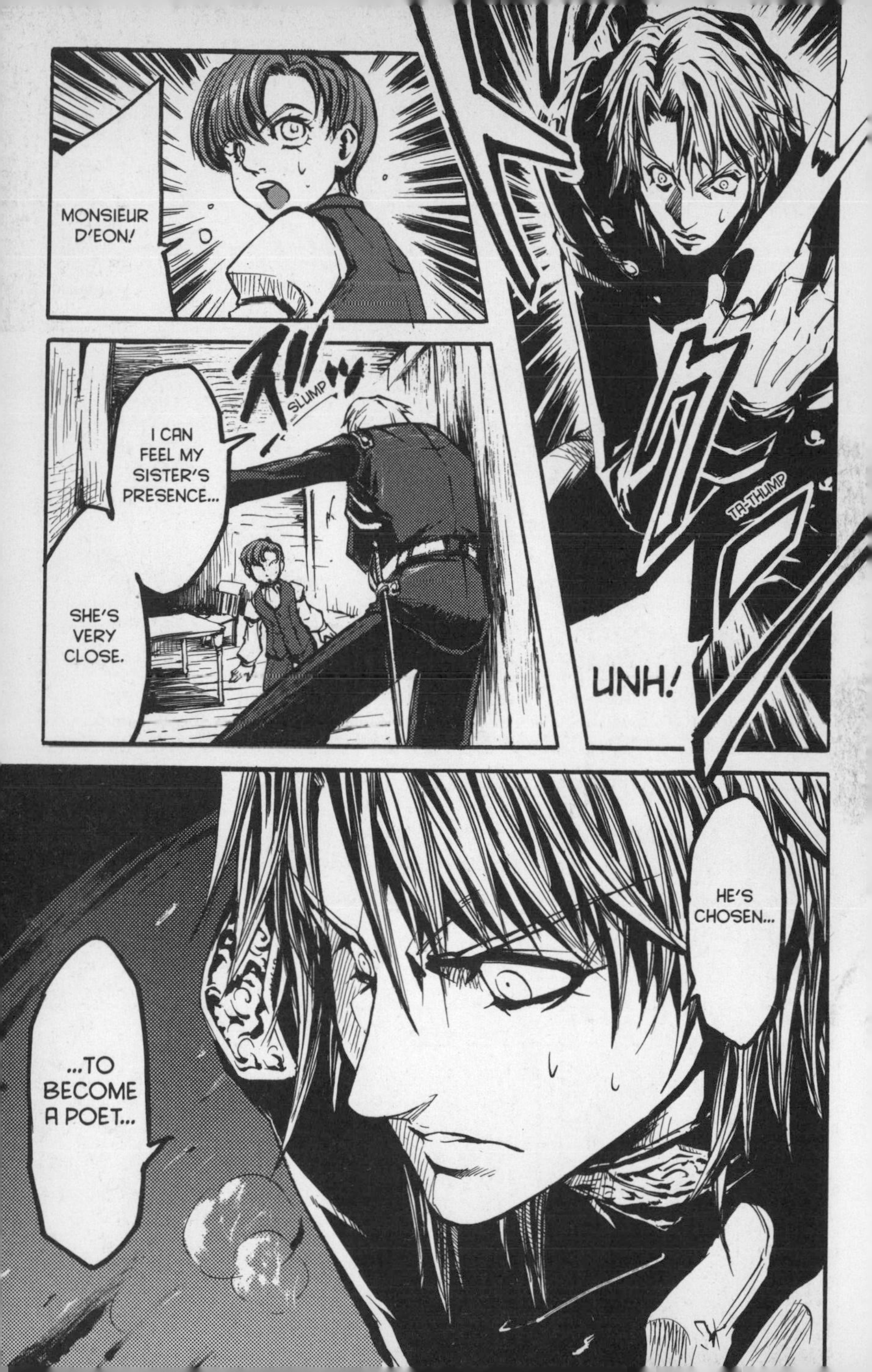
TA-THUMP
UNH!
MONSIEUR D'EON!
SLUMP
I CAN FEEL MY SISTER'S PRESENCE...
SHE'S VERY CLOSE.
HE'S CHOSEN...
...TO BECOME A POET...

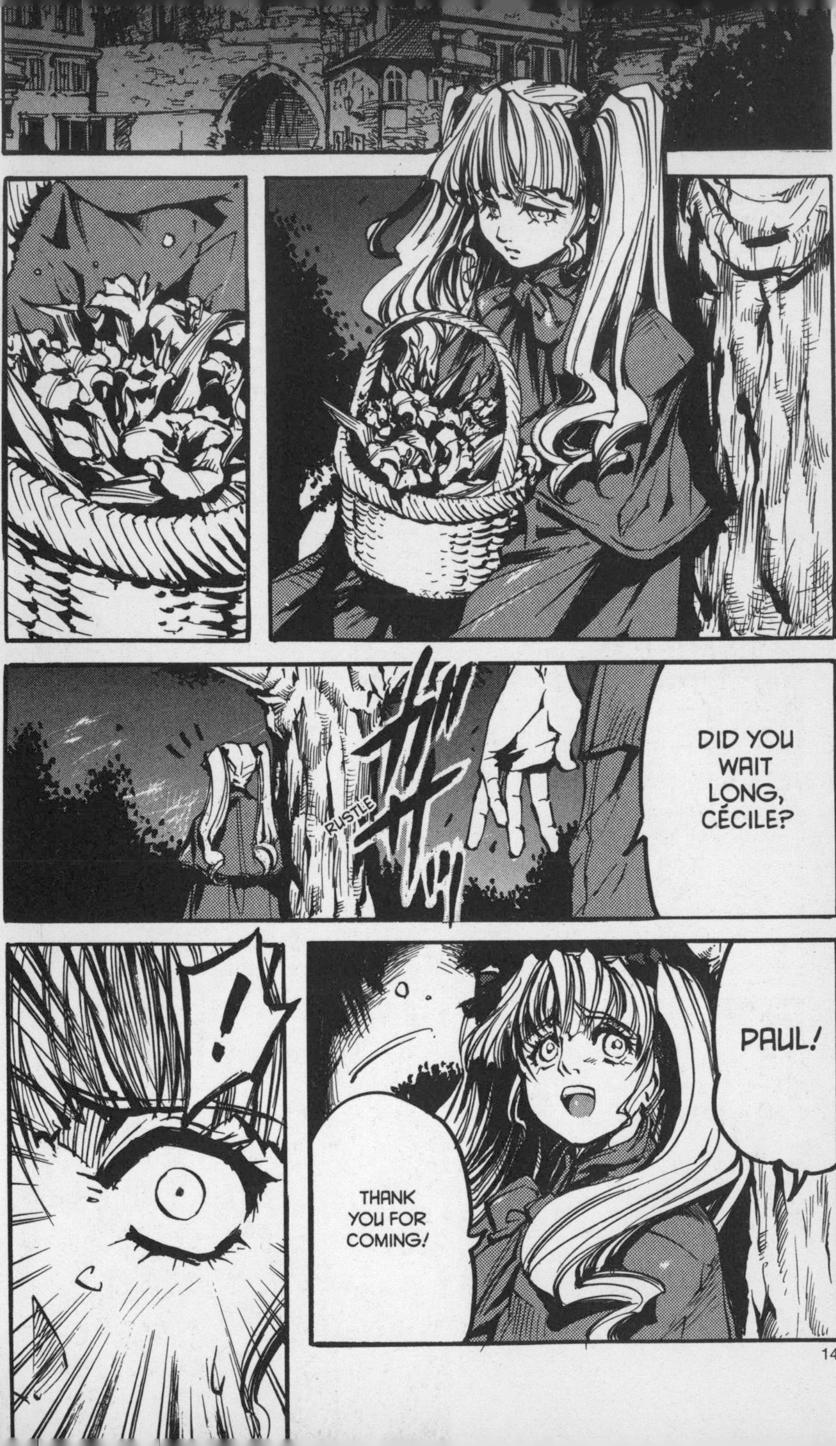
DID YOU WAIT LONG, CÉCILE?
RUSTLE
PAUL!
THANK YOU FOR COMING!
!

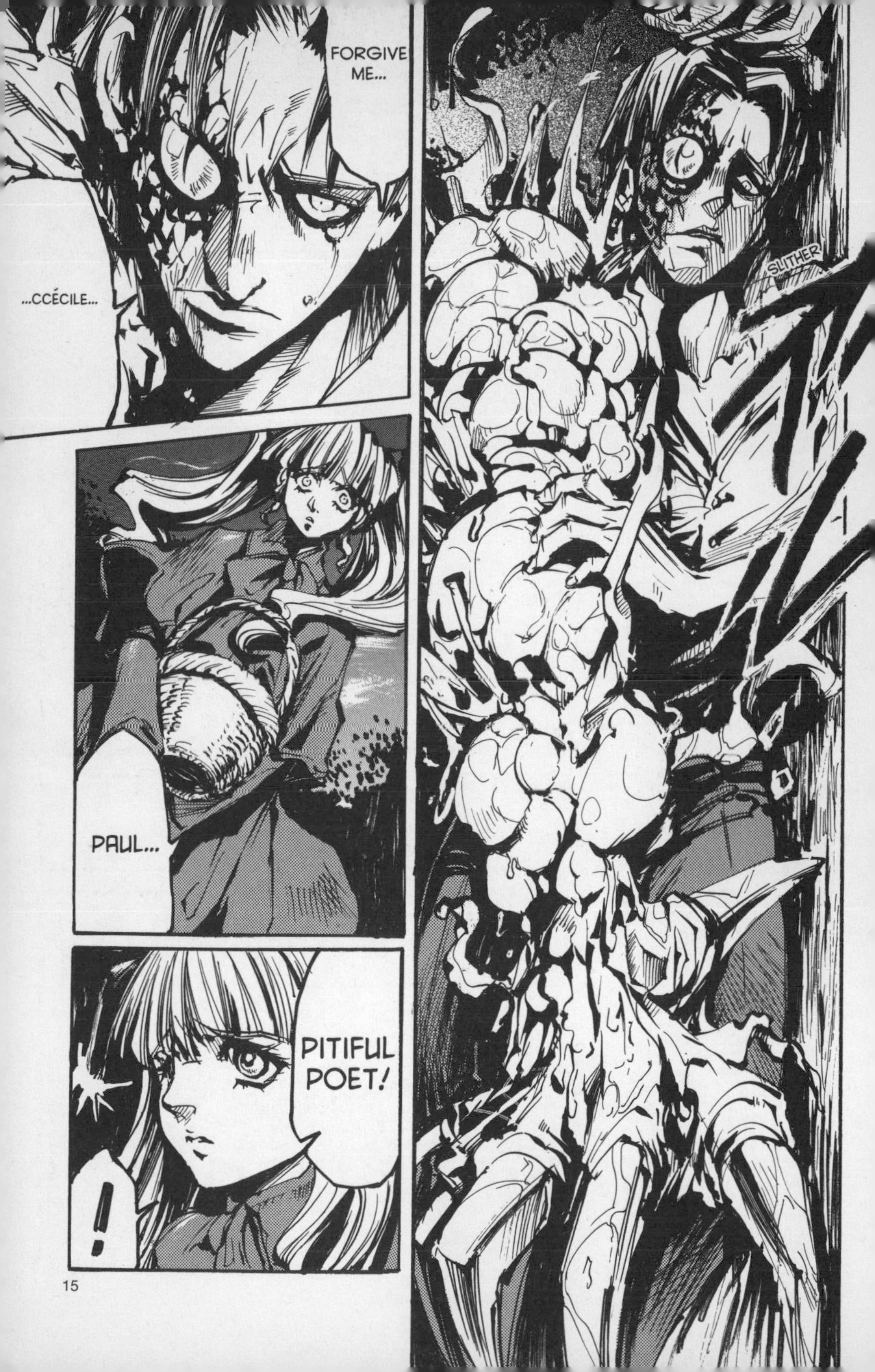
SLITHER
FORGIVE ME...
...CCÉCILE...
PAUL...
PITIFUL POET!
!

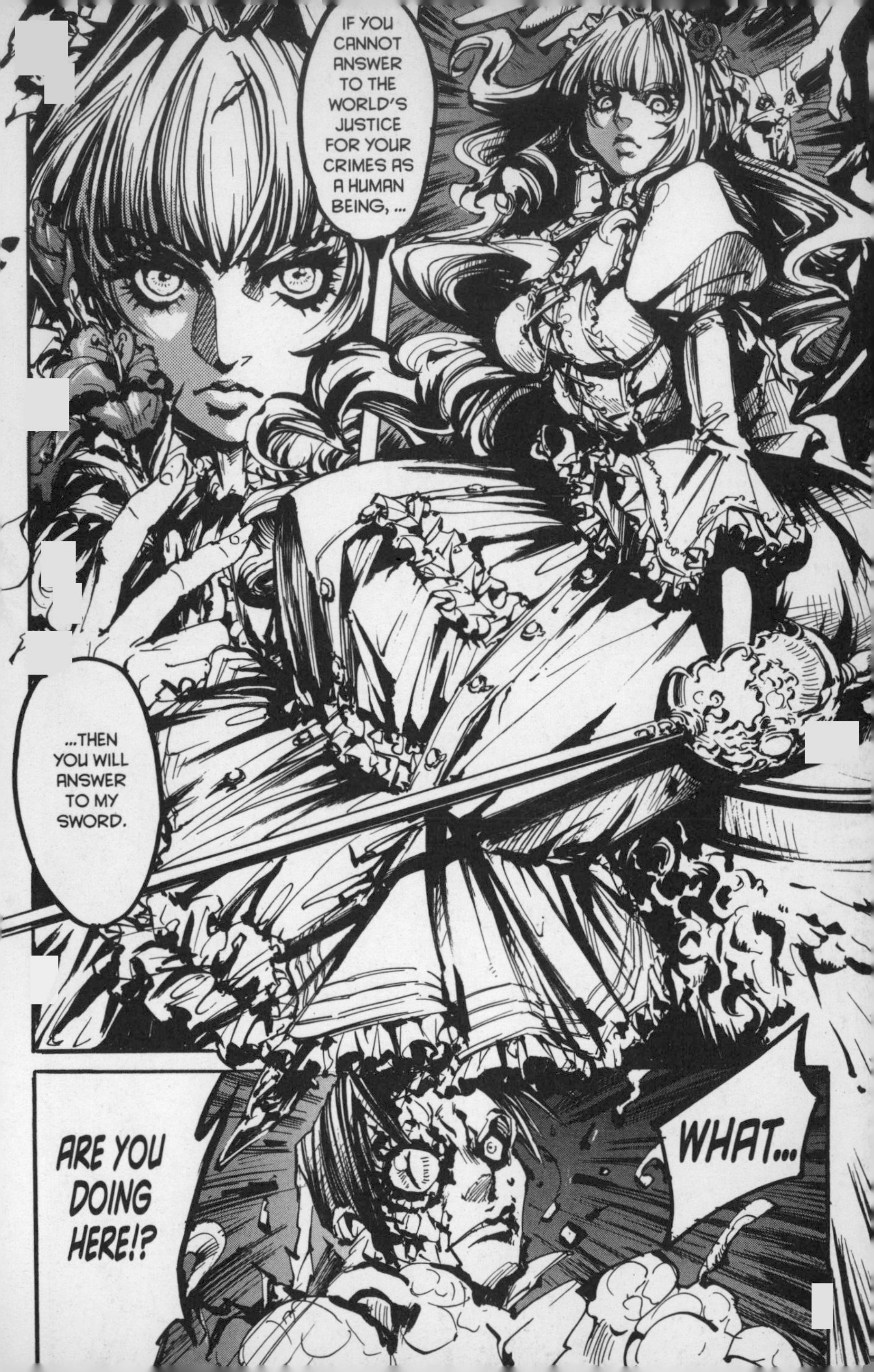
IF YOU CANNOT ANSWER TO THE WORLD'S JUSTICE FOR YOUR CRIMES AS A HUMAN BEING, ...
...THEN YOU WILL ANSWER TO MY SWORD.
WHAT...
ARE YOU DOING HERE!?

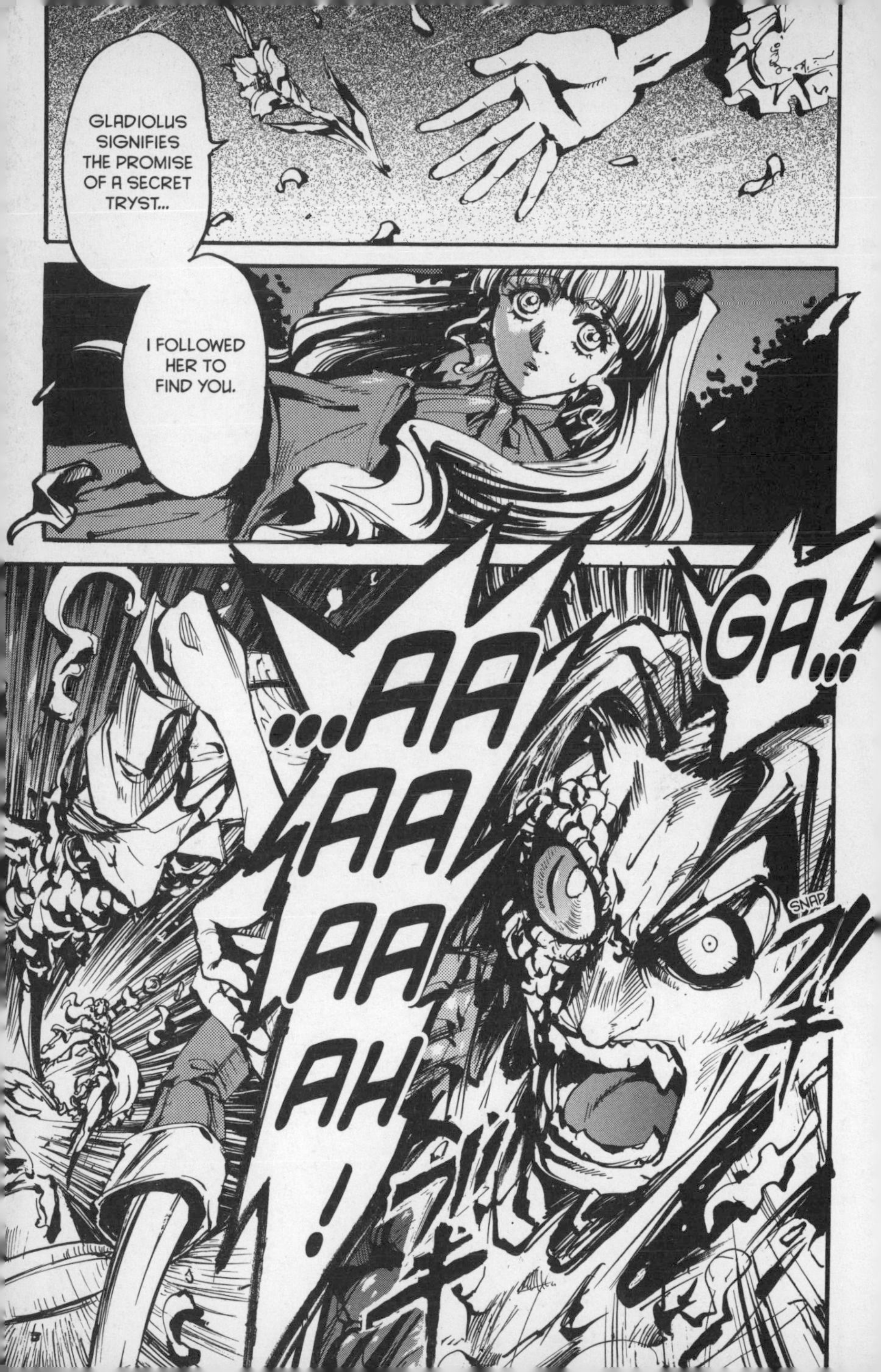
GLADIOLUS SIGNIFIES THE PROMISE OF A SECRET TRYST...
I FOLLOWED HER TO FIND YOU.
GA...!
SNAP
...AAAAAAAAH!

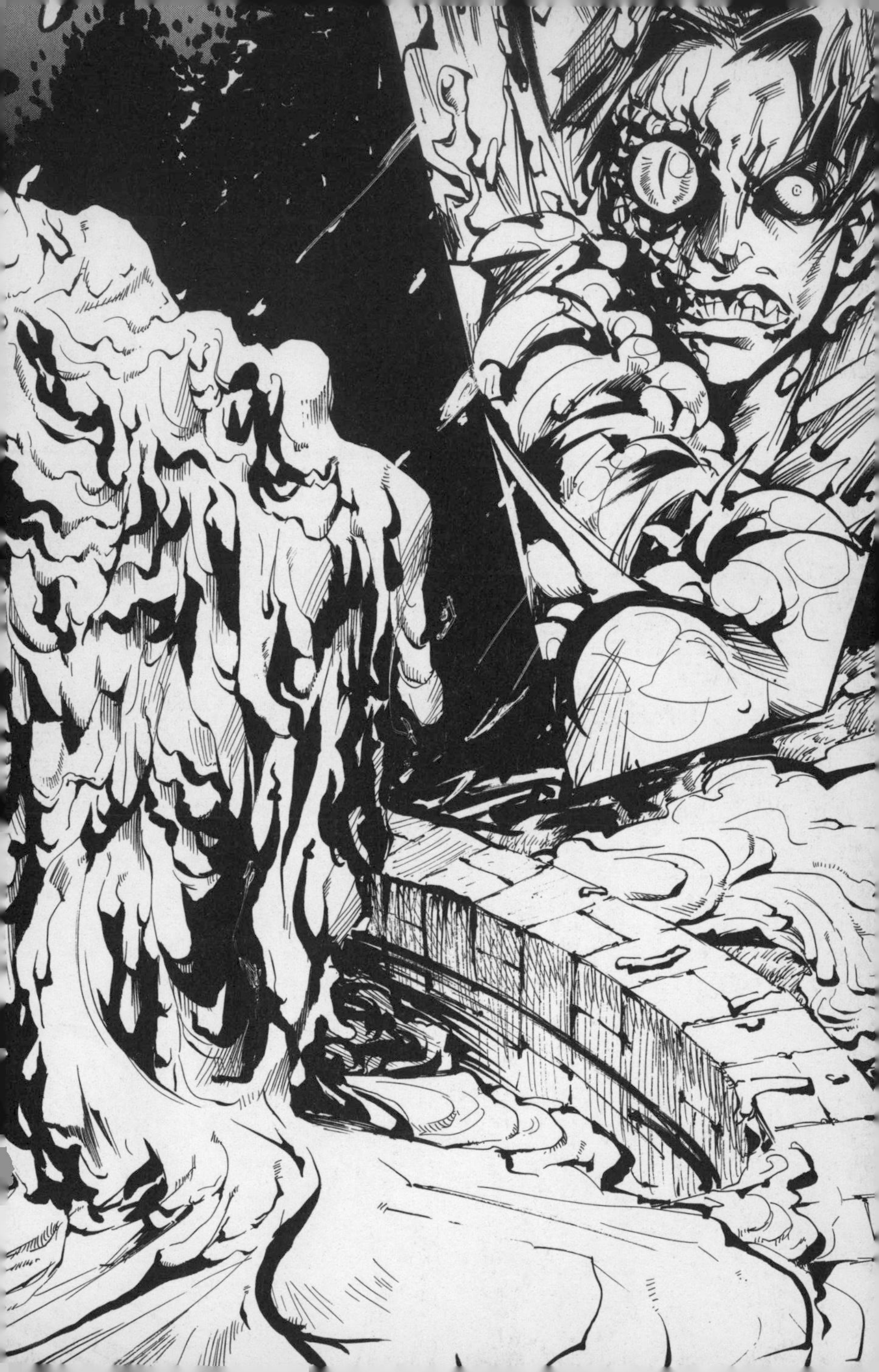

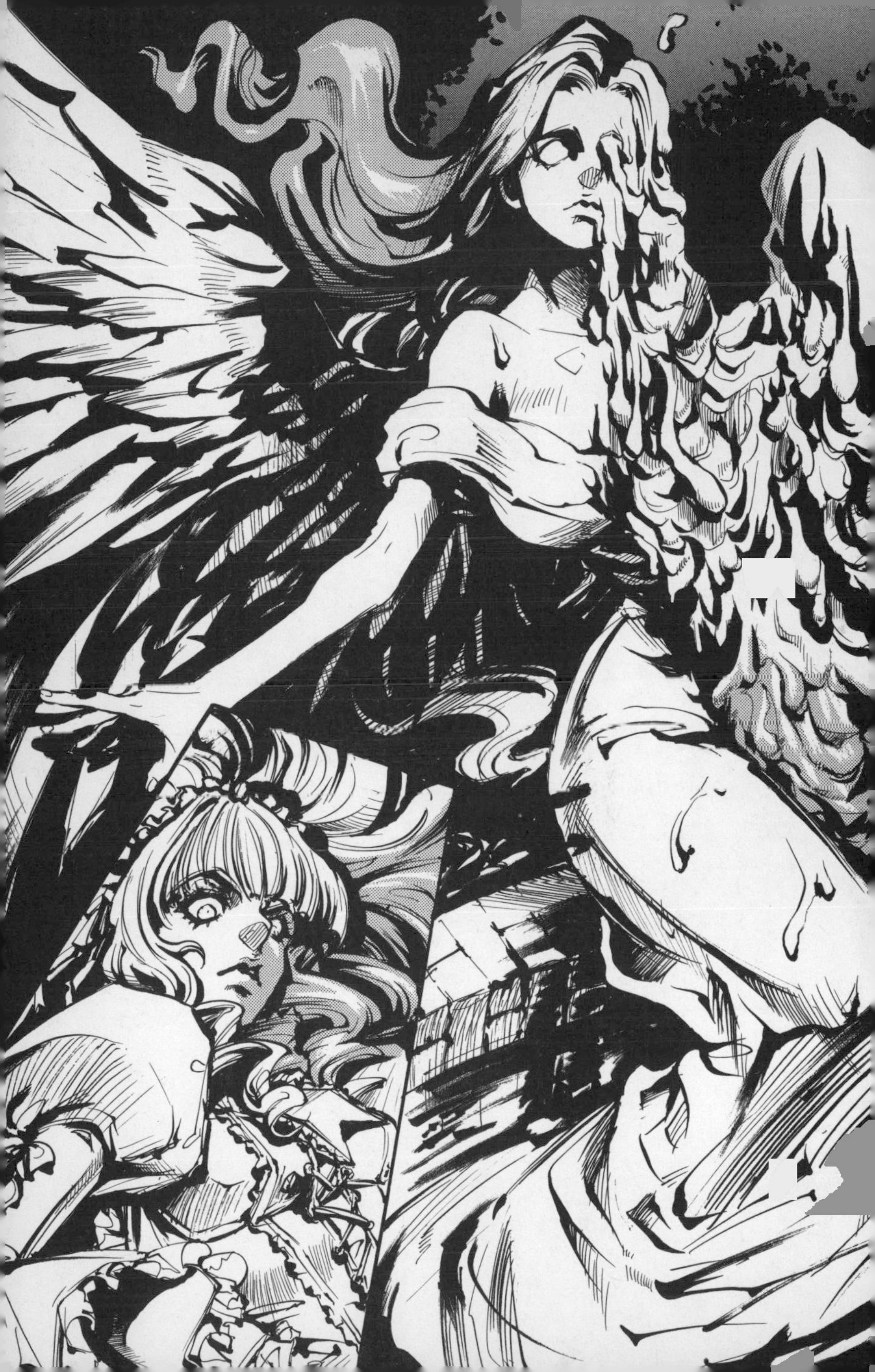

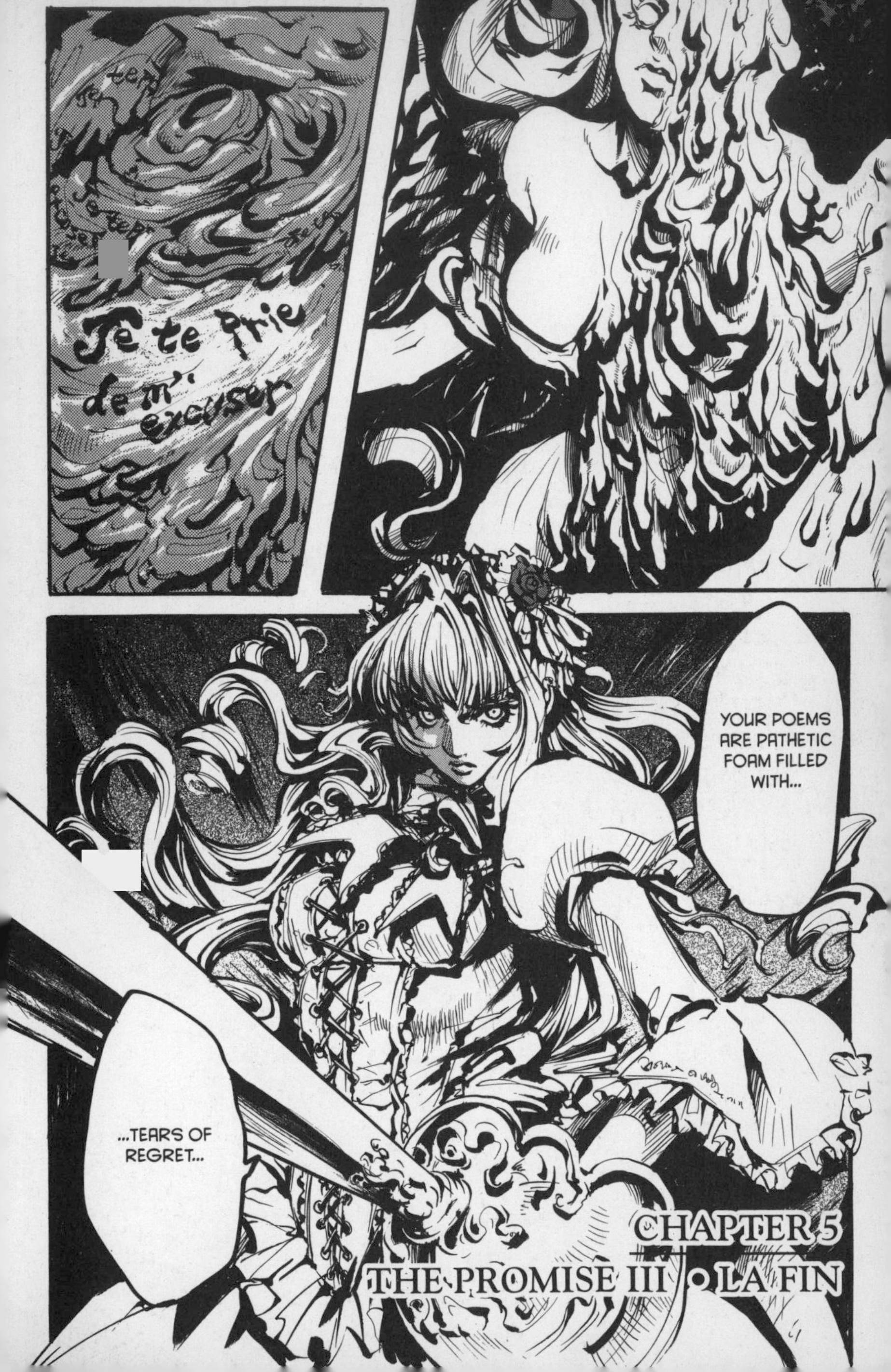
Je te prie de m'excuser
YOUR POEMS ARE PATHETIC FOAM FILLED WITH...
...TEARS OF REGRET...
CHAPTER 5
THE PROMISE III • LA FIN

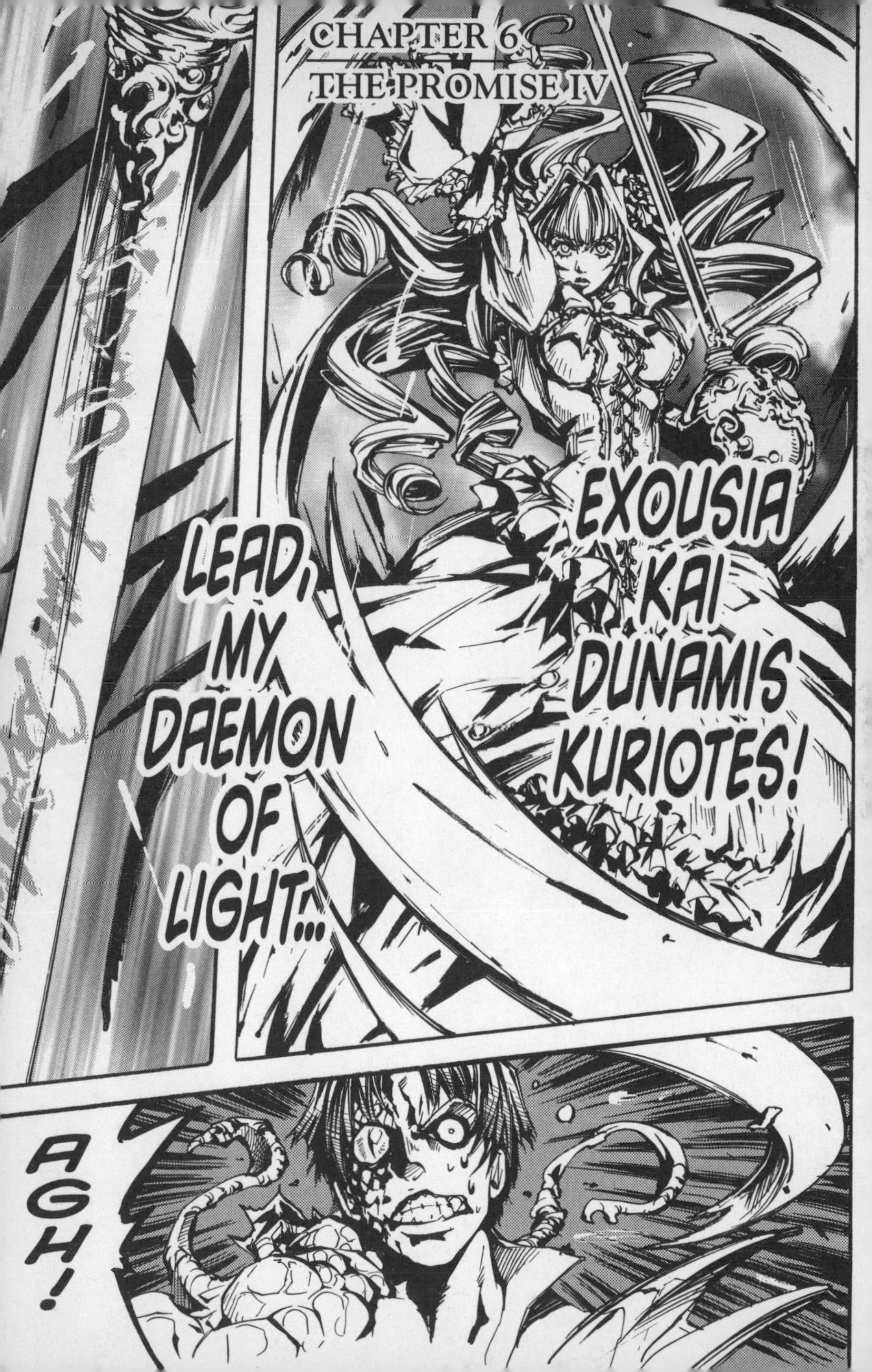
CHAPTER 6
THE PROMISE IV
EXOUSIA KAI DUNAMIS KURIOTES!
LEAD, MY DAEMON OF LIGHT...
AGH!

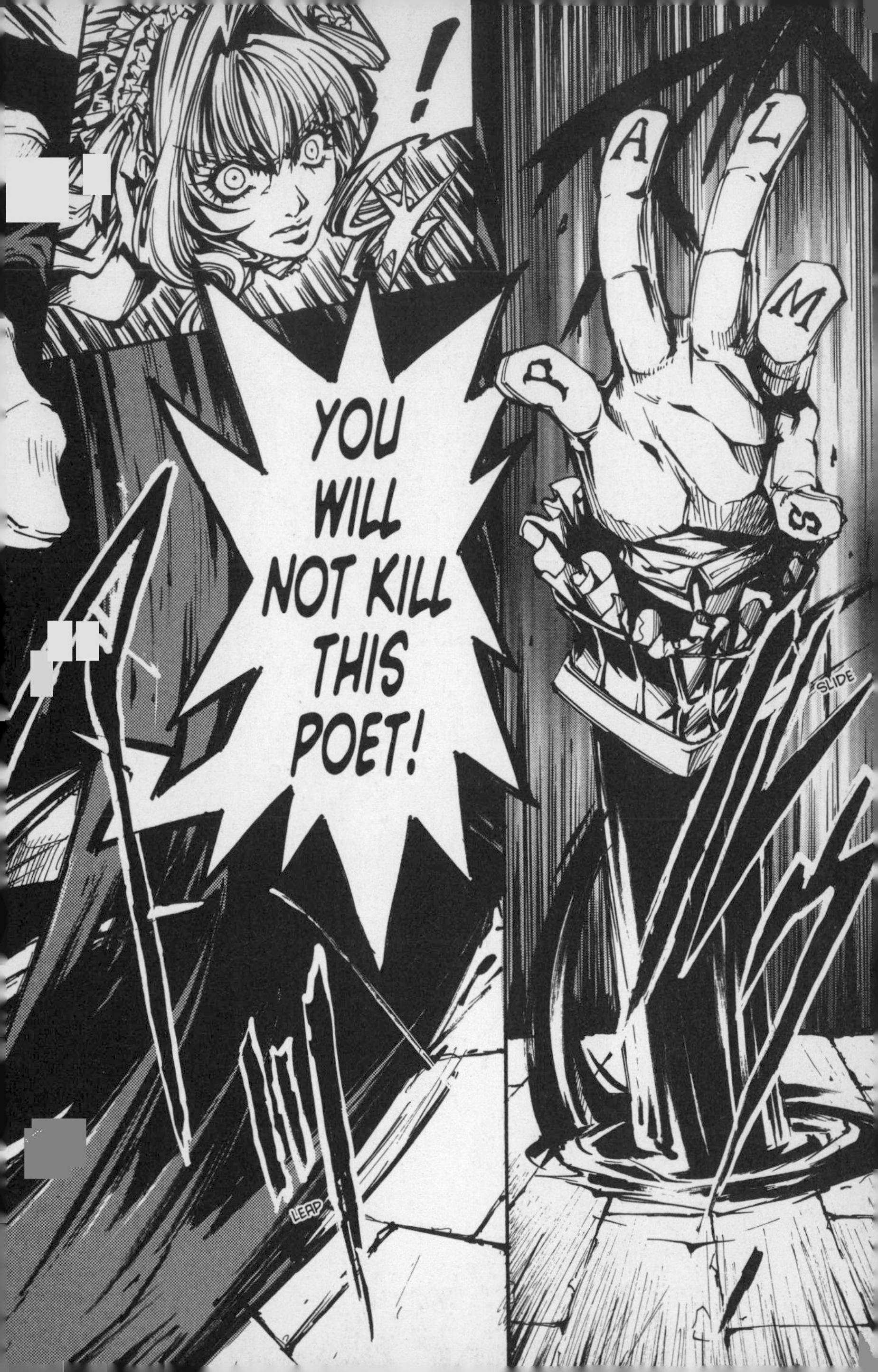
SLIDE
!
YOU WILL NOT KILL THIS POET!
LEAP

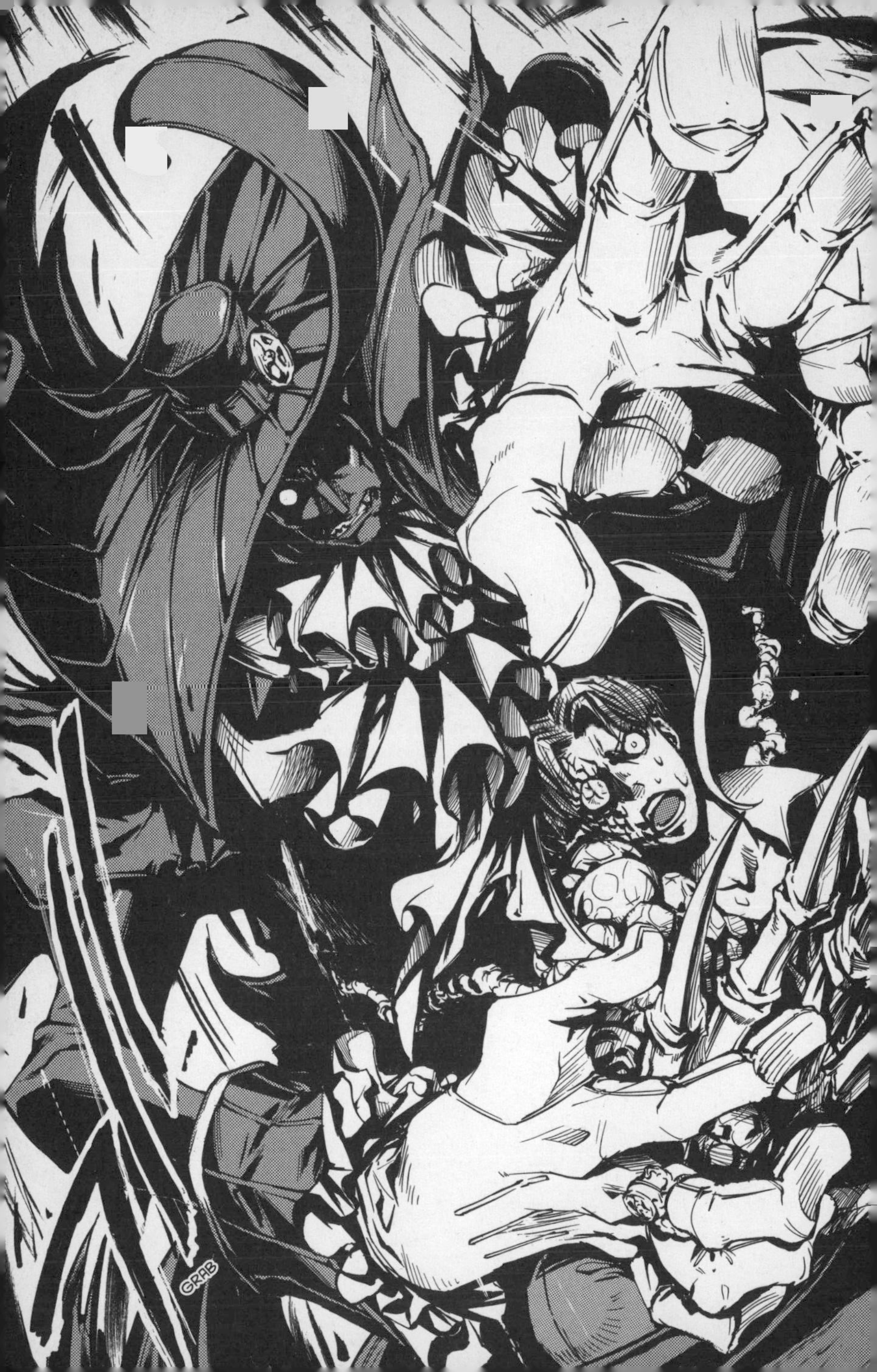
GRAB

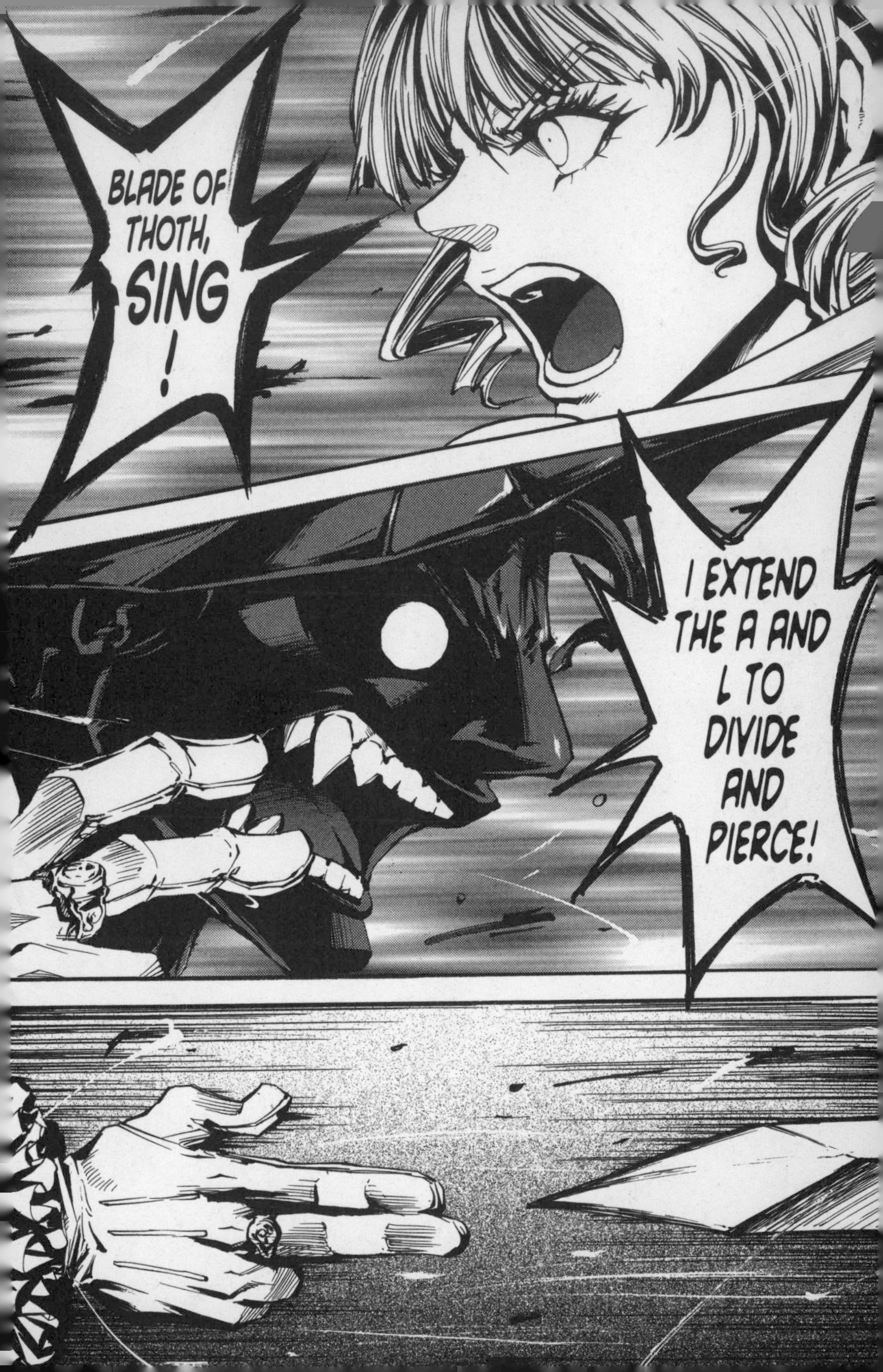
BLADE OF THOTH, SING!
I EXTEND THE A AND L TO DIVIDE AND PIERCE!

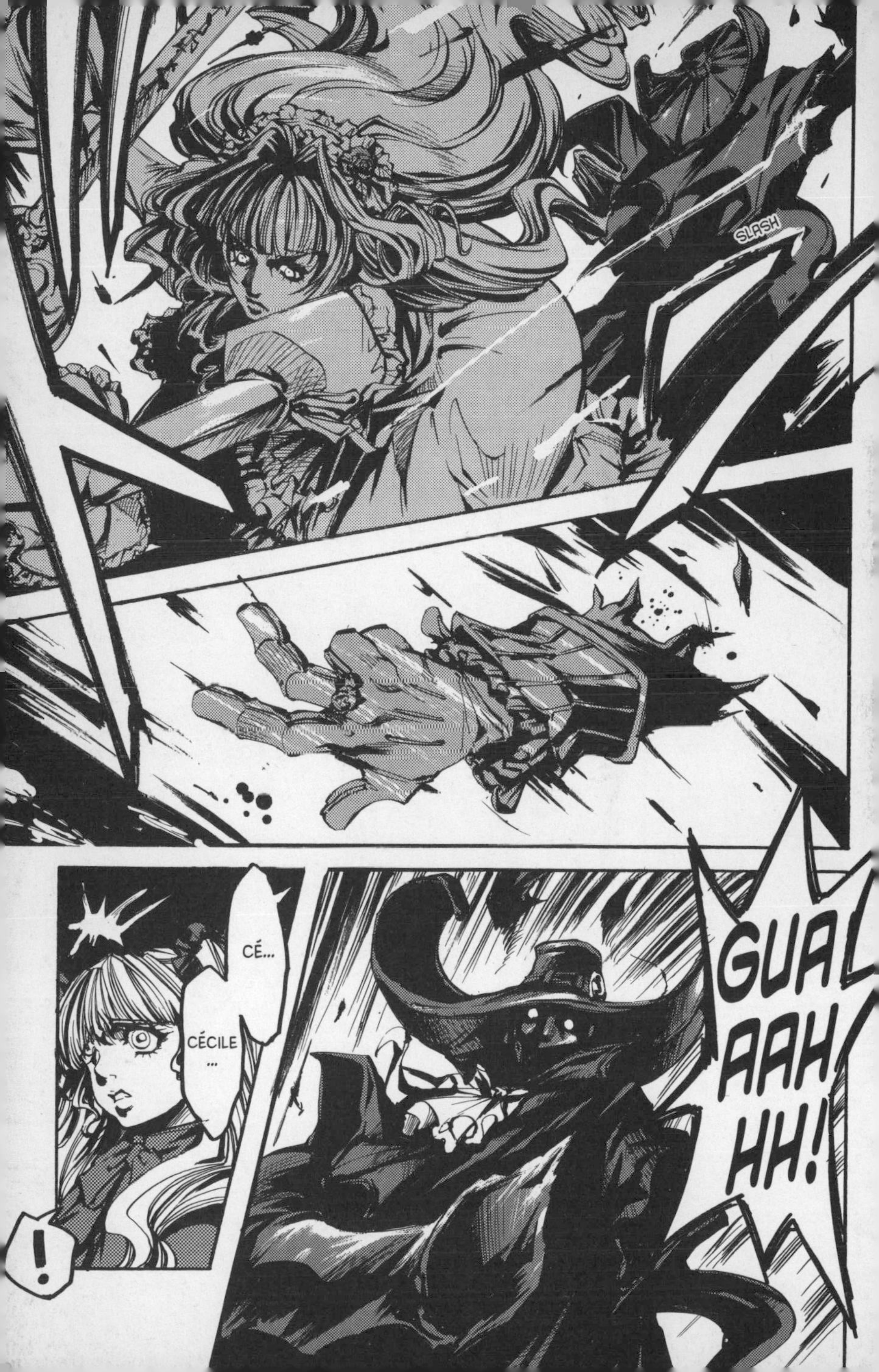
SLASH
GUAAAHHH!
CÉ...
CÉCILE...
!

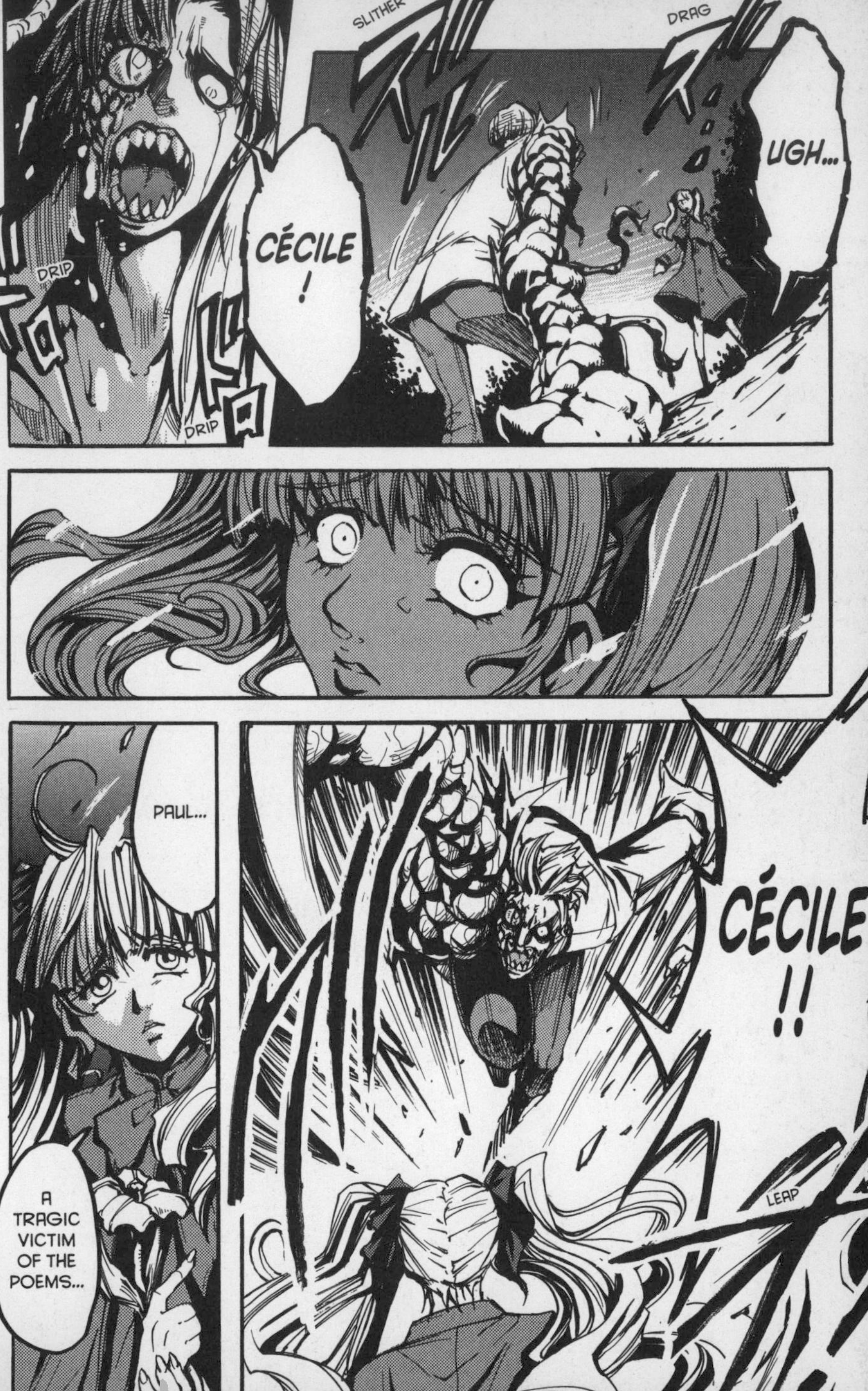
DRAG
UGH...
SLITHER
CÉCILE!
DRIP
DRIP
CÉCILE!!
LEAP
PAUL...
A TRAGIC VICTIM OF THE POEMS...

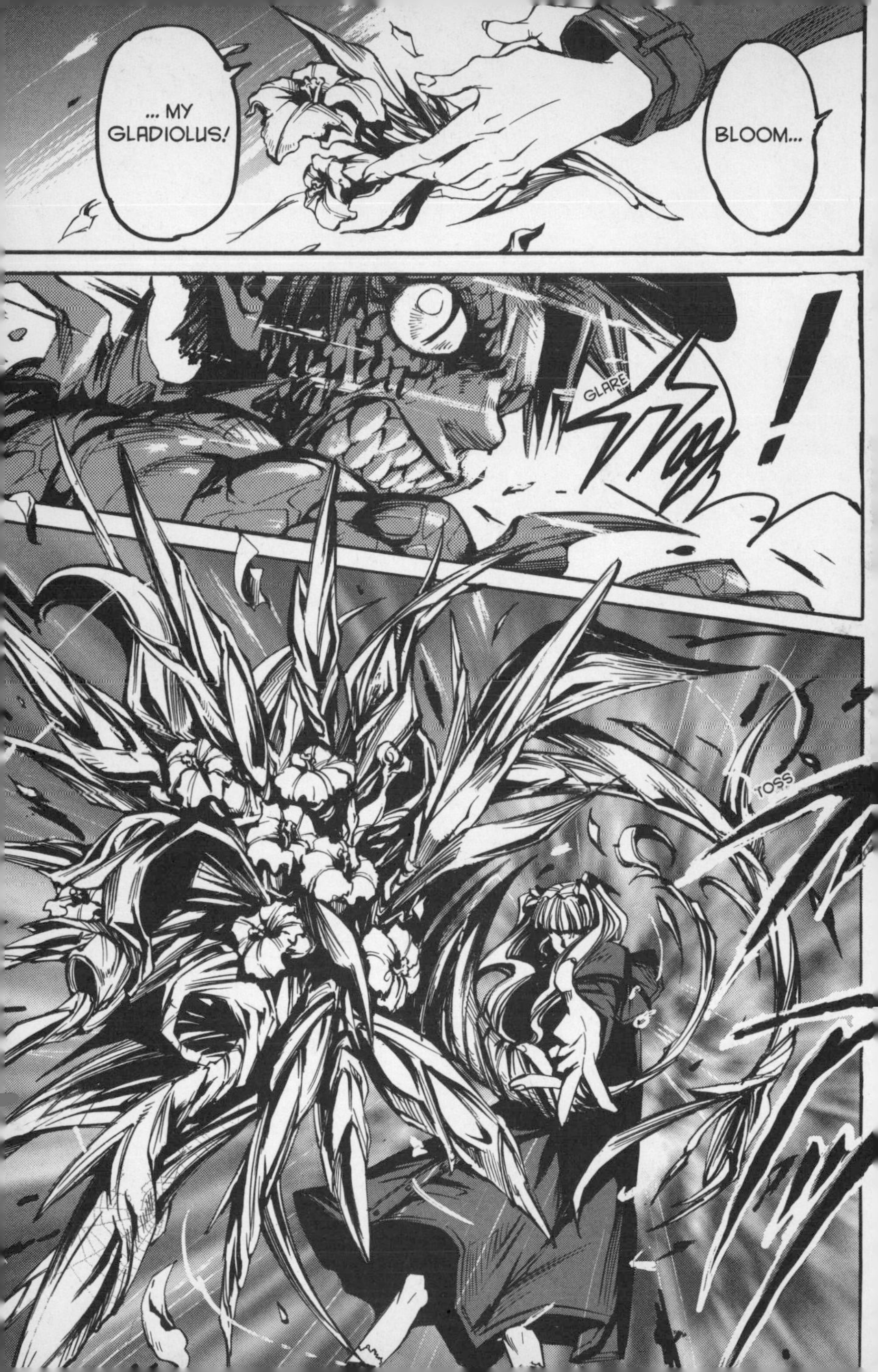
BLOOM...
... MY GLADIOLUS!
GLARE
TOSS

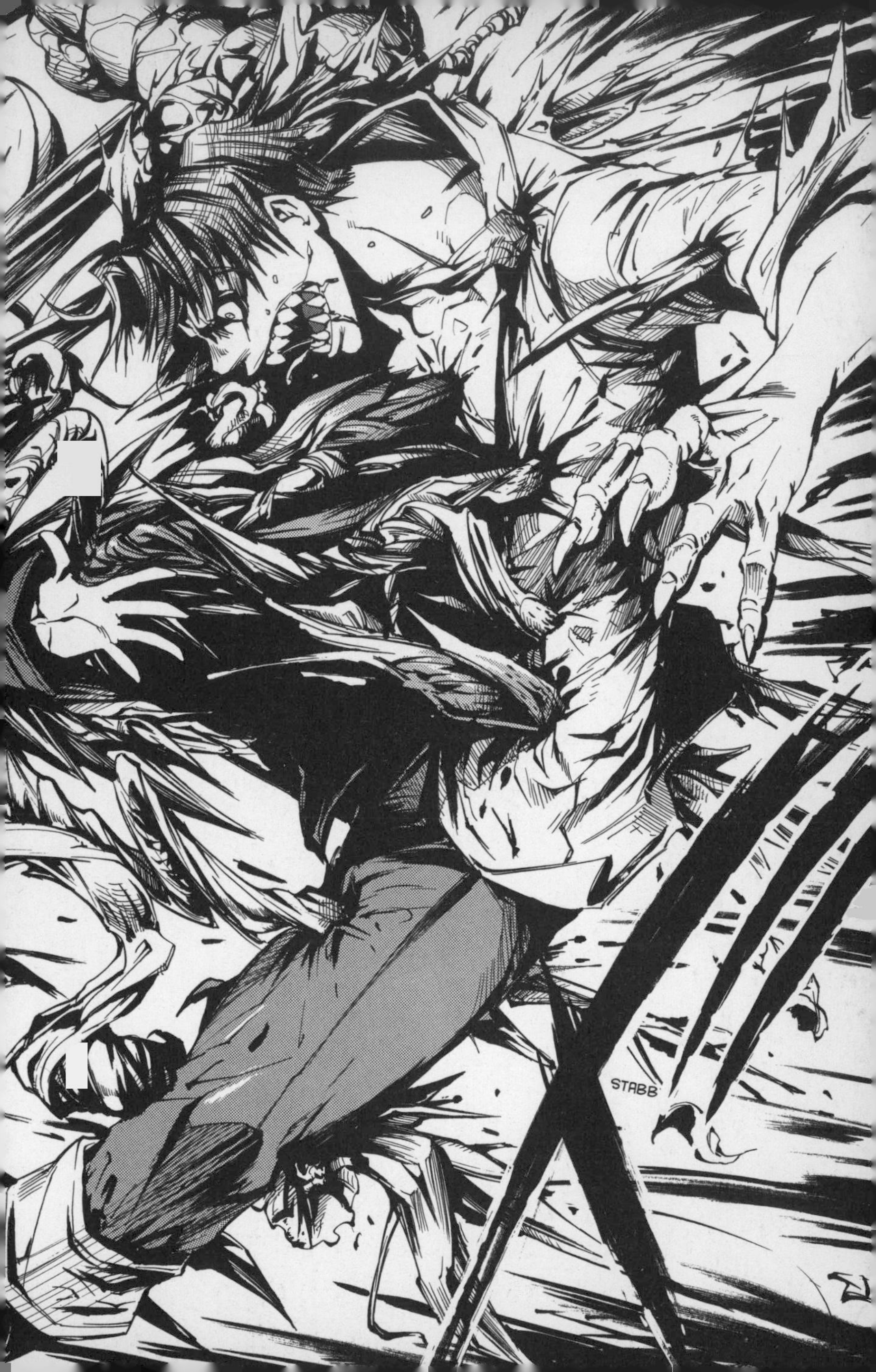
STABB

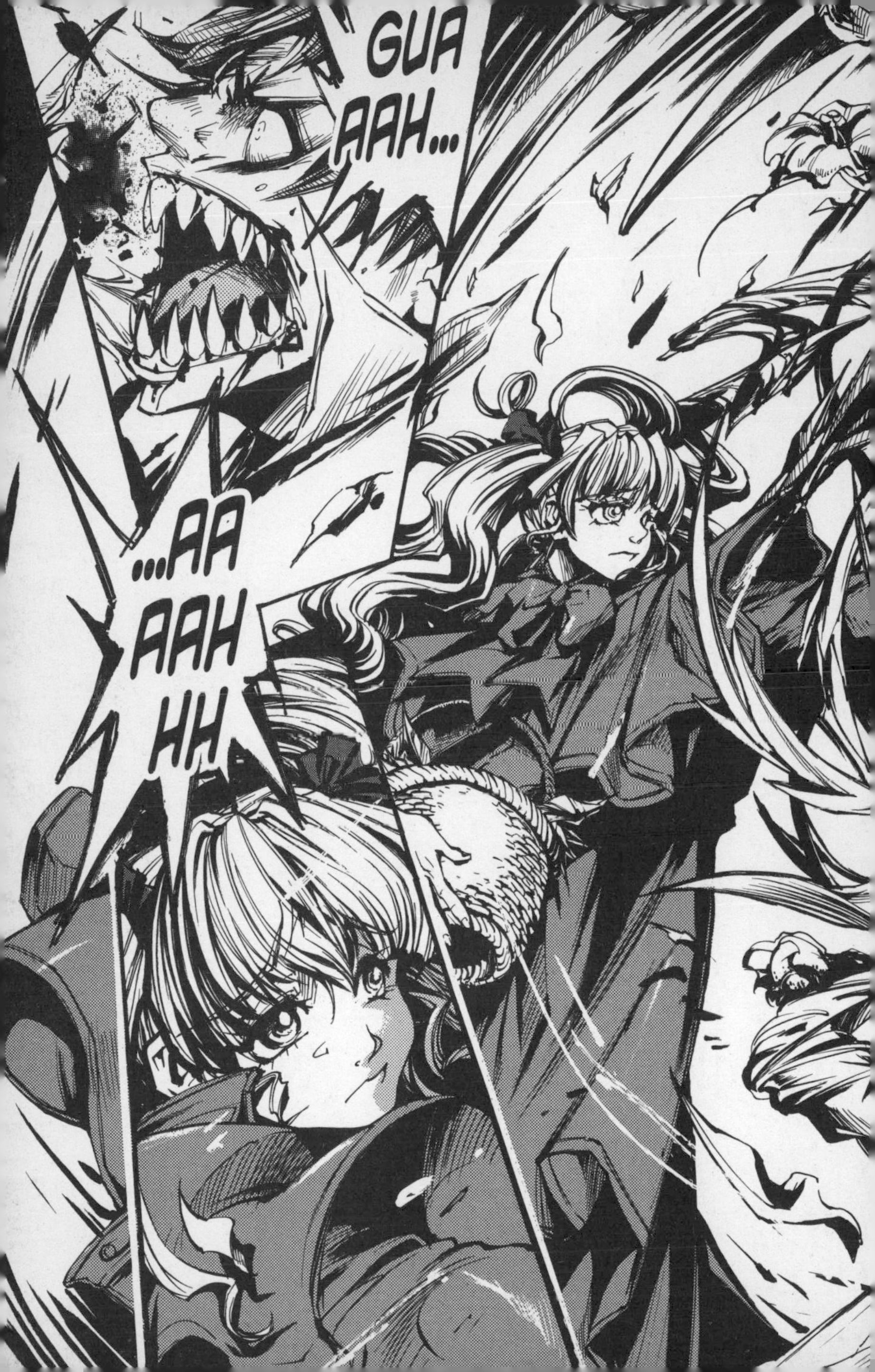
GUA AAH...
...AA AAH HH

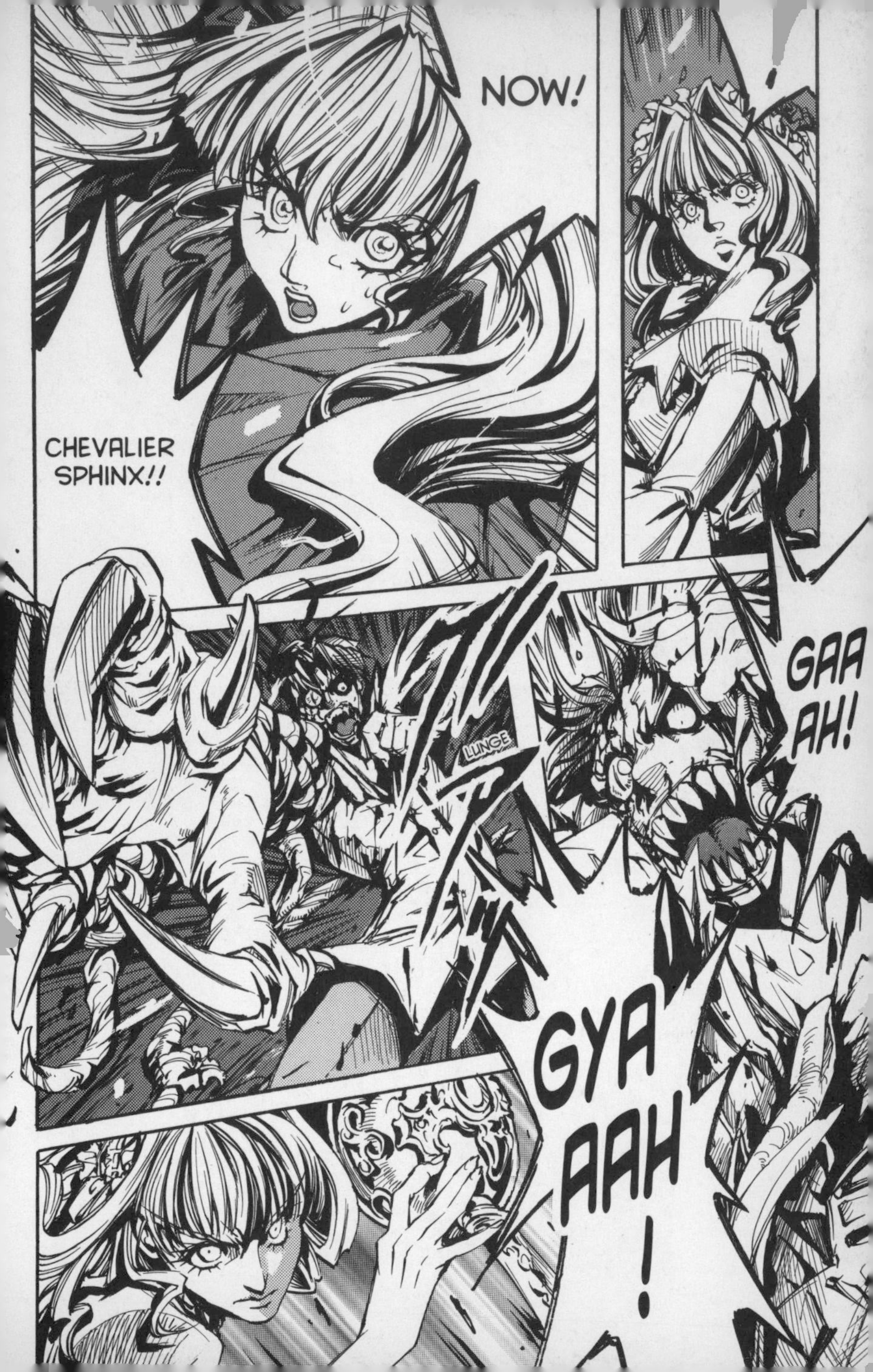
NOW!
CHEVALIER SPHINX!!
GAA AH!
LUNGE
GYA AAH!

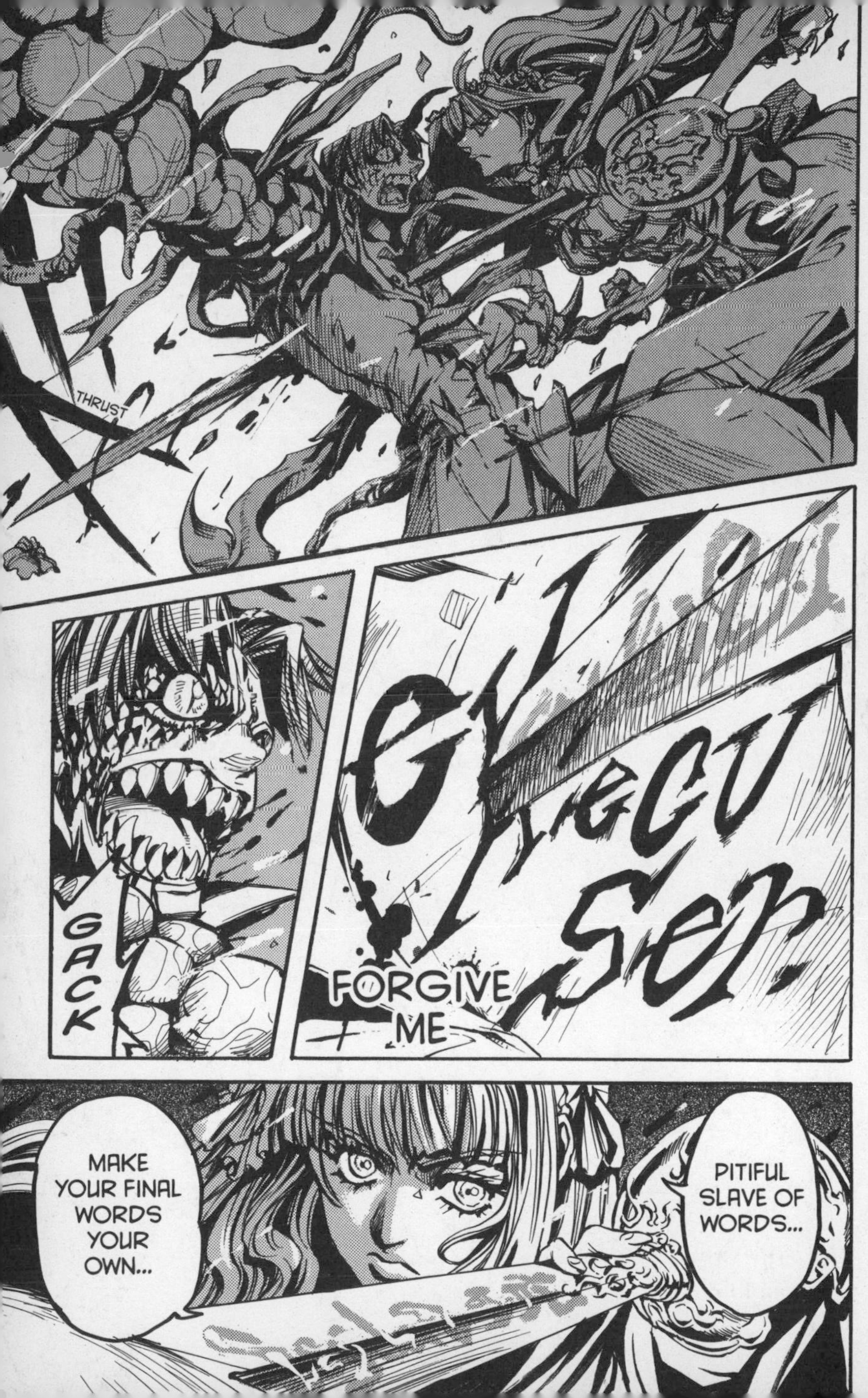
THRUST
FORGIVE ME
GACK
PITIFUL SLAVE OF WORDS...
MAKE YOUR FINAL WORDS YOUR OWN...

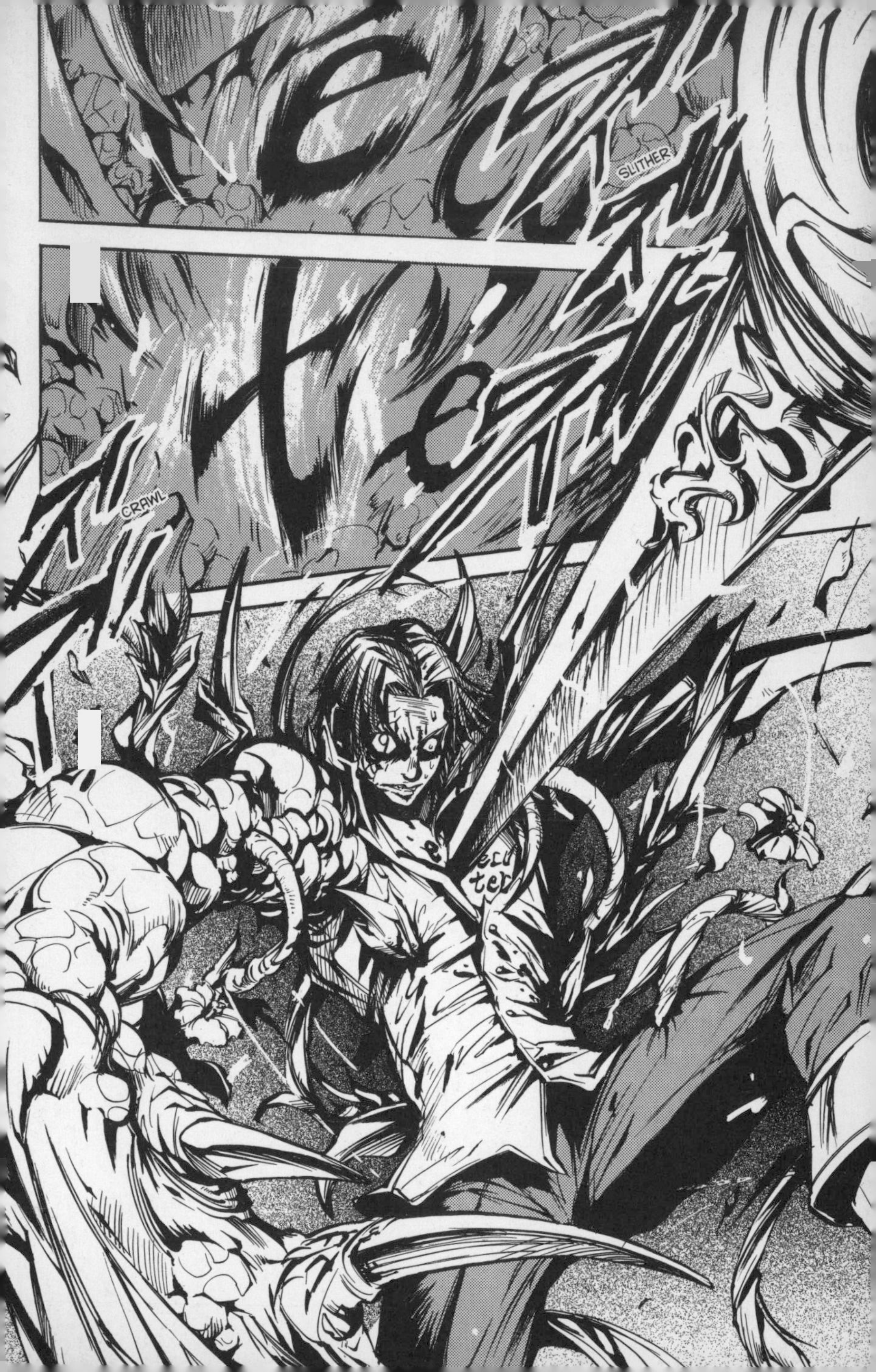
SLITHER
CRAWL

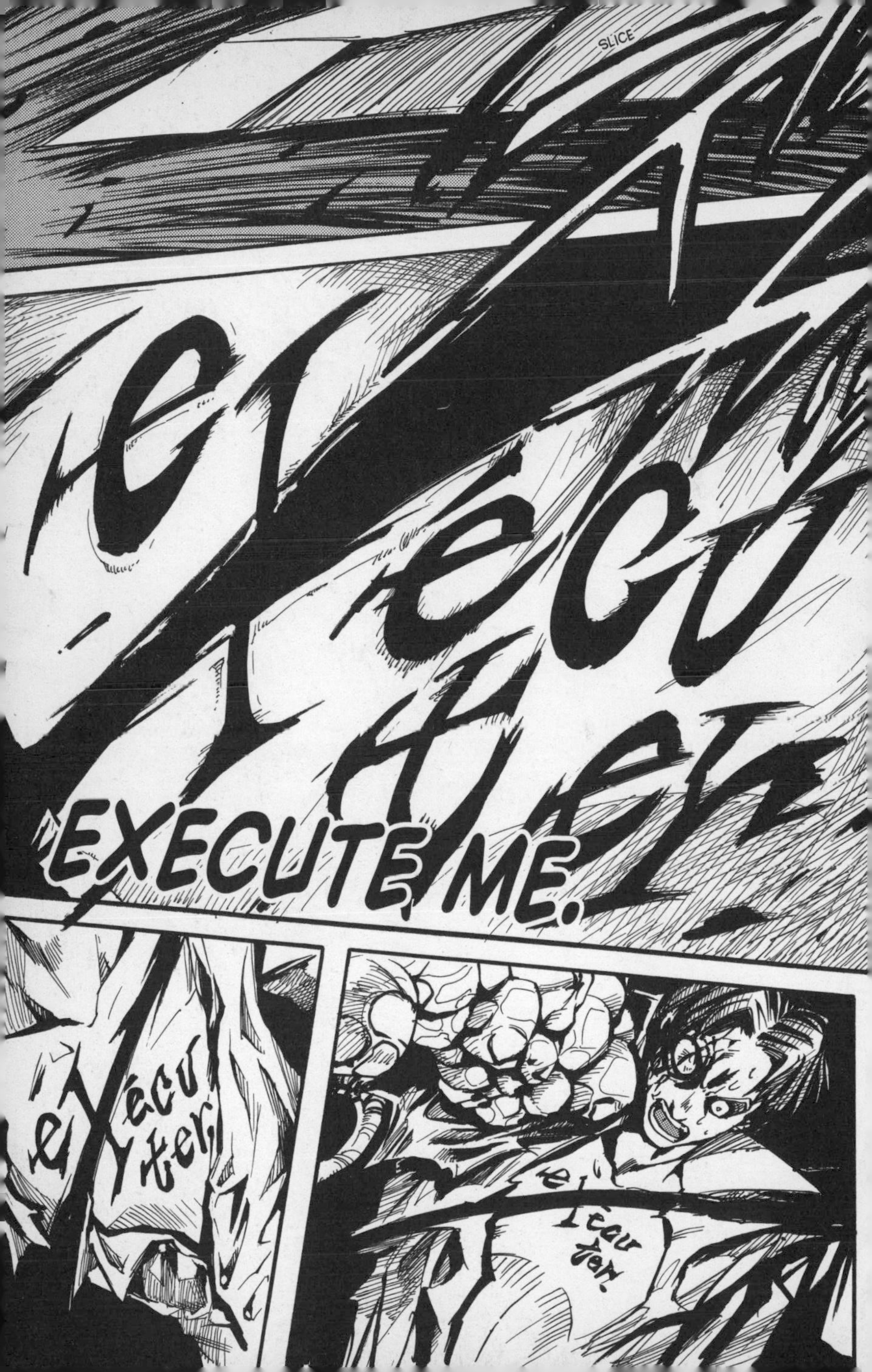
SLICE
EXECUTE ME.
exécuter.
exécuter,

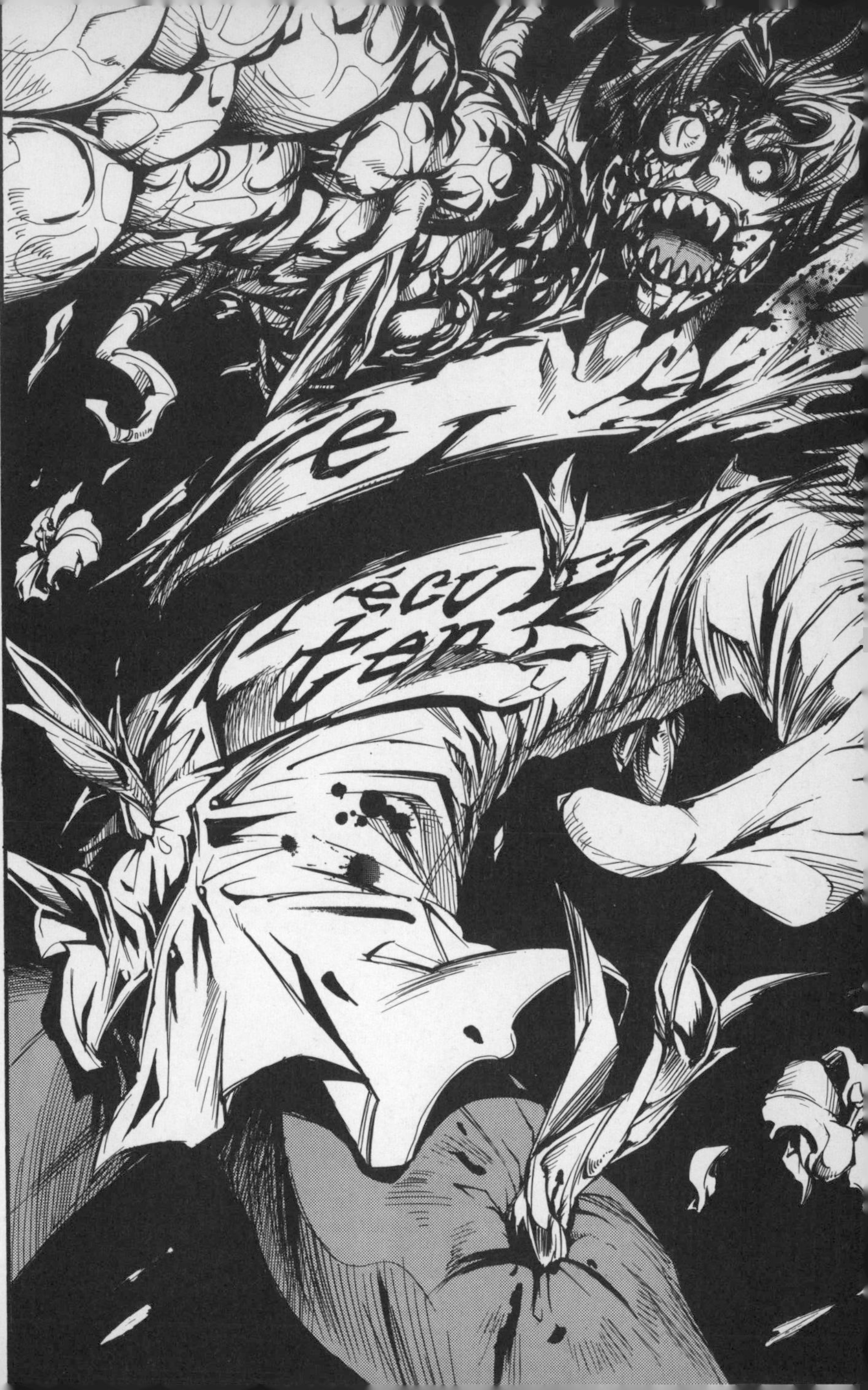

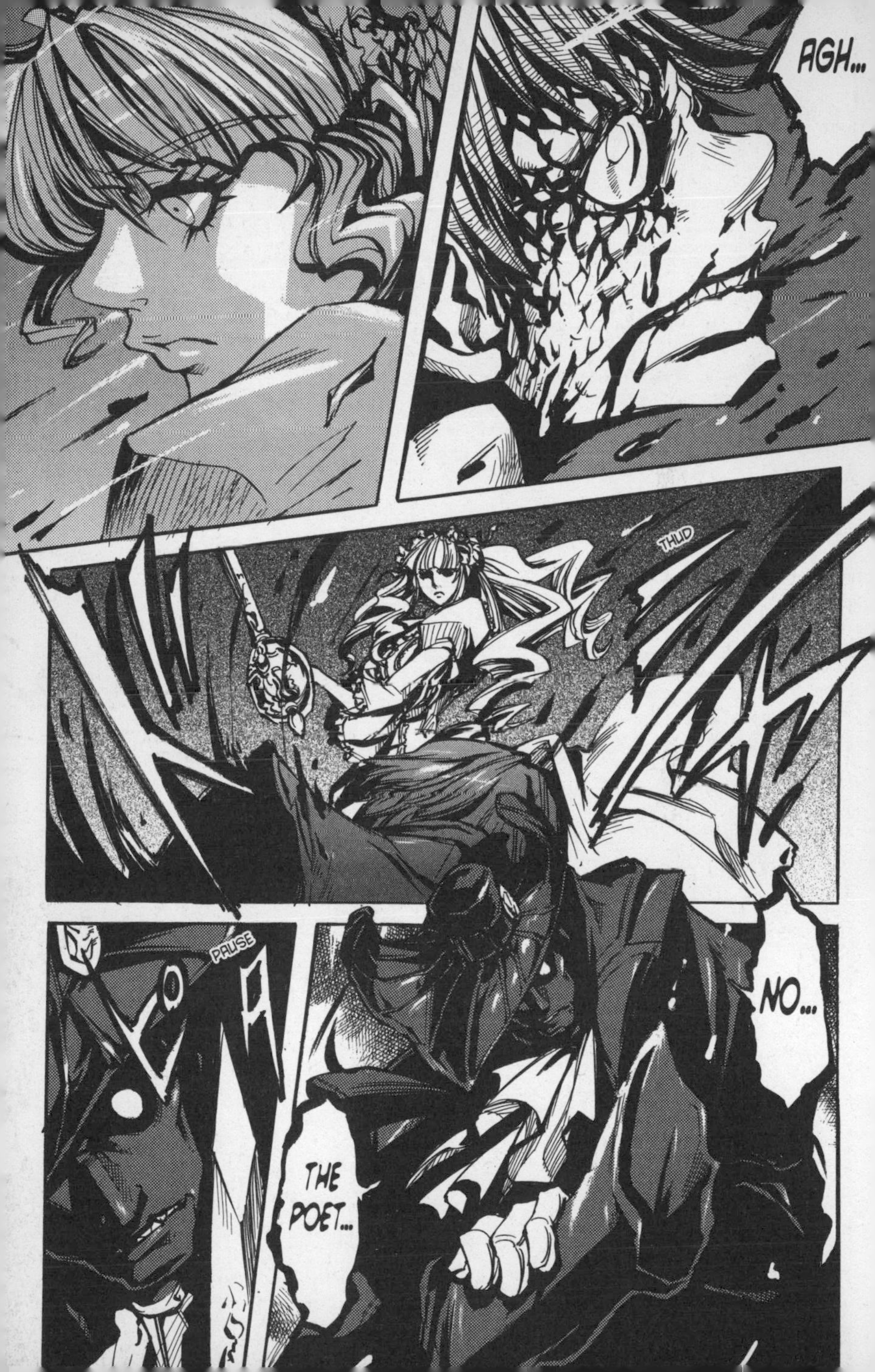
AGH...
THUD
NO...
THE POET...
PAUSE

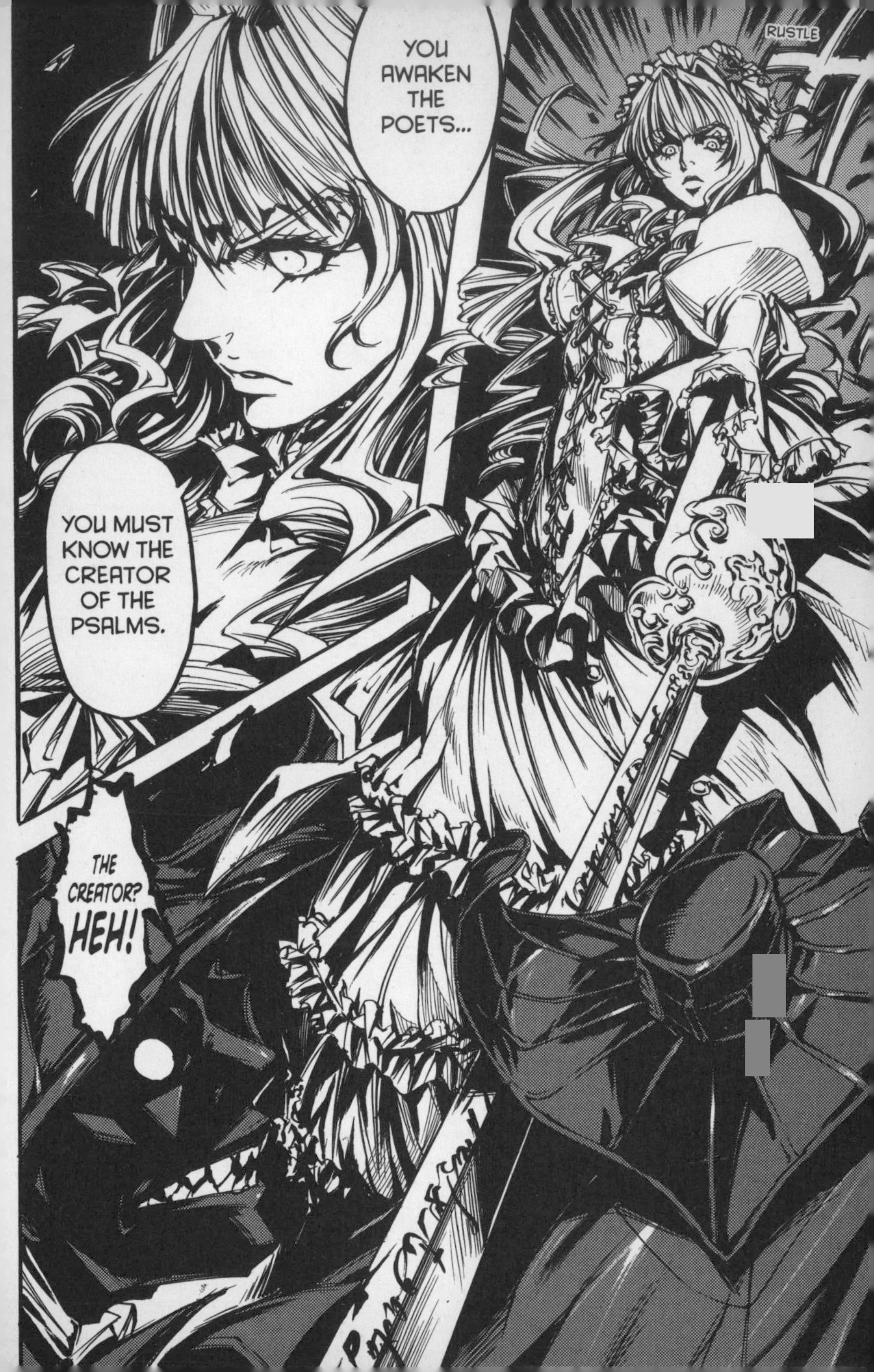
RUSTLE
YOU AWAKEN THE POETS...
YOU MUST KNOW THE CREATOR OF THE PSALMS.
THE CREATOR? HEH!

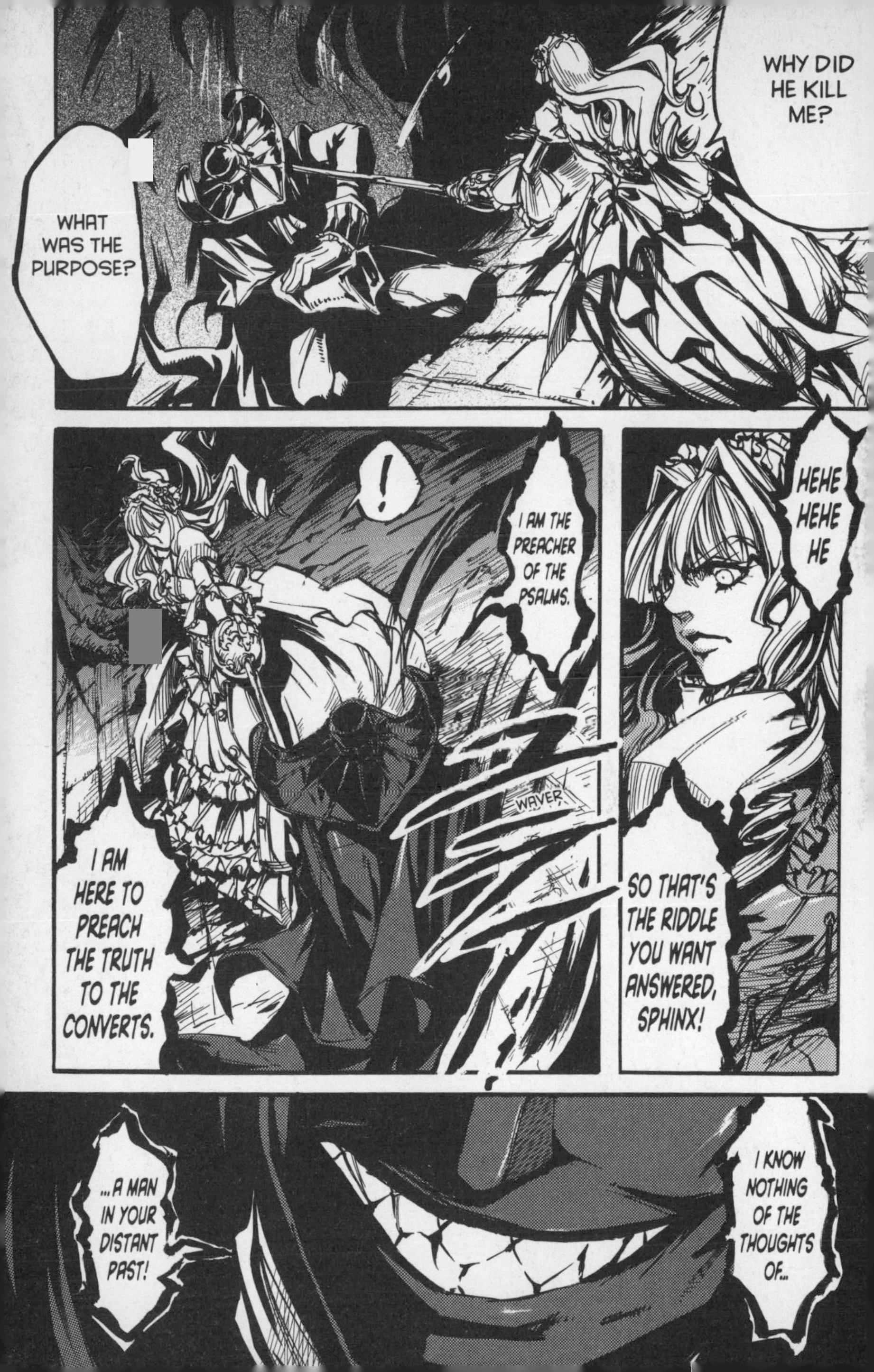
WHY DID HE KILL ME?
WHAT WAS THE PURPOSE?
HEHE HEHE HE
SO THAT'S THE RIDDLE YOU WANT ANSWERED, SPHINX!
!
I AM THE PREACHER OF THE PSALMS.
WAVER
I AM HERE TO PREACH THE TRUTH TO THE CONVERTS.
I KNOW NOTHING OF THE THOUGHTS OF...
...A MAN IN YOUR DISTANT PAST!

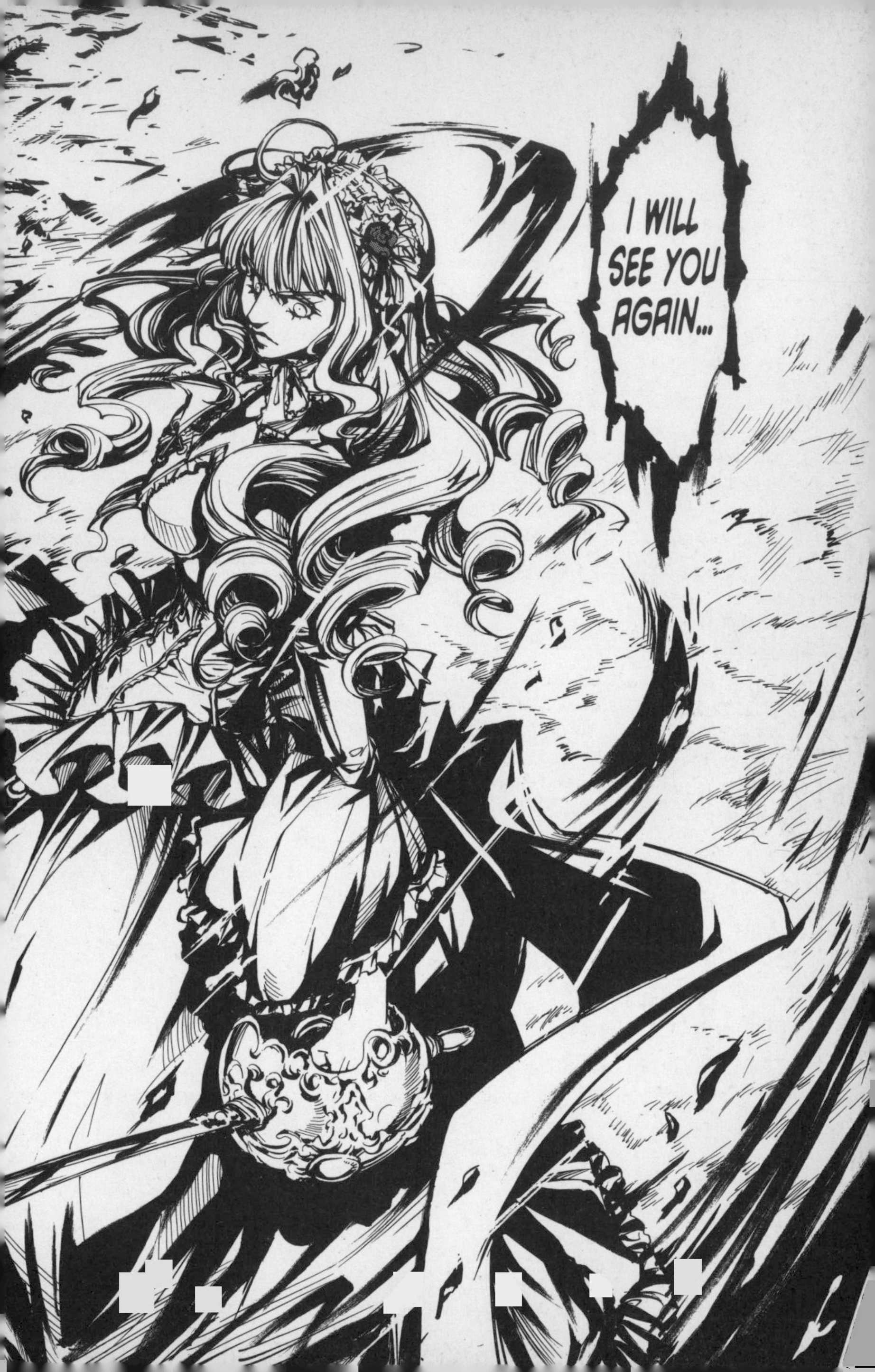
I WILL SEE YOU AGAIN...

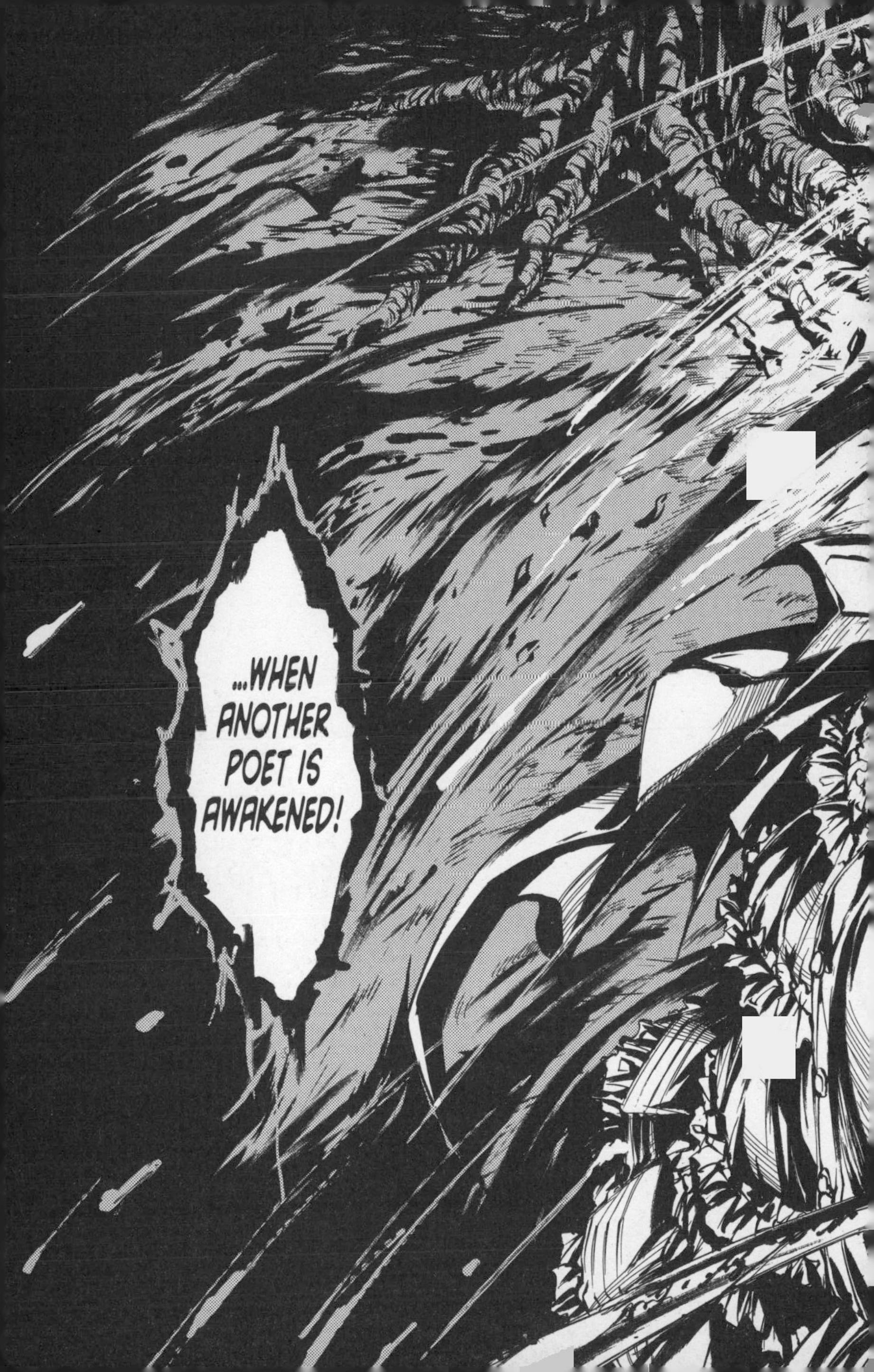
...WHEN ANOTHER POET IS AWAKENED!

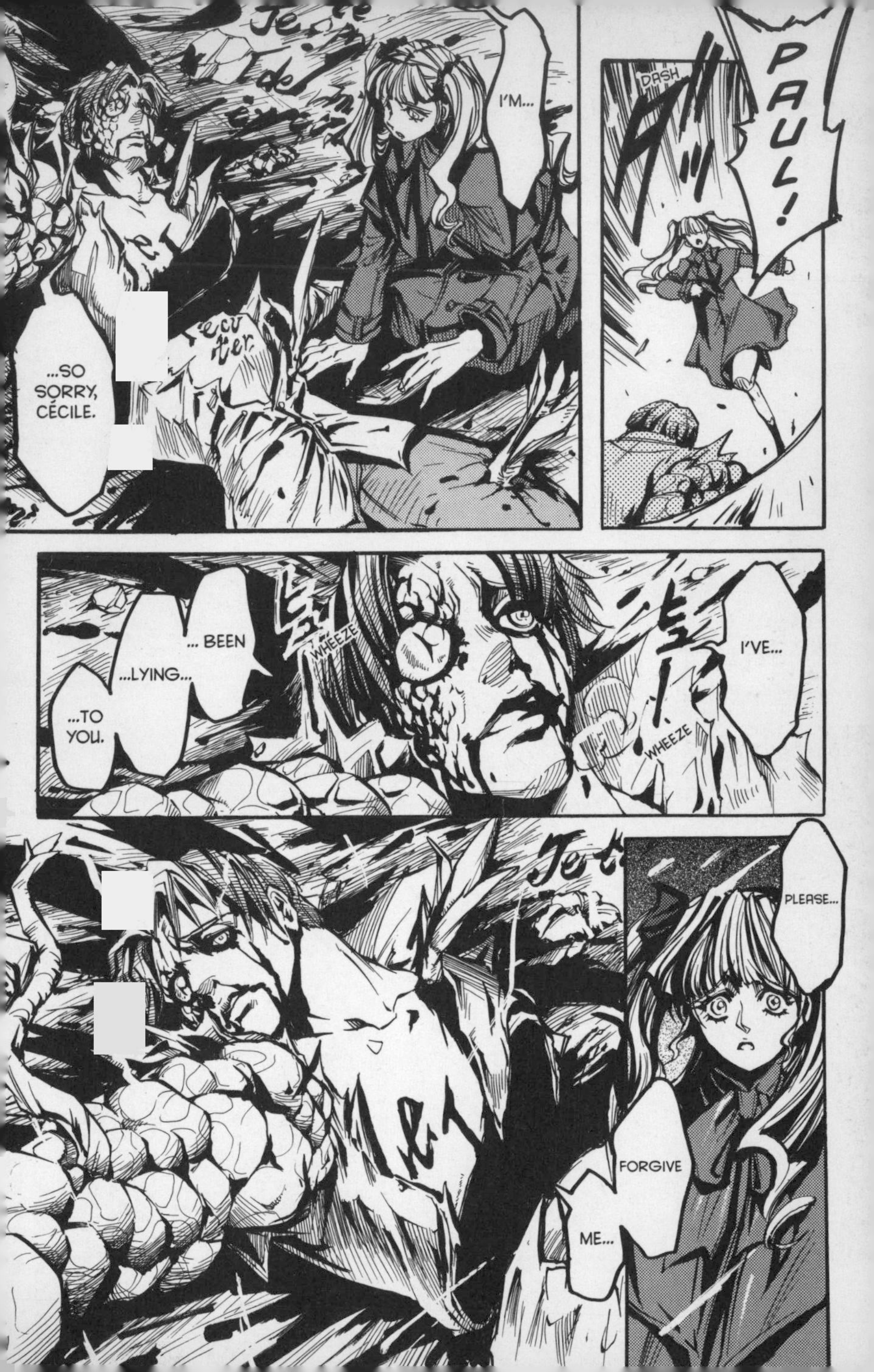
DASH
PAUL!
I'M...
...SO SORRY, CÉCILE.
I'VE...
WHEEZE
WHEEZE
... BEEN
...LYING...
...TO YOU.
PLEASE...
FORGIVE
ME...

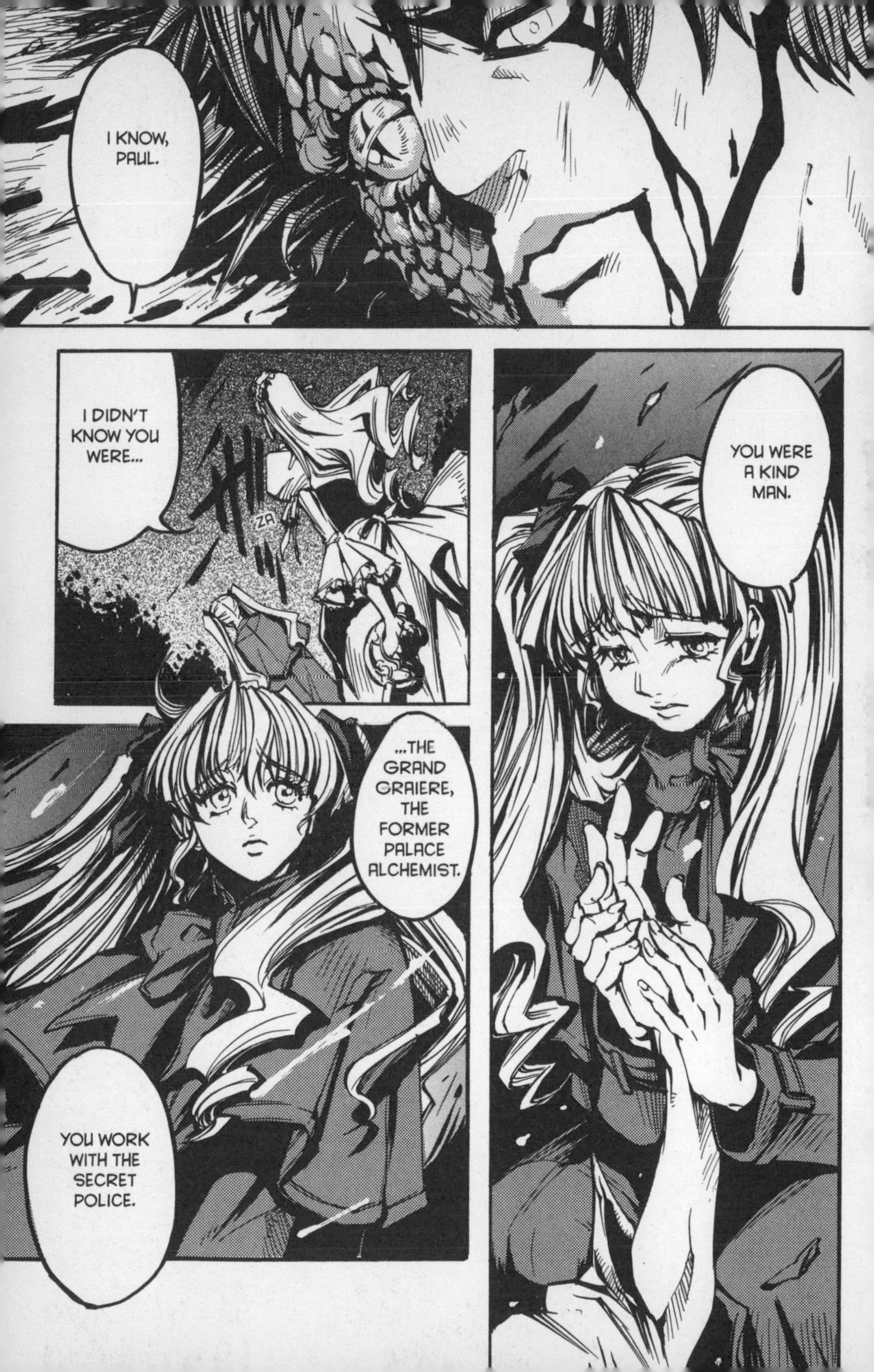
I KNOW, PAUL.
YOU WERE A KIND MAN.
I DIDN'T KNOW YOU WERE...
ZA
...THE GRAND GRAIERE, THE FORMER PALACE ALCHEMIST.
YOU WORK WITH THE SECRET POLICE.

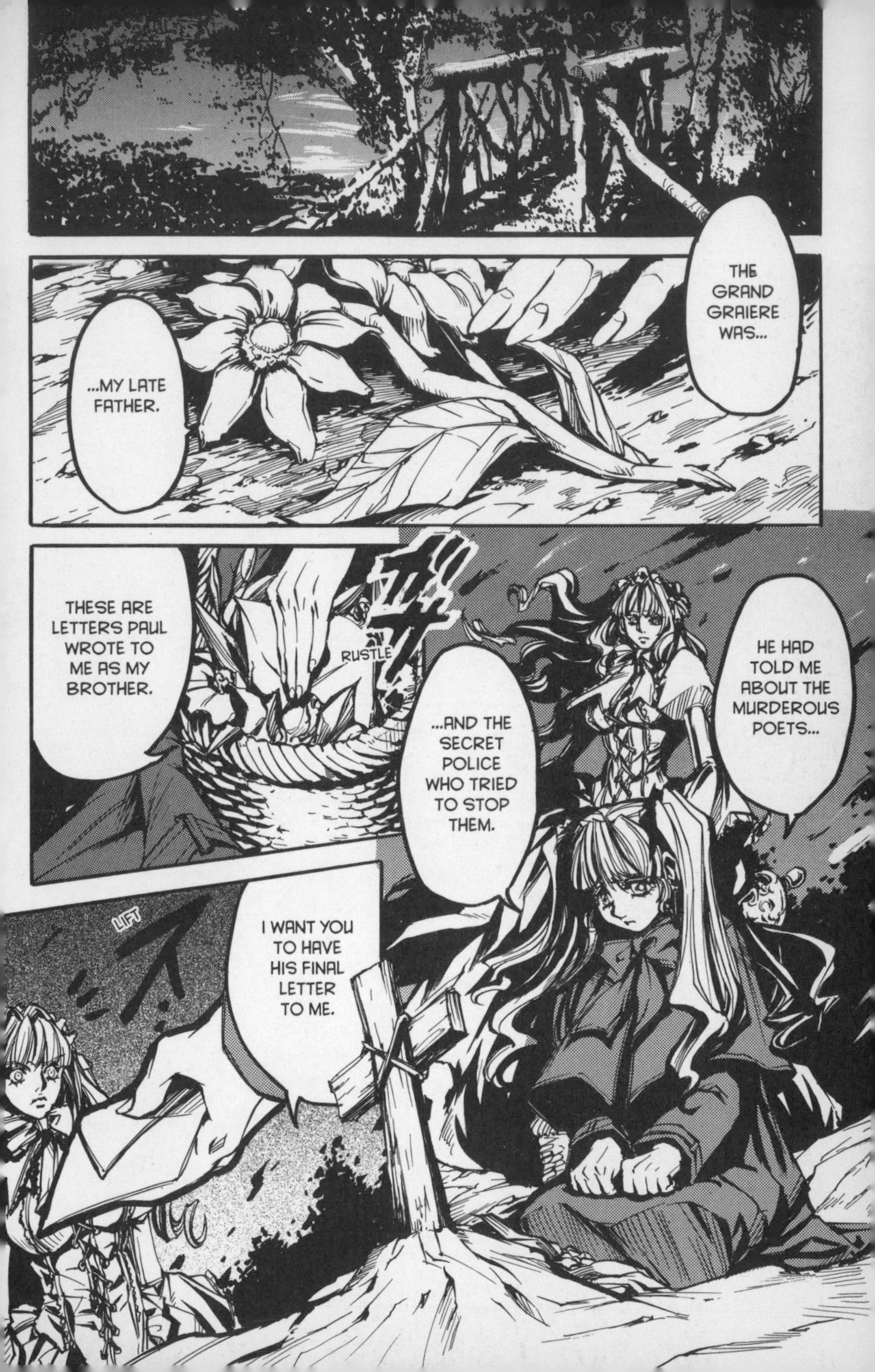
THE GRAND GRAIERE WAS...
...MY LATE FATHER.
HE HAD TOLD ME ABOUT THE MURDEROUS POETS...
...AND THE SECRET POLICE WHO TRIED TO STOP THEM.
RUSTLE
THESE ARE LETTERS PAUL WROTE TO ME AS MY BROTHER.
LIFT
I WANT YOU TO HAVE HIS FINAL LETTER TO ME.

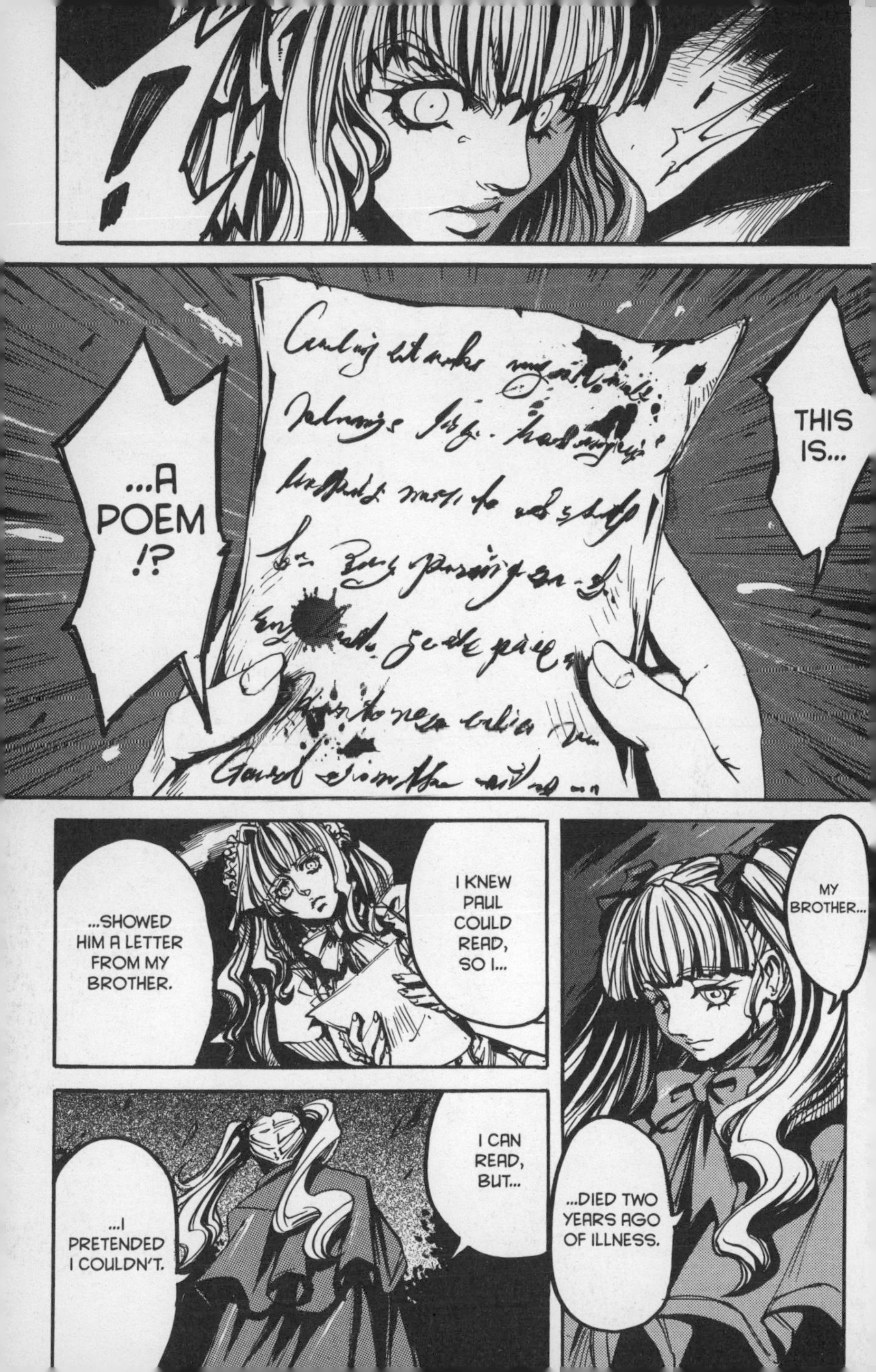
THIS IS...
...A POEM!?
MY BROTHER...
...DIED TWO YEARS AGO OF ILLNESS.
I KNEW PAUL COULD READ, SO I...
...SHOWED HIM A LETTER FROM MY BROTHER.
I CAN READ, BUT...
...I PRETENDED I COULDN'T.

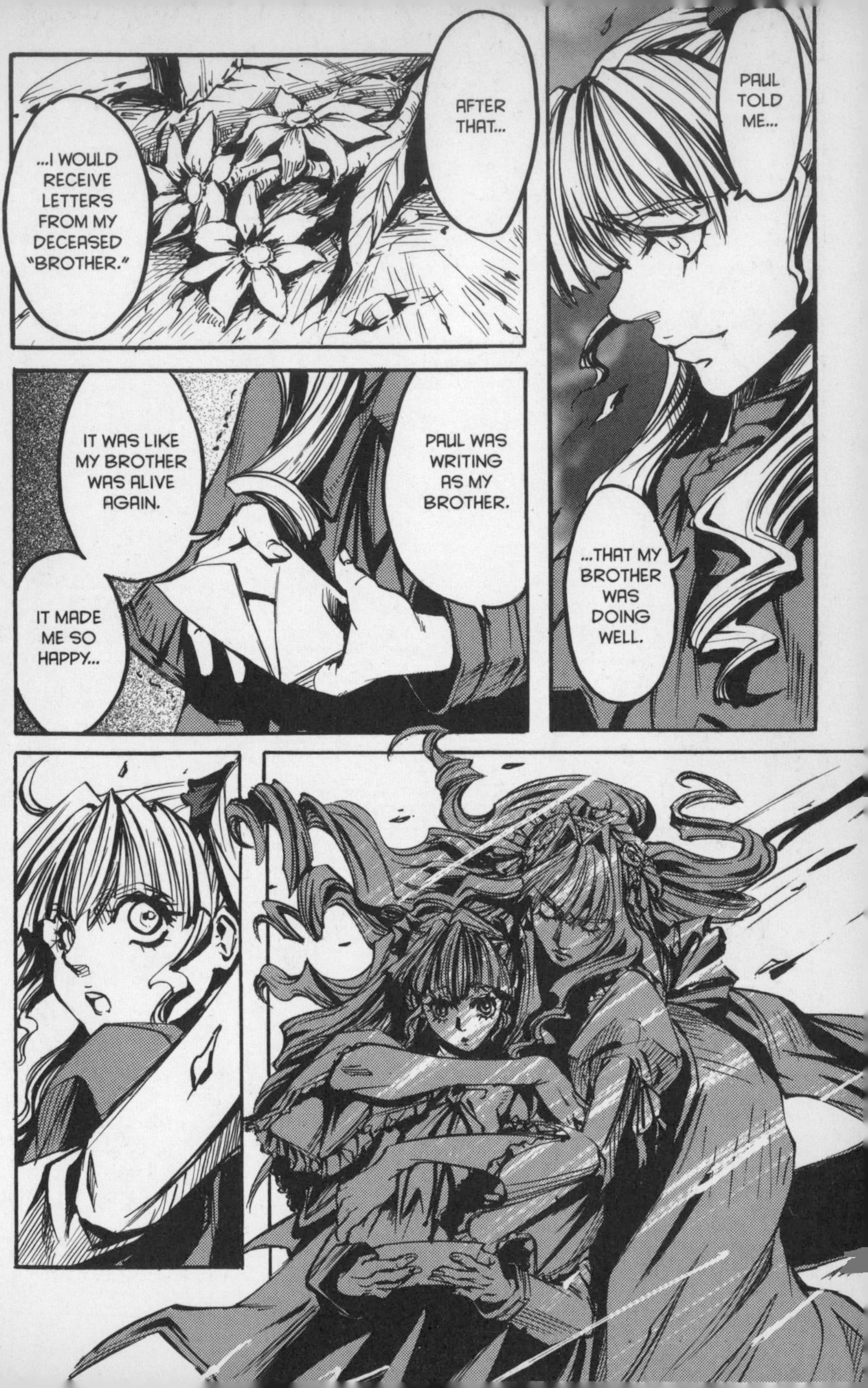
PAUL TOLD ME...
...THAT MY BROTHER WAS DOING WELL.
AFTER THAT...
...I WOULD RECEIVE LETTERS FROM MY DECEASED "BROTHER."
PAUL WAS WRITING AS MY BROTHER.
IT WAS LIKE MY BROTHER WAS ALIVE AGAIN.
IT MADE ME SO HAPPY...

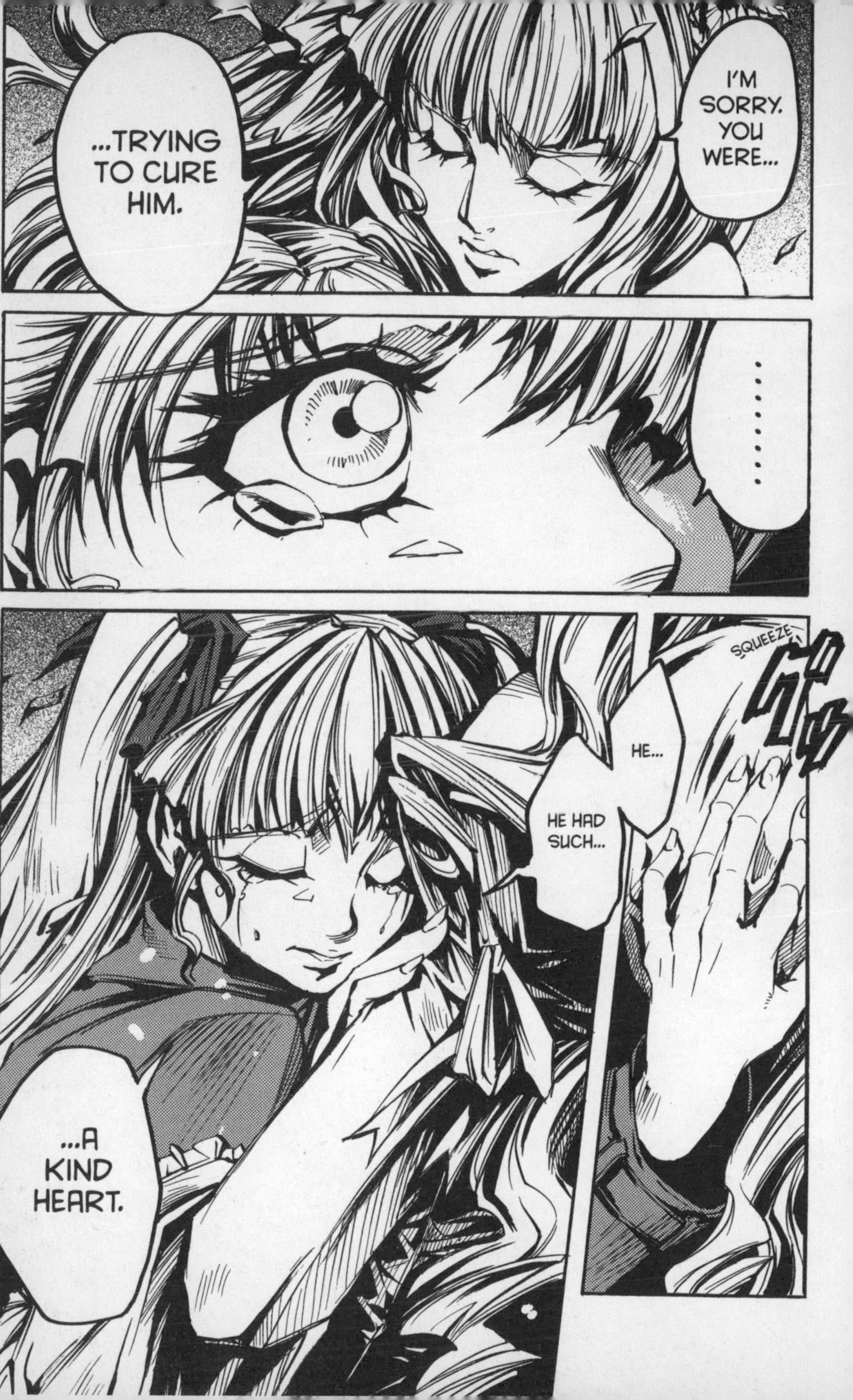
I'M SORRY. YOU WERE...
...TRYING TO CURE HIM.
......
SQUEEZE
HE...
HE HAD SUCH...
...A KIND HEART.

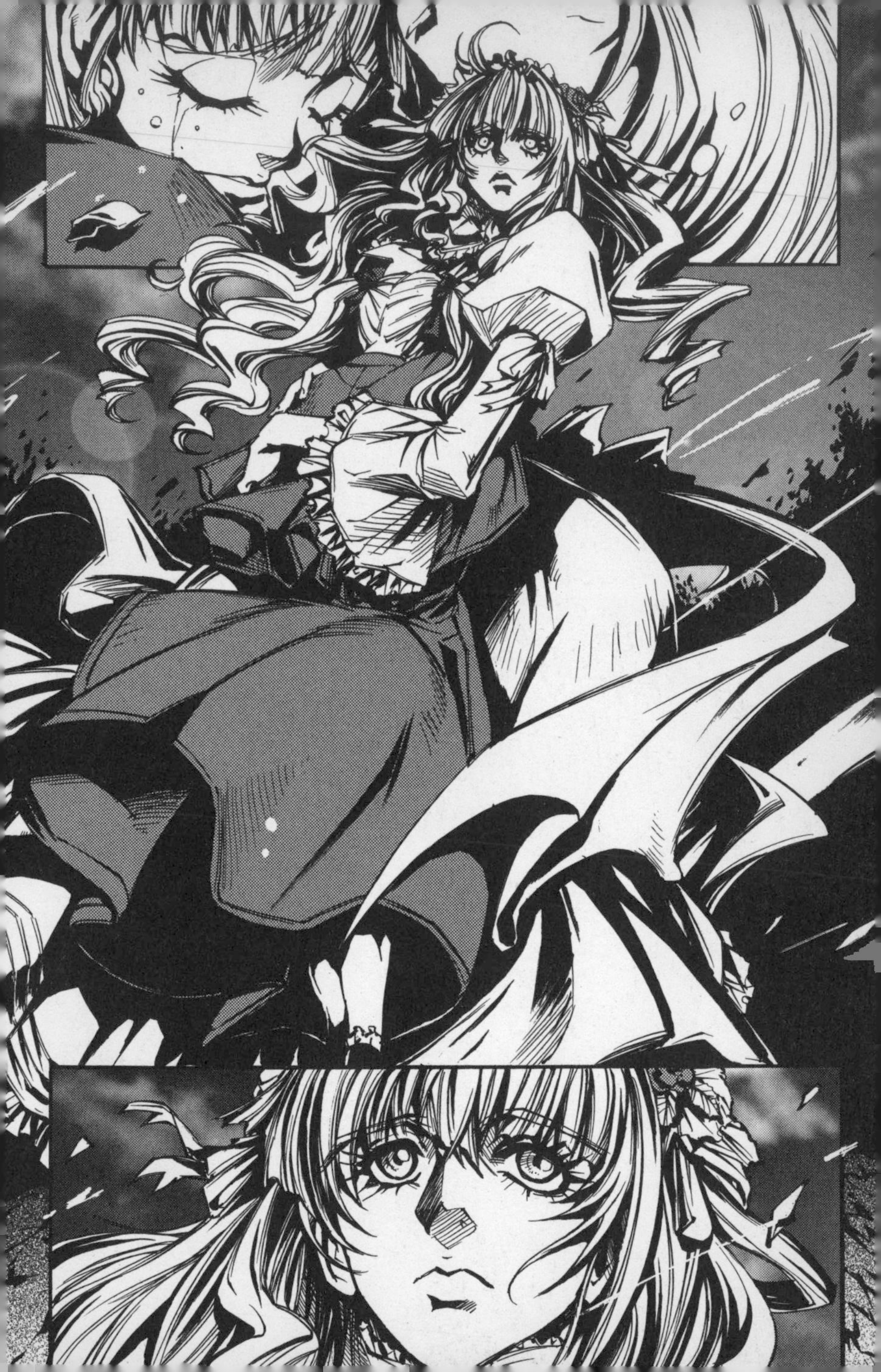

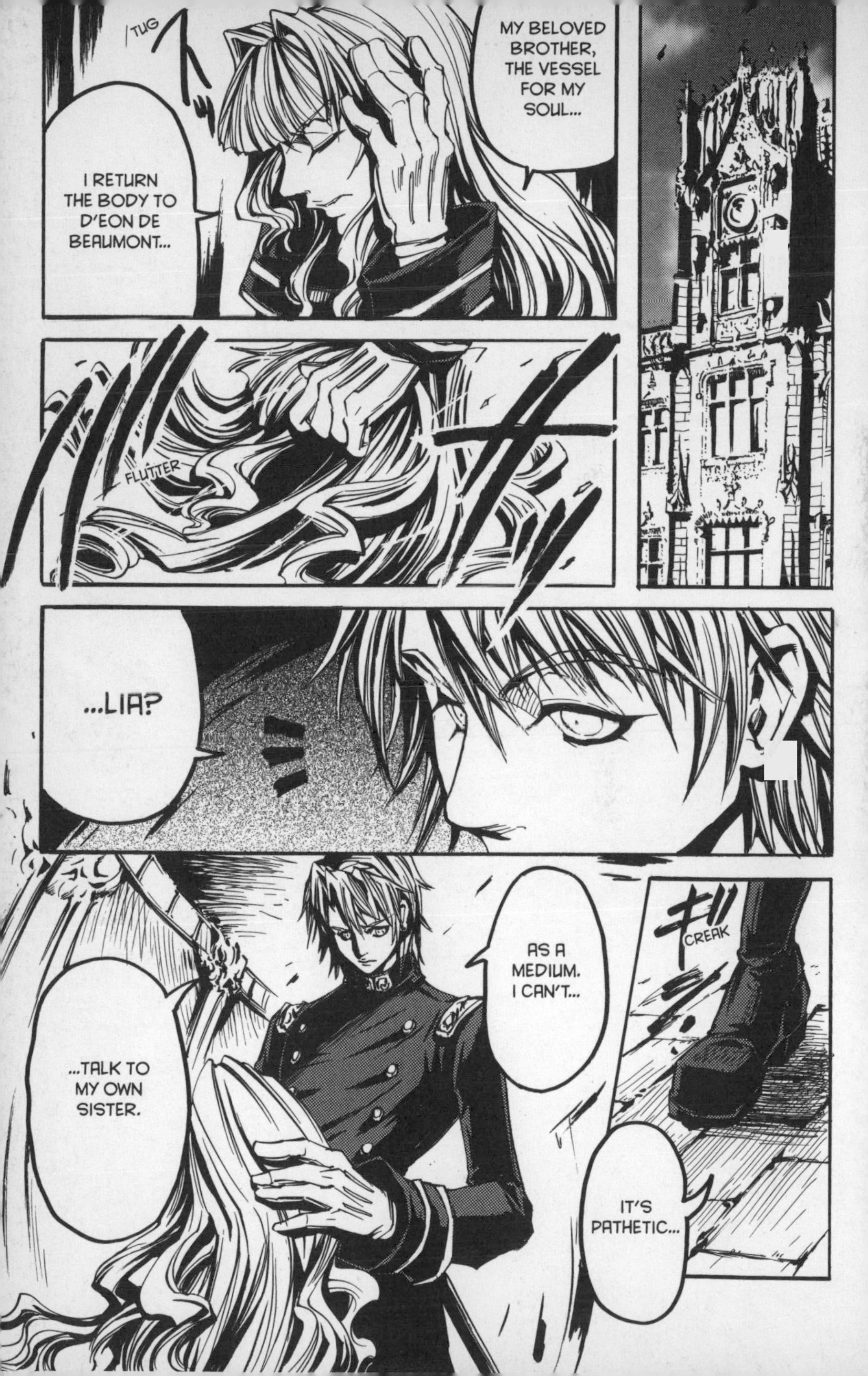
MY BELOVED BROTHER, THE VESSEL FOR MY SOUL...
TUG
I RETURN THE BODY TO D'EON DE BEAUMONT...
FLUTTER
...LIA?
CREAK
IT'S PATHETIC...
AS A MEDIUM. I CAN'T...
...TALK TO MY OWN SISTER.

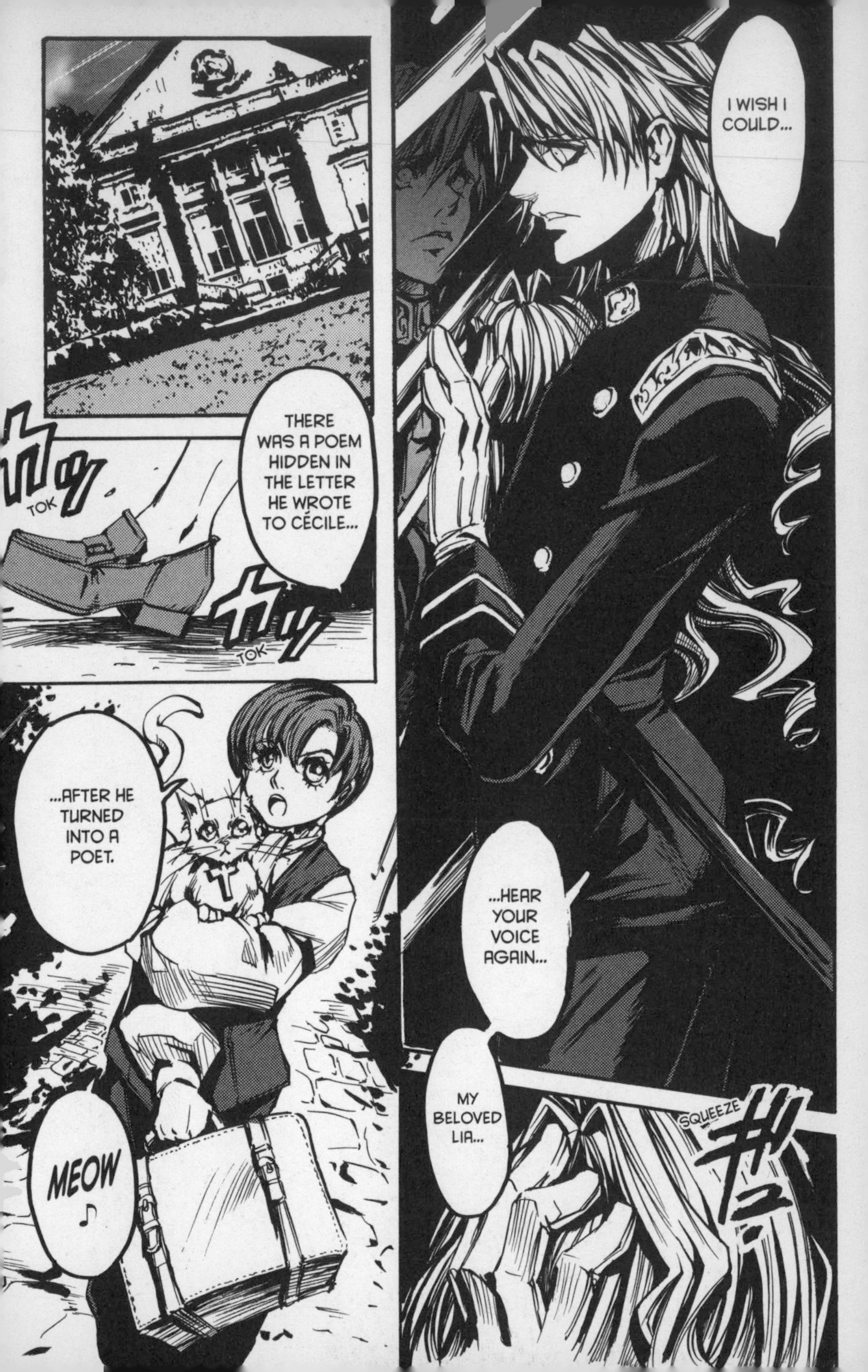

I WISH I COULD...
...HEAR YOUR VOICE AGAIN...
MY BELOVED LIA...
SQUEEZE
THERE WAS A POEM HIDDEN IN THE LETTER HE WROTE TO CÉCILE...
TOK
TOK
...AFTER HE TURNED INTO A POET.
MEOW ♪

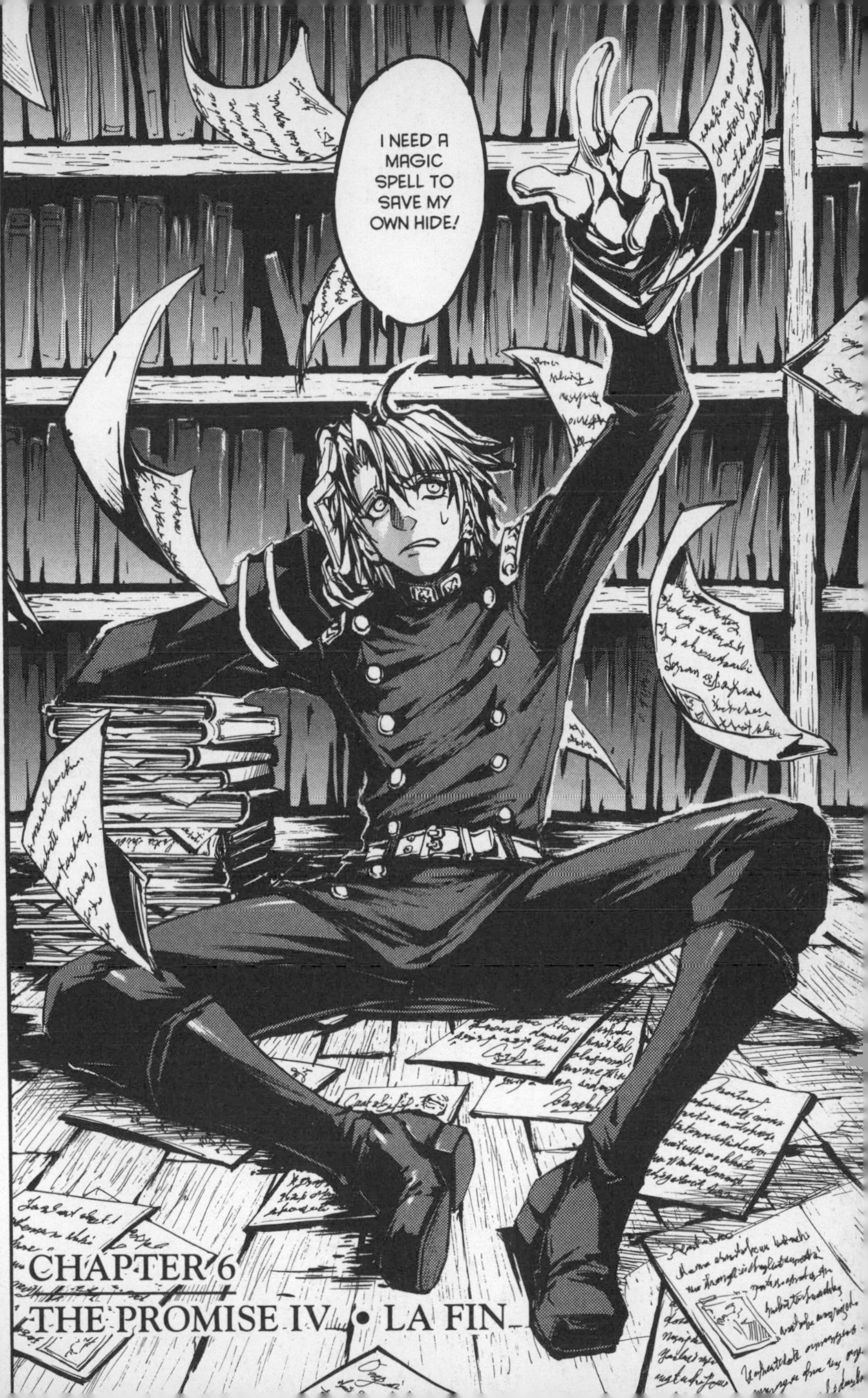
I NEED A MAGIC SPELL TO SAVE MY OWN HIDE!
CHAPTER 6
THE PROMISE IV • LA FIN

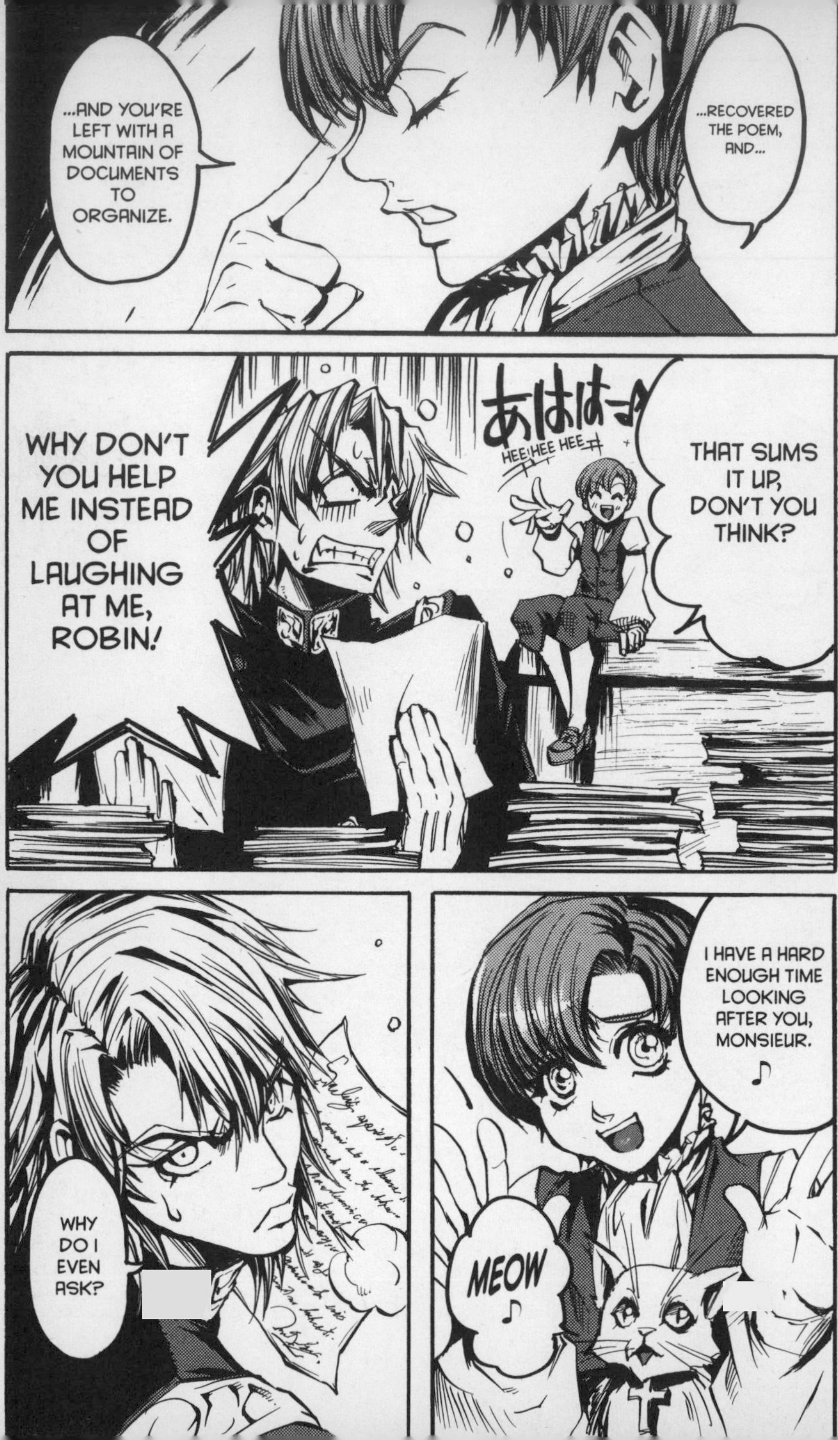
...RECOVERED THE POEM, AND...
...AND YOU'RE LEFT WITH A MOUNTAIN OF DOCUMENTS TO ORGANIZE.
THAT SUMS IT UP, DON'T YOU THINK?
あははー♪
HEE HEE HEE
WHY DON'T YOU HELP ME INSTEAD OF LAUGHING AT ME, ROBIN!
I HAVE A HARD ENOUGH TIME LOOKING AFTER YOU, MONSIEUR. ♪
MEOW ♪
WHY DO I EVEN ASK?

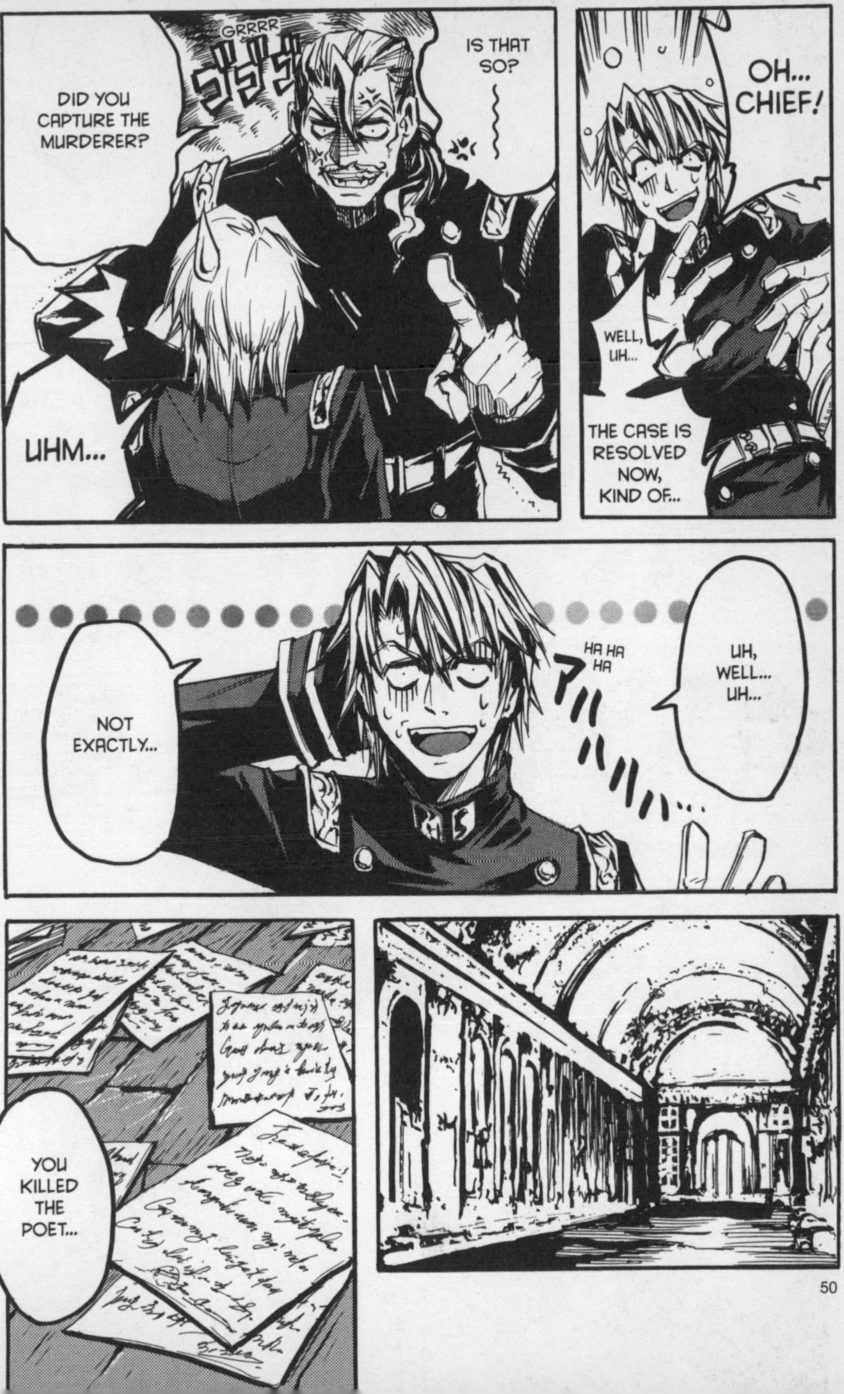
OH... CHIEF!
WELL, UH...
THE CASE IS RESOLVED NOW, KIND OF...
IS THAT SO?
GRRRR
DID YOU CAPTURE THE MURDERER?
UHM...
UH, WELL... UH...
HA HA HA
NOT EXACTLY...
YOU KILLED THE POET...

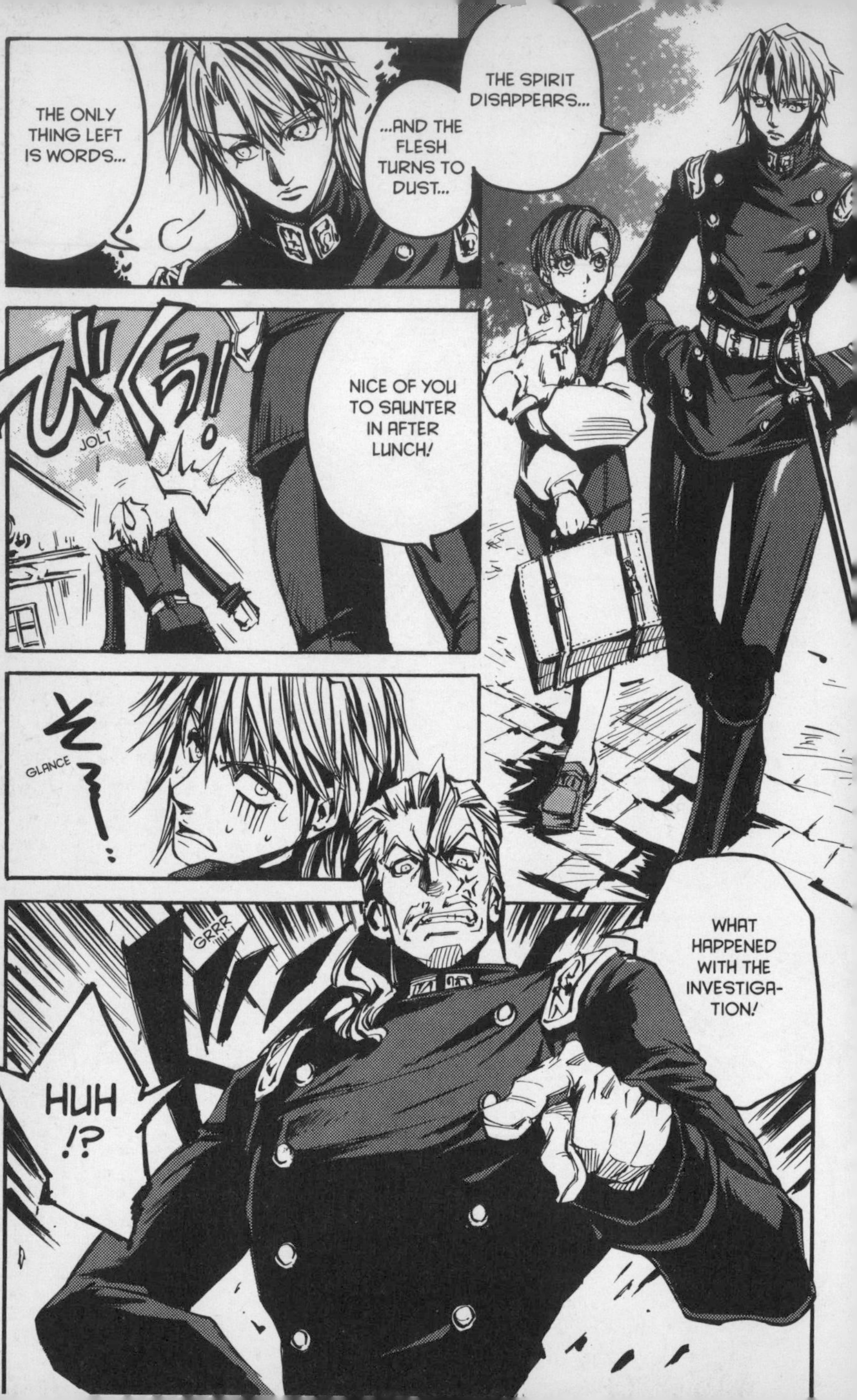
THE SPIRIT DISAPPEARS...
...AND THE FLESH TURNS TO DUST...
THE ONLY THING LEFT IS WORDS...
NICE OF YOU TO SAUNTER IN AFTER LUNCH!
JOLT
GLANCE
WHAT HAPPENED WITH THE INVESTIGA-TION!
GRRR
HUH !?

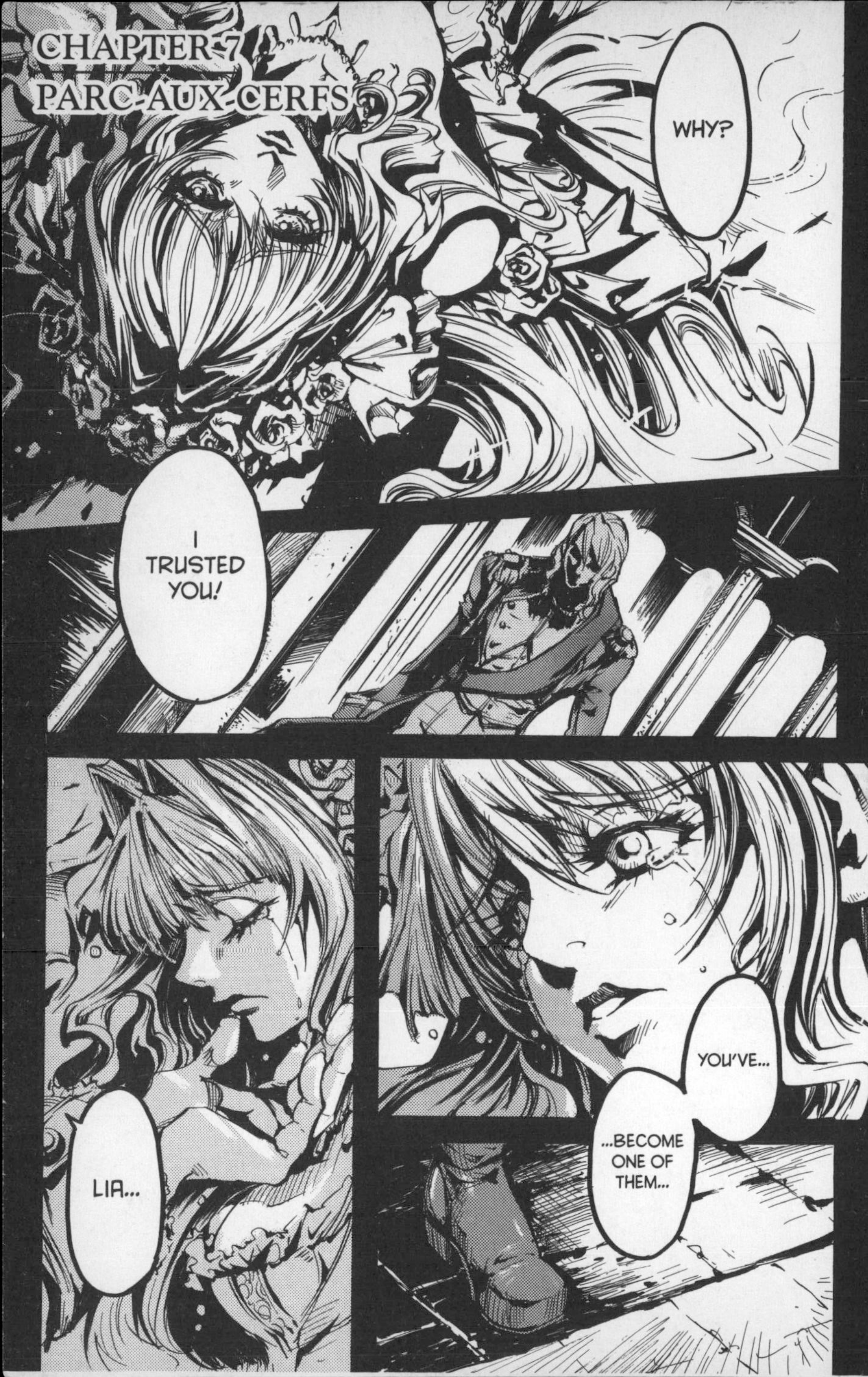
CHAPTER 7
PARC-AUX-CERFS
WHY?
I TRUSTED YOU!
YOU'VE...
...BECOME ONE OF THEM...
LIA...

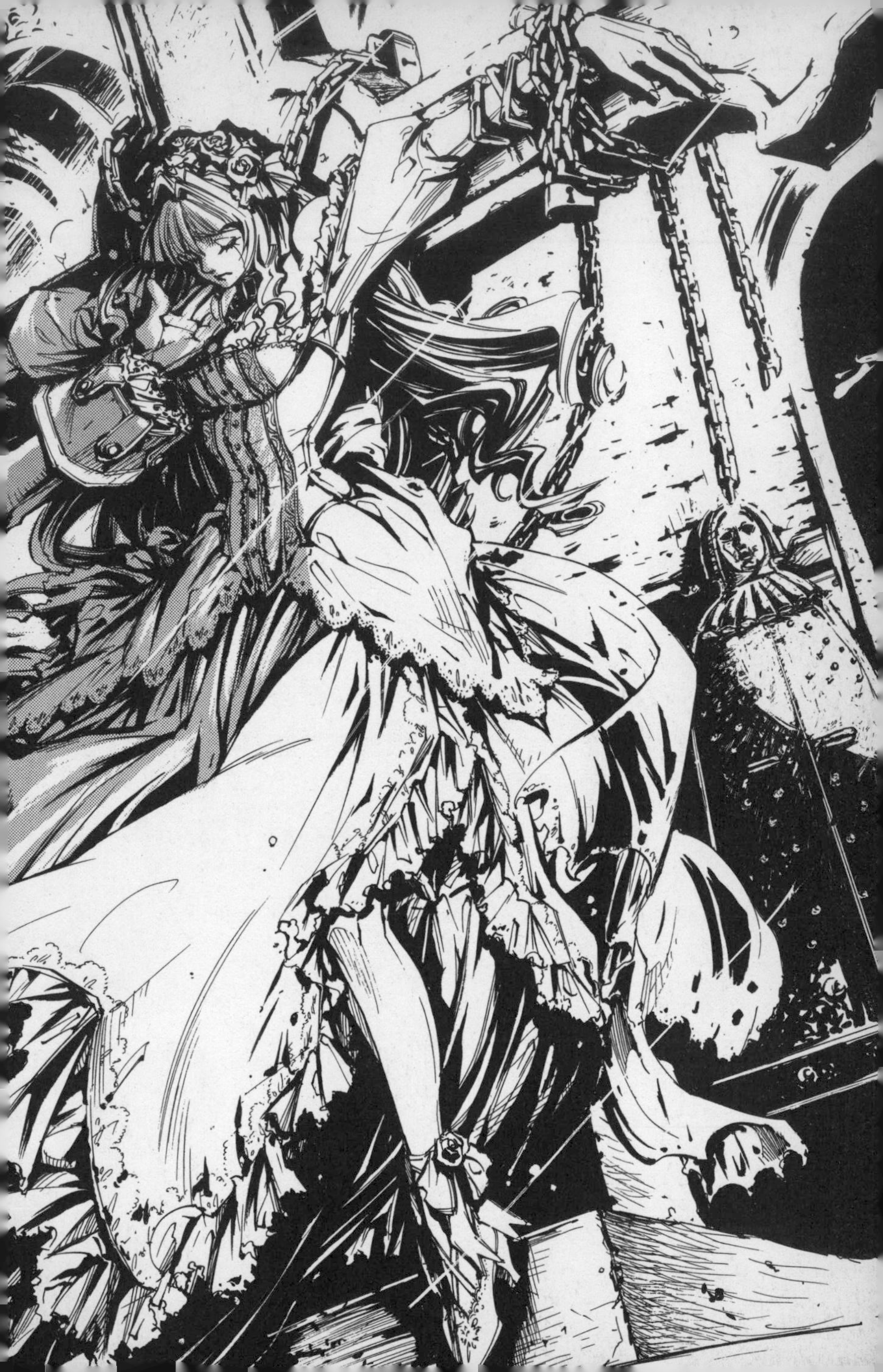

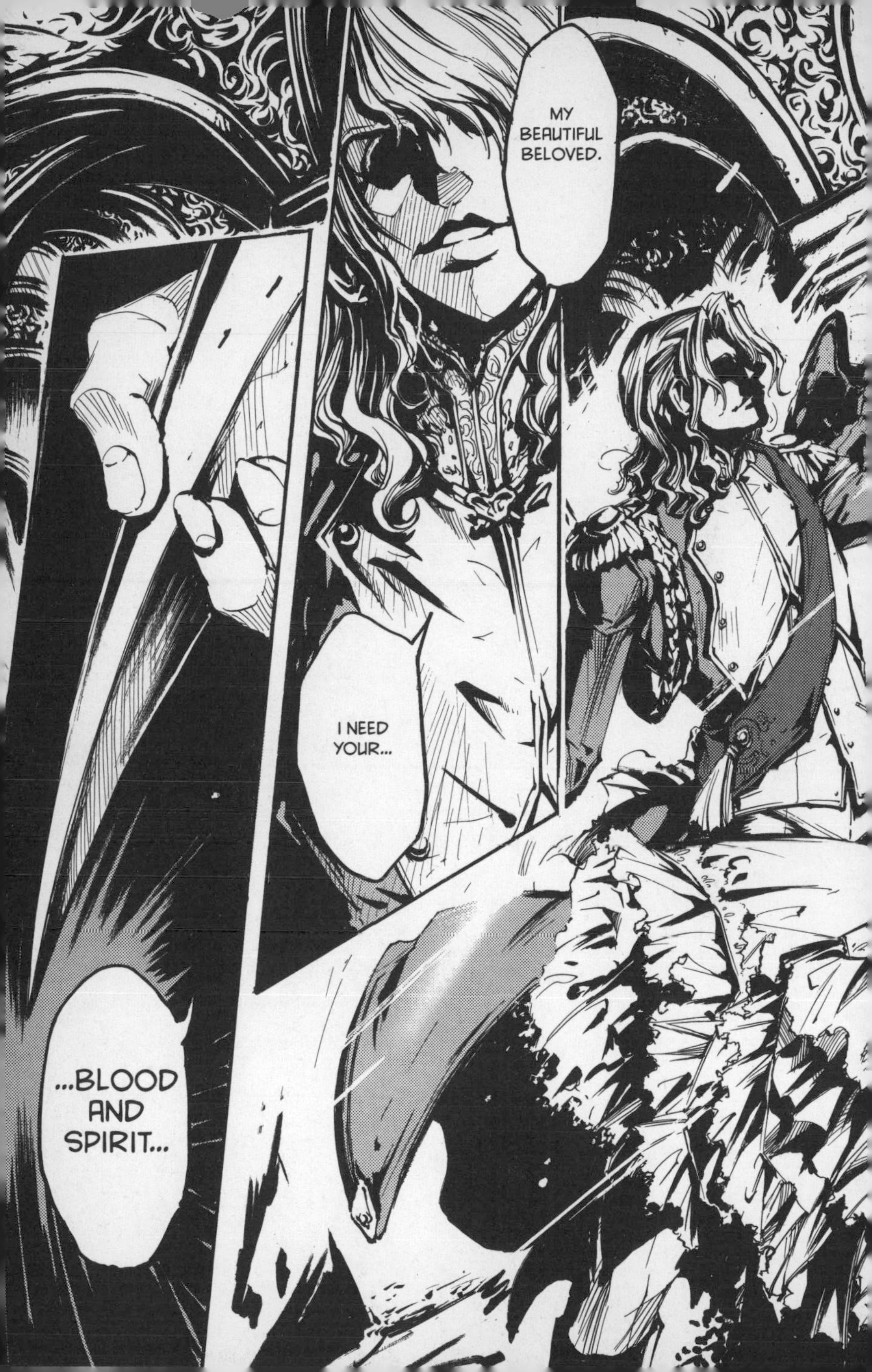
MY BEAUTIFUL BELOVED.
I NEED YOUR...
...BLOOD AND SPIRIT...

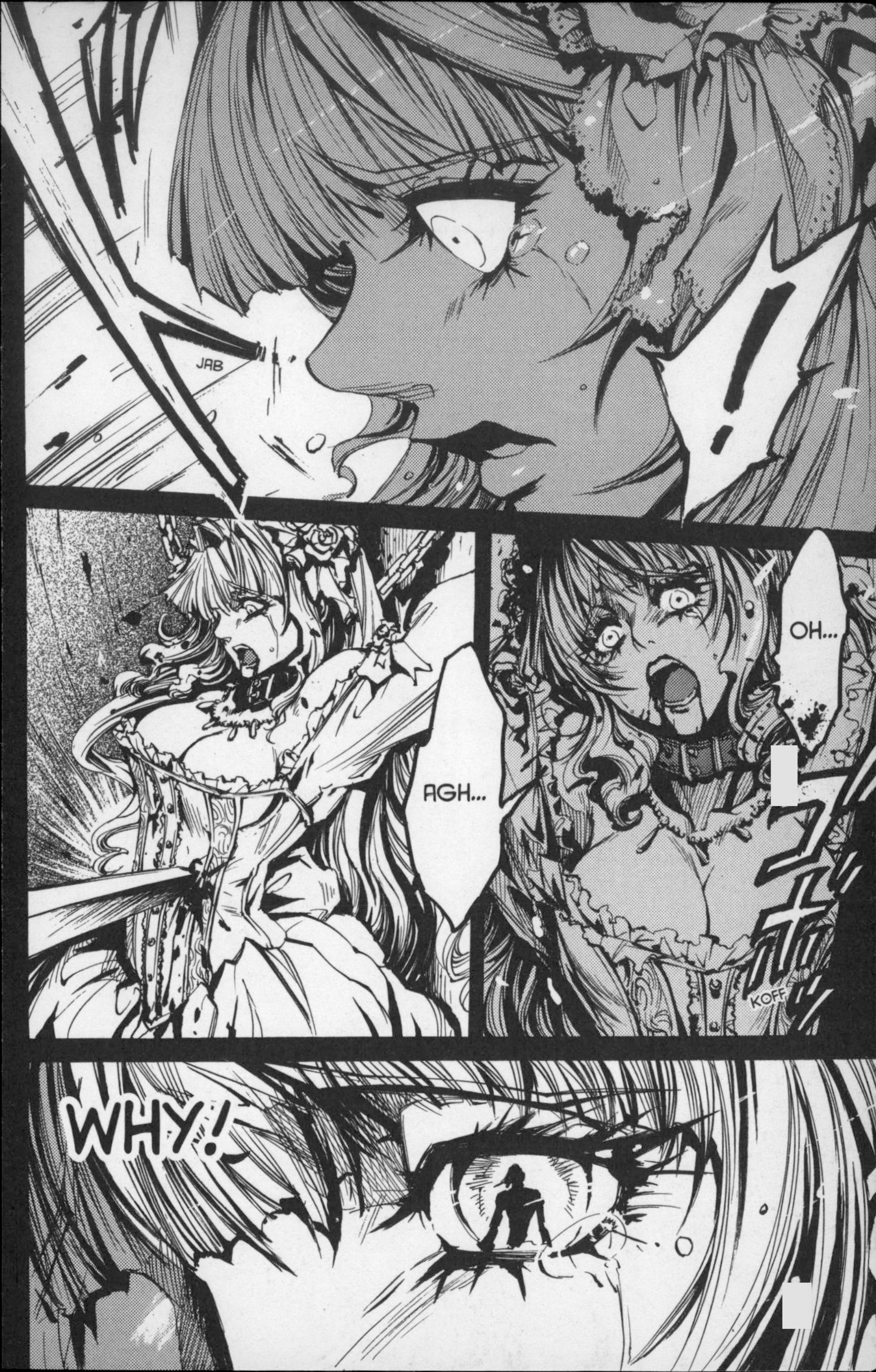
JAB
OH...
KOFF
AGH...
WHY!

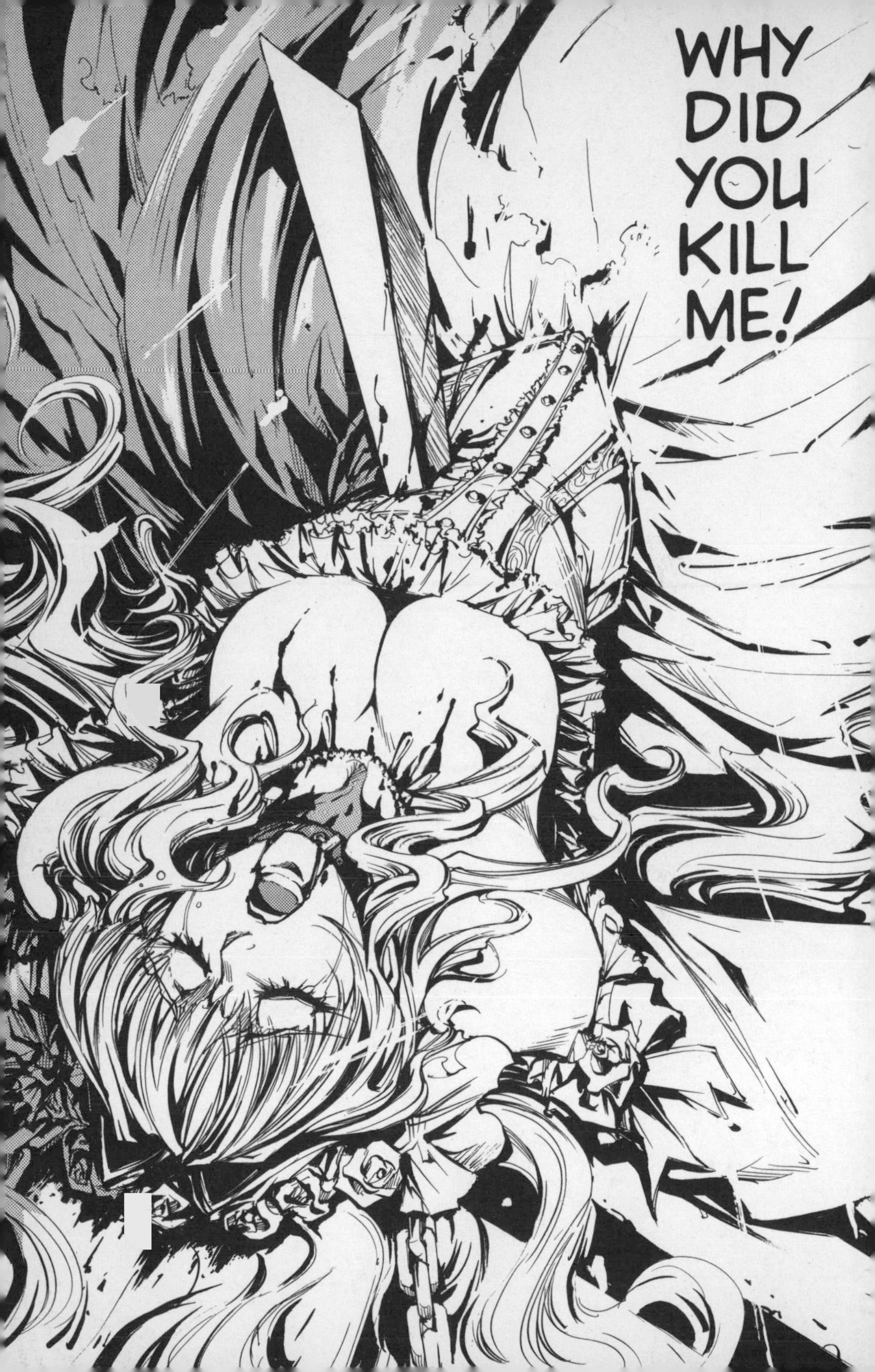
WHY DID YOU KILL ME!

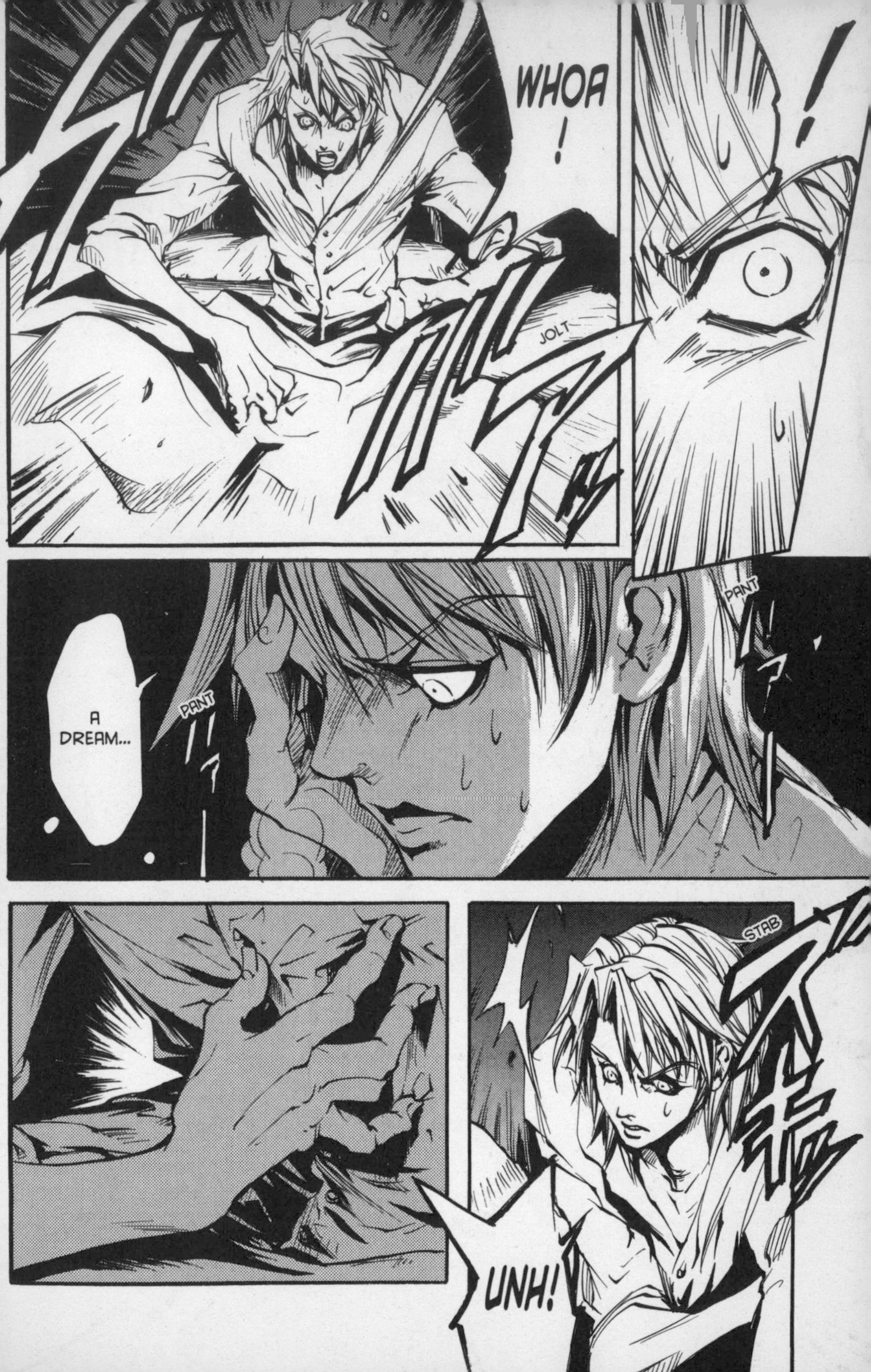
WHOA!
JOLT
PANT
A DREAM...
PANT
STAB
UNH!

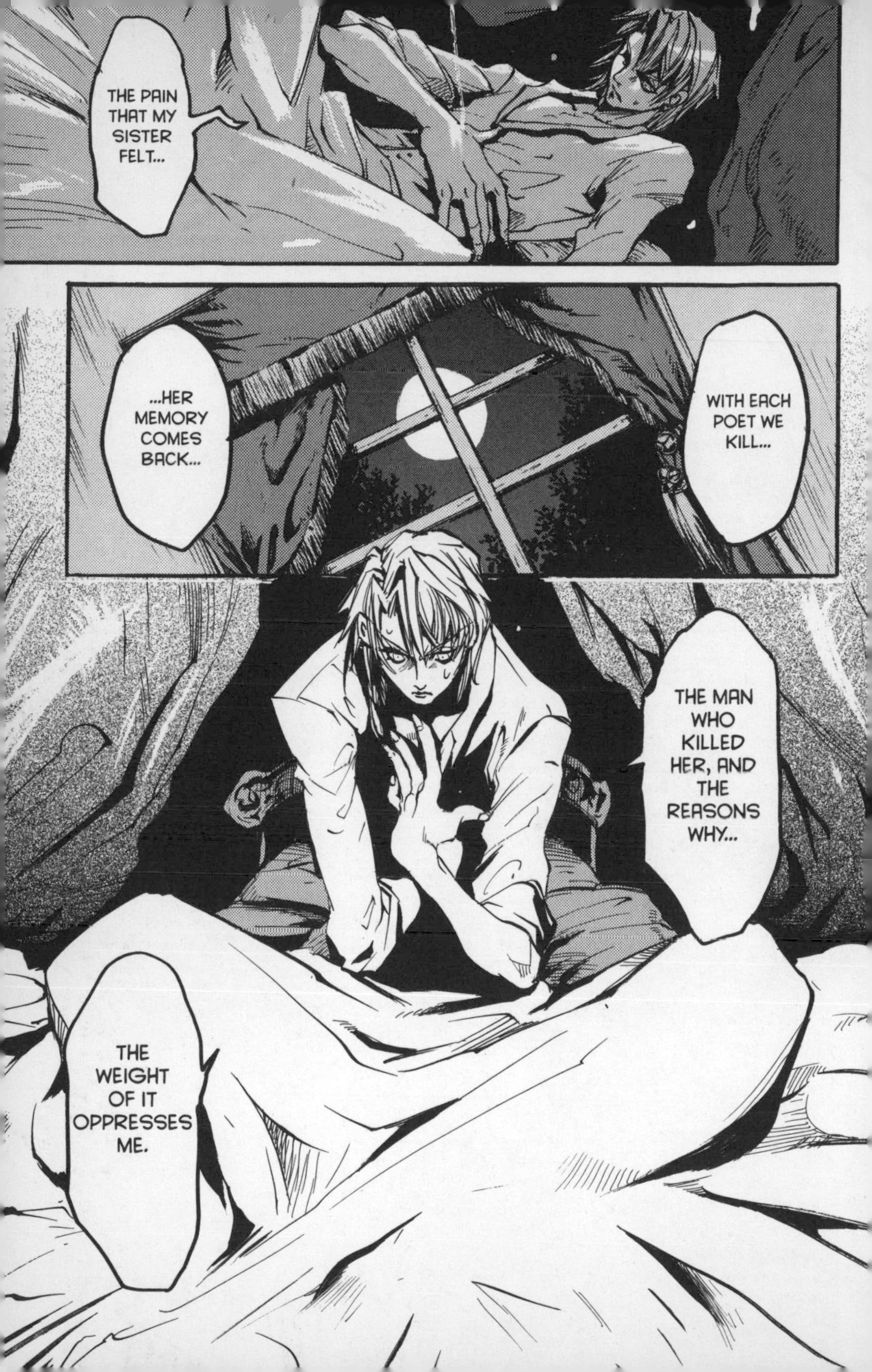
THE PAIN THAT MY SISTER FELT...
WITH EACH POET WE KILL...
...HER MEMORY COMES BACK...
THE MAN WHO KILLED HER, AND THE REASONS WHY...
THE WEIGHT OF IT OPPRESSES ME.

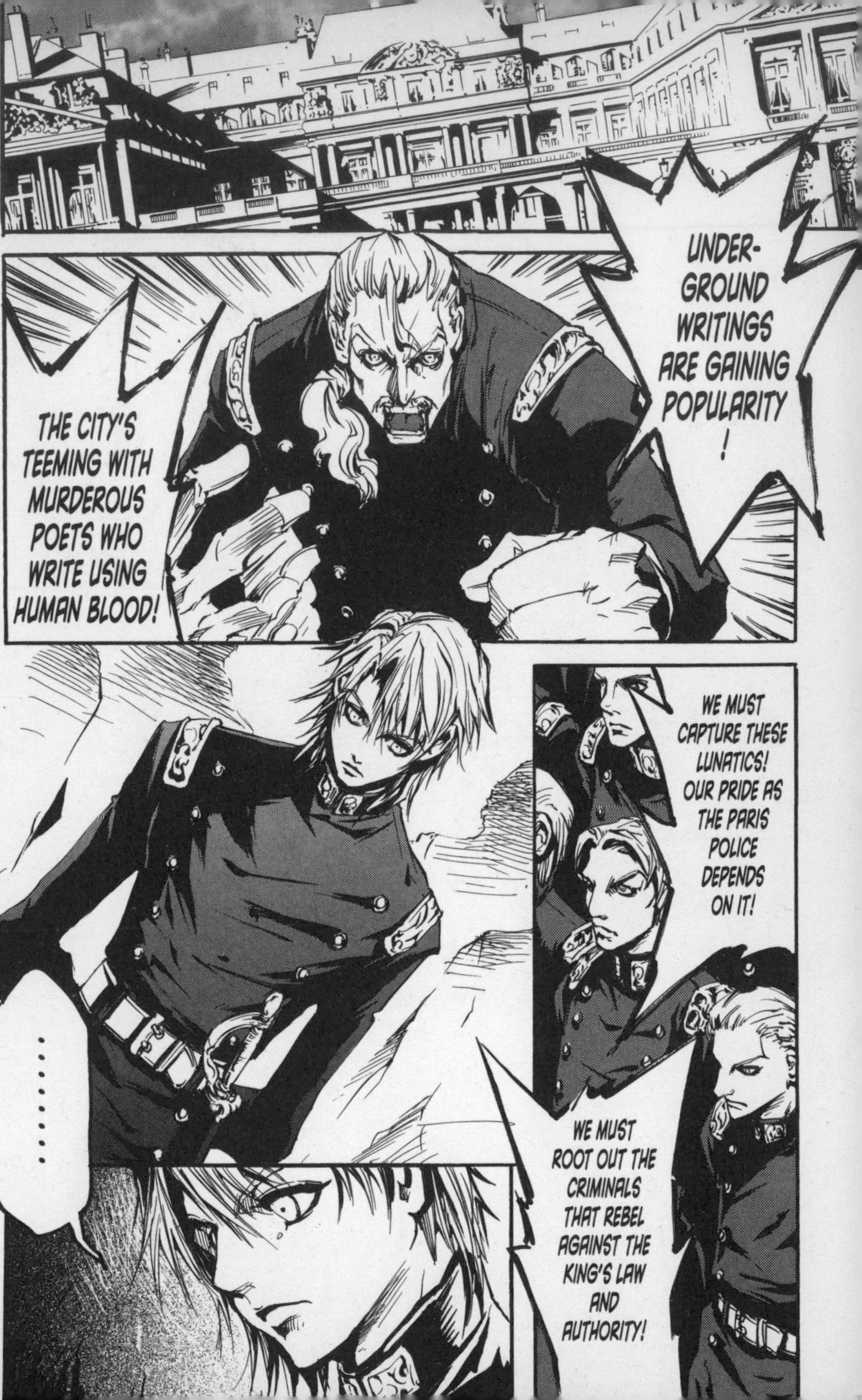
UNDER-GROUND WRITINGS ARE GAINING POPULARITY!
THE CITY'S TEEMING WITH MURDEROUS POETS WHO WRITE USING HUMAN BLOOD!
WE MUST CAPTURE THESE LUNATICS! OUR PRIDE AS THE PARIS POLICE DEPENDS ON IT!
WE MUST ROOT OUT THE CRIMINALS THAT REBEL AGAINST THE KING'S LAW AND AUTHORITY!
......

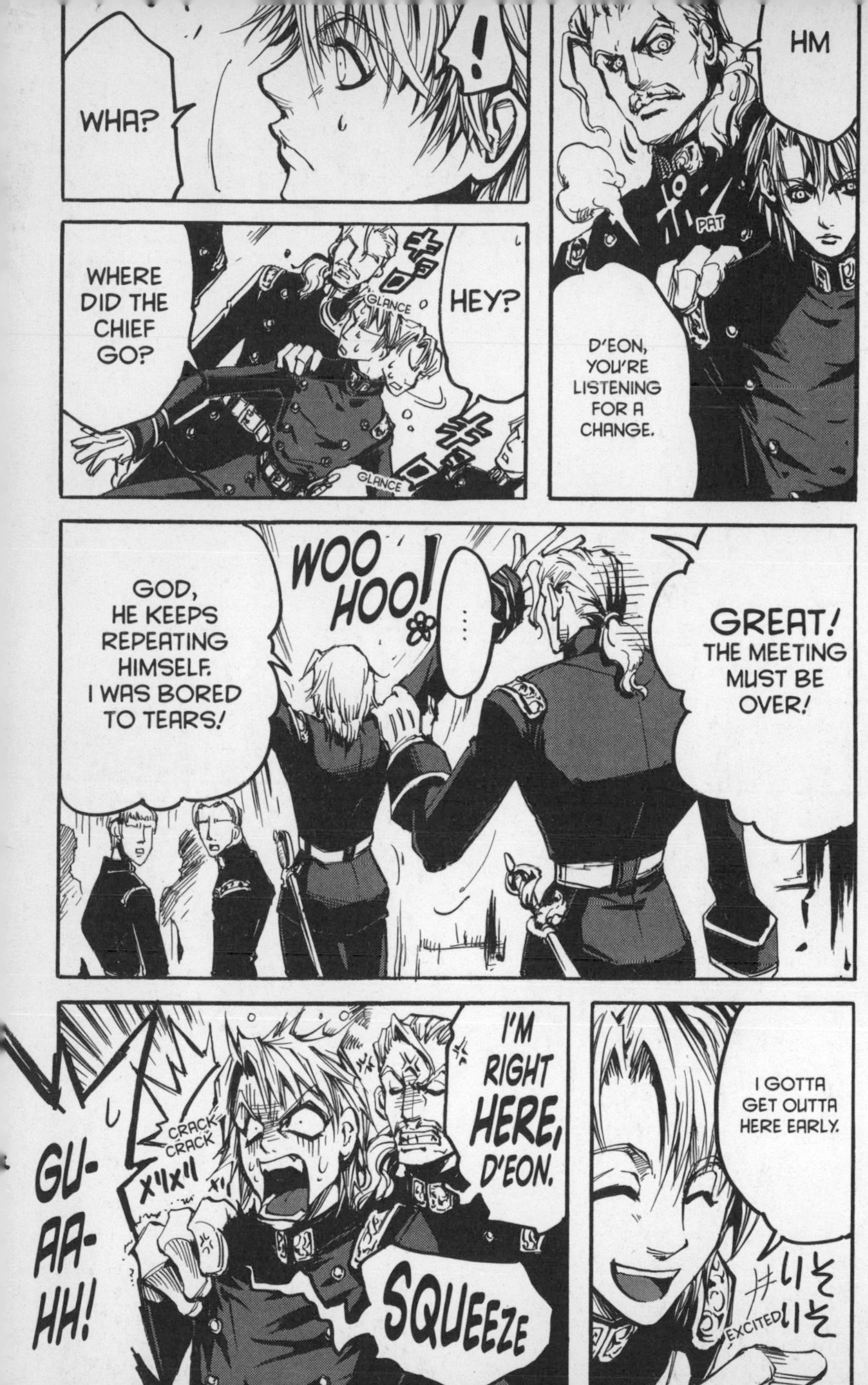
HM
PAT
D'EON, YOU'RE LISTENING FOR A CHANGE.
!
WHA?
HEY?
GLANCE
WHERE DID THE CHIEF GO?
GLANCE
GREAT! THE MEETING MUST BE OVER!
....
WOO HOO!
GOD, HE KEEPS REPEATING HIMSELF. I WAS BORED TO TEARS!
I GOTTA GET OUTTA HERE EARLY.
いそいそ
EXCITED
I'M RIGHT HERE, D'EON.
CRACK CRACK
GU-AA-HH!
SQUEEZE

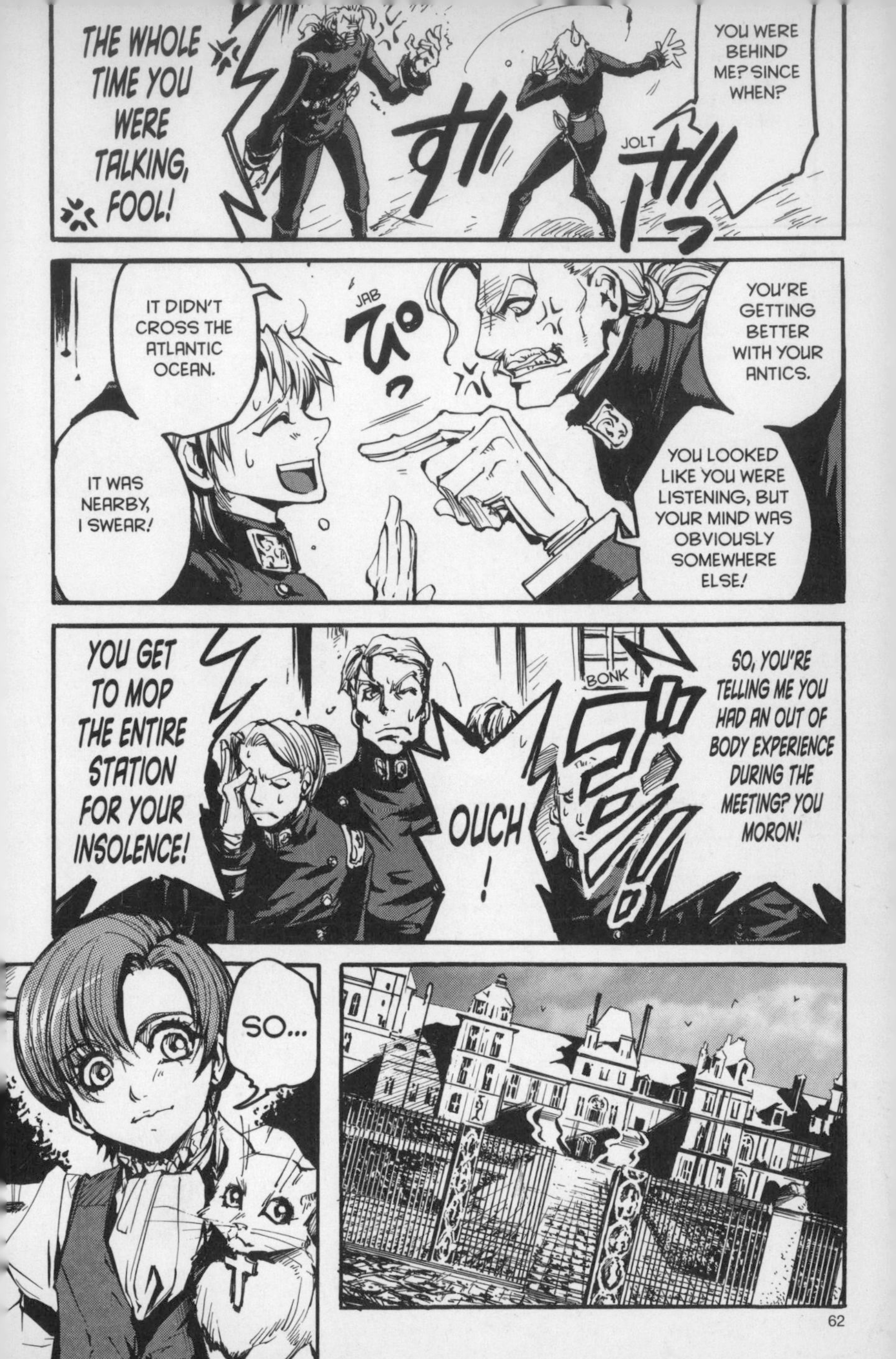
YOU WERE BEHIND ME? SINCE WHEN?
JOLT
THE WHOLE TIME YOU WERE TALKING, FOOL!
YOU'RE GETTING BETTER WITH YOUR ANTICS.
YOU LOOKED LIKE YOU WERE LISTENING, BUT YOUR MIND WAS OBVIOUSLY SOMEWHERE ELSE!
JAB
IT DIDN'T CROSS THE ATLANTIC OCEAN.
IT WAS NEARBY, I SWEAR!
SO, YOU'RE TELLING ME YOU HAD AN OUT OF BODY EXPERIENCE DURING THE MEETING? YOU MORON!
BONK
OUCH!
YOU GET TO MOP THE ENTIRE STATION FOR YOUR INSOLENCE!
SO...

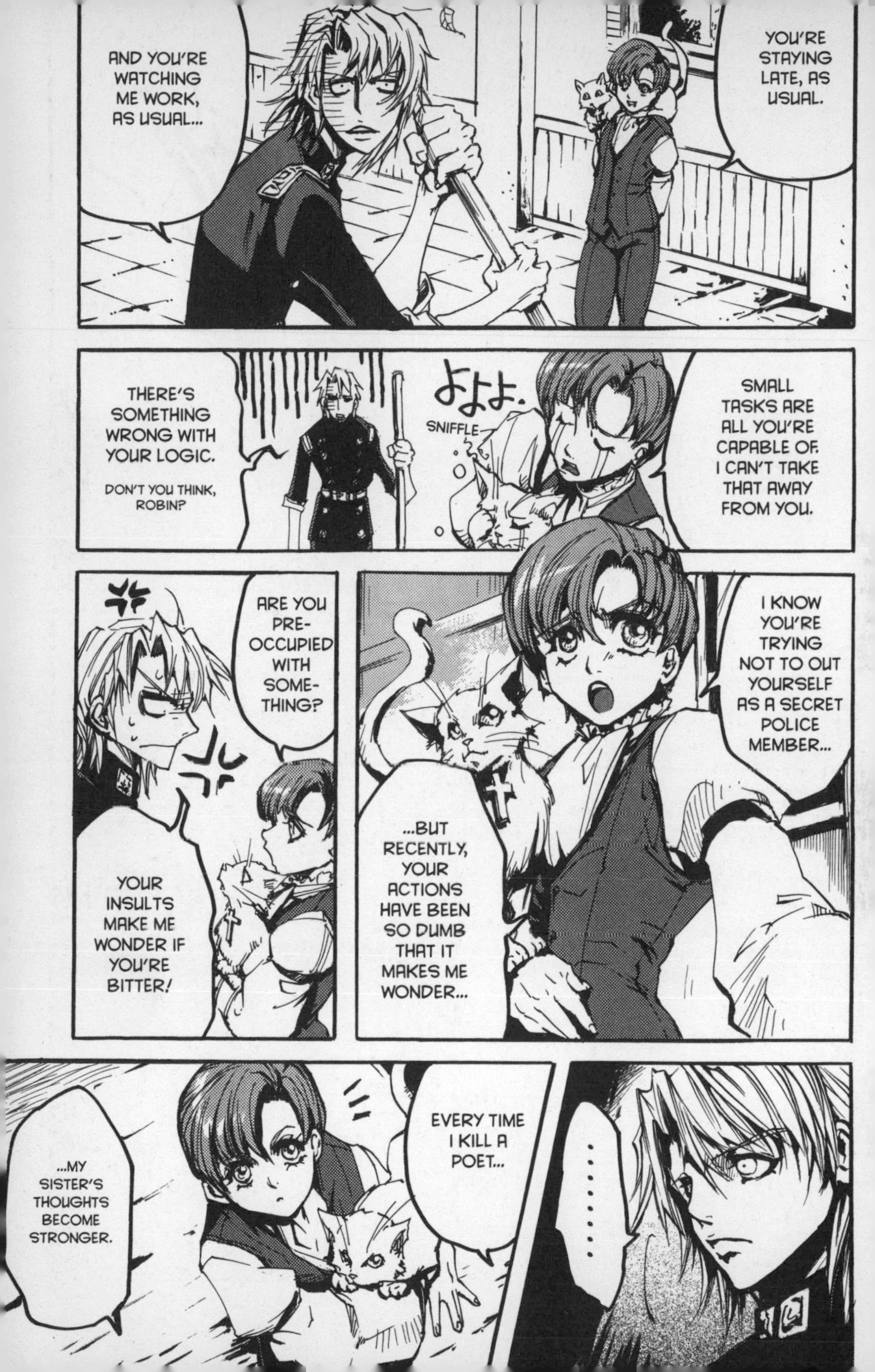
YOU'RE STAYING LATE, AS USUAL.
AND YOU'RE WATCHING ME WORK, AS USUAL...
SMALL TASKS ARE ALL YOU'RE CAPABLE OF. I CAN'T TAKE THAT AWAY FROM YOU.
よよよ.
SNIFFLE
THERE'S SOMETHING WRONG WITH YOUR LOGIC.
DON'T YOU THINK, ROBIN?
I KNOW YOU'RE TRYING NOT TO OUT YOURSELF AS A SECRET POLICE MEMBER...
...BUT RECENTLY, YOUR ACTIONS HAVE BEEN SO DUMB THAT IT MAKES ME WONDER...
ARE YOU PRE-OCCUPIED WITH SOME-THING?
YOUR INSULTS MAKE ME WONDER IF YOU'RE BITTER!
......
EVERY TIME I KILL A POET...
...MY SISTER'S THOUGHTS BECOME STRONGER.

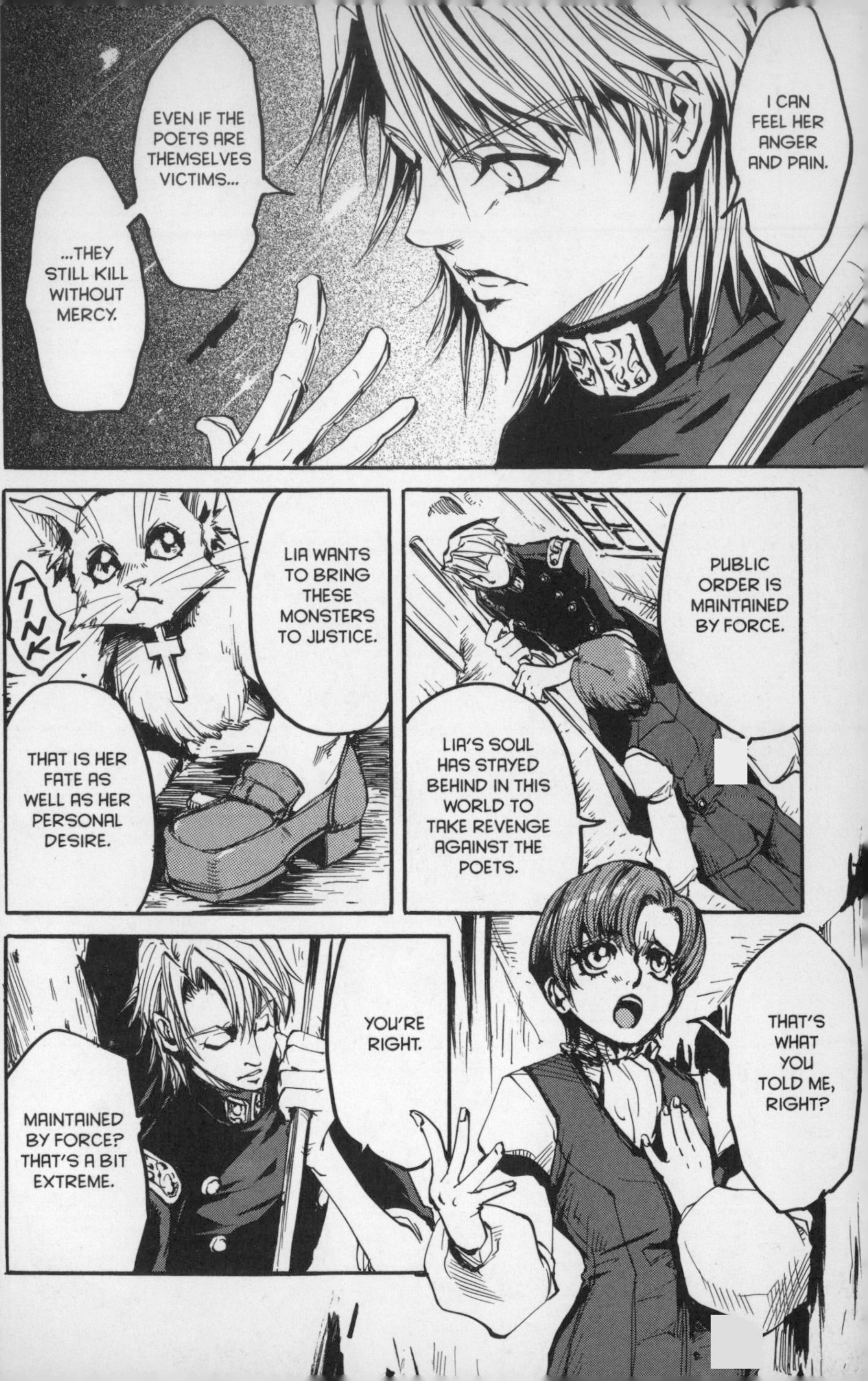
I CAN FEEL HER ANGER AND PAIN.
EVEN IF THE POETS ARE THEMSELVES VICTIMS...
...THEY STILL KILL WITHOUT MERCY.
PUBLIC ORDER IS MAINTAINED BY FORCE.
LIA'S SOUL HAS STAYED BEHIND IN THIS WORLD TO TAKE REVENGE AGAINST THE POETS.
LIA WANTS TO BRING THESE MONSTERS TO JUSTICE.
TINK
THAT IS HER FATE AS WELL AS HER PERSONAL DESIRE.
THAT'S WHAT YOU TOLD ME, RIGHT?
YOU'RE RIGHT.
MAINTAINED BY FORCE? THAT'S A BIT EXTREME.

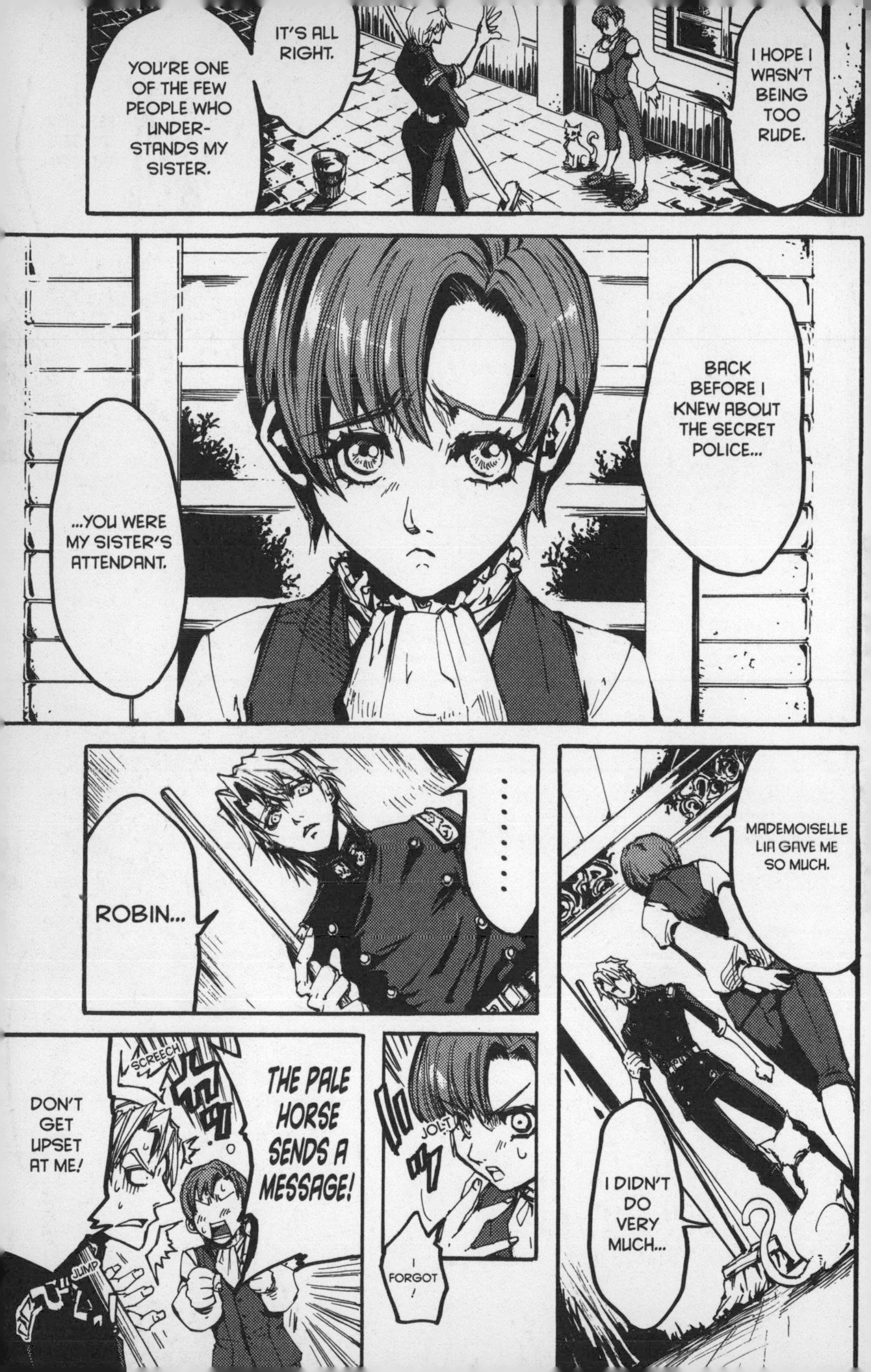
I HOPE I WASN'T BEING TOO RUDE.
IT'S ALL RIGHT.
YOU'RE ONE OF THE FEW PEOPLE WHO UNDER-STANDS MY SISTER.
BACK BEFORE I KNEW ABOUT THE SECRET POLICE...
...YOU WERE MY SISTER'S ATTENDANT.
MADEMOISELLE LIA GAVE ME SO MUCH.
I DIDN'T DO VERY MUCH...
......
ROBIN...
JOLT
I FORGOT!
SCREECH
THE PALE HORSE SENDS A MESSAGE!
DON'T GET UPSET AT ME!
JUMP

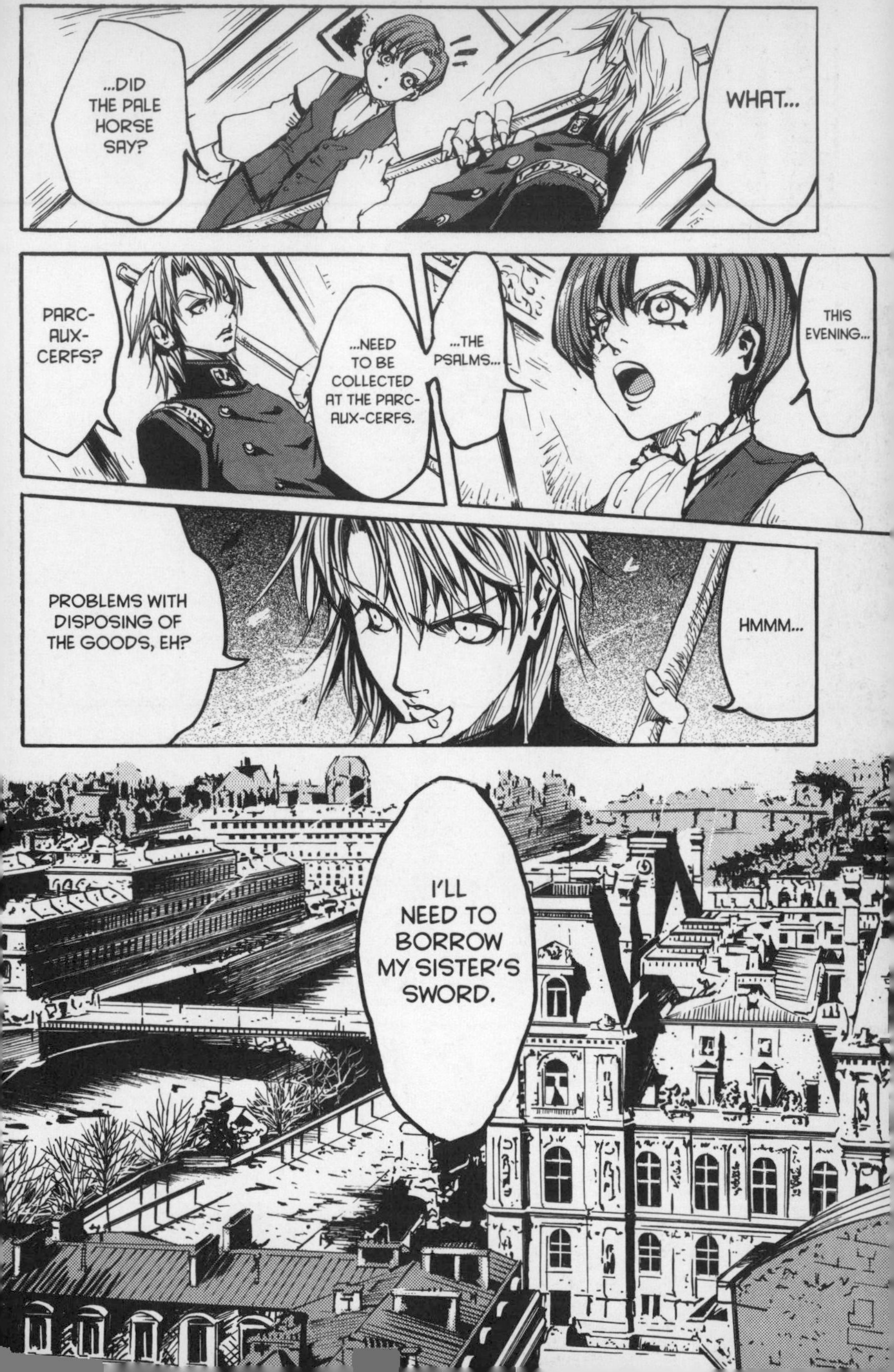
WHAT...
...DID THE PALE HORSE SAY?
THIS EVENING...
...THE PSALMS...
...NEED TO BE COLLECTED AT THE PARC-AUX-CERFS.
PARC-AUX-CERFS?
HMMM...
PROBLEMS WITH DISPOSING OF THE GOODS, EH?
I'LL NEED TO BORROW MY SISTER'S SWORD.

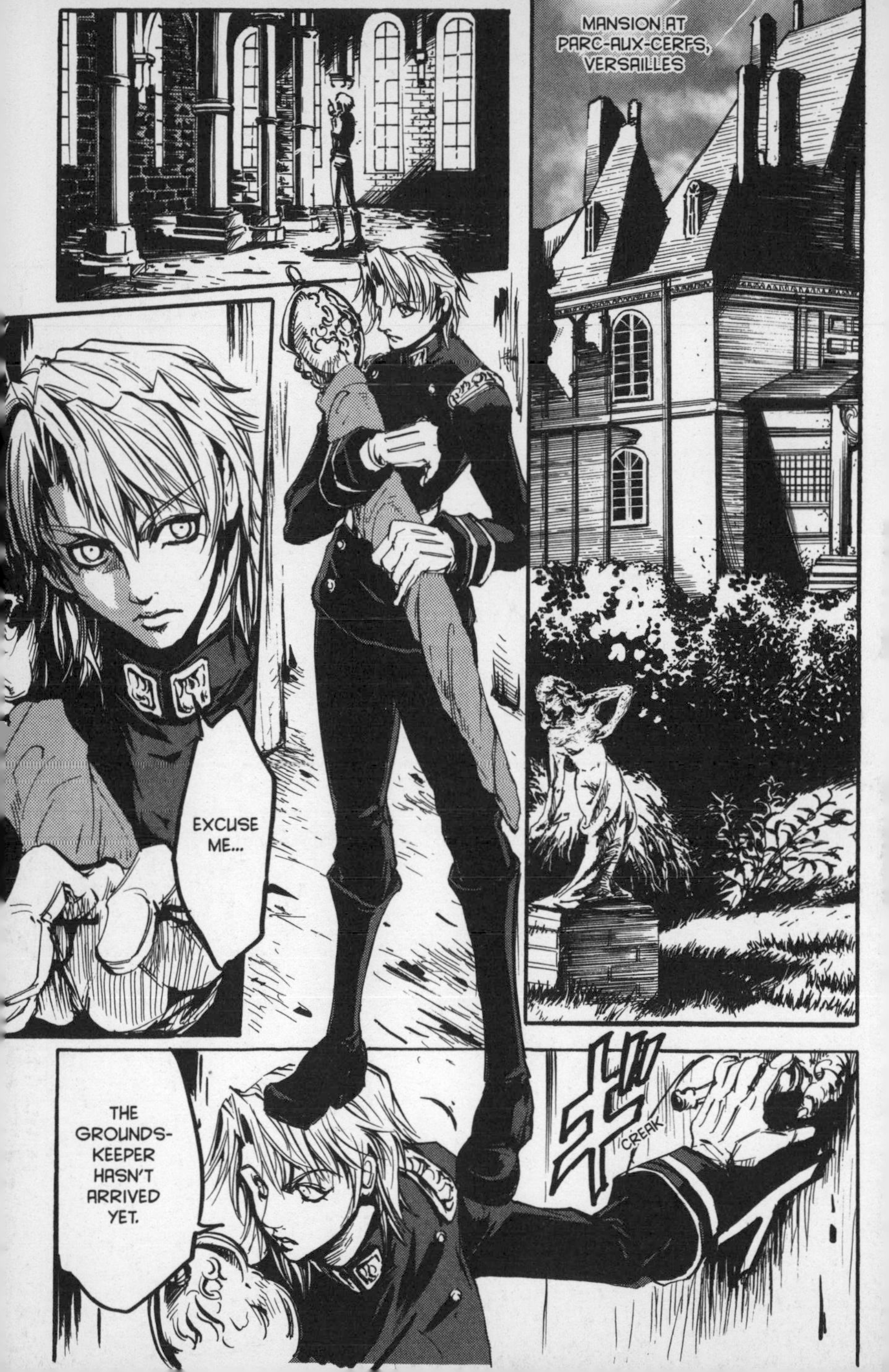
MANSION AT PARC-AUX-CERFS, VERSAILLES
EXCUSE ME...
CREAK
THE GROUNDS-KEEPER HASN'T ARRIVED YET.

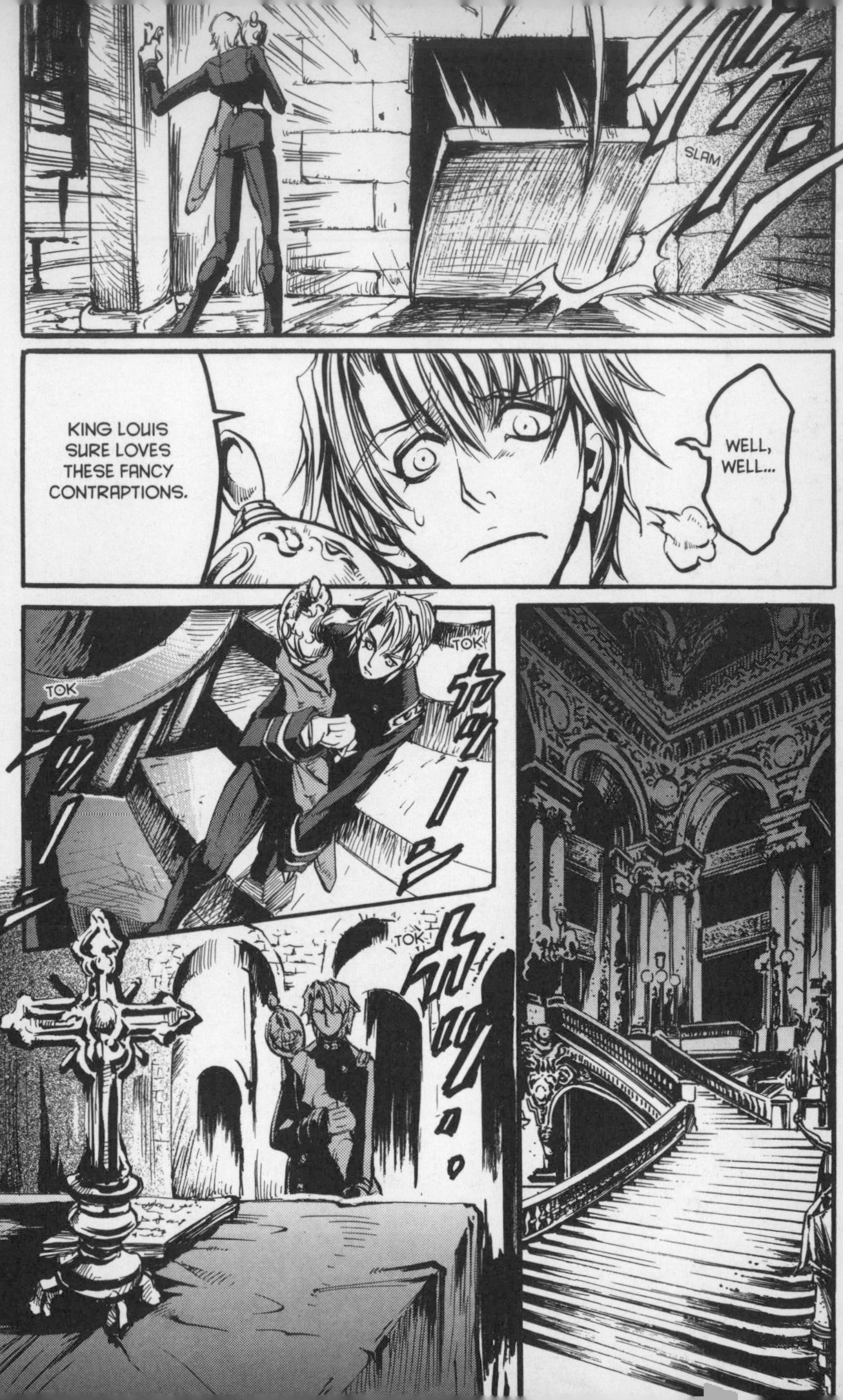
SLAM
WELL, WELL...
KING LOUIS SURE LOVES THESE FANCY CONTRAPTIONS.
TOK
TOK
TOK

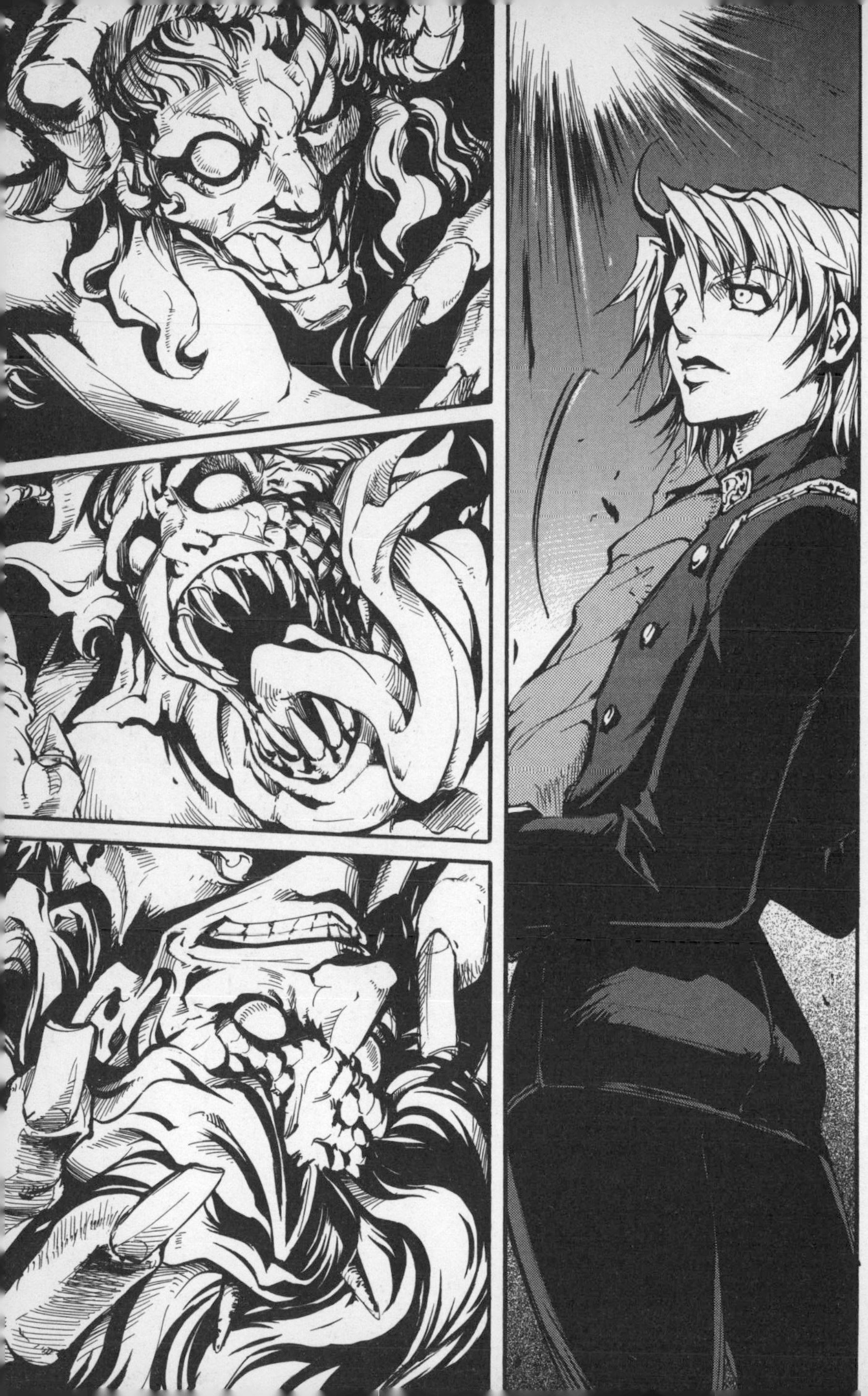

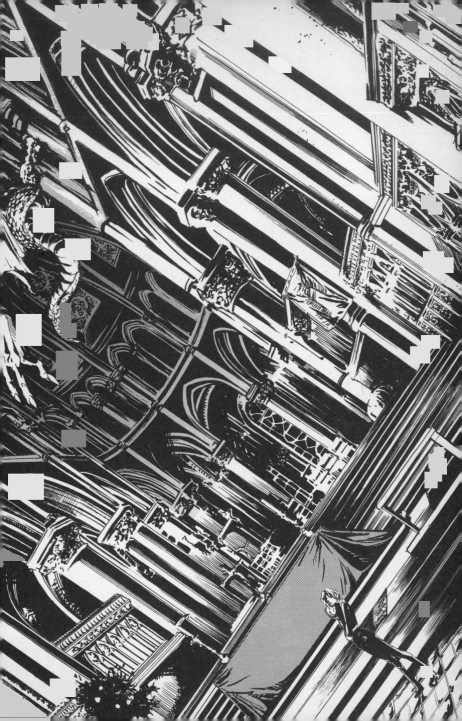

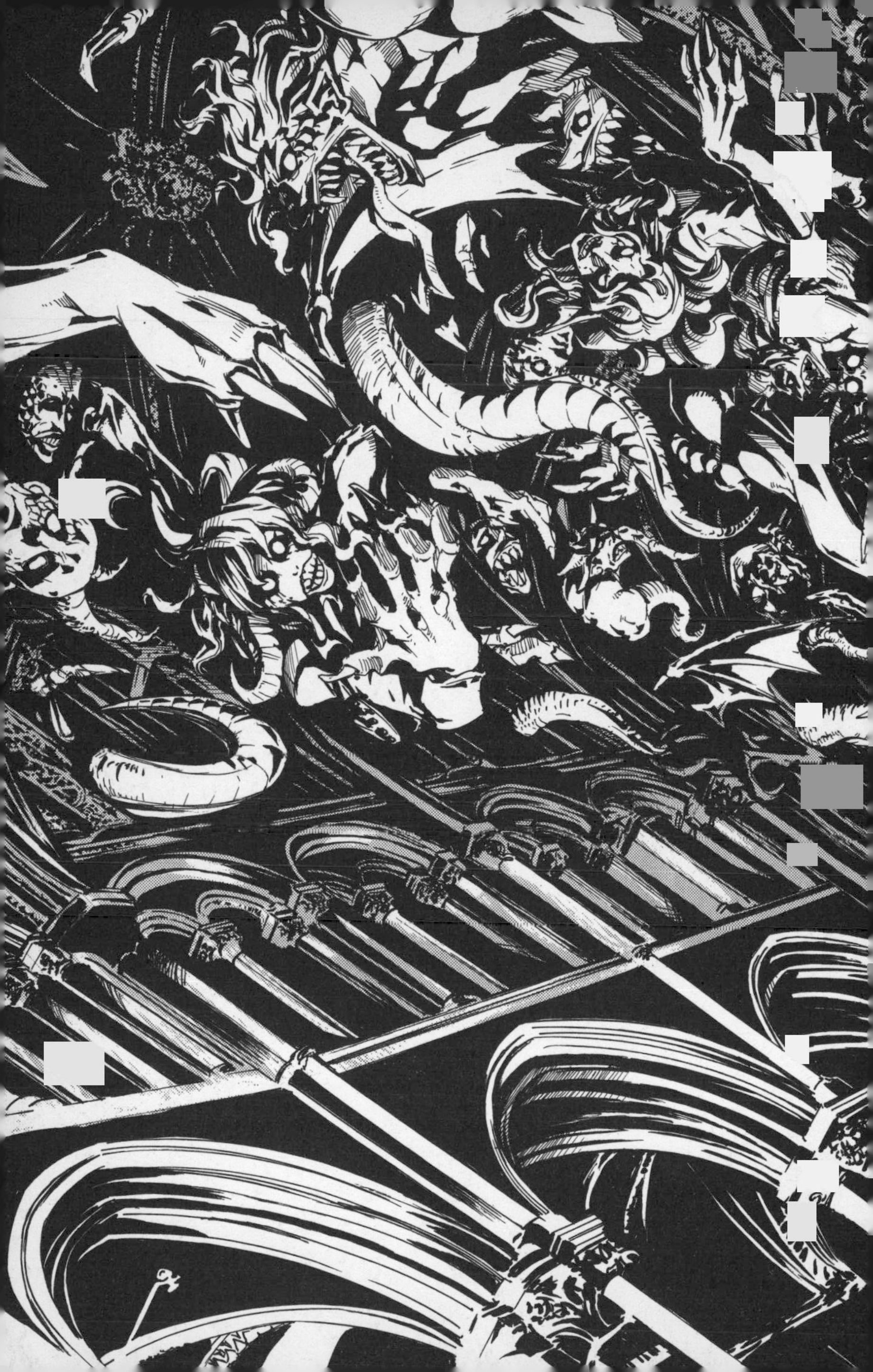

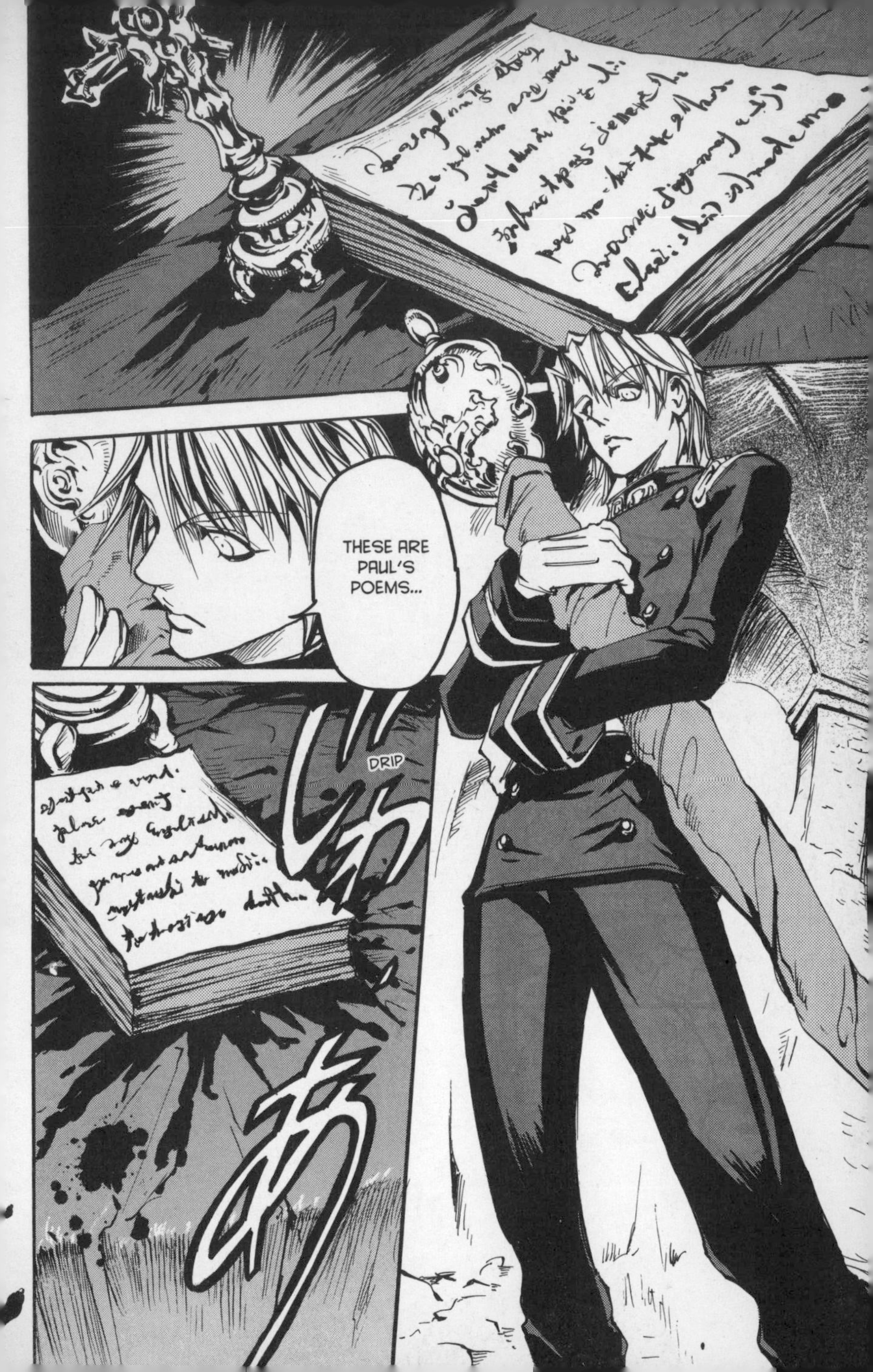
THESE ARE PAUL'S POEMS...
DRIP

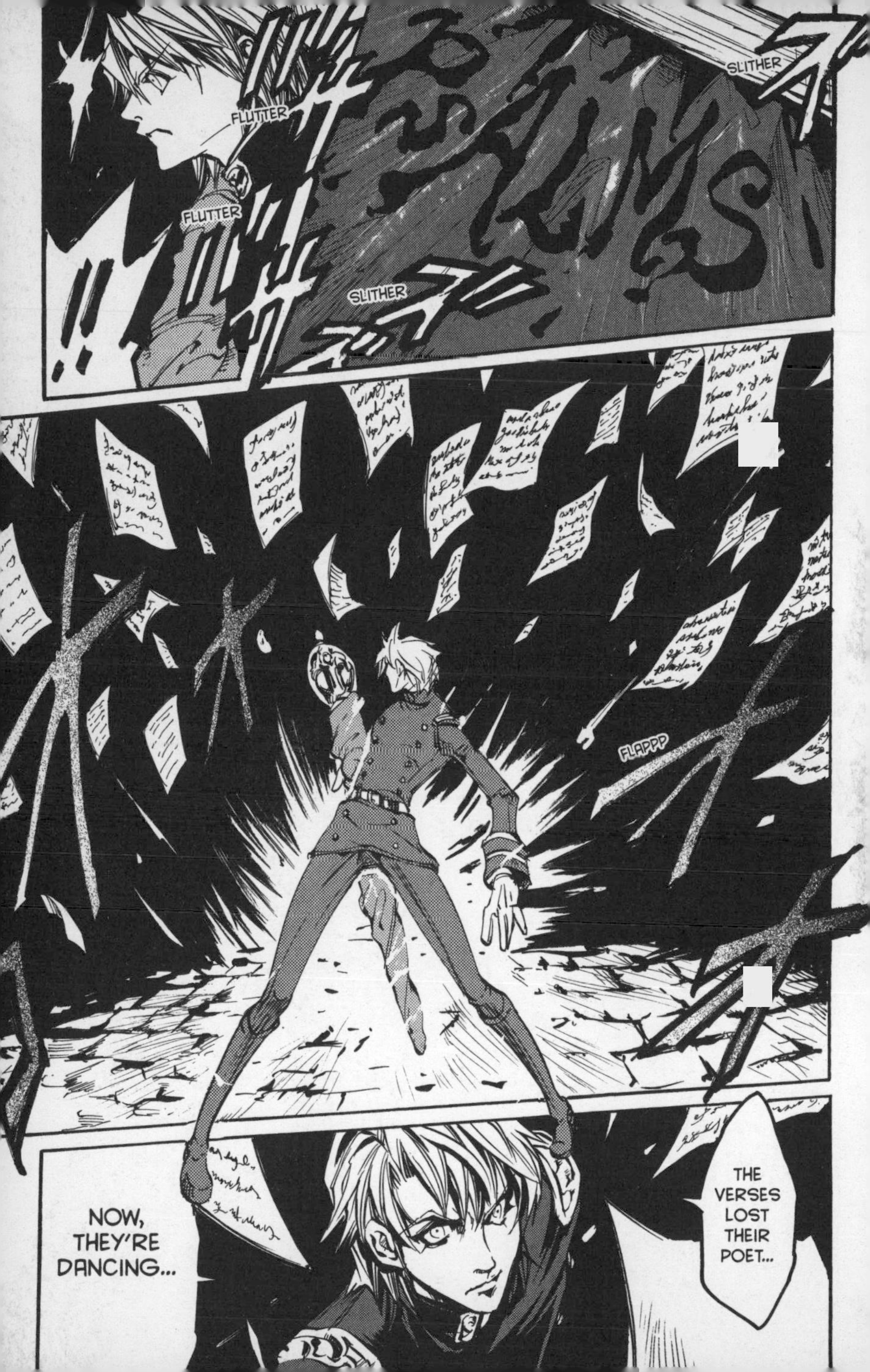
SLITHER
FLUTTER
FLUTTER
SLITHER
FLAPPP
THE VERSES LOST THEIR POET...
NOW, THEY'RE DANCING...

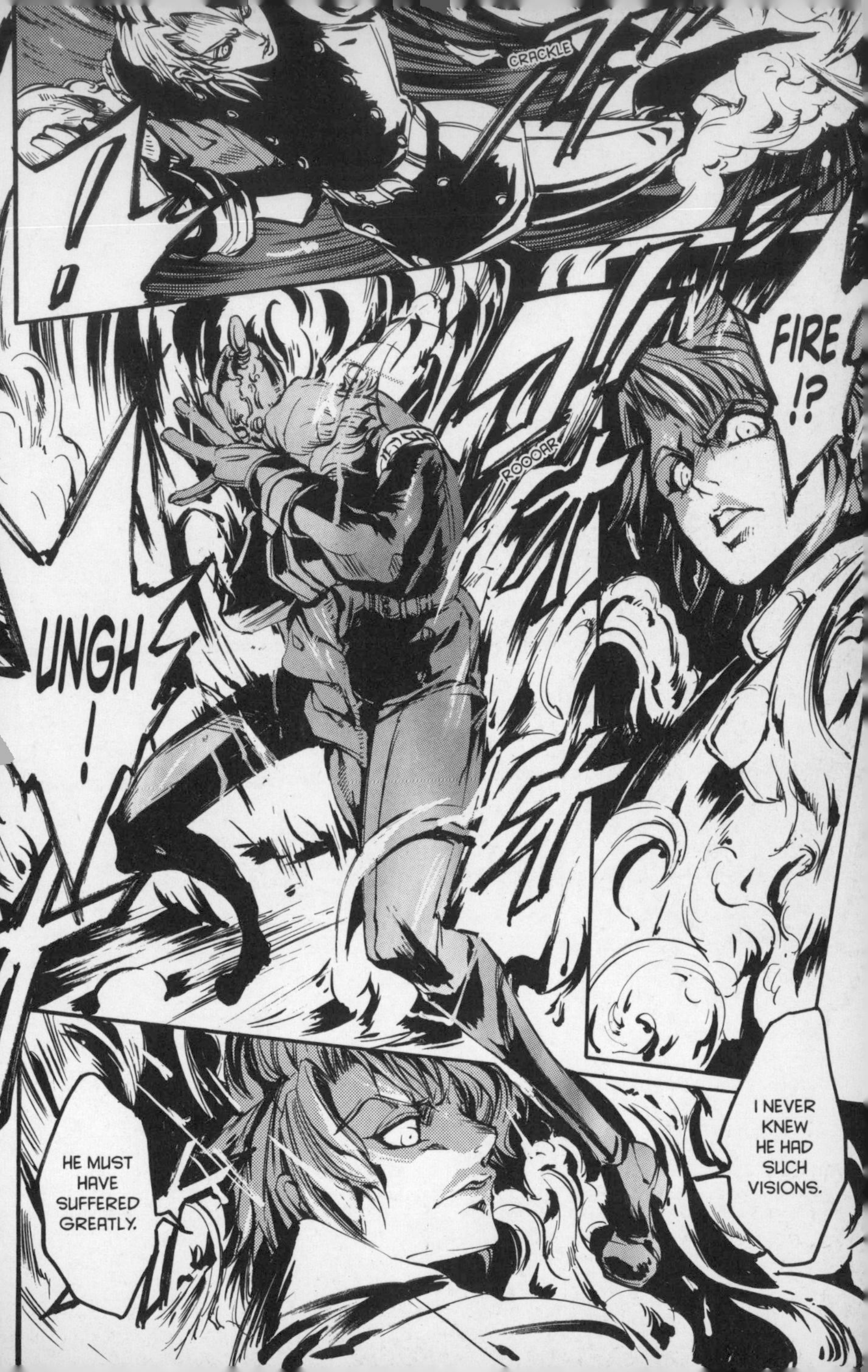
CRACKLE
FIRE!?
ROOOAR
UNGH!
I NEVER KNEW HE HAD SUCH VISIONS.
HE MUST HAVE SUFFERED GREATLY.

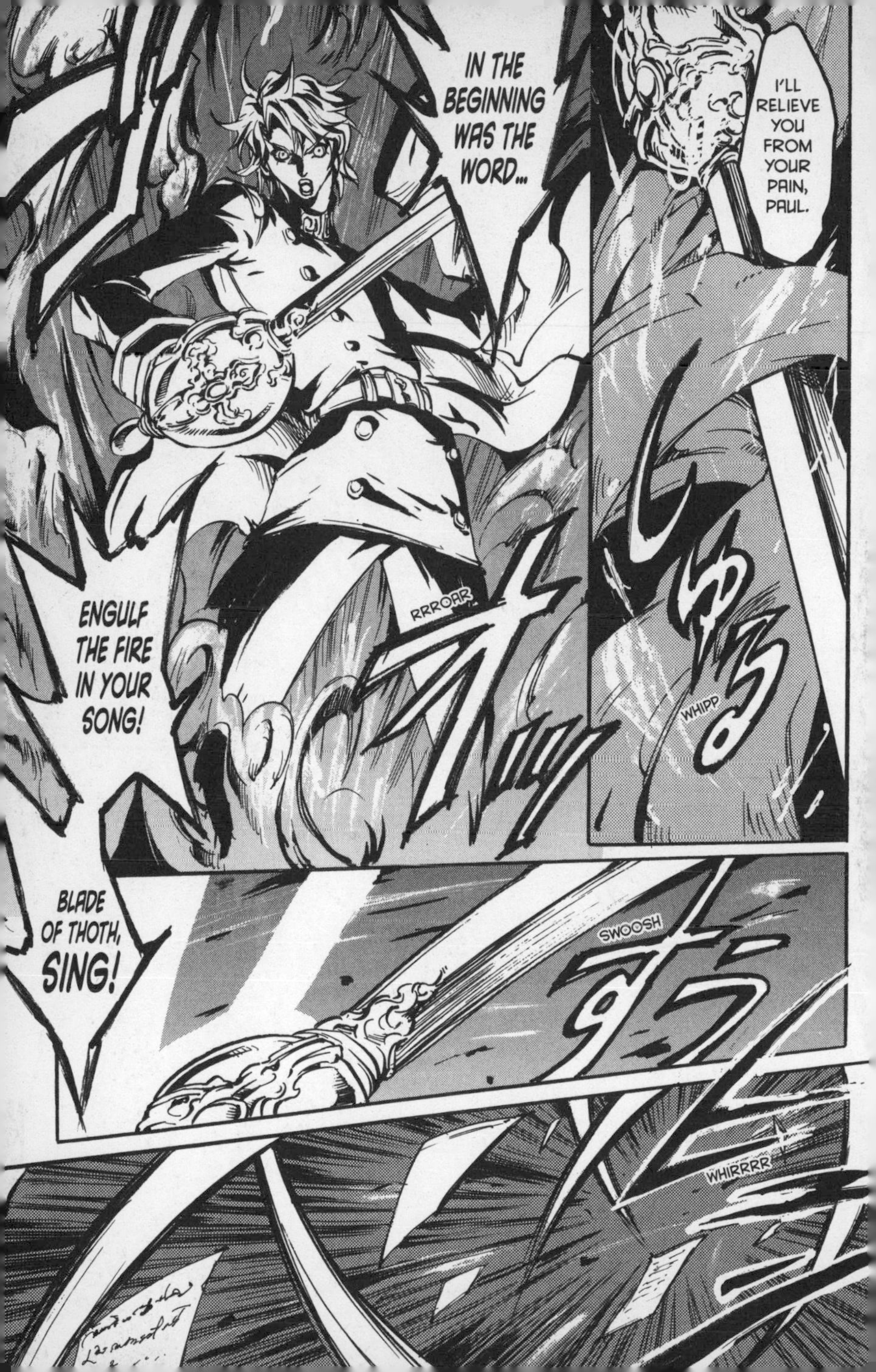
I'LL RELIEVE YOU FROM YOUR PAIN, PAUL.
WHIPP
IN THE BEGINNING WAS THE WORD...
RRROAR
ENGULF THE FIRE IN YOUR SONG!
SWOOSH
BLADE OF THOTH, SING!
WHIRRRR

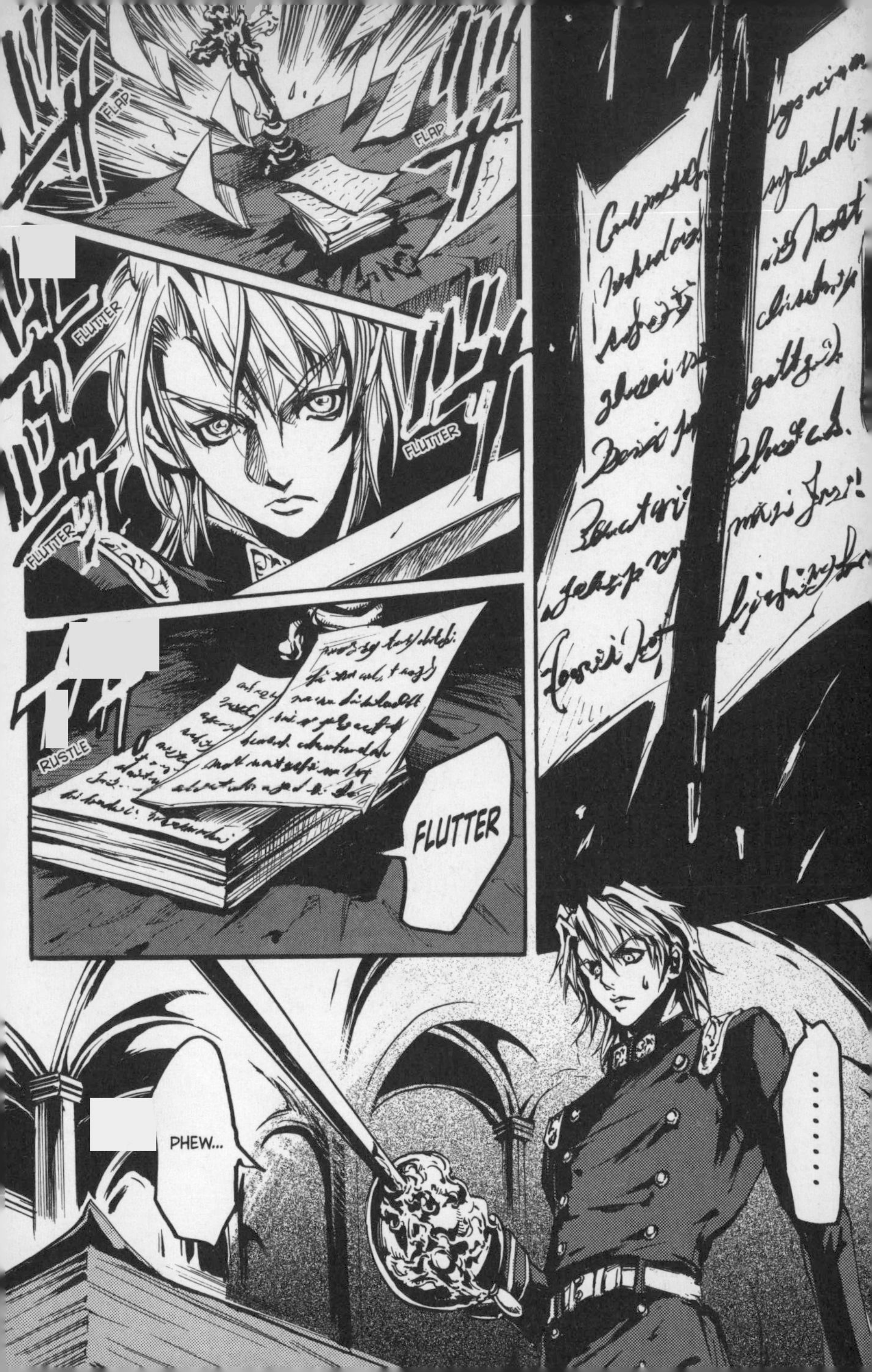
FLAP
FLAP
FLUTTER
FLUTTER
FLUTTER
RUSTLE
FLUTTER
......
PHEW...

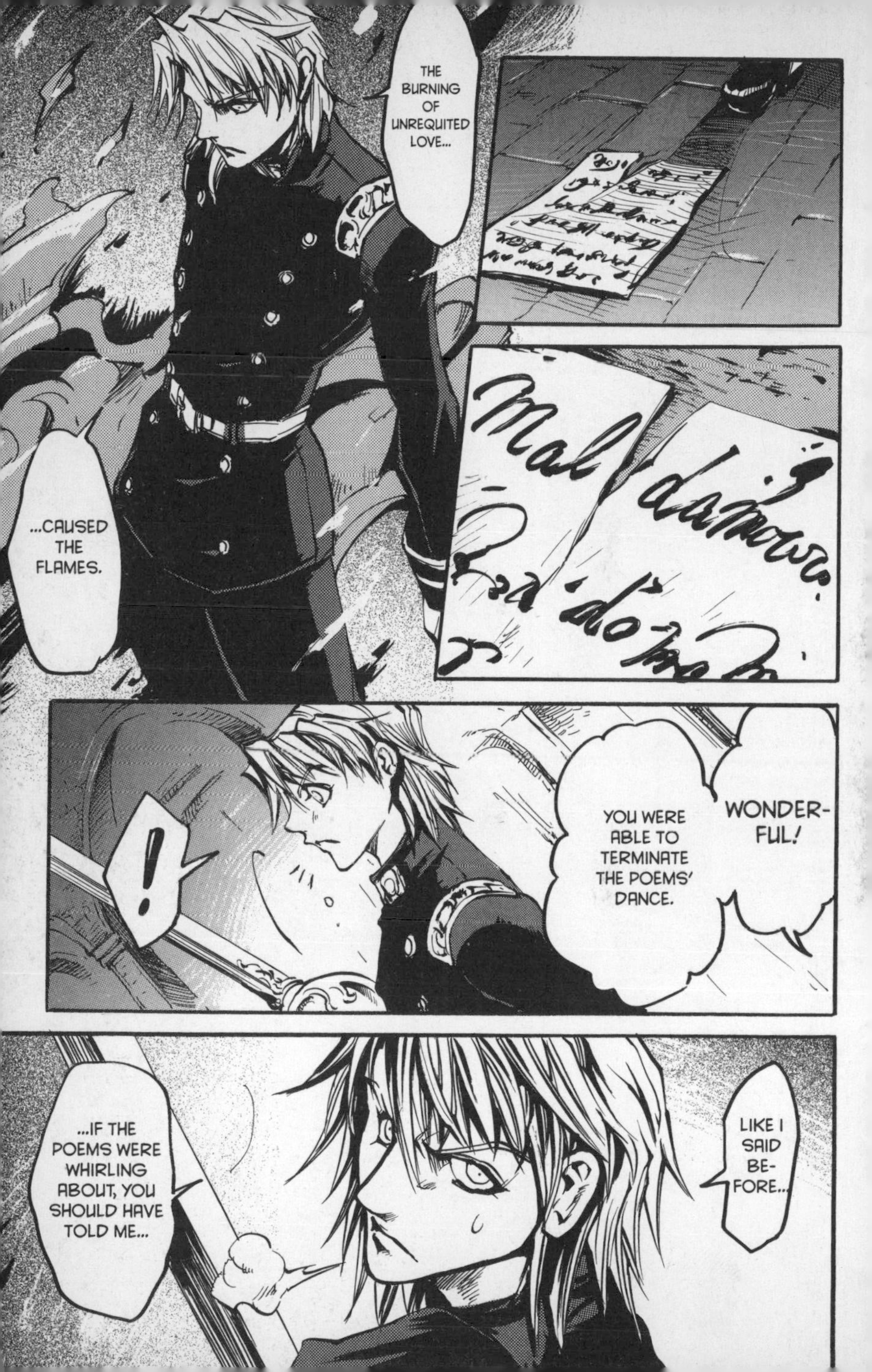
THE BURNING OF UNREQUITED LOVE...
...CAUSED THE FLAMES.
WONDERFUL!
YOU WERE ABLE TO TERMINATE THE POEMS' DANCE.
!
LIKE I SAID BEFORE...
...IF THE POEMS WERE WHIRLING ABOUT, YOU SHOULD HAVE TOLD ME...

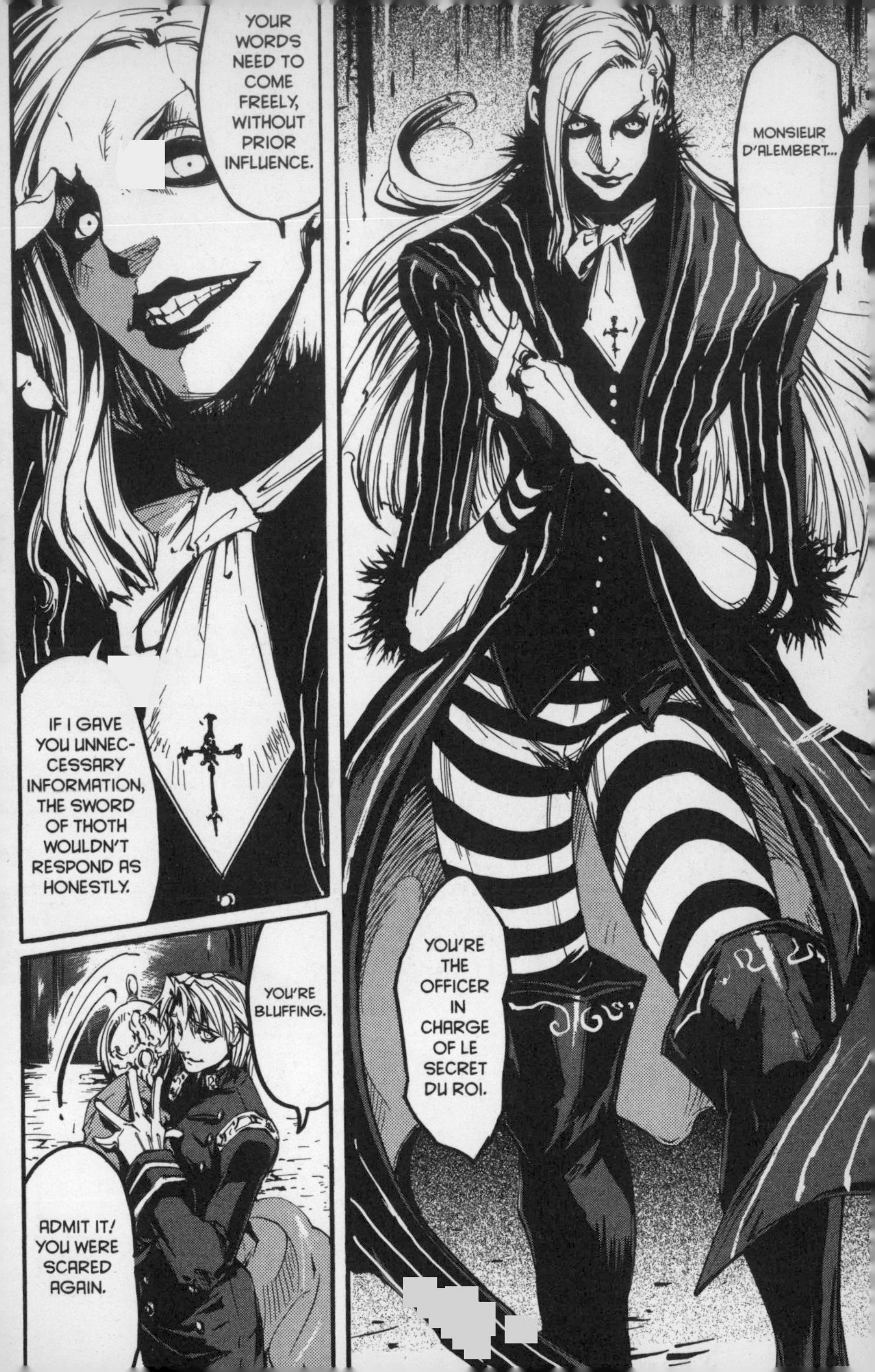
MONSIEUR D'ALEMBERT...
YOU'RE THE OFFICER IN CHARGE OF LE SECRET DU ROI.
YOUR WORDS NEED TO COME FREELY, WITHOUT PRIOR INFLUENCE.
IF I GAVE YOU UNNEC-CESSARY INFORMATION, THE SWORD OF THOTH WOULDN'T RESPOND AS HONESTLY.
YOU'RE BLUFFING.
ADMIT IT! YOU WERE SCARED AGAIN.

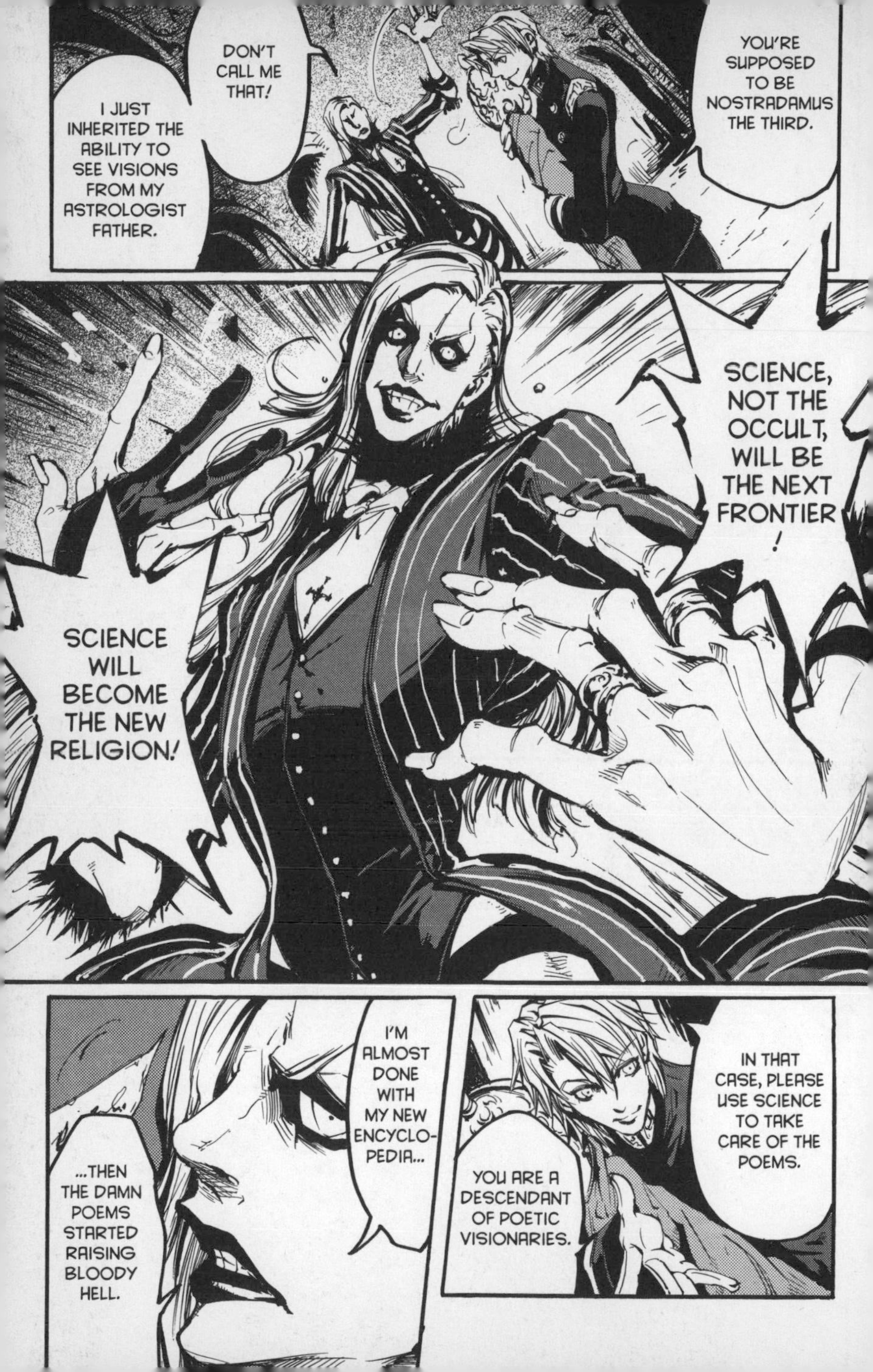
YOU'RE SUPPOSED TO BE NOSTRADAMUS THE THIRD.
DON'T CALL ME THAT!
I JUST INHERITED THE ABILITY TO SEE VISIONS FROM MY ASTROLOGIST FATHER.
SCIENCE, NOT THE OCCULT, WILL BE THE NEXT FRONTIER!
SCIENCE WILL BECOME THE NEW RELIGION!
IN THAT CASE, PLEASE USE SCIENCE TO TAKE CARE OF THE POEMS.
YOU ARE A DESCENDANT OF POETIC VISIONARIES.
I'M ALMOST DONE WITH MY NEW ENCYCLO-PEDIA...
...THEN THE DAMN POEMS STARTED RAISING BLOODY HELL.

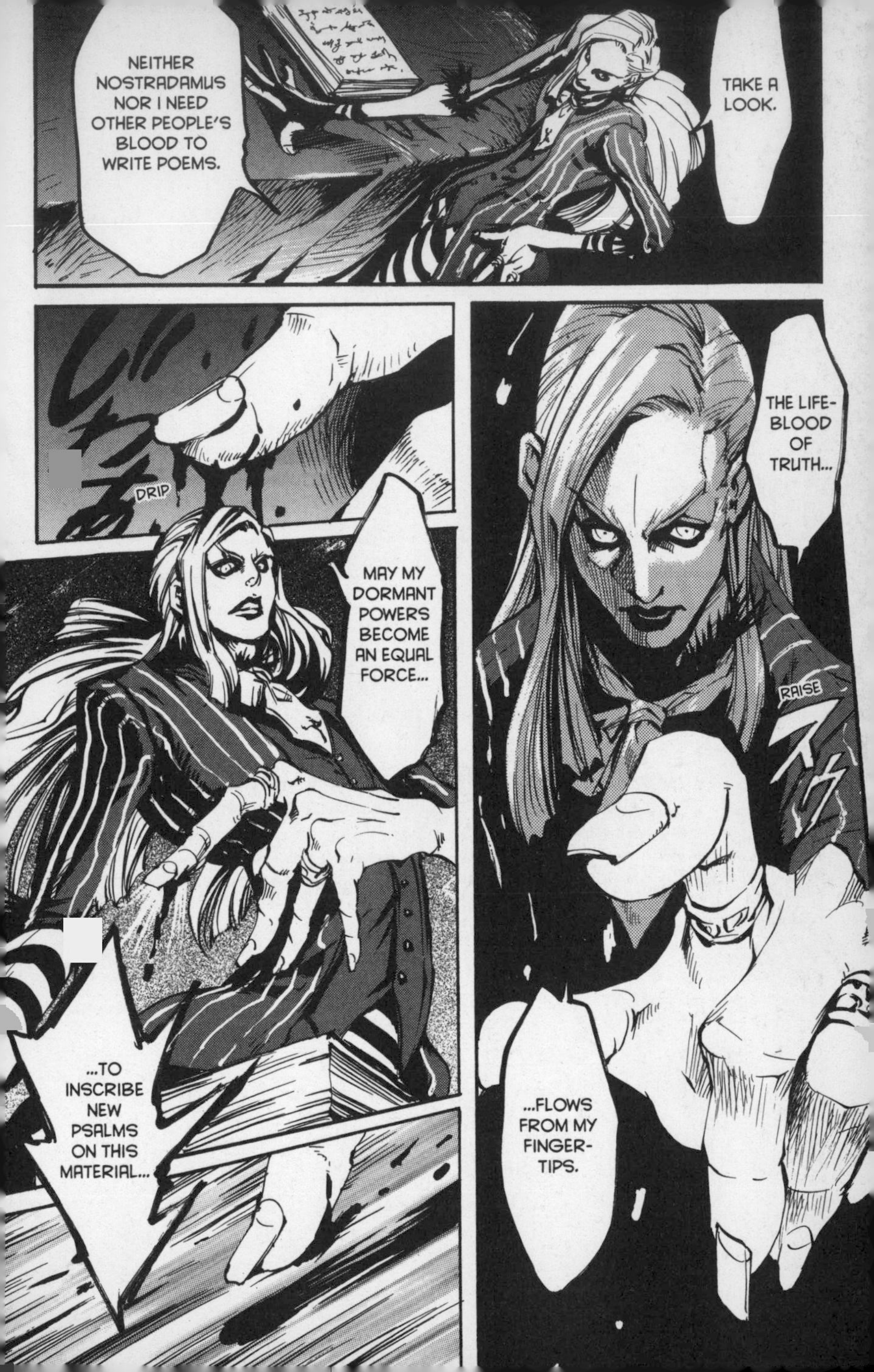
NEITHER NOSTRADAMUS NOR I NEED OTHER PEOPLE'S BLOOD TO WRITE POEMS.
TAKE A LOOK.
THE LIFE-BLOOD OF TRUTH...
RAISE
...FLOWS FROM MY FINGER-TIPS.
DRIP
MAY MY DORMANT POWERS BECOME AN EQUAL FORCE...
...TO INSCRIBE NEW PSALMS ON THIS MATERIAL...

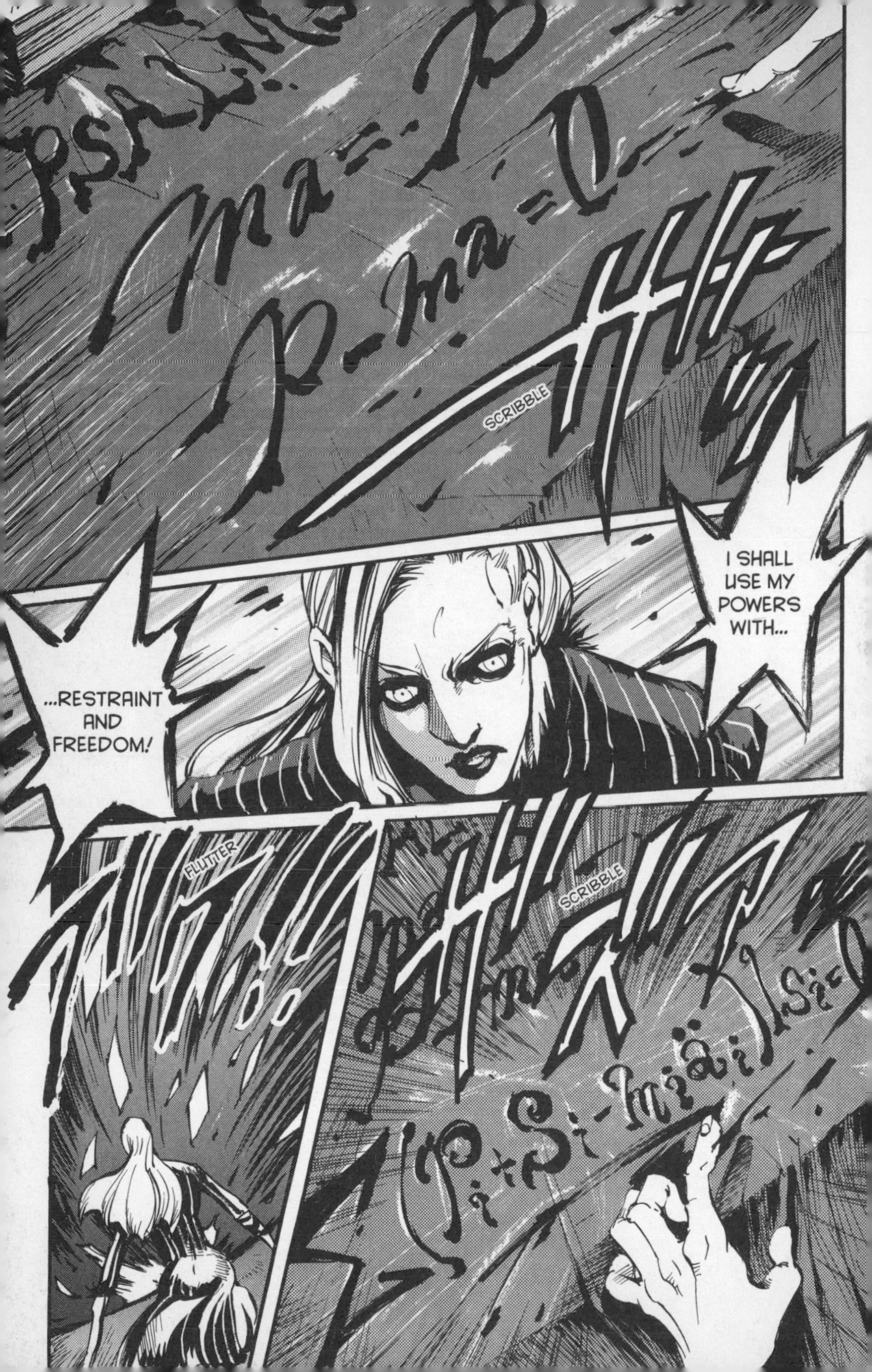
SCRIBBLE
I SHALL USE MY POWERS WITH...
...RESTRAINT AND FREEDOM!
SCRIBBLE
FLUTTER

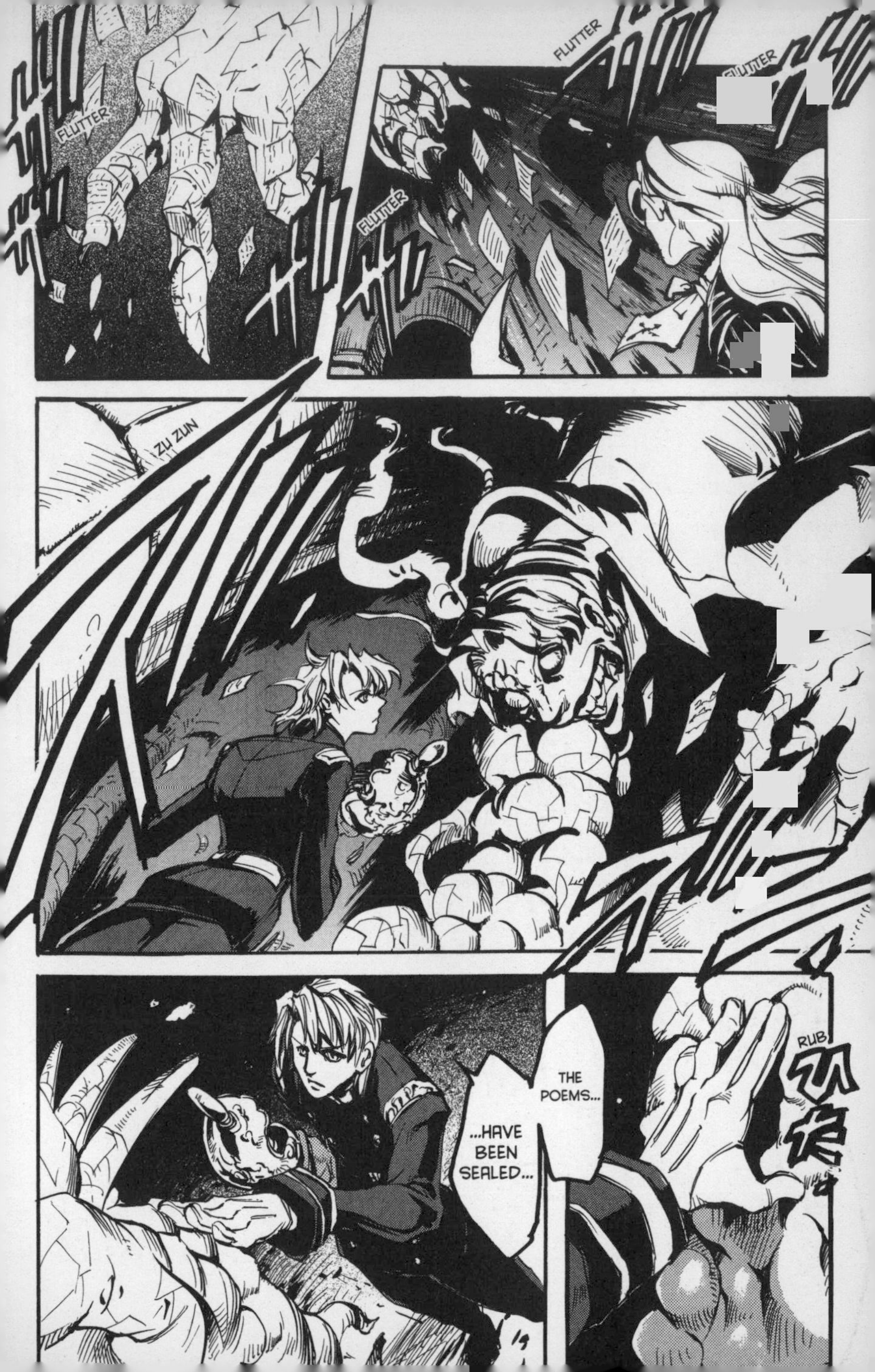
FLUTTER
FLUTTER
FLUTTER
FLUTTER
ZU ZUN
RUB
THE POEMS...
...HAVE BEEN SEALED...

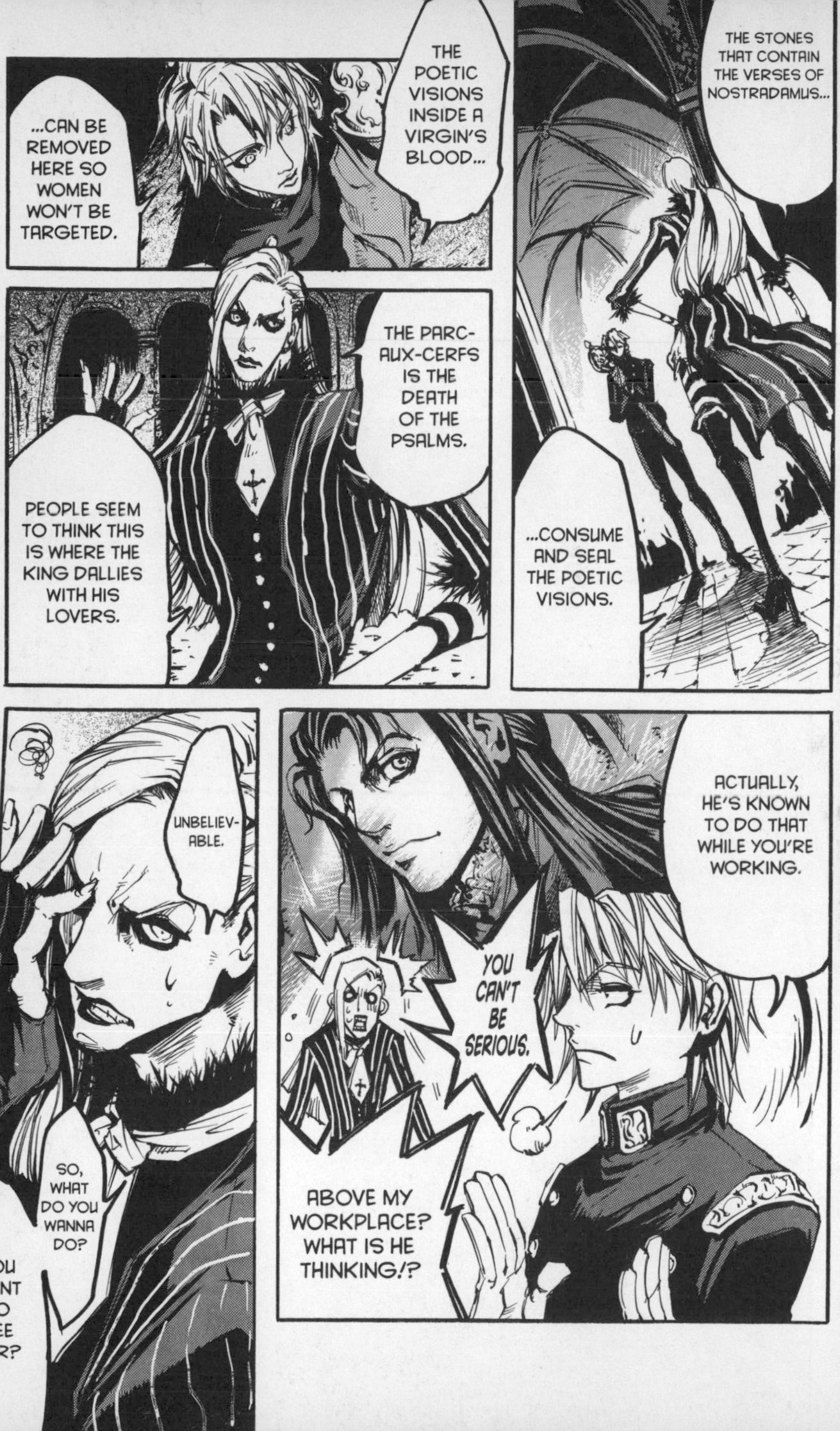
THE STONES THAT CONTAIN THE VERSES OF NOSTRADAMUS...
...CONSUME AND SEAL THE POETIC VISIONS.
THE POETIC VISIONS INSIDE A VIRGIN'S BLOOD...
...CAN BE REMOVED HERE SO WOMEN WON'T BE TARGETED.
THE PARC-AUX-CERFS IS THE DEATH OF THE PSALMS.
PEOPLE SEEM TO THINK THIS IS WHERE THE KING DALLIES WITH HIS LOVERS.
ACTUALLY, HE'S KNOWN TO DO THAT WHILE YOU'RE WORKING.
YOU CAN'T BE SERIOUS.
ABOVE MY WORKPLACE? WHAT IS HE THINKING!?
UNBELIEVABLE.
SO, WHAT DO YOU WANNA DO?
YOU WANT TO SEE HER?

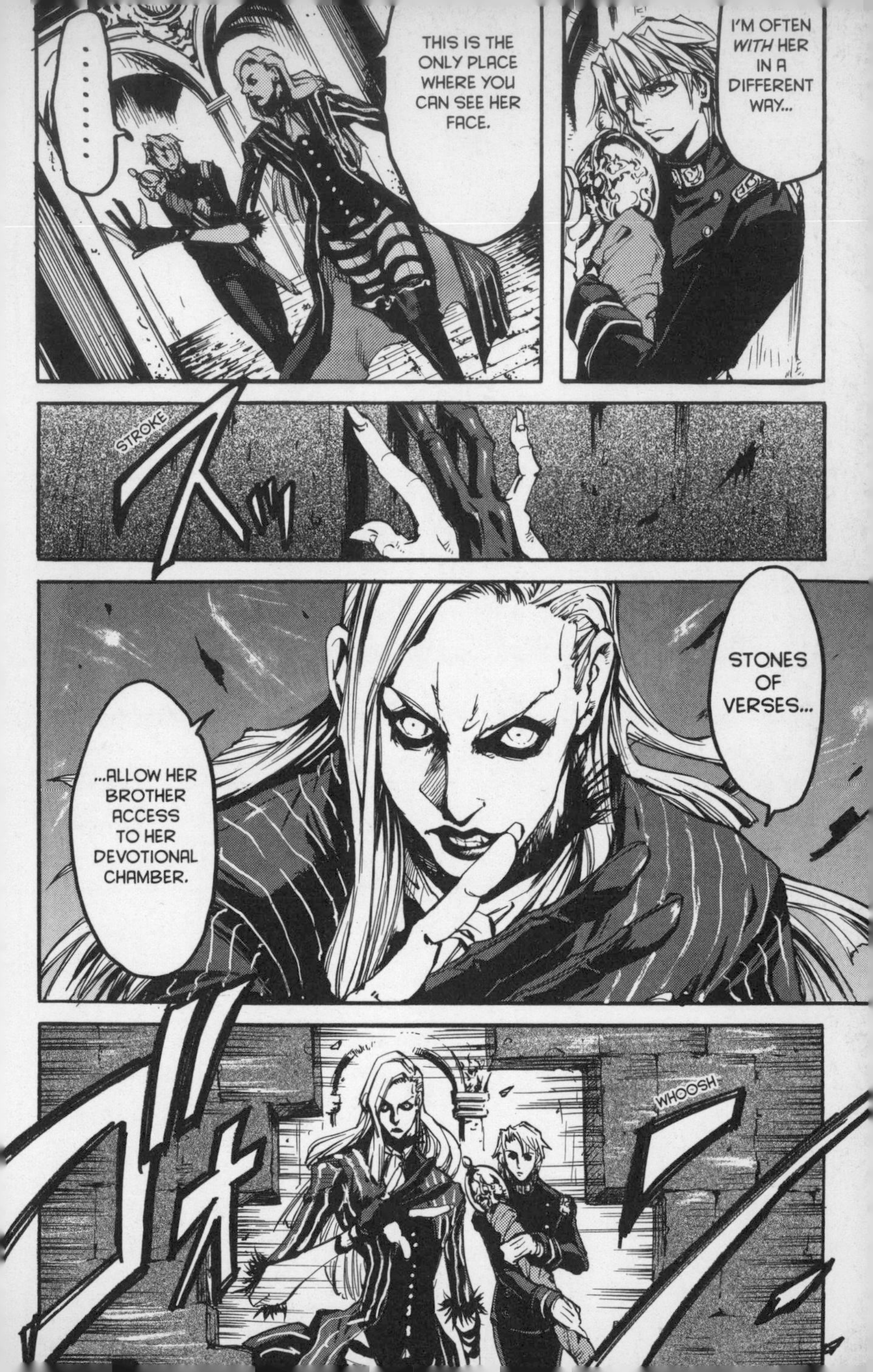
I'M OFTEN *WITH* HER IN A DIFFERENT WAY...
THIS IS THE ONLY PLACE WHERE YOU CAN SEE HER FACE.
......
STROKE
STONES OF VERSES...
...ALLOW HER BROTHER ACCESS TO HER DEVOTIONAL CHAMBER.
WHOOSH

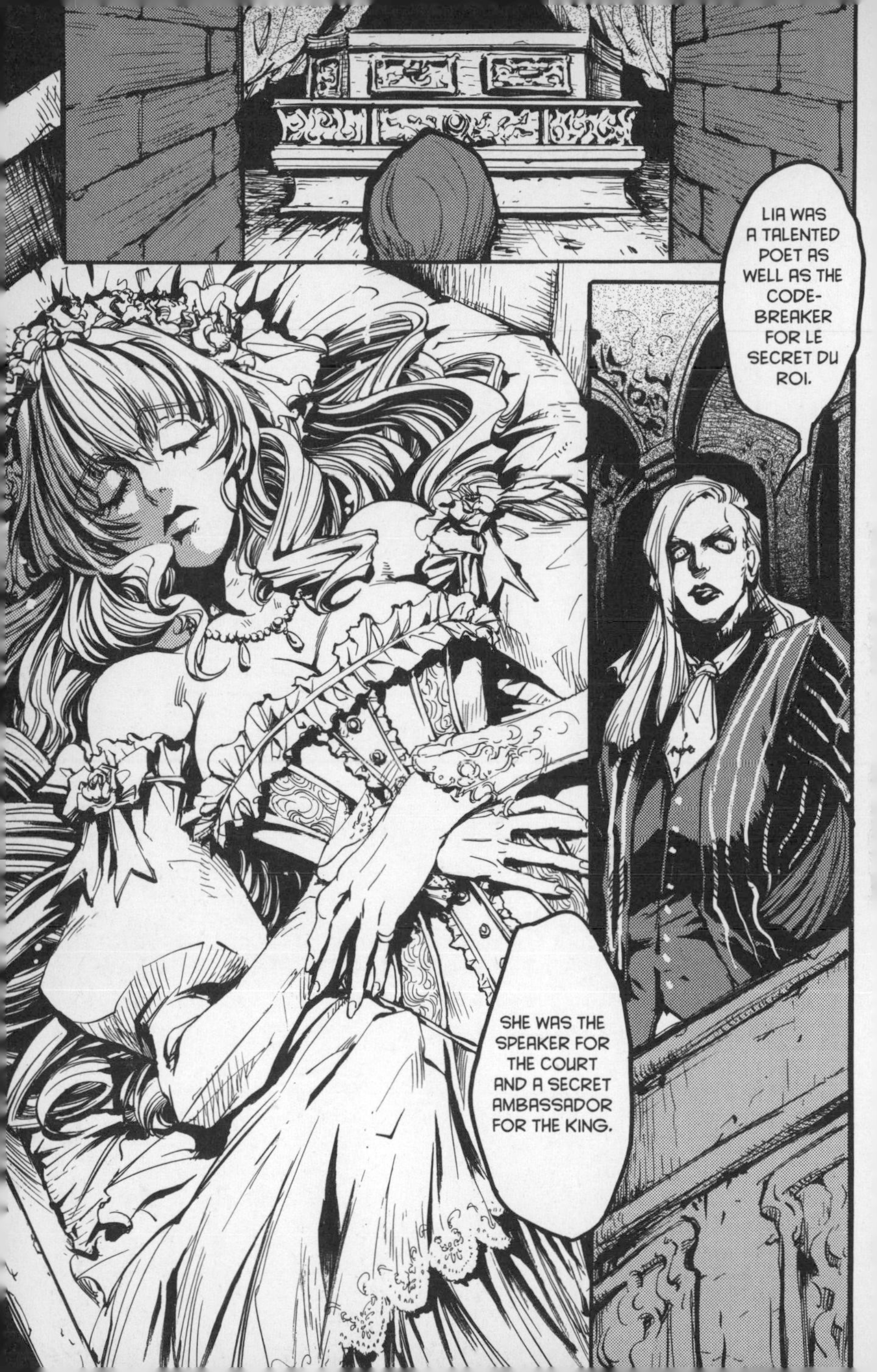
LIA WAS A TALENTED POET AS WELL AS THE CODE-BREAKER FOR LE SECRET DU ROI.
SHE WAS THE SPEAKER FOR THE COURT AND A SECRET AMBASSADOR FOR THE KING.

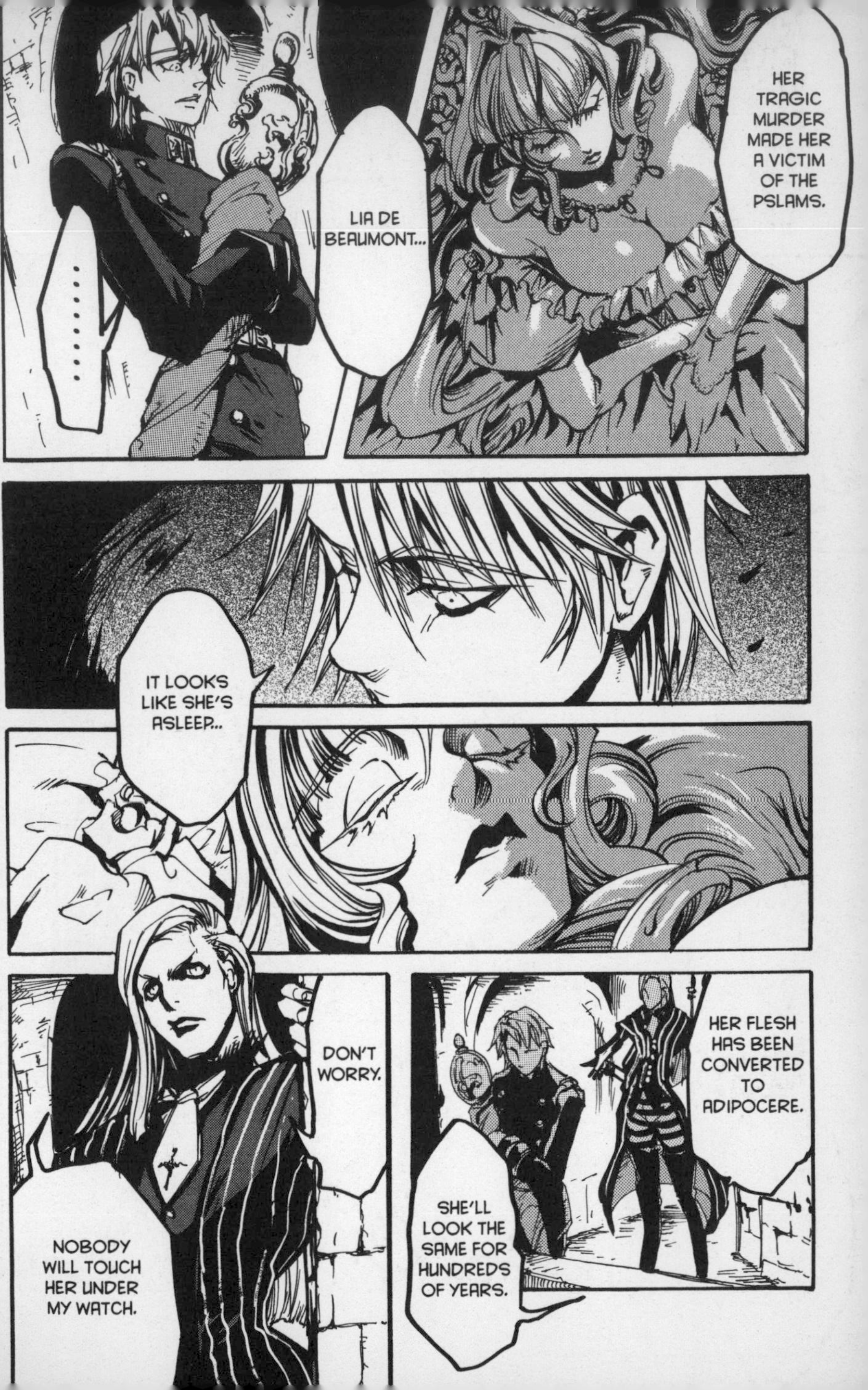
HER TRAGIC MURDER MADE HER A VICTIM OF THE PSLAMS.
LIA DE BEAUMONT...
......
IT LOOKS LIKE SHE'S ASLEEP...
HER FLESH HAS BEEN CONVERTED TO ADIPOCERE.
SHE'LL LOOK THE SAME FOR HUNDREDS OF YEARS.
DON'T WORRY.
NOBODY WILL TOUCH HER UNDER MY WATCH.

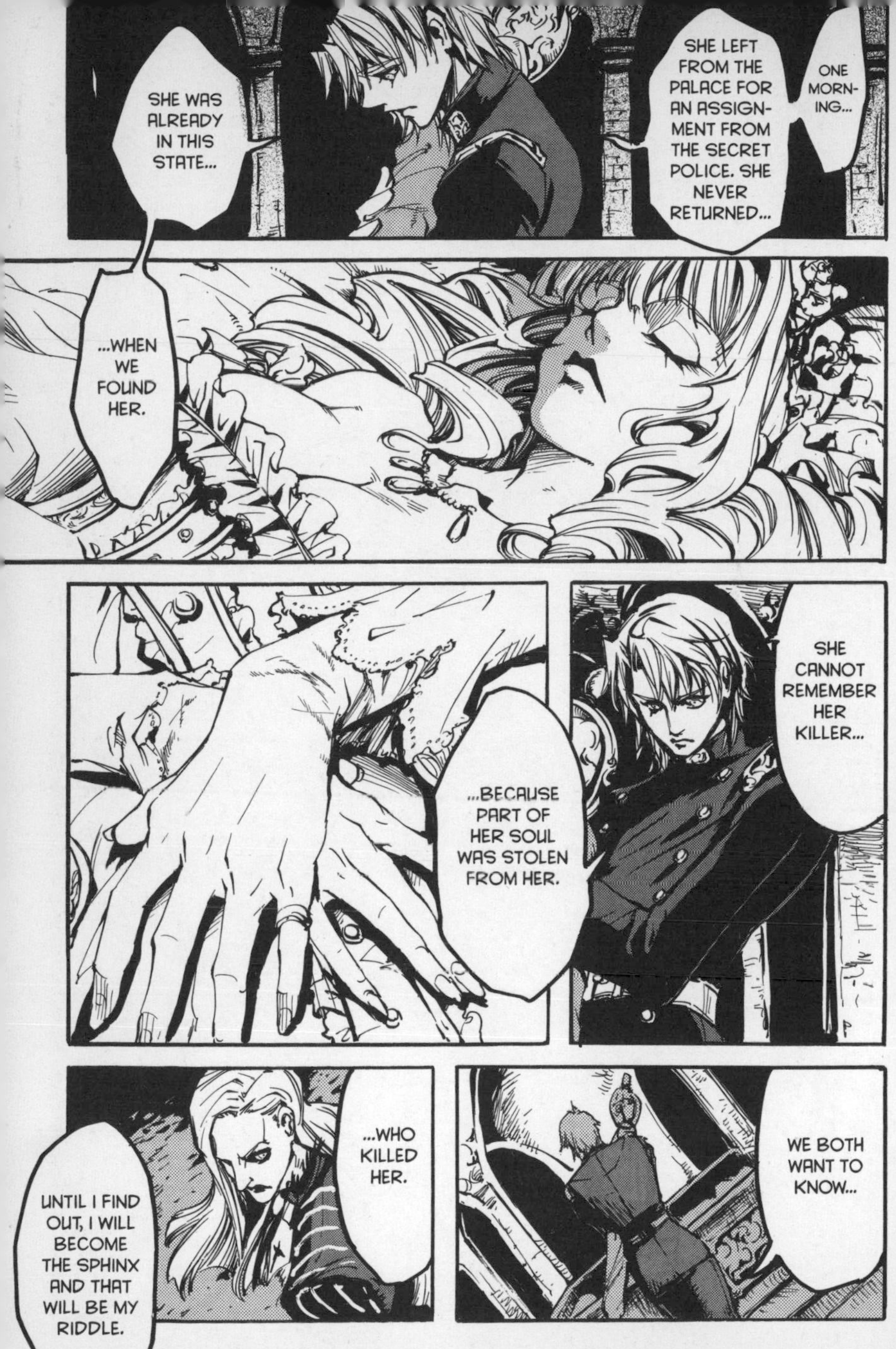
ONE MORNING...
SHE LEFT FROM THE PALACE FOR AN ASSIGNMENT FROM THE SECRET POLICE. SHE NEVER RETURNED...
SHE WAS ALREADY IN THIS STATE...
...WHEN WE FOUND HER.
SHE CANNOT REMEMBER HER KILLER...
...BECAUSE PART OF HER SOUL WAS STOLEN FROM HER.
WE BOTH WANT TO KNOW...
...WHO KILLED HER.
UNTIL I FIND OUT, I WILL BECOME THE SPHINX AND THAT WILL BE MY RIDDLE.

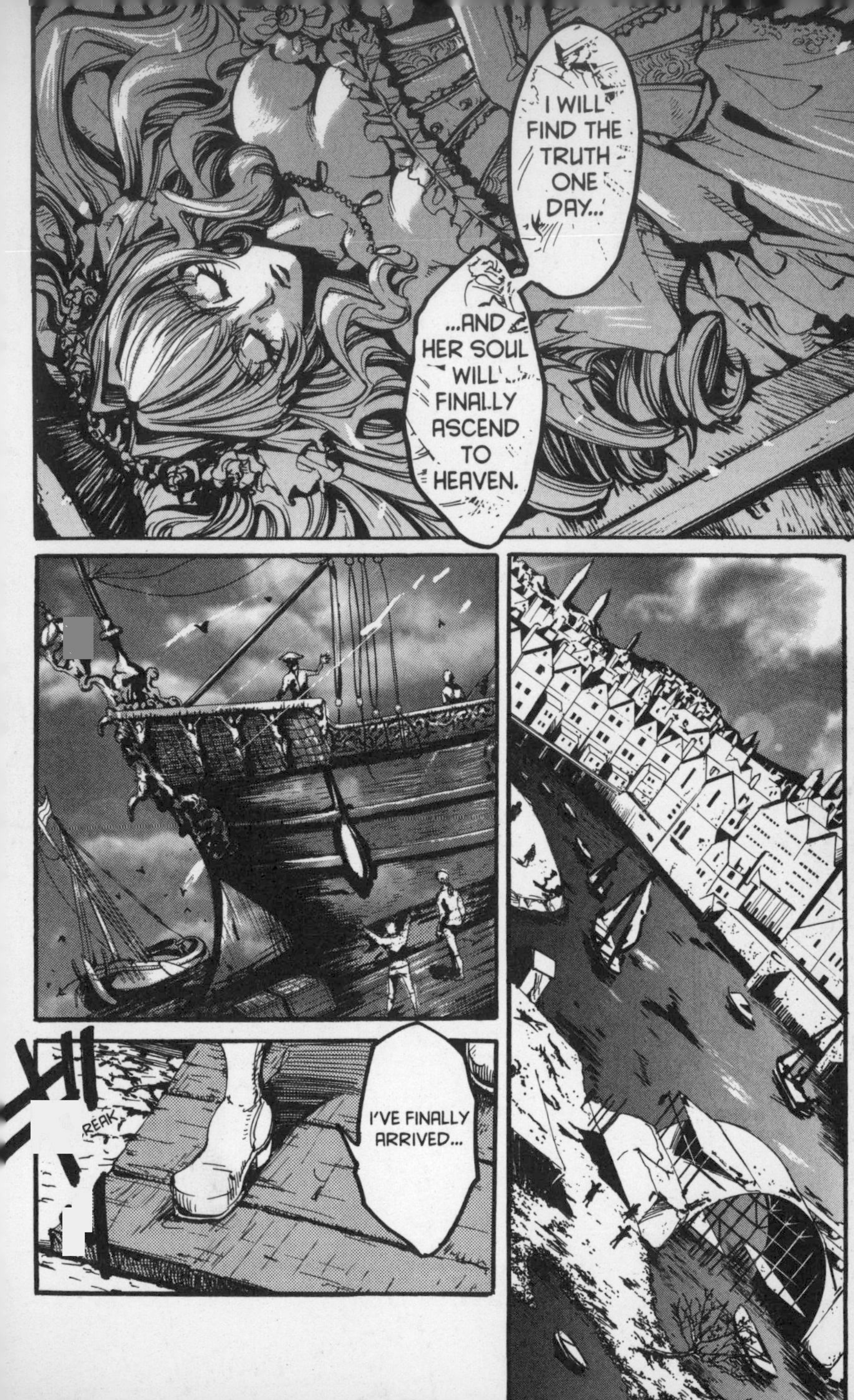
I WILL FIND THE TRUTH ONE DAY...
...AND HER SOUL WILL FINALLY ASCEND TO HEAVEN.
REAK
I'VE FINALLY ARRIVED...

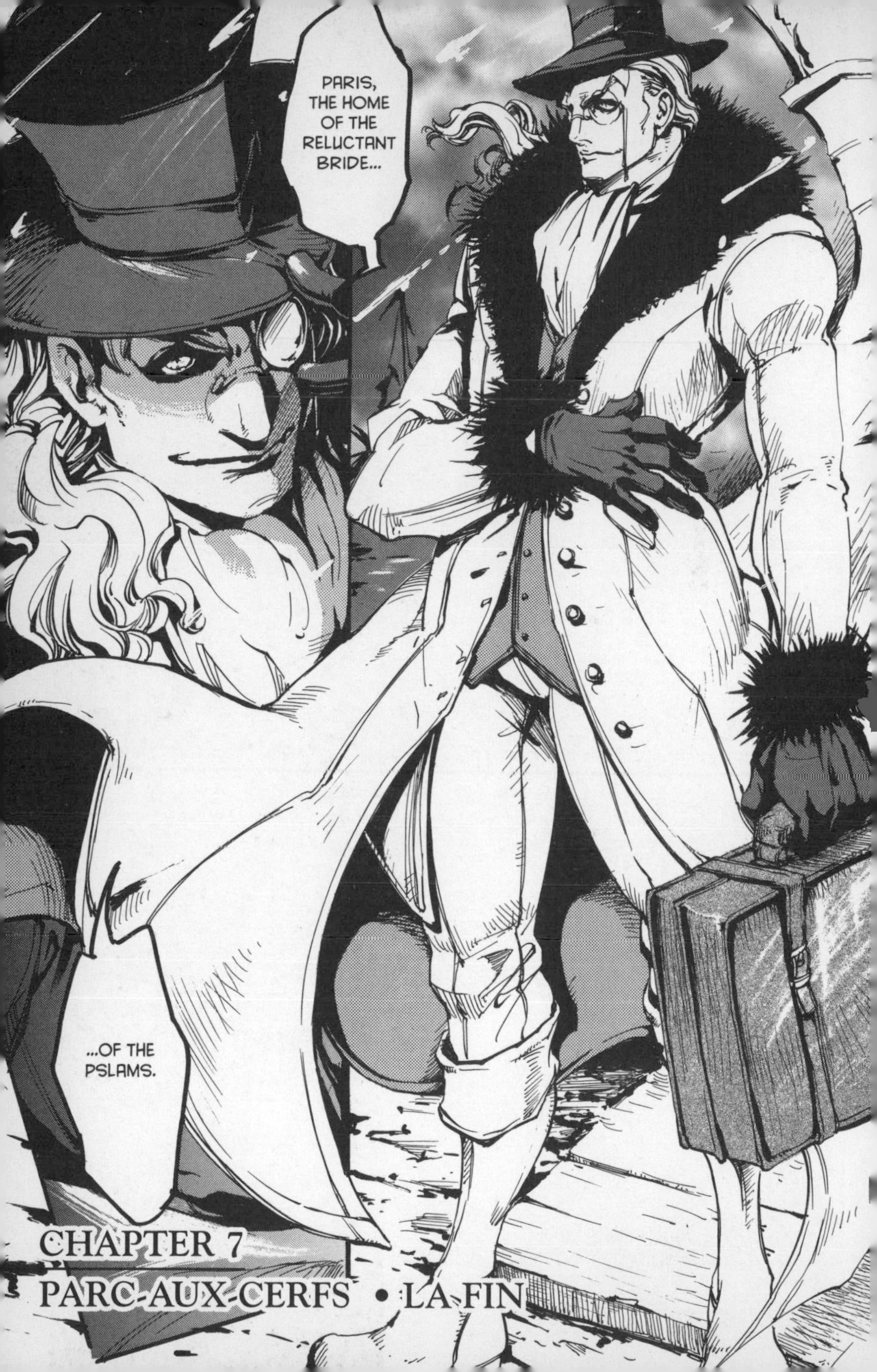
PARIS, THE HOME OF THE RELUCTANT BRIDE...
...OF THE PSLAMS.
CHAPTER 7
PARC-AUX-CERFS • LA FIN

CHEVALIER

CHAPTER 8
HIERARCHY OF POETS

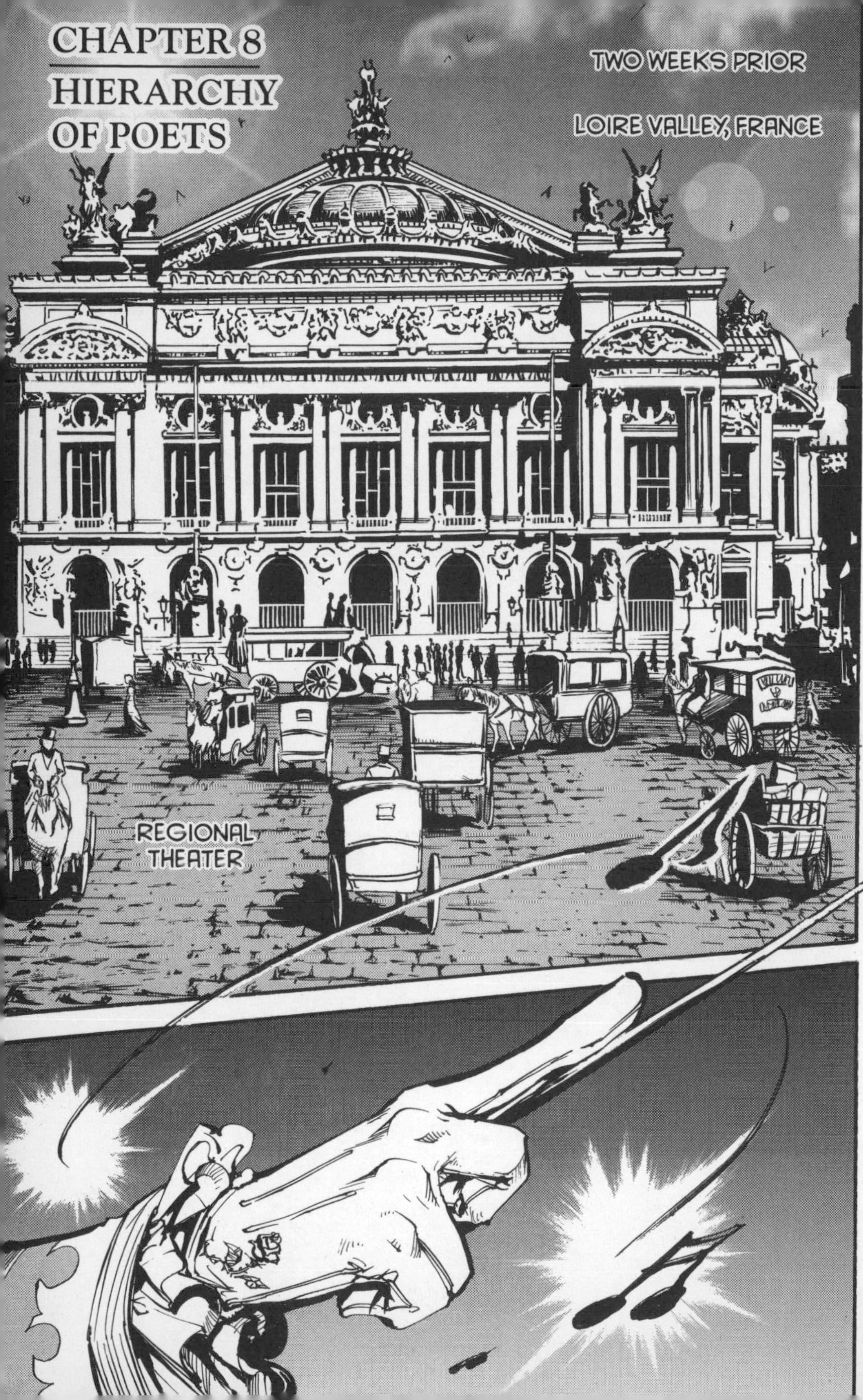
TWO WEEKS PRIOR
LOIRE VALLEY, FRANCE
REGIONAL THEATER

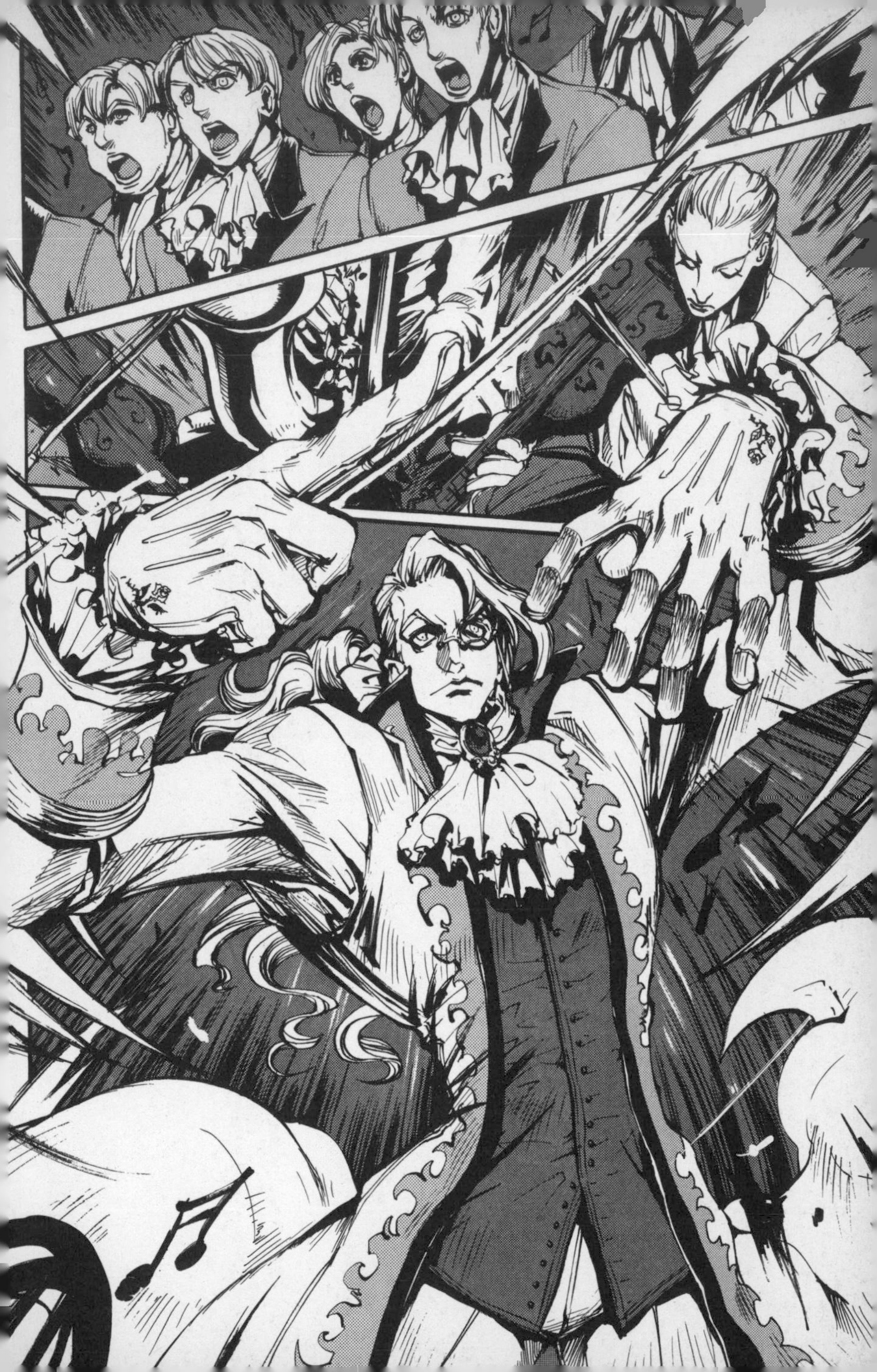

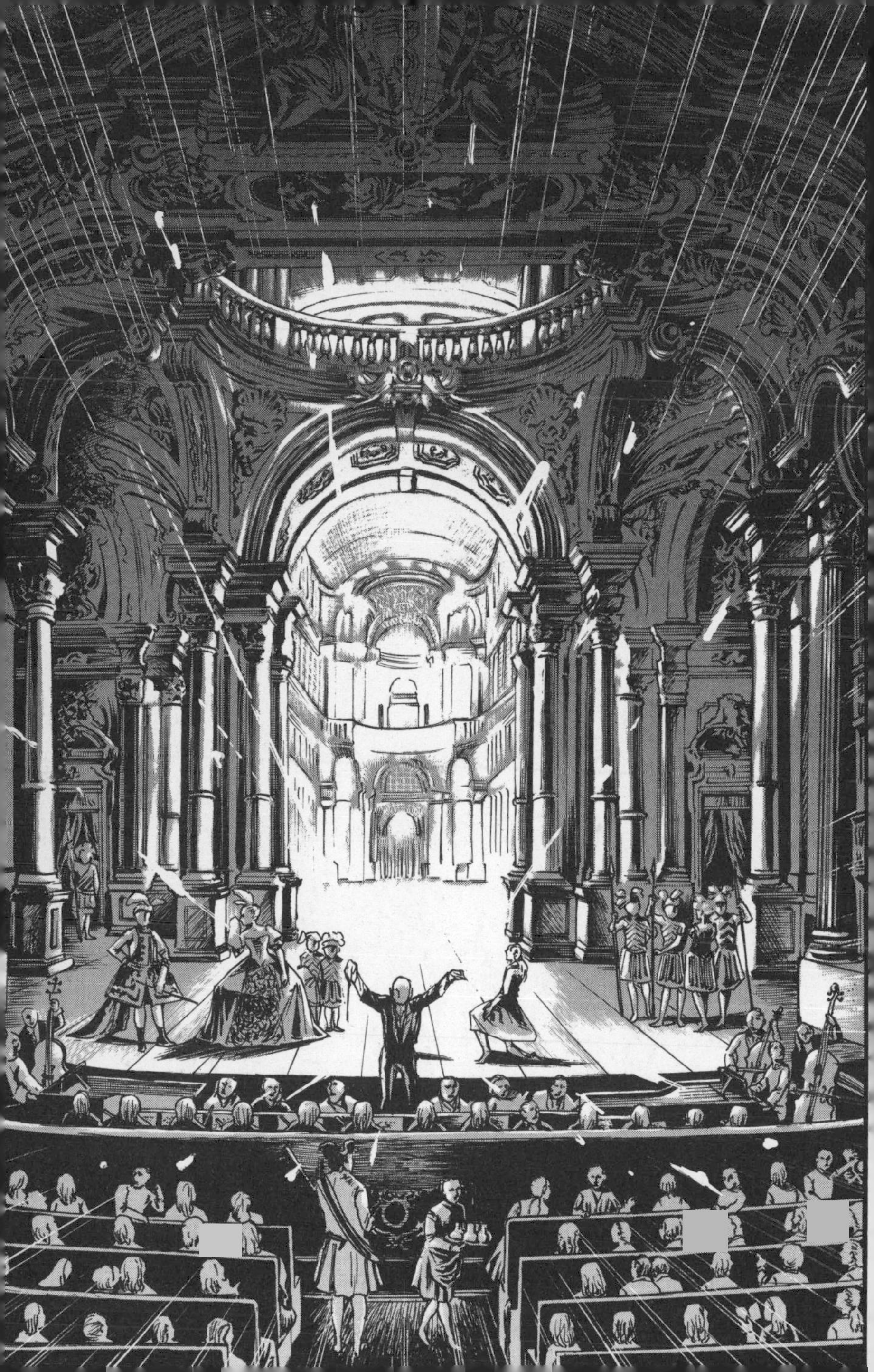

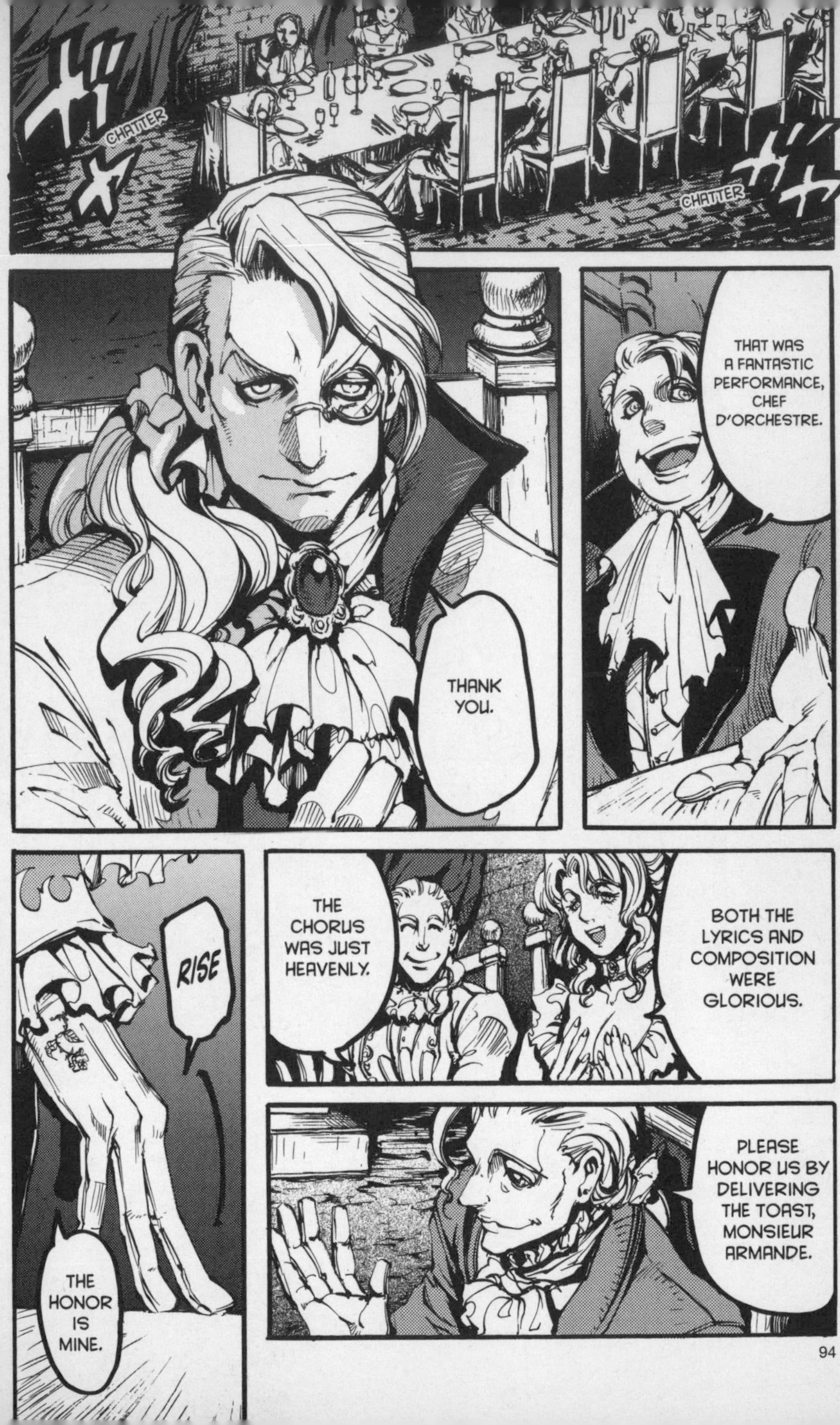
CHATTER
CHATTER
THAT WAS A FANTASTIC PERFORMANCE, CHEF D'ORCHESTRE.
THANK YOU.
BOTH THE LYRICS AND COMPOSITION WERE GLORIOUS.
THE CHORUS WAS JUST HEAVENLY.
PLEASE HONOR US BY DELIVERING THE TOAST, MONSIEUR ARMANDE.
RISE
THE HONOR IS MINE.

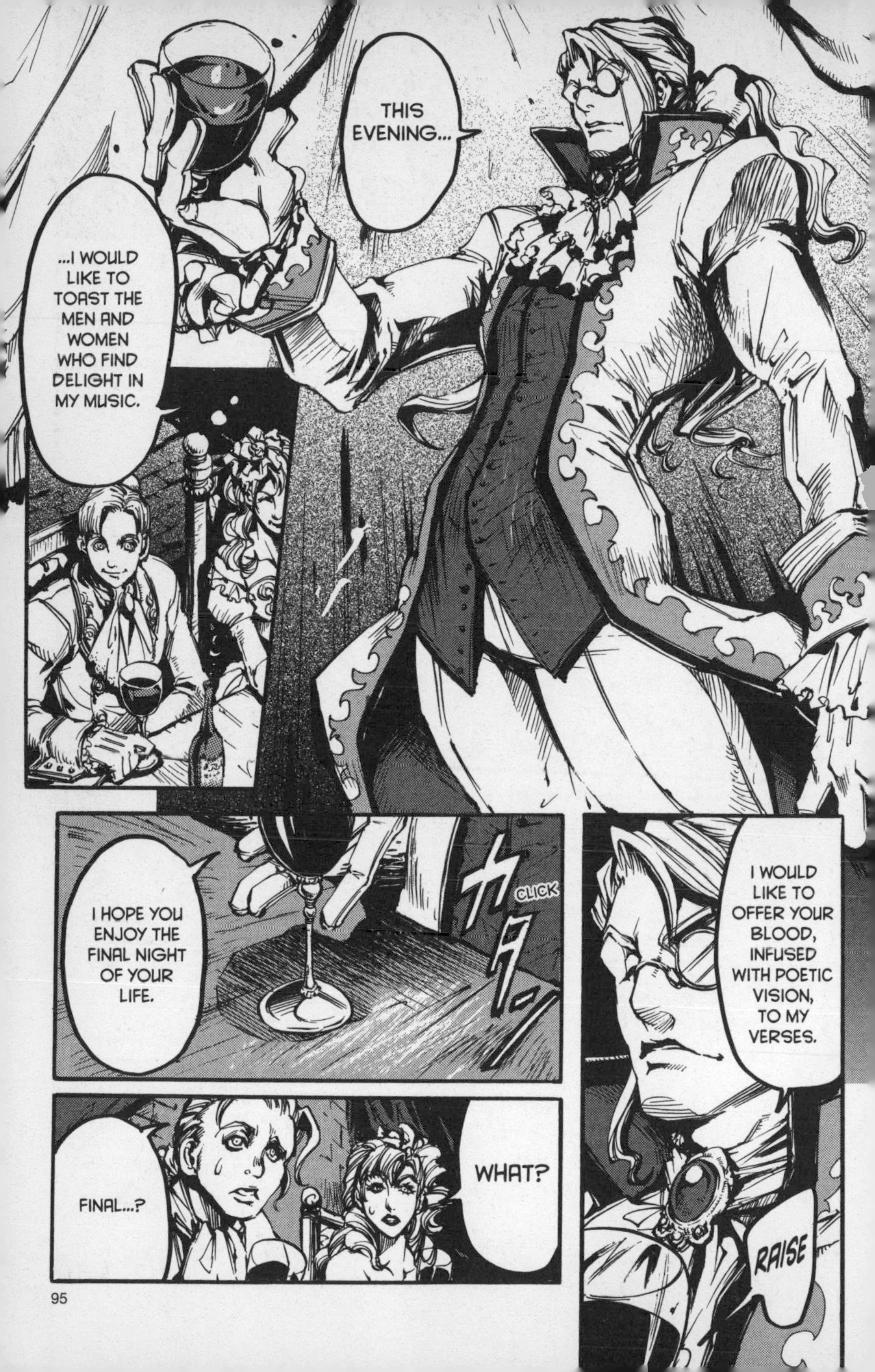
THIS EVENING...
...I WOULD LIKE TO TOAST THE MEN AND WOMEN WHO FIND DELIGHT IN MY MUSIC.
I WOULD LIKE TO OFFER YOUR BLOOD, INFUSED WITH POETIC VISION, TO MY VERSES.
RAISE
CLICK
I HOPE YOU ENJOY THE FINAL NIGHT OF YOUR LIFE.
WHAT?
FINAL...?

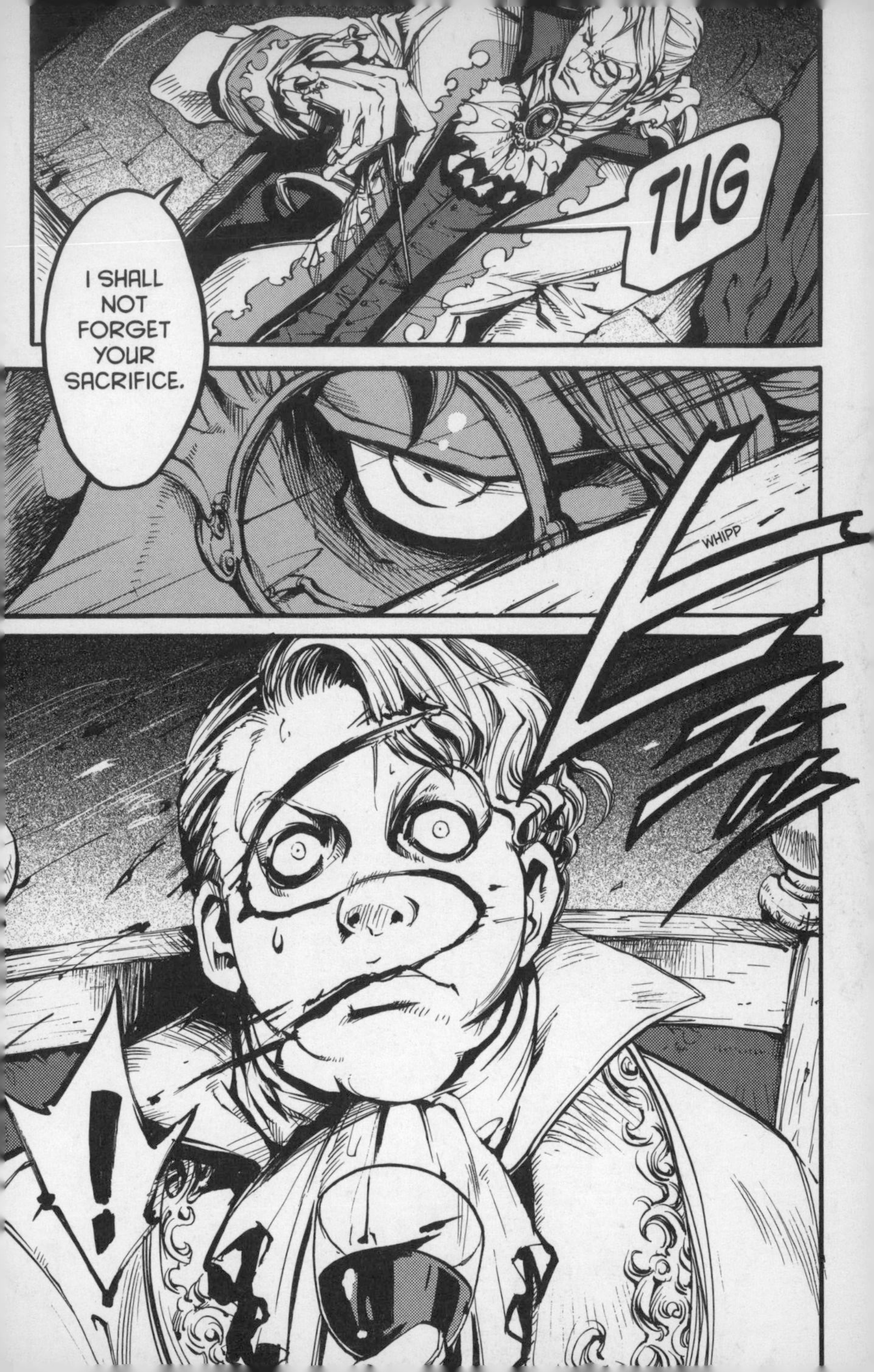
TUG
I SHALL NOT FORGET YOUR SACRIFICE.
WHIPP
!

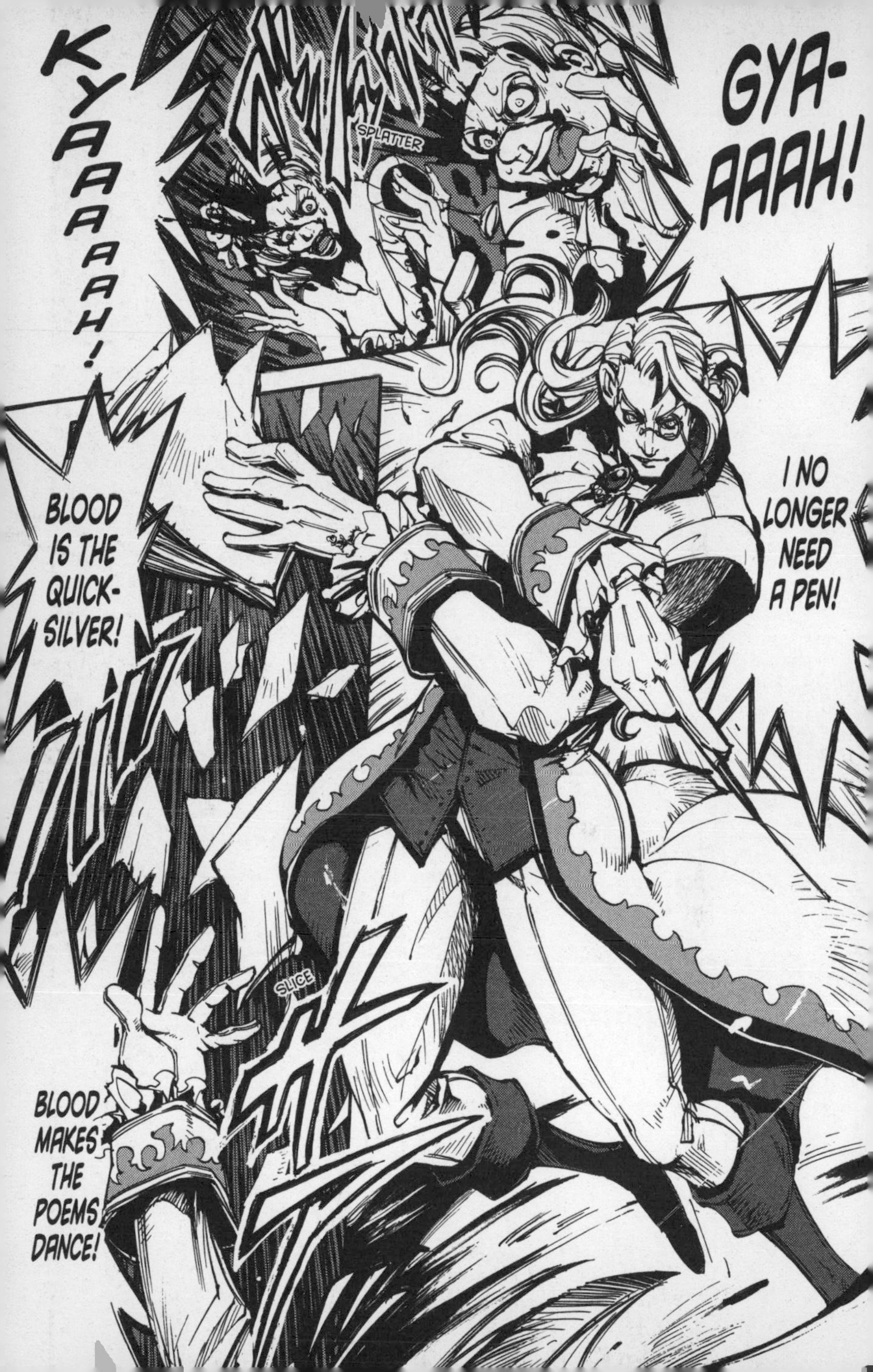
GYA-AAAH!
SPLATTER
KYAAAAAAH!
I NO LONGER NEED A PEN!
BLOOD IS THE QUICK-SILVER!
SLICE
BLOOD MAKES THE POEMS DANCE!

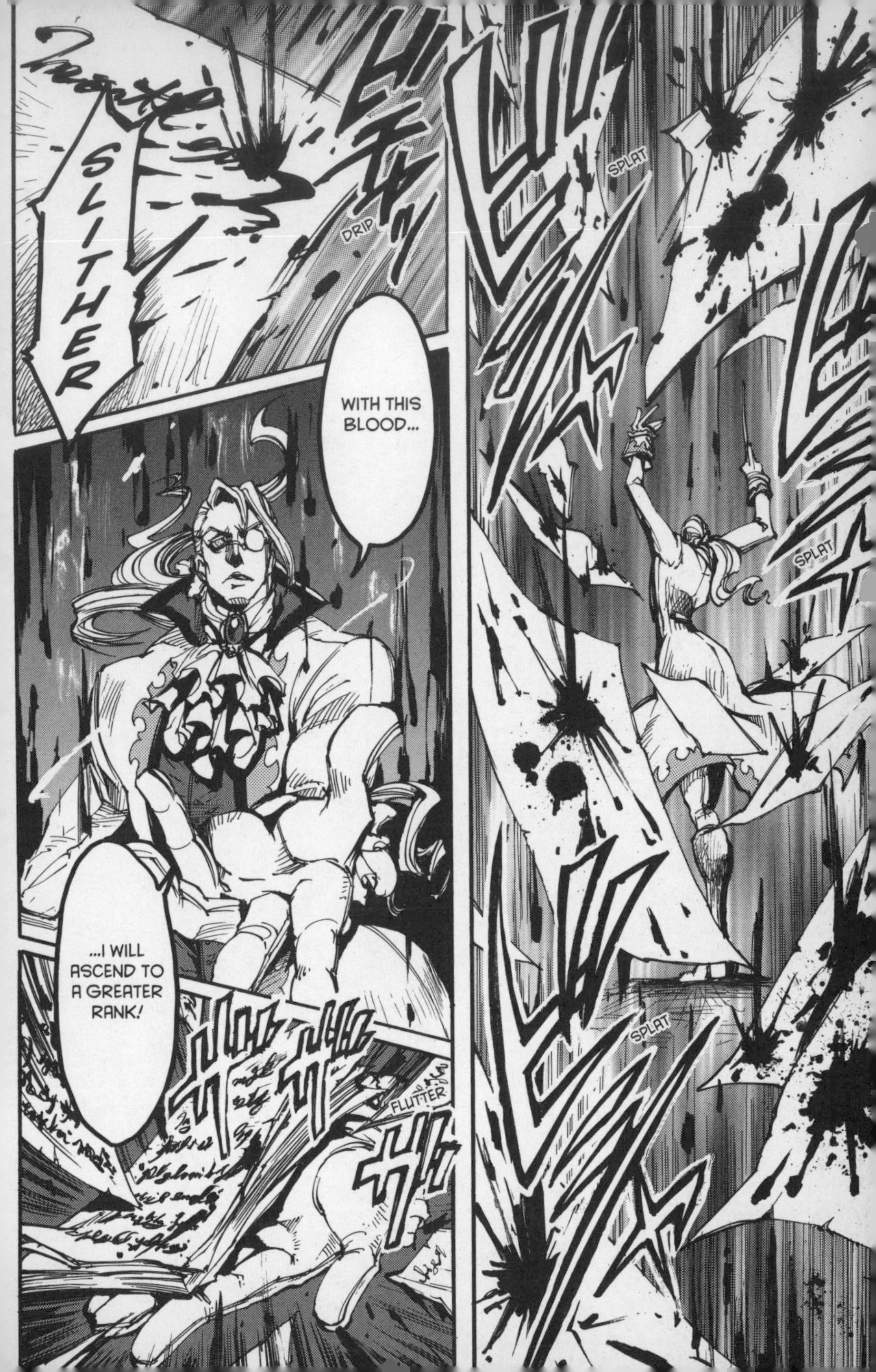
SPLAT
SPLAT
SPLAT
DRIP
SLITHER
WITH THIS BLOOD...
...I WILL ASCEND TO A GREATER RANK!
FLUTTER

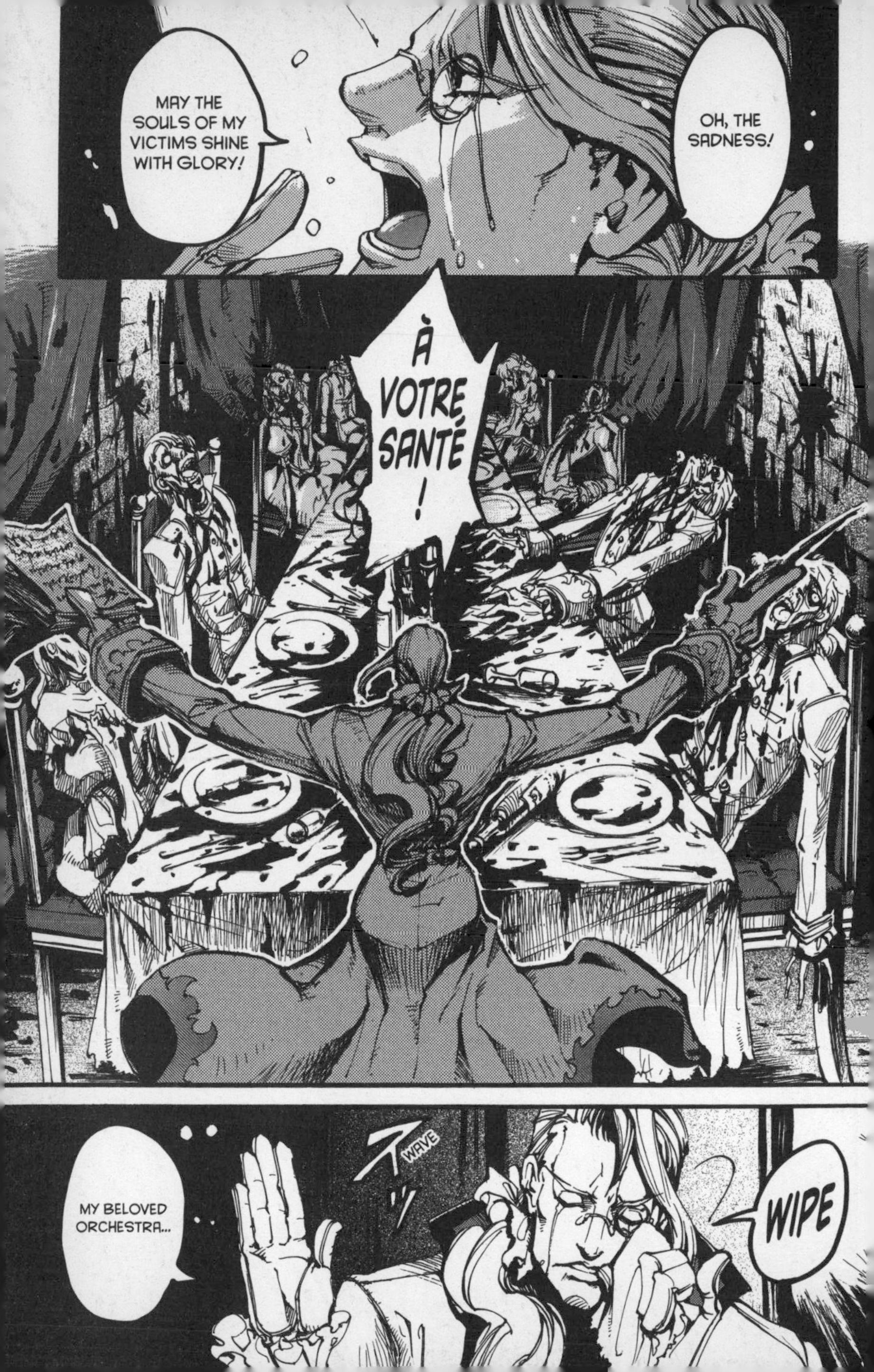
OH, THE SADNESS!
MAY THE SOULS OF MY VICTIMS SHINE WITH GLORY!
À VOTRE SANTÉ!
WIPE
WAVE
MY BELOVED ORCHESTRA...

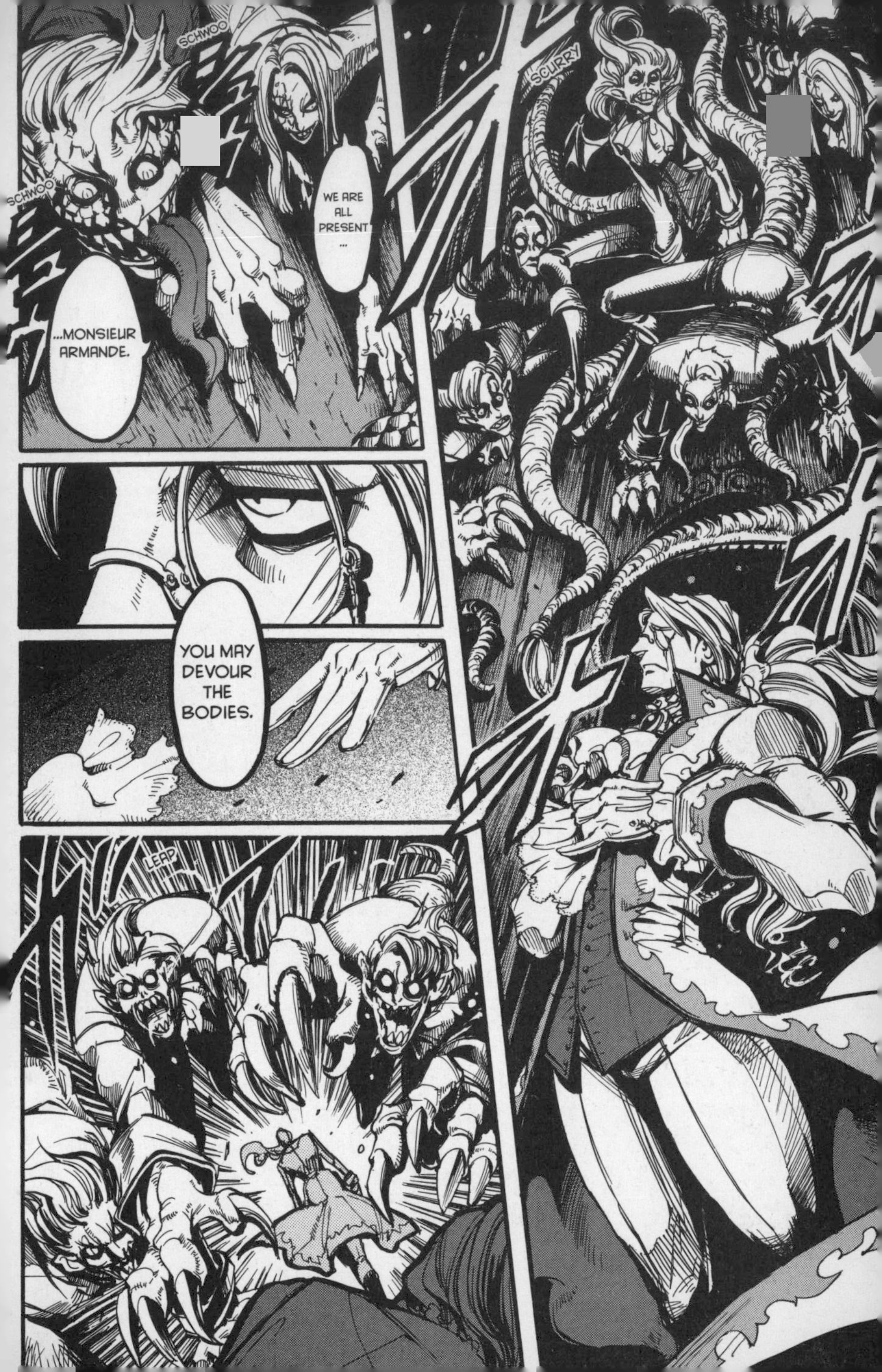
SCURRY
SCHWOO
SCHWOO
WE ARE ALL PRESENT ...
...MONSIEUR ARMANDE.
YOU MAY DEVOUR THE BODIES.
LEAP

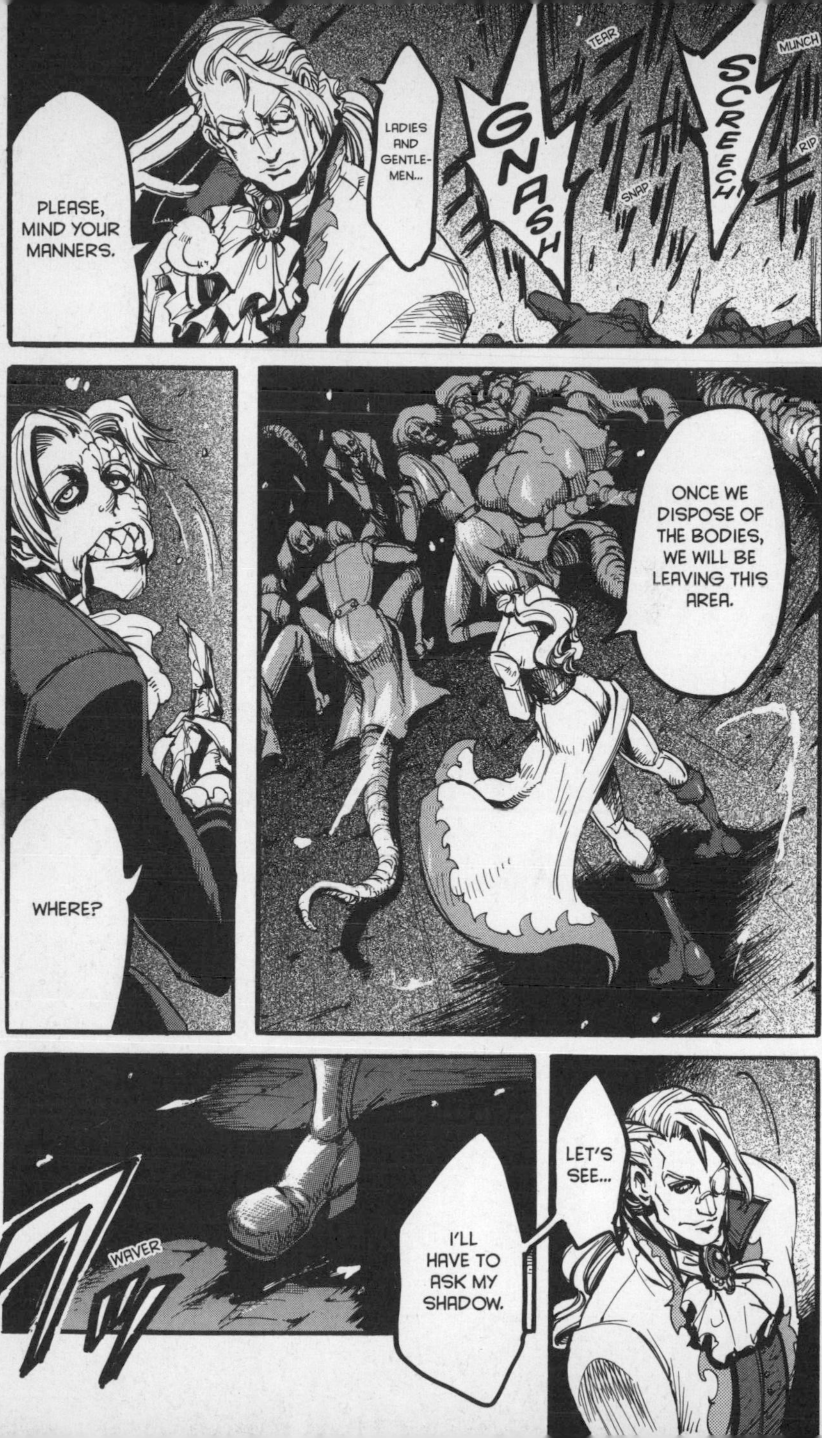
MUNCH
SCREECH
RIP
TEAR
GNASH
SNAP
LADIES AND GENTLE-MEN...
PLEASE, MIND YOUR MANNERS.
ONCE WE DISPOSE OF THE BODIES, WE WILL BE LEAVING THIS AREA.
WHERE?
LET'S SEE...
I'LL HAVE TO ASK MY SHADOW.
WAVER

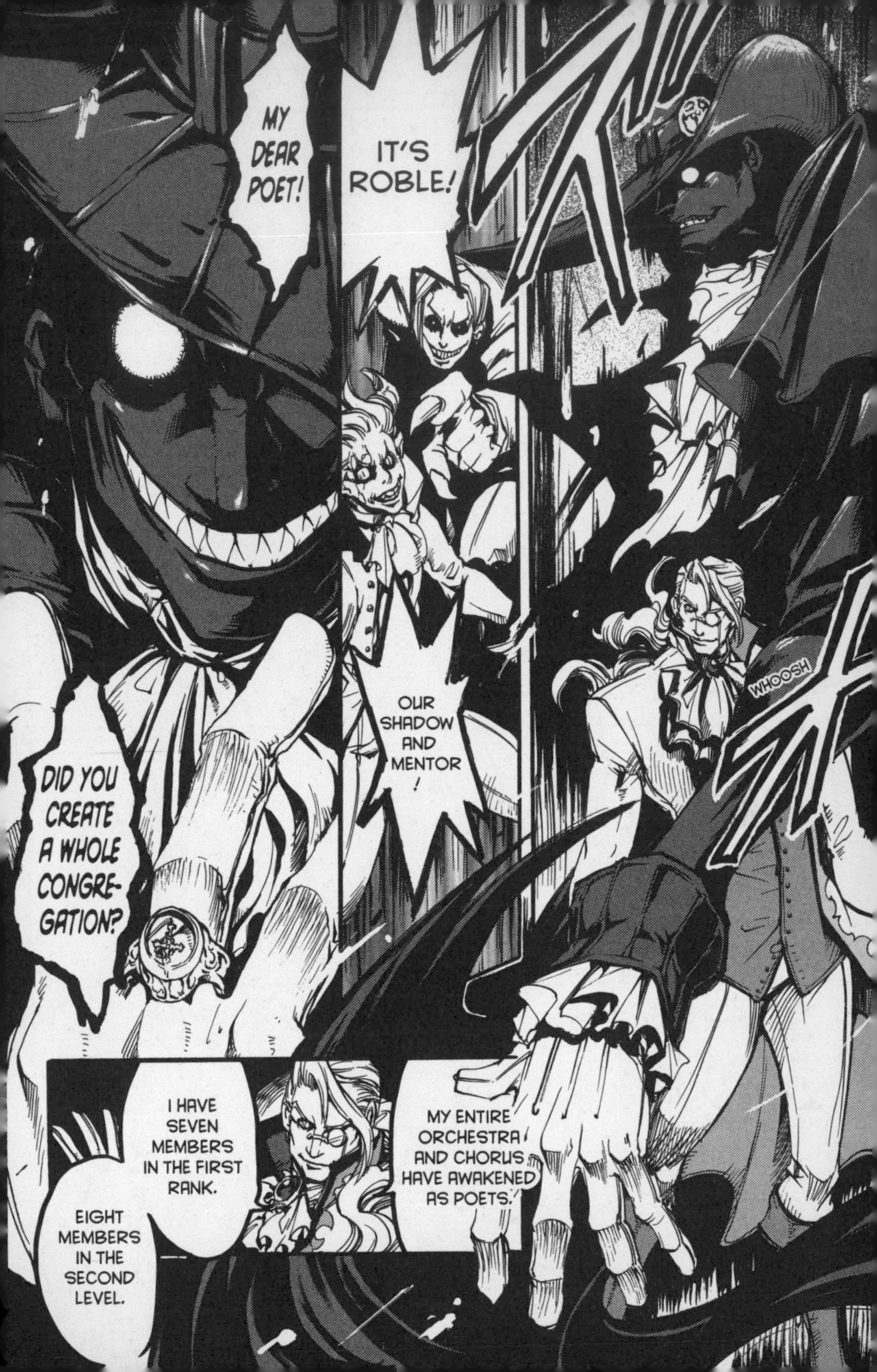

WHOOSH
IT'S ROBLE!
OUR SHADOW AND MENTOR!
MY DEAR POET!
DID YOU CREATE A WHOLE CONGREGATION?
MY ENTIRE ORCHESTRA AND CHORUS HAVE AWAKENED AS POETS.
I HAVE SEVEN MEMBERS IN THE FIRST RANK.
EIGHT MEMBERS IN THE SECOND LEVEL.

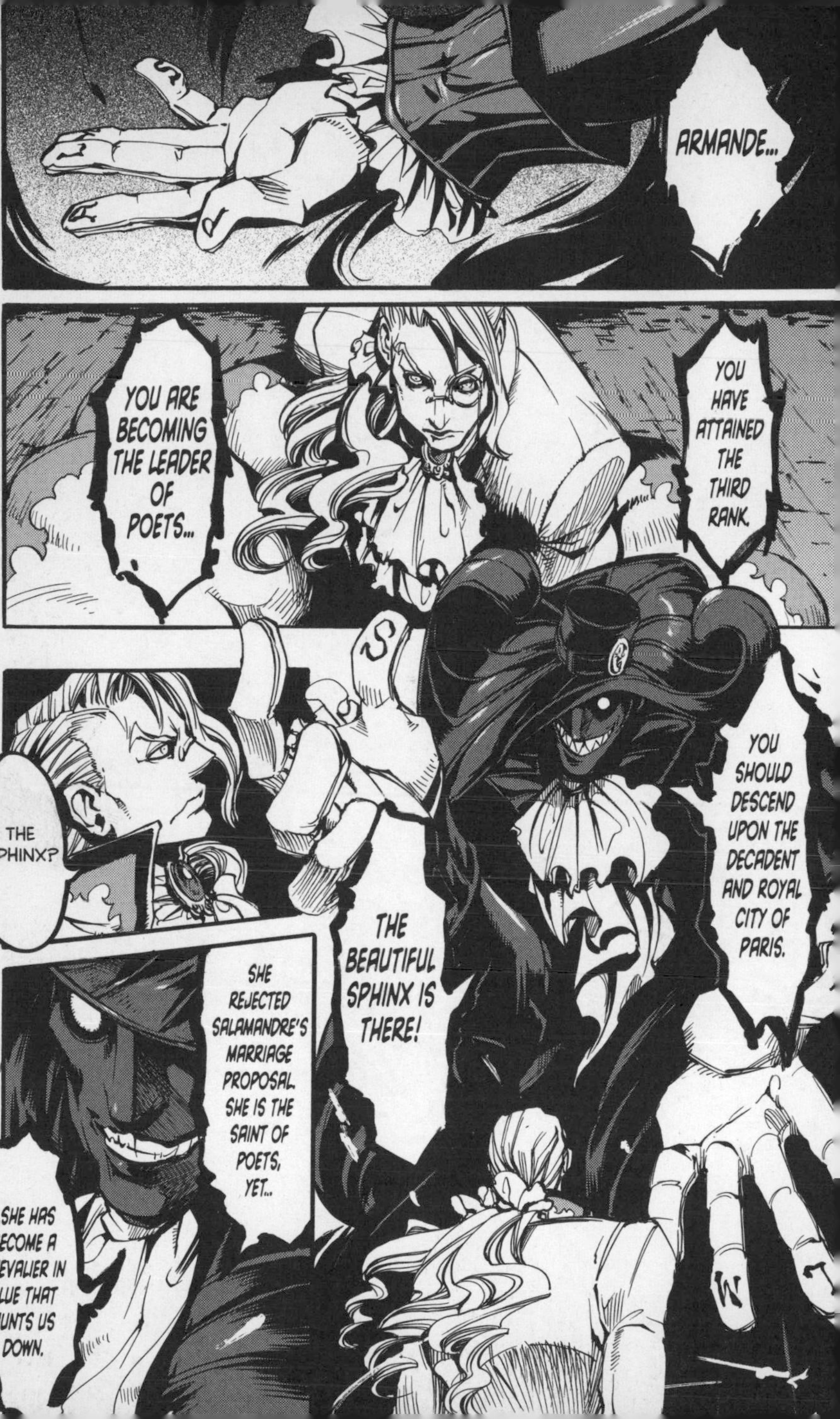
ARMANDE...
YOU HAVE ATTAINED THE THIRD RANK.
YOU ARE BECOMING THE LEADER OF POETS...
YOU SHOULD DESCEND UPON THE DECADENT AND ROYAL CITY OF PARIS.
THE BEAUTIFUL SPHINX IS THERE!
THE SPHINX?
SHE REJECTED SALAMANDRE'S MARRIAGE PROPOSAL. SHE IS THE SAINT OF POETS, YET...
...SHE HAS BECOME A CHEVALIER IN BLUE THAT HUNTS US DOWN.

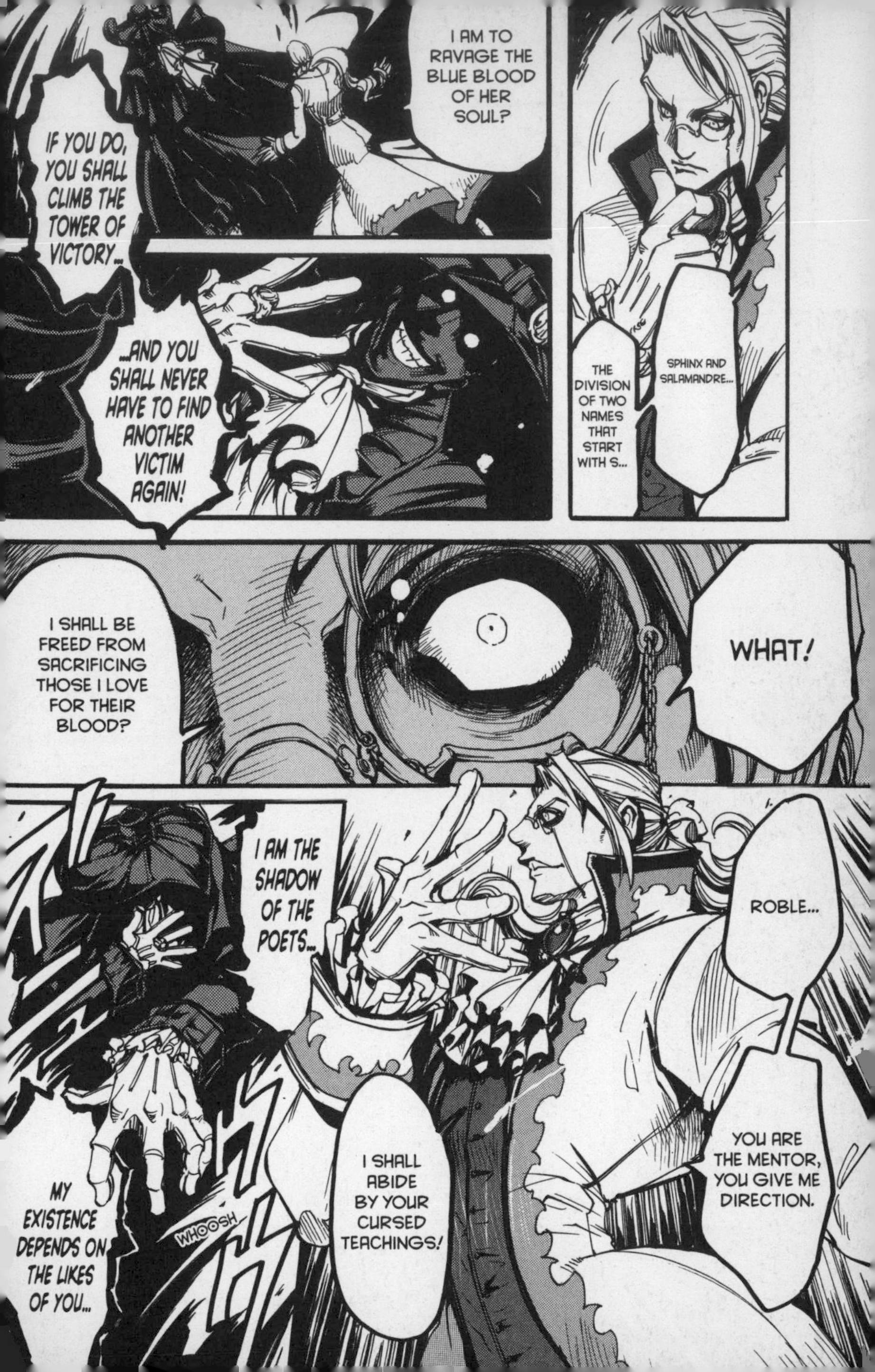
SPHINX AND SALAMANDRE...
THE DIVISION OF TWO NAMES THAT START WITH S...
I AM TO RAVAGE THE BLUE BLOOD OF HER SOUL?
IF YOU DO, YOU SHALL CLIMB THE TOWER OF VICTORY...
...AND YOU SHALL NEVER HAVE TO FIND ANOTHER VICTIM AGAIN!
WHAT!
I SHALL BE FREED FROM SACRIFICING THOSE I LOVE FOR THEIR BLOOD?
ROBLE...
I AM THE SHADOW OF THE POETS...
YOU ARE THE MENTOR, YOU GIVE ME DIRECTION.
I SHALL ABIDE BY YOUR CURSED TEACHINGS!
WHOOSH
MY EXISTENCE DEPENDS ON THE LIKES OF YOU...

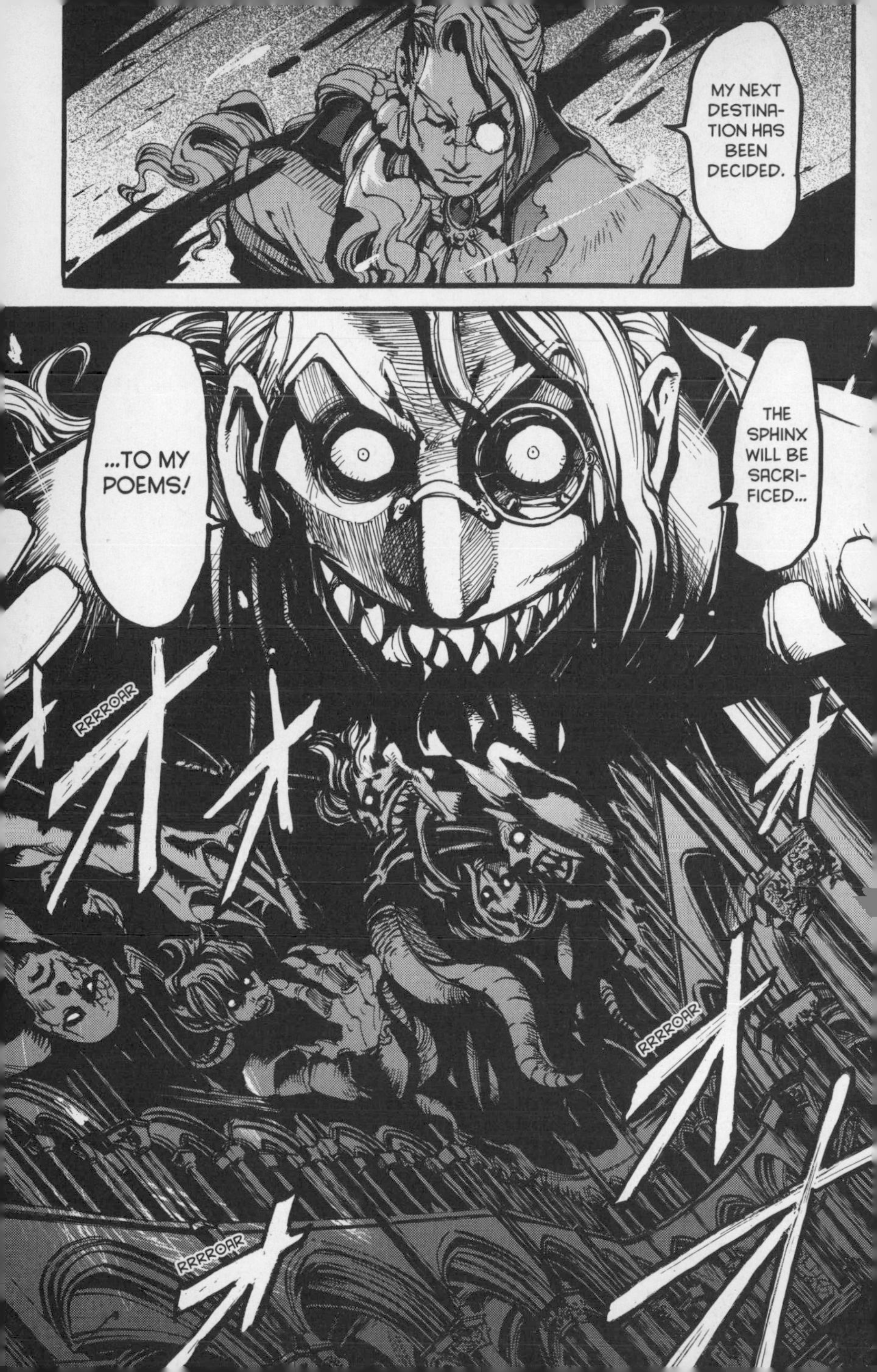
MY NEXT DESTINATION HAS BEEN DECIDED.
THE SPHINX WILL BE SACRIFICED...
...TO MY POEMS!
RRRROAR
RRRROAR
RRRROAR

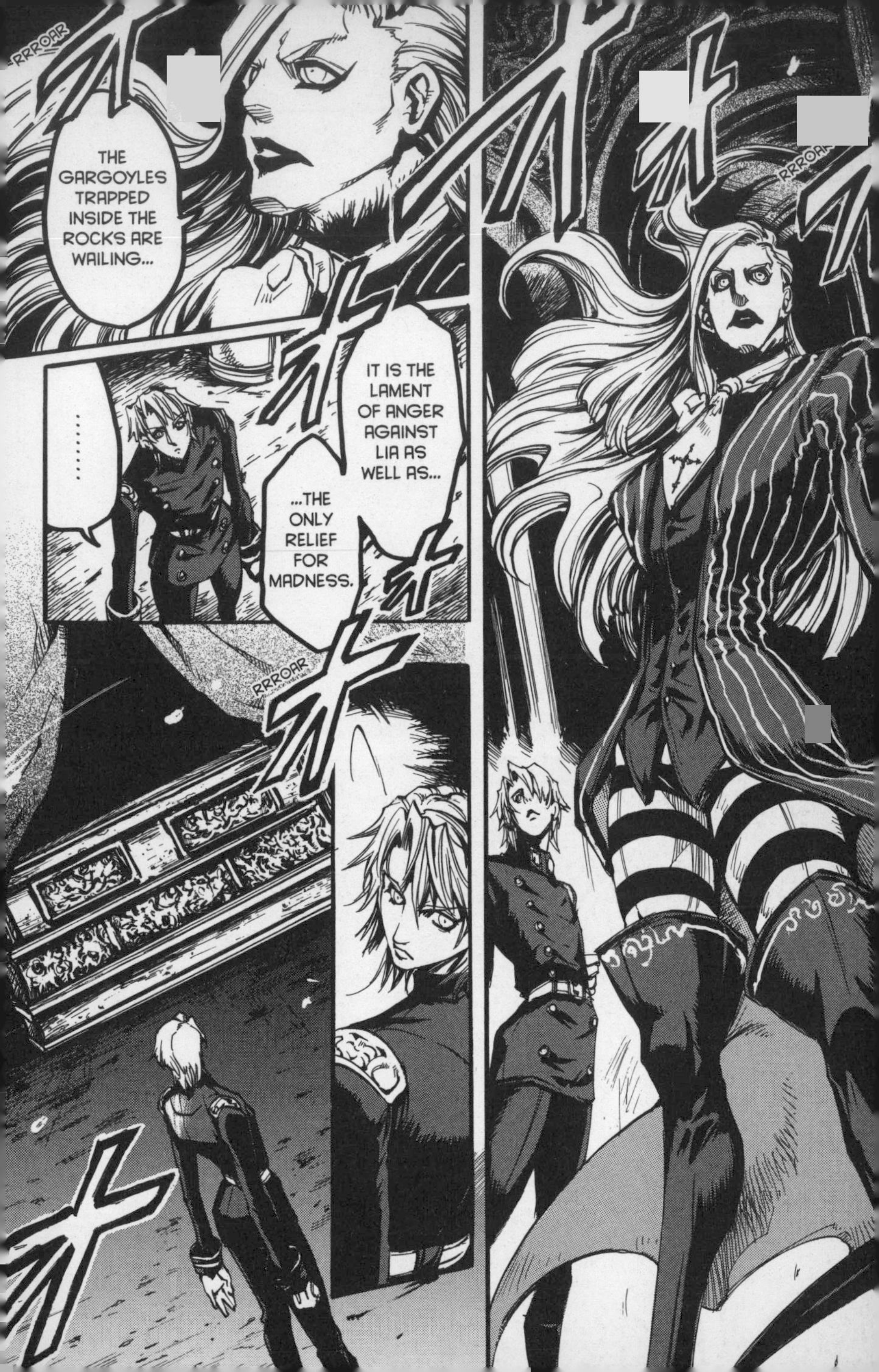
RRROAR
RRROAR
THE GARGOYLES TRAPPED INSIDE THE ROCKS ARE WAILING...
IT IS THE LAMENT OF ANGER AGAINST LIA AS WELL AS...
...THE ONLY RELIEF FOR MADNESS.
......
RRROAR

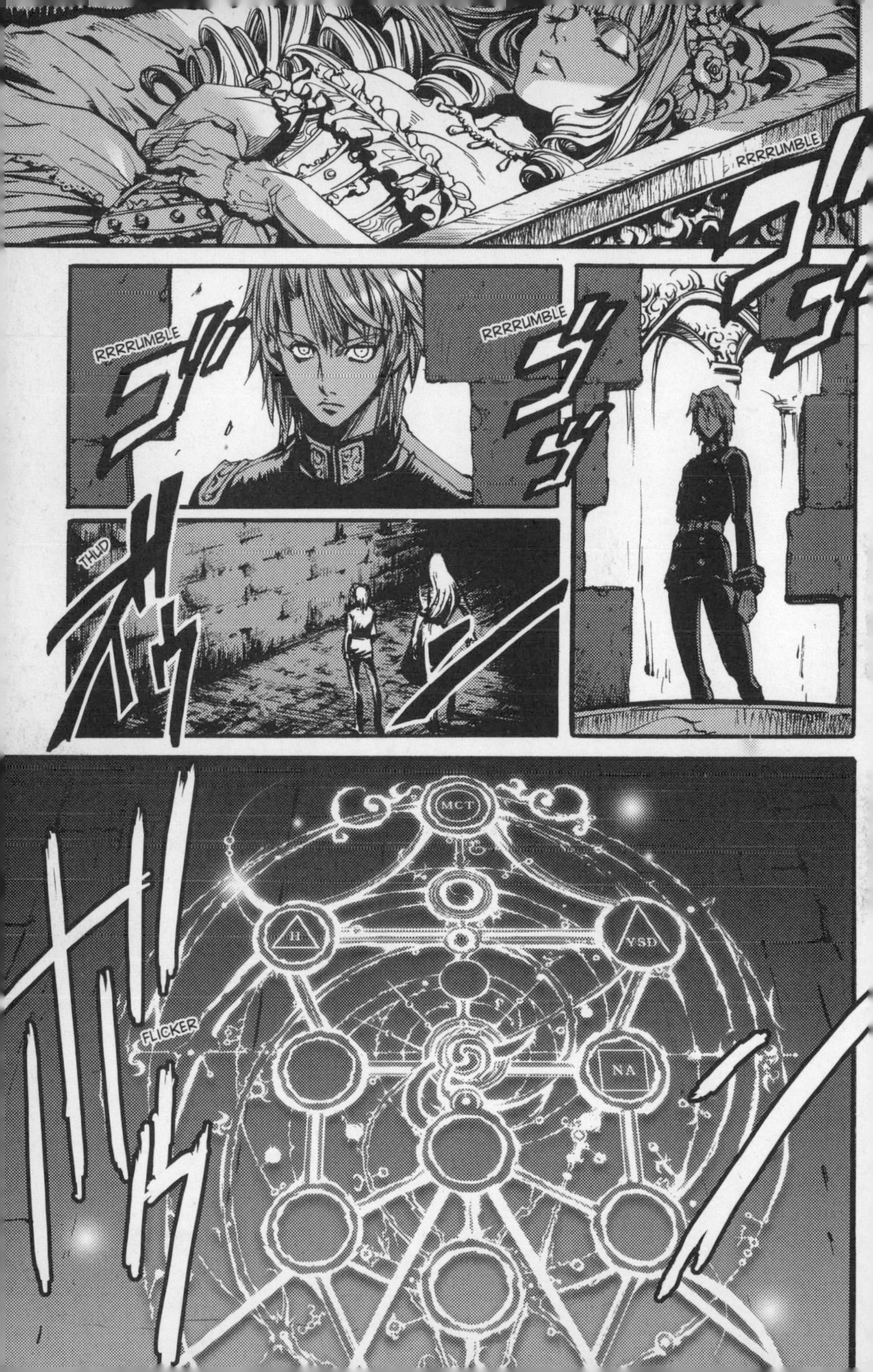
RRRRUMBLE
RRRRUMBLE
RRRRUMBLE
THUD
FLICKER
MCT
YSD
H
NA

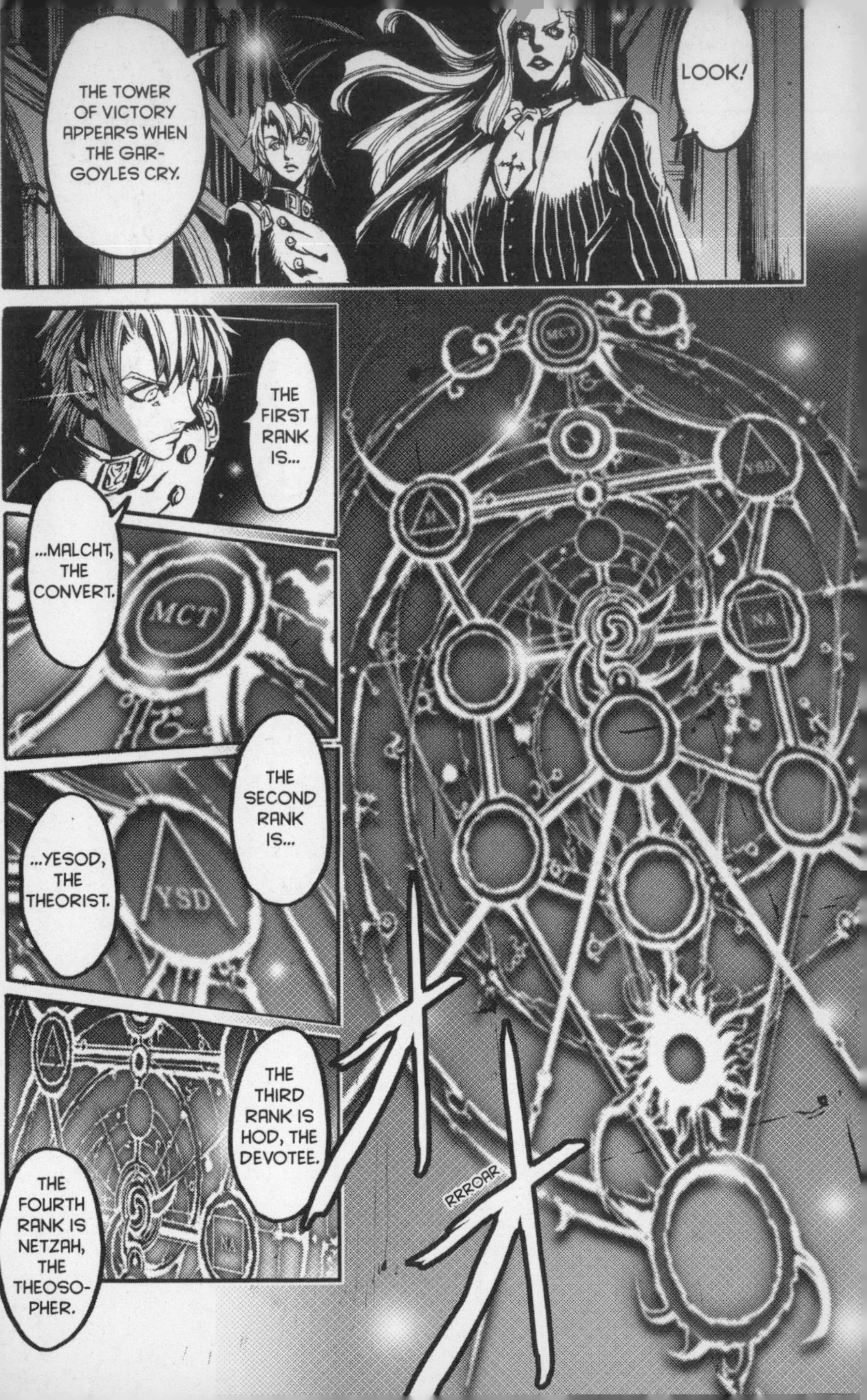
LOOK!
THE TOWER OF VICTORY APPEARS WHEN THE GAR-GOYLES CRY.
RRROAR
THE FIRST RANK IS...
...MALCHT, THE CONVERT.
THE SECOND RANK IS...
...YESOD, THE THEORIST.
THE THIRD RANK IS HOD, THE DEVOTEE.
THE FOURTH RANK IS NETZAH, THE THEOSO-PHER.

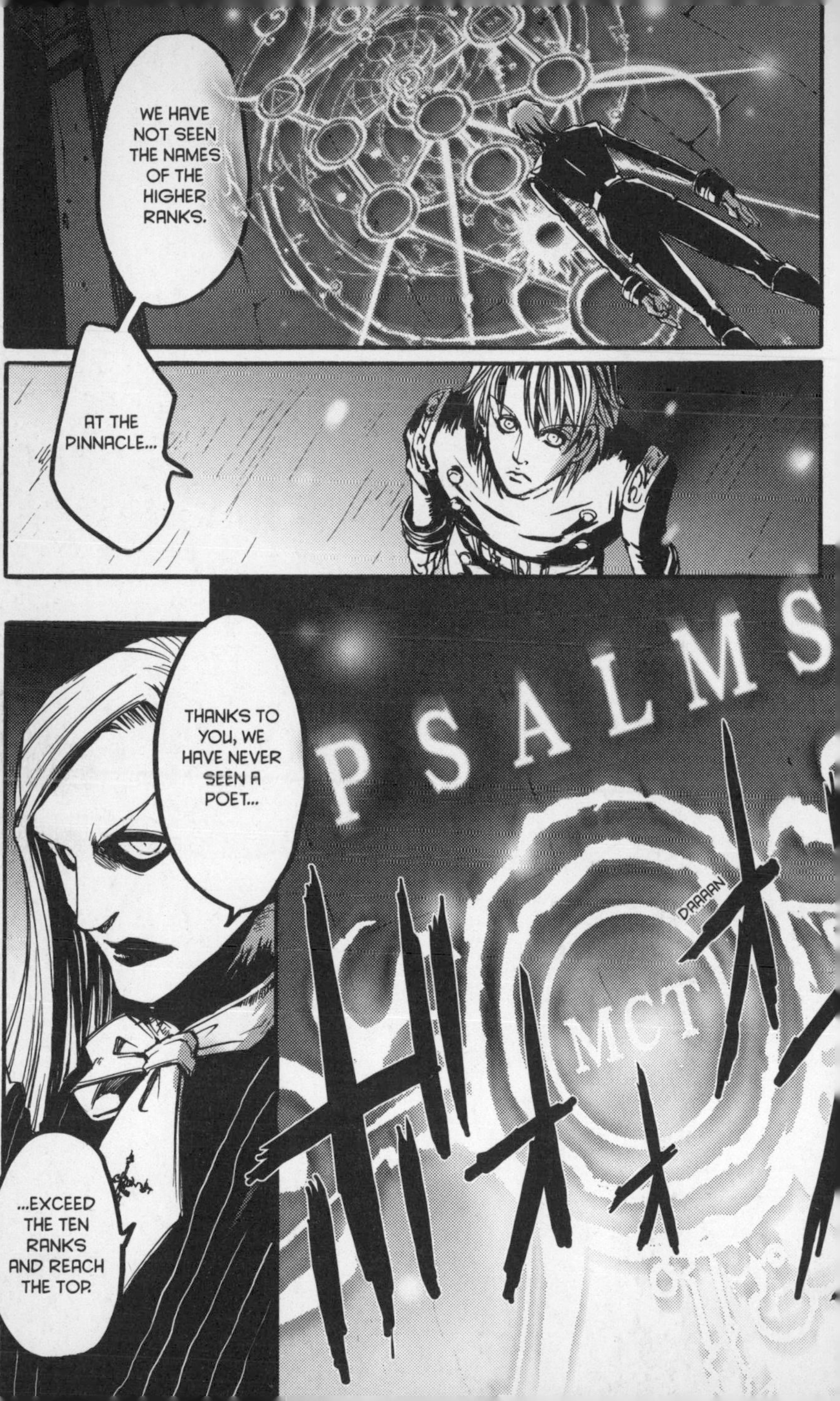
WE HAVE NOT SEEN THE NAMES OF THE HIGHER RANKS.
AT THE PINNACLE...
THANKS TO YOU, WE HAVE NEVER SEEN A POET...
...EXCEED THE TEN RANKS AND REACH THE TOP.
PSALMS
MCT
DAAAAN

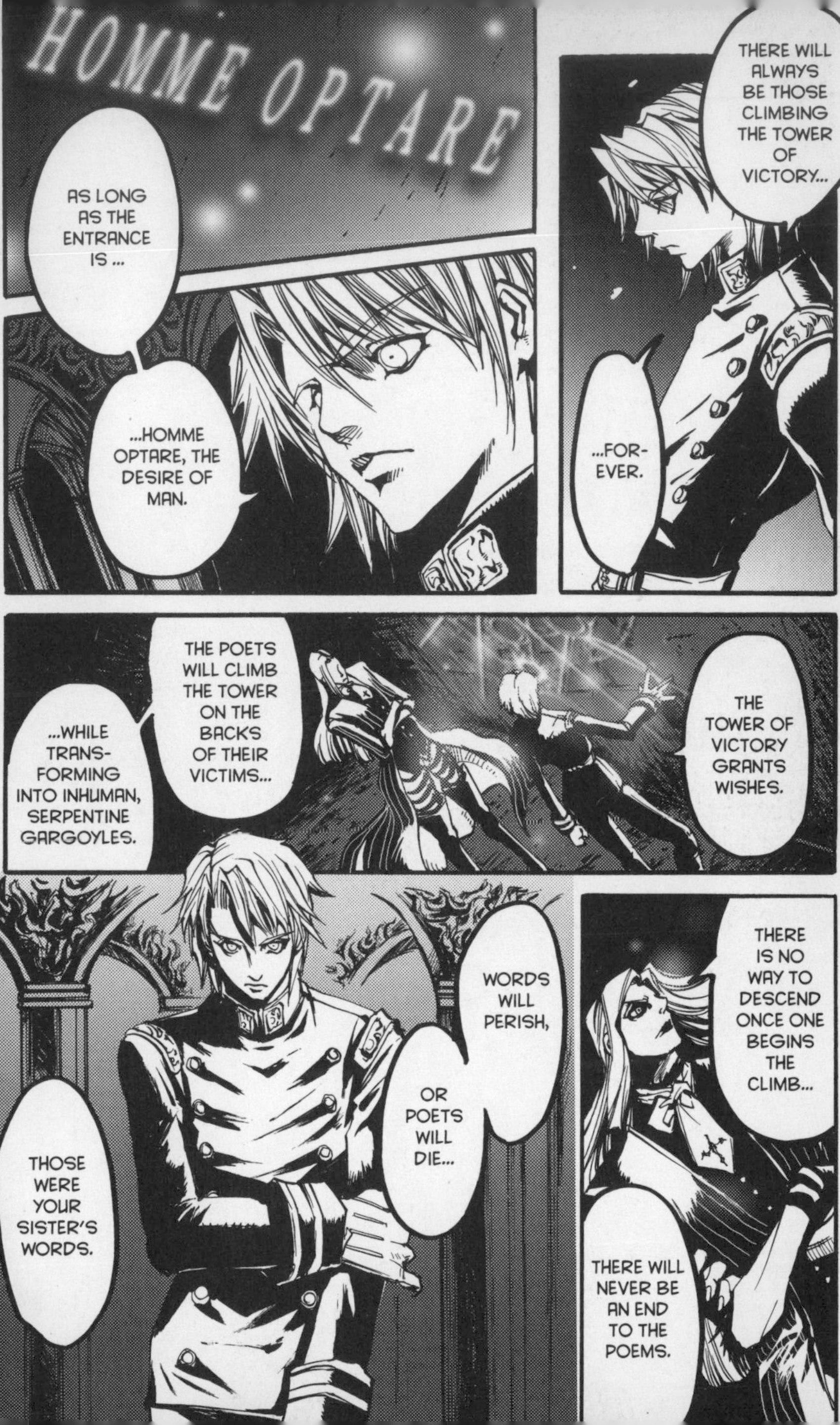
THERE WILL ALWAYS BE THOSE CLIMBING THE TOWER OF VICTORY...
...FOR-EVER.
HOMME OPTARE
AS LONG AS THE ENTRANCE IS ...
...HOMME OPTARE, THE DESIRE OF MAN.
THE TOWER OF VICTORY GRANTS WISHES.
THE POETS WILL CLIMB THE TOWER ON THE BACKS OF THEIR VICTIMS...
...WHILE TRANS-FORMING INTO INHUMAN, SERPENTINE GARGOYLES.
THERE IS NO WAY TO DESCEND ONCE ONE BEGINS THE CLIMB...
THERE WILL NEVER BE AN END TO THE POEMS.
WORDS WILL PERISH,
OR POETS WILL DIE...
THOSE WERE YOUR SISTER'S WORDS.

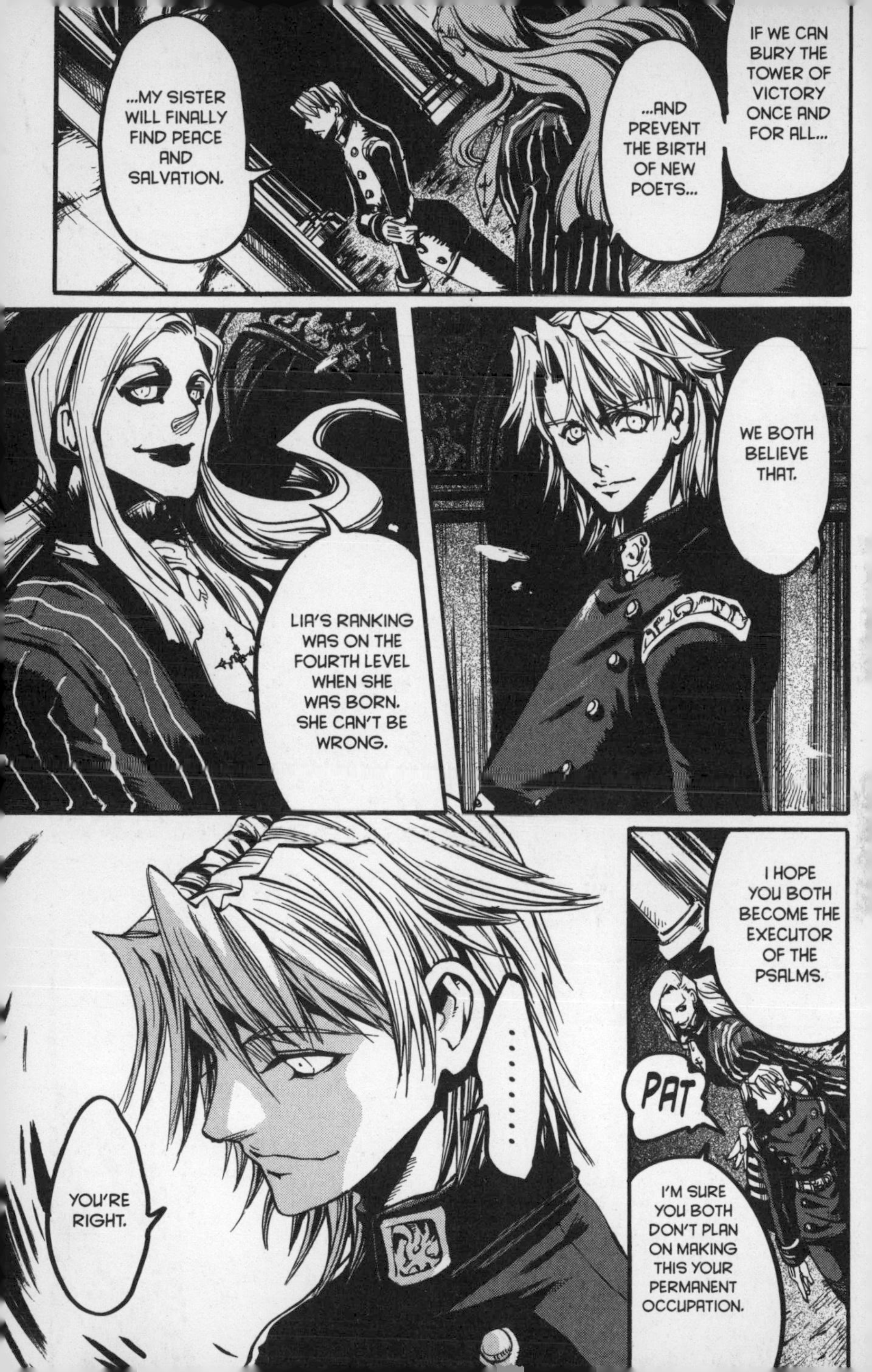
IF WE CAN BURY THE TOWER OF VICTORY ONCE AND FOR ALL...
...AND PREVENT THE BIRTH OF NEW POETS...
...MY SISTER WILL FINALLY FIND PEACE AND SALVATION.
WE BOTH BELIEVE THAT.
LIA'S RANKING WAS ON THE FOURTH LEVEL WHEN SHE WAS BORN. SHE CAN'T BE WRONG.
I HOPE YOU BOTH BECOME THE EXECUTOR OF THE PSALMS.
PAT
I'M SURE YOU BOTH DON'T PLAN ON MAKING THIS YOUR PERMANENT OCCUPATION.
......
YOU'RE RIGHT.

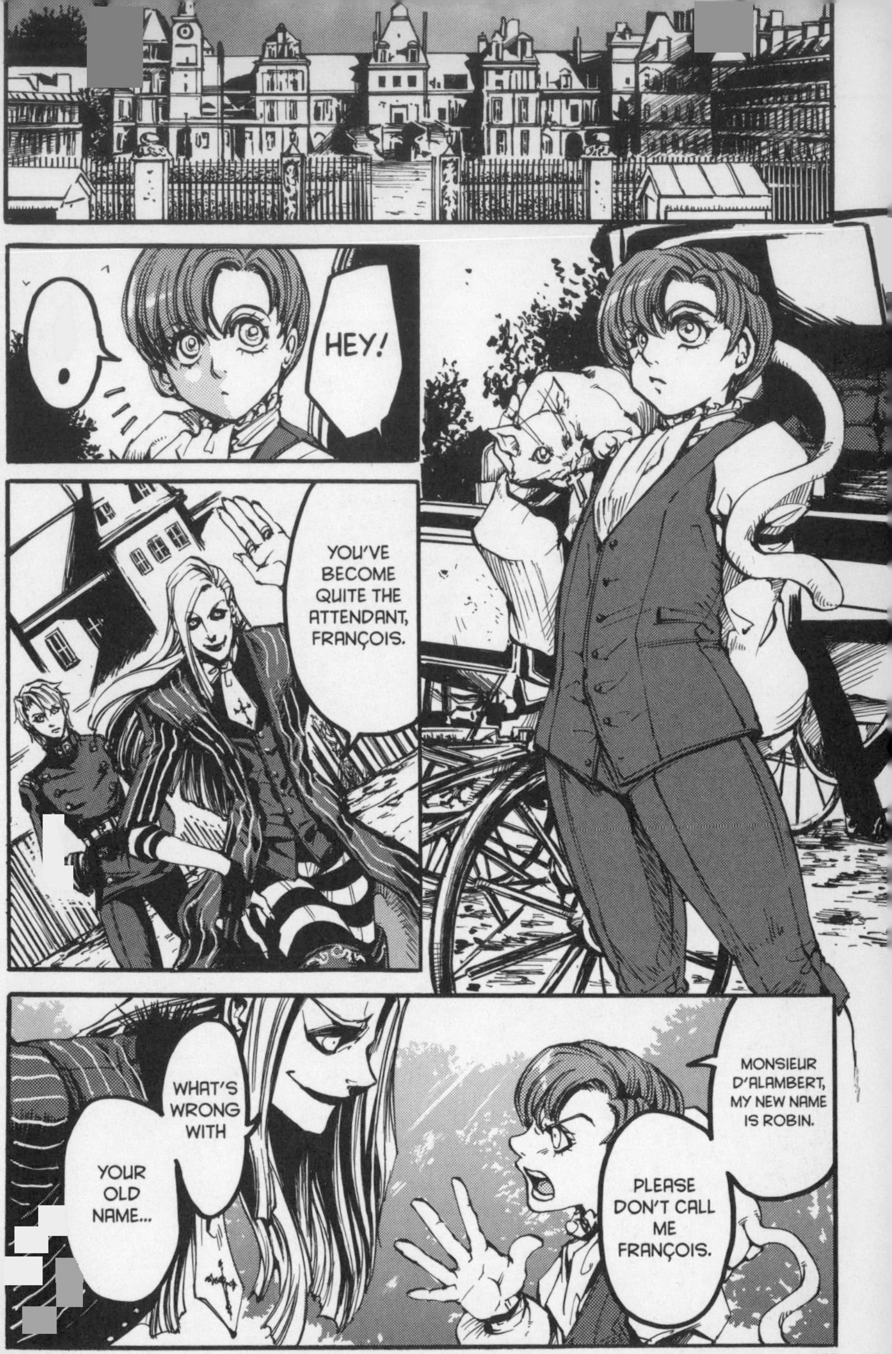
HEY!
YOU'VE BECOME QUITE THE ATTENDANT, FRANÇOIS.
MONSIEUR D'ALAMBERT, MY NEW NAME IS ROBIN.
PLEASE DON'T CALL ME FRANÇOIS.
WHAT'S WRONG WITH
YOUR OLD NAME...

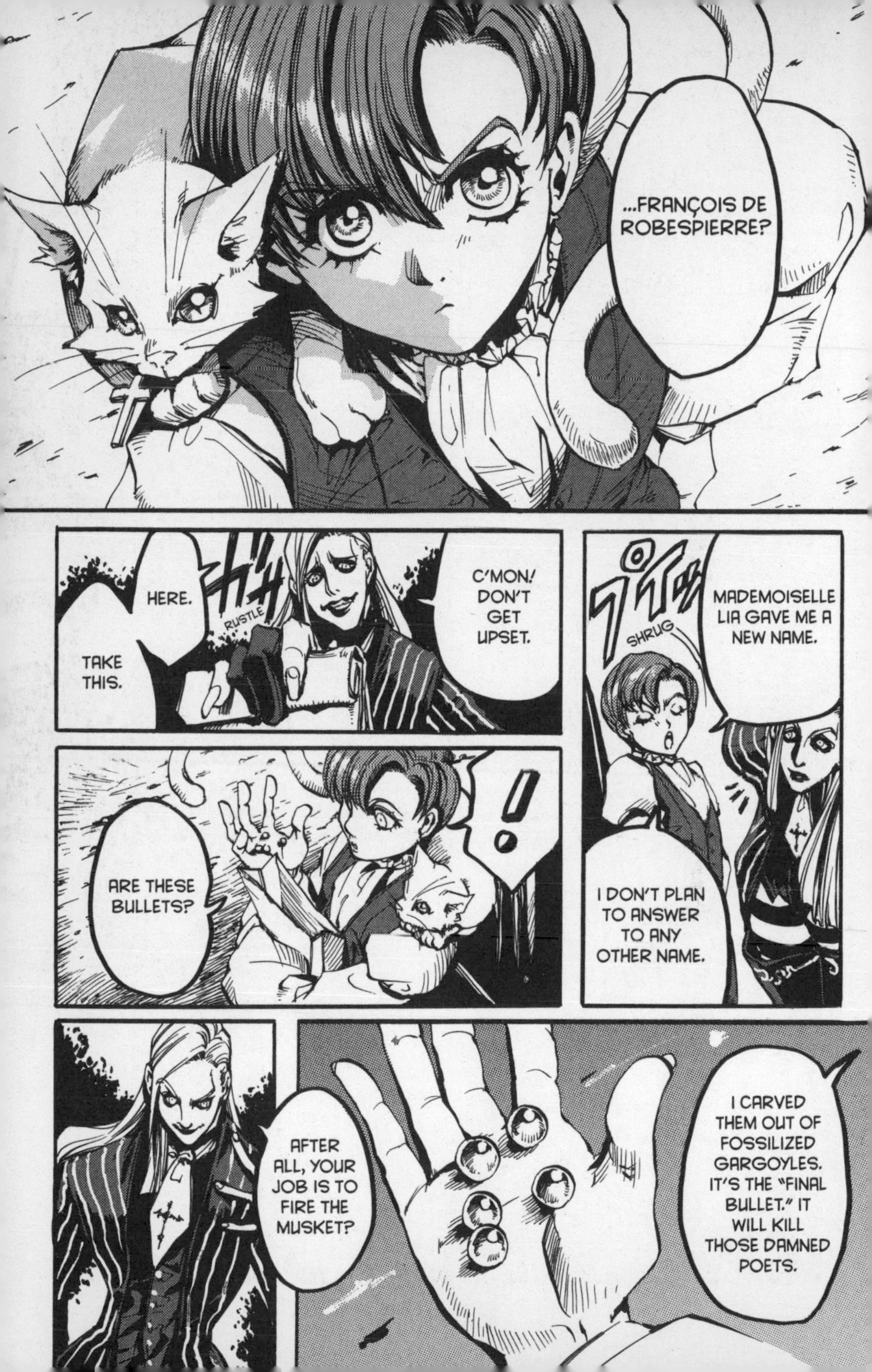
...FRANÇOIS DE ROBESPIERRE?
SHRUG
MADEMOISELLE LIA GAVE ME A NEW NAME.
I DON'T PLAN TO ANSWER TO ANY OTHER NAME.
C'MON! DON'T GET UPSET.
RUSTLE
HERE.
TAKE THIS.
!
ARE THESE BULLETS?
I CARVED THEM OUT OF FOSSILIZED GARGOYLES. IT'S THE "FINAL BULLET." IT WILL KILL THOSE DAMNED POETS.
AFTER ALL, YOUR JOB IS TO FIRE THE MUSKET?

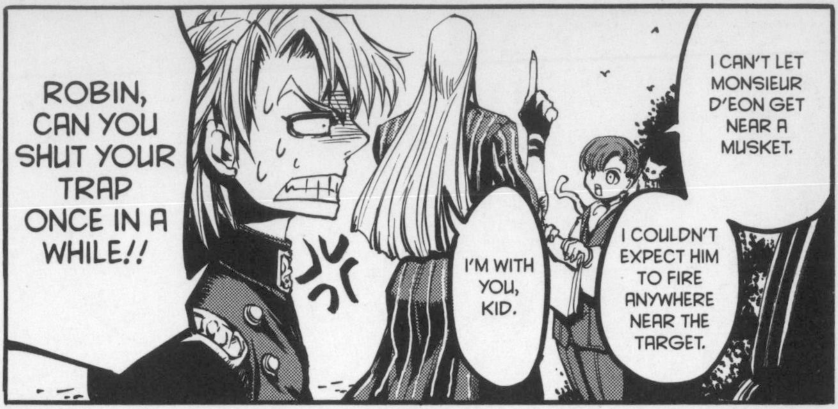
I CAN'T LET MONSIEUR D'EON GET NEAR A MUSKET.
I COULDN'T EXPECT HIM TO FIRE ANYWHERE NEAR THE TARGET.
I'M WITH YOU, KID.
ROBIN, CAN YOU SHUT YOUR TRAP ONCE IN A WHILE!!

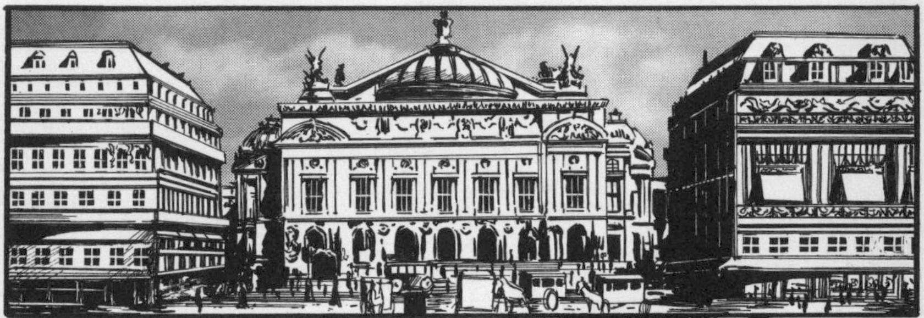

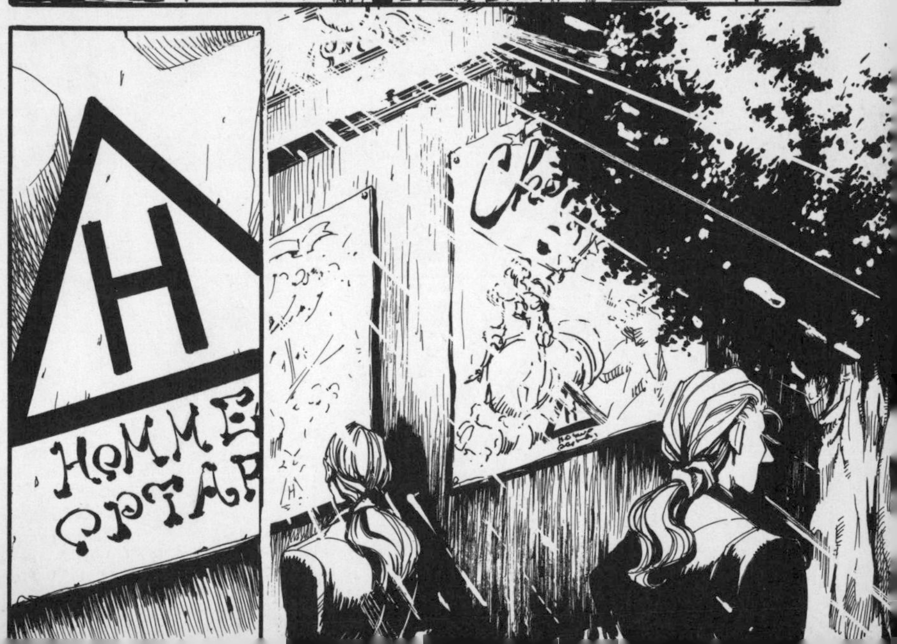
H

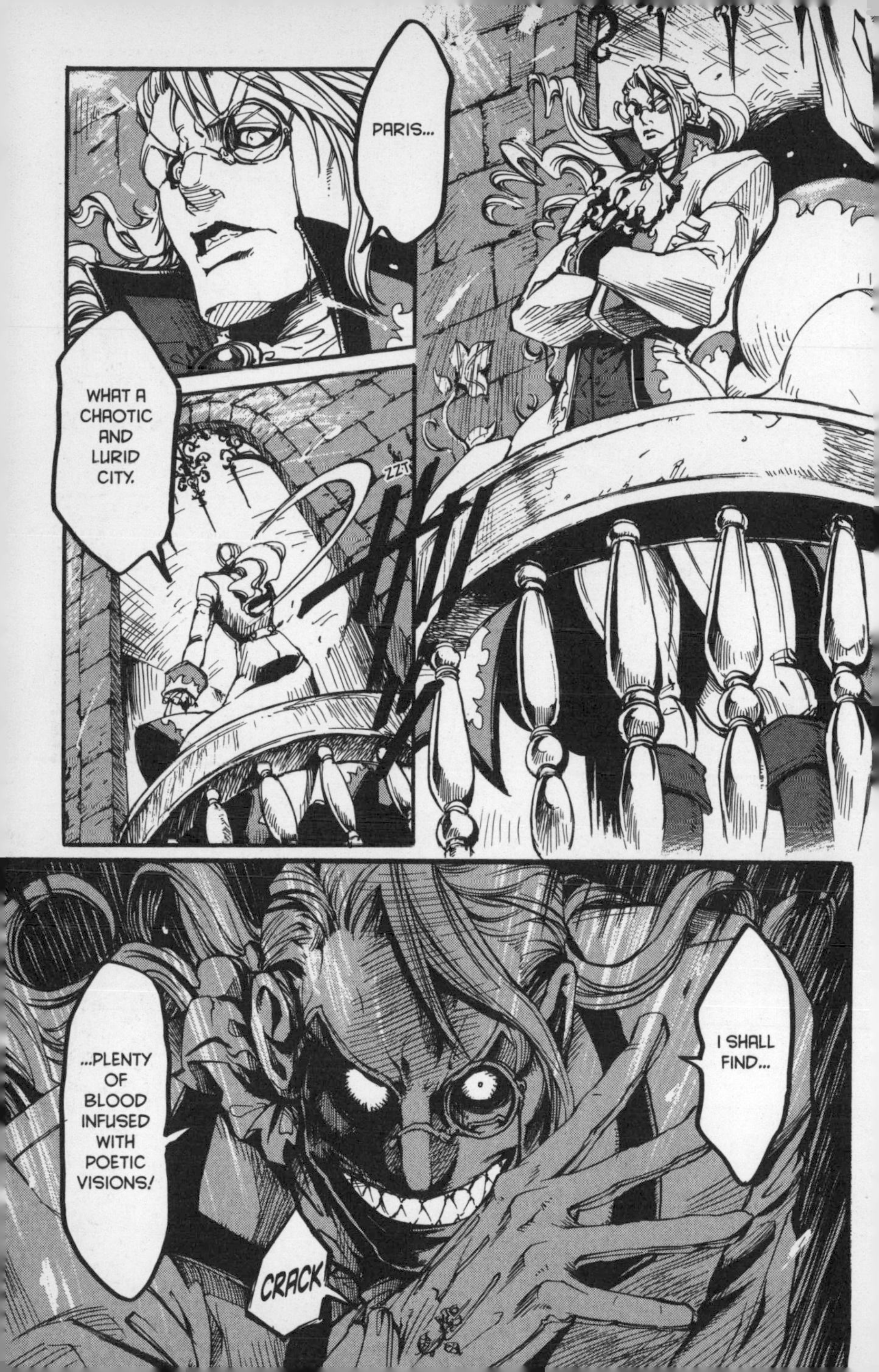
PARIS...
WHAT A CHAOTIC AND LURID CITY.
ZZT
I SHALL FIND...
...PLENTY OF BLOOD INFUSED WITH POETIC VISIONS!
CRACK!

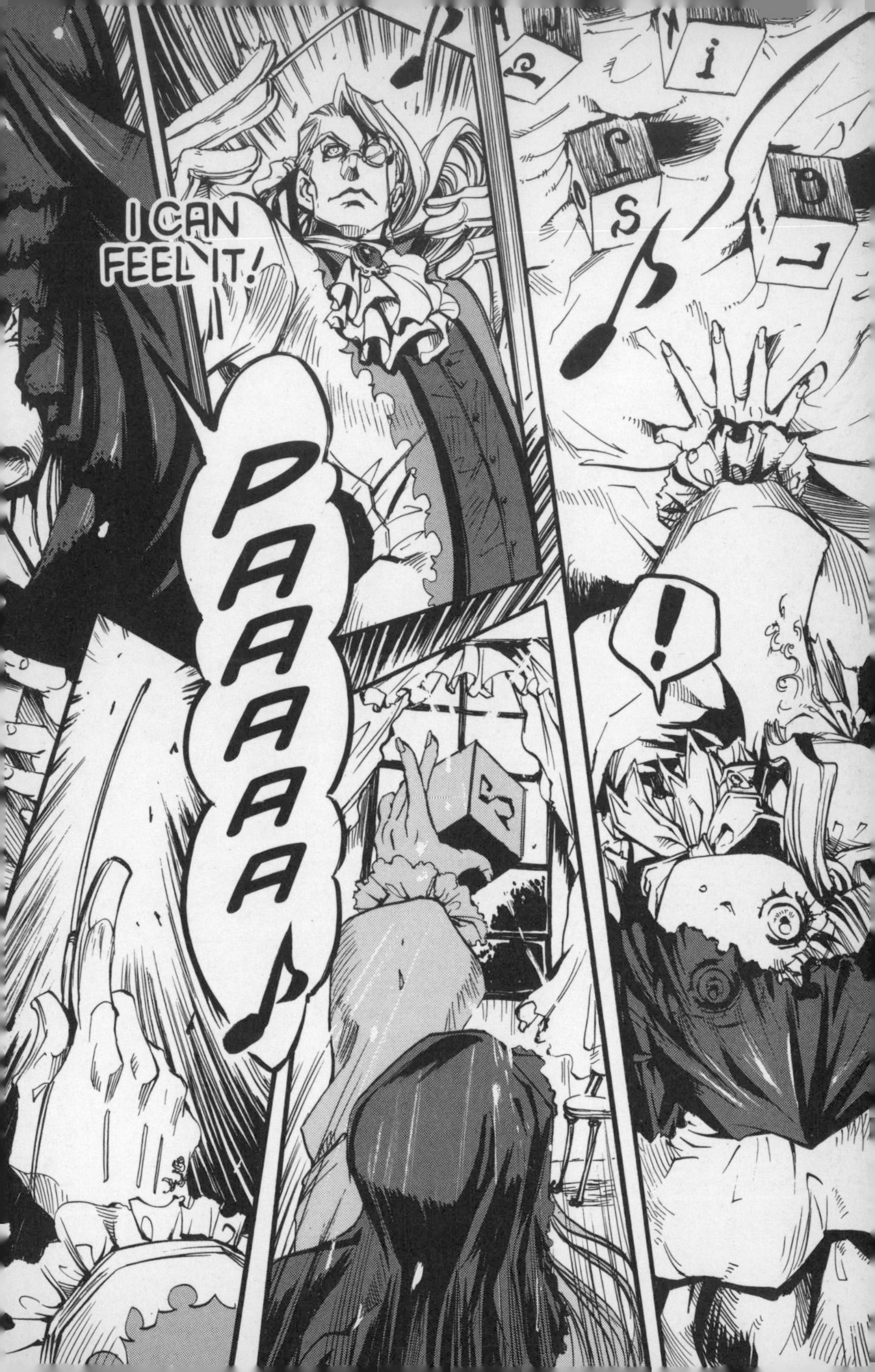
!
I CAN FEEL IT!
PAAAAAA♪

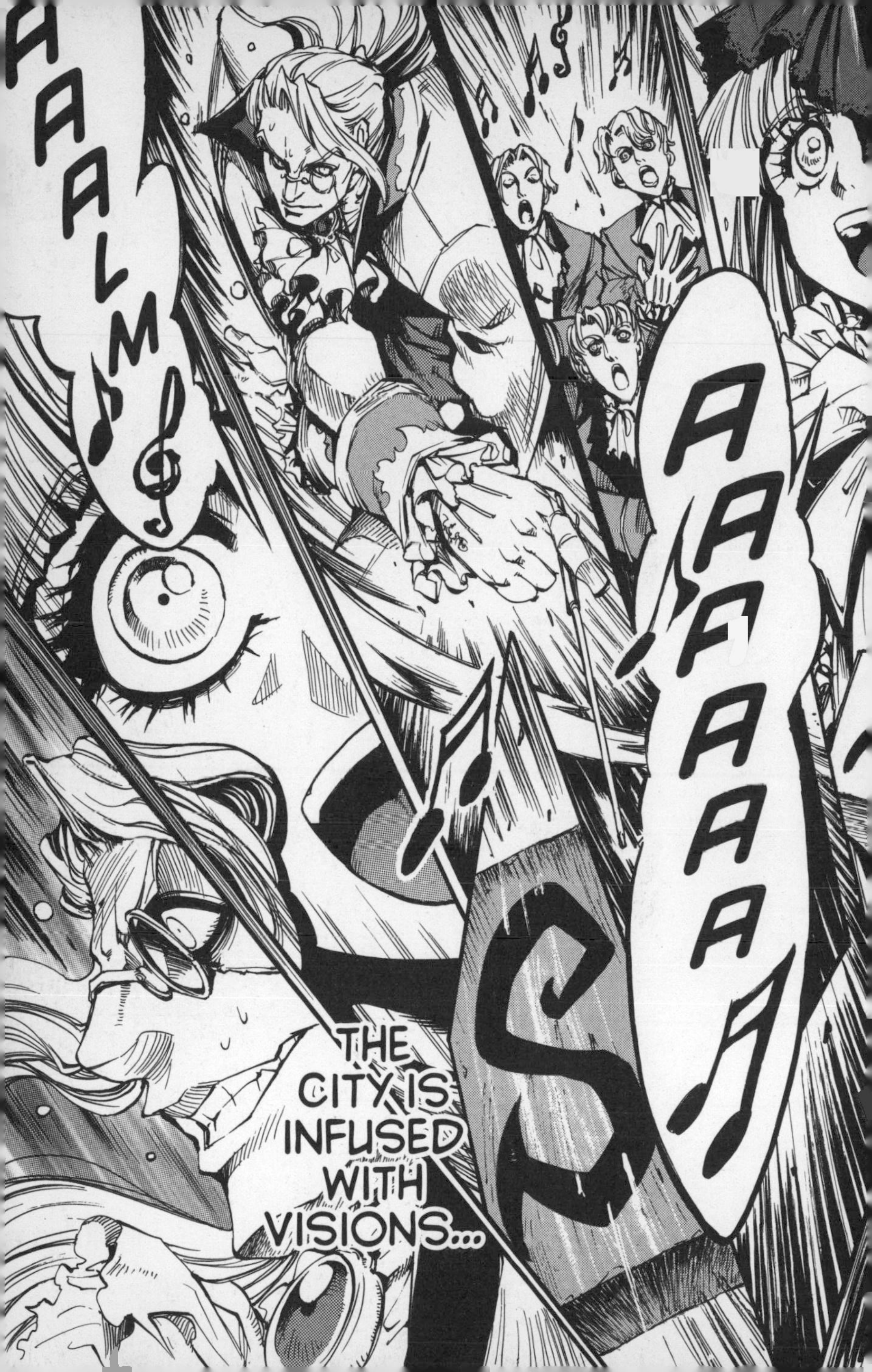
AAAAAAA
AAALM!
S
THE CITY IS INFUSED WITH VISIONS...

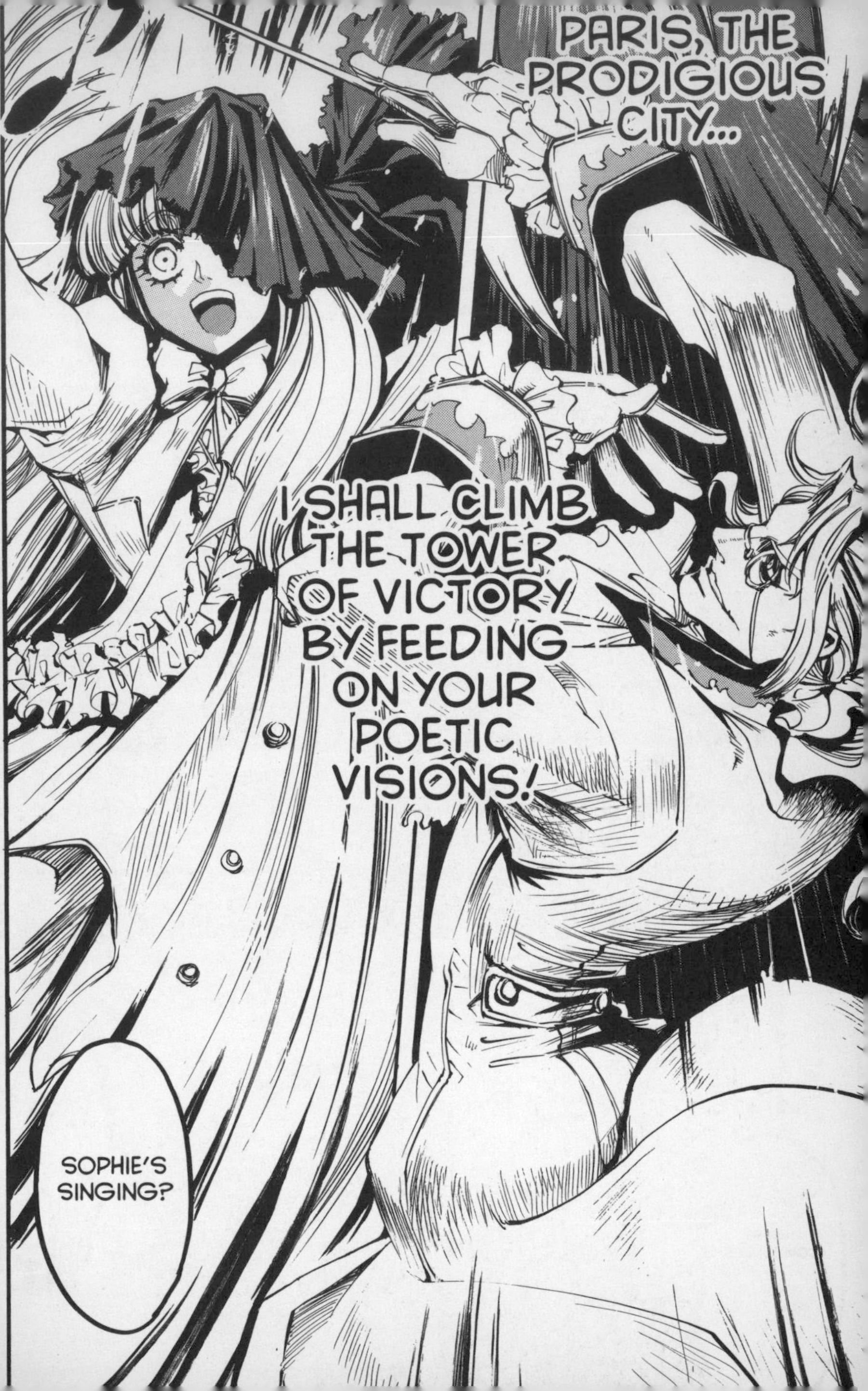
PARIS, THE PRODIGIOUS CITY...
I SHALL CLIMB THE TOWER OF VICTORY BY FEEDING ON YOUR POETIC VISIONS!
SOPHIE'S SINGING?

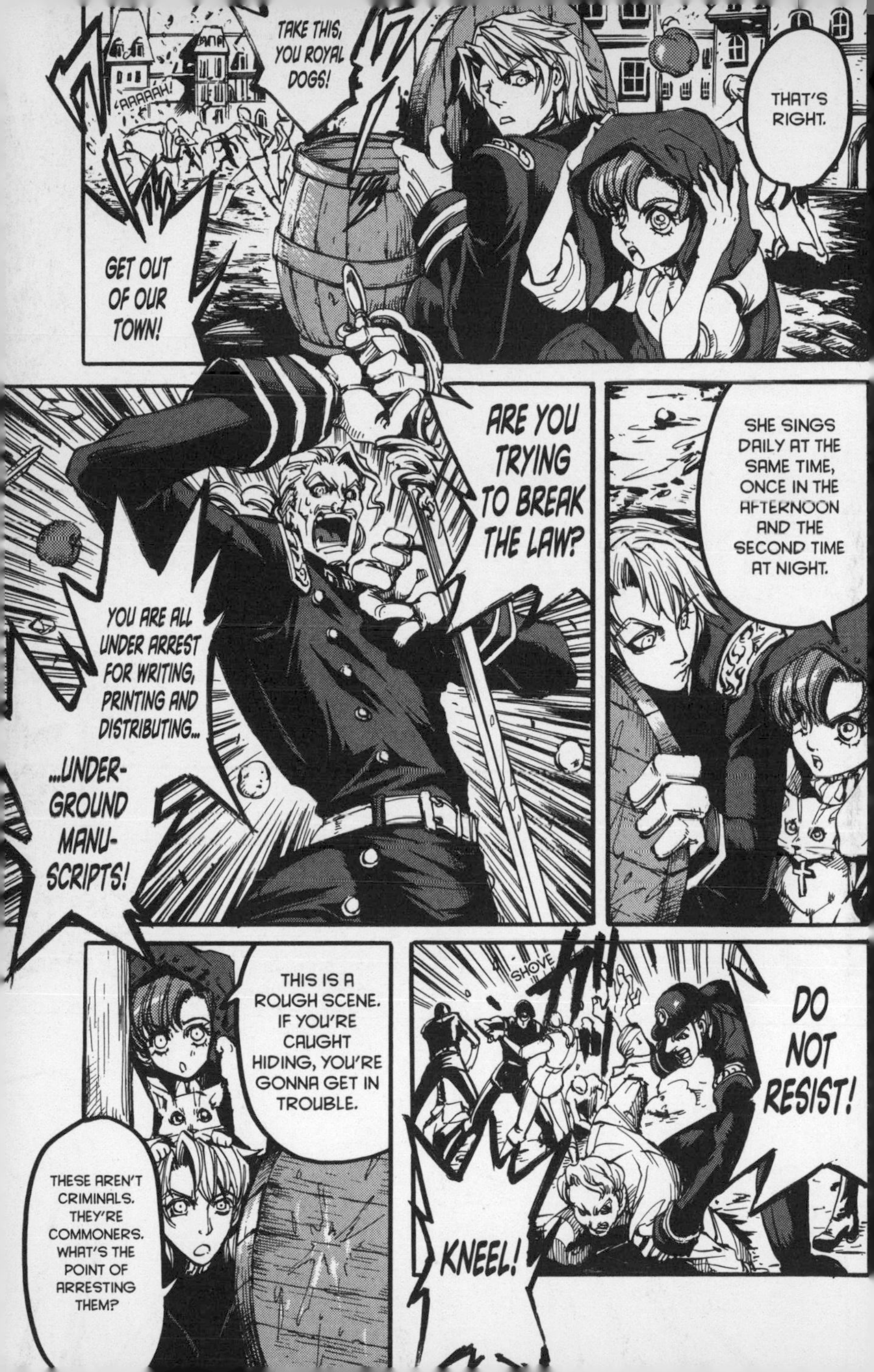
THAT'S RIGHT.
TAKE THIS, YOU ROYAL DOGS!
AAAAAH!
GET OUT OF OUR TOWN!
SHE SINGS DAILY AT THE SAME TIME, ONCE IN THE AFTERNOON AND THE SECOND TIME AT NIGHT.
ARE YOU TRYING TO BREAK THE LAW?
YOU ARE ALL UNDER ARREST FOR WRITING, PRINTING AND DISTRIBUTING...
...UNDER-GROUND MANU-SCRIPTS!
SHOVE
DO NOT RESIST!
KNEEL!
THIS IS A ROUGH SCENE. IF YOU'RE CAUGHT HIDING, YOU'RE GONNA GET IN TROUBLE.
THESE AREN'T CRIMINALS. THEY'RE COMMONERS. WHAT'S THE POINT OF ARRESTING THEM?

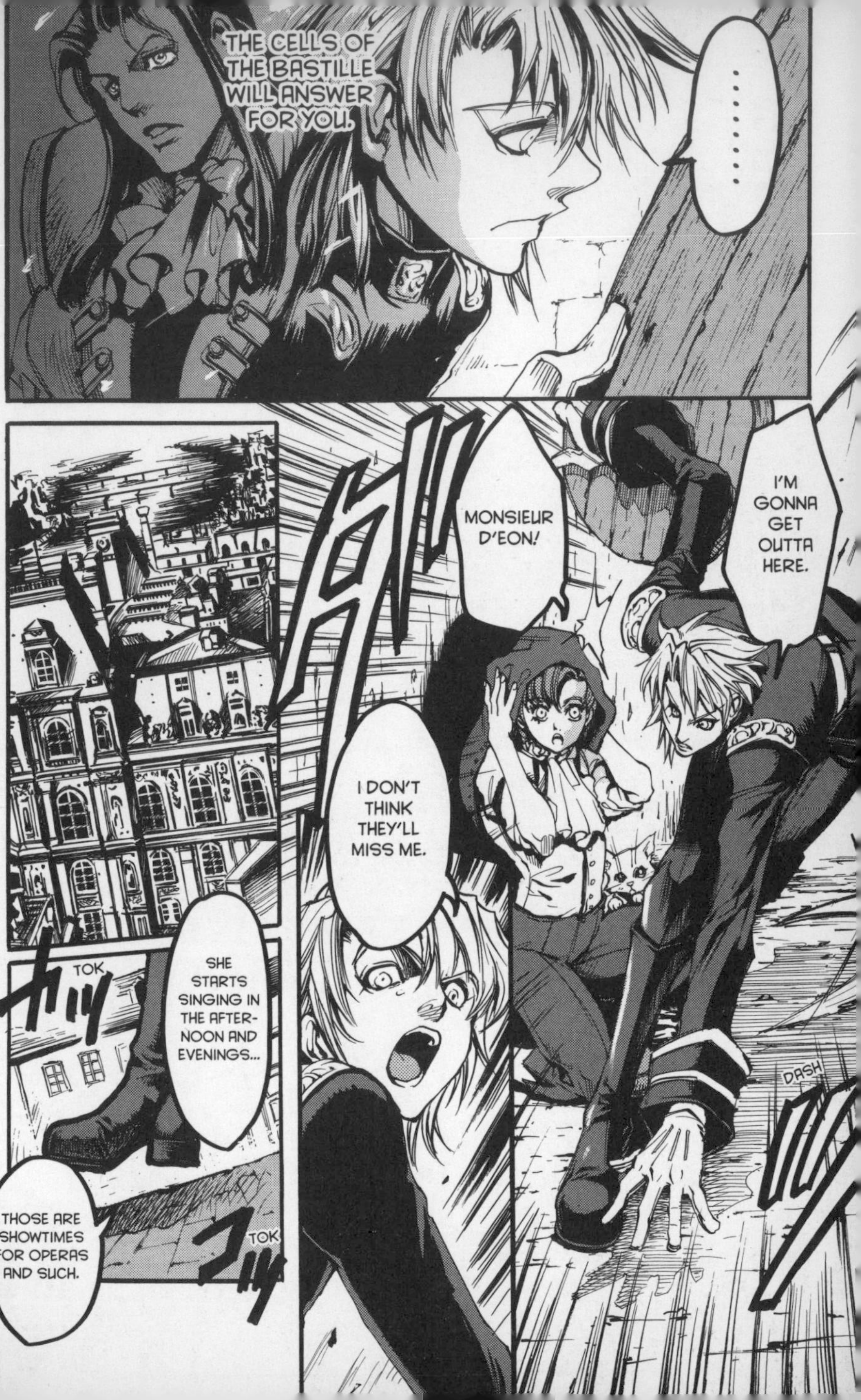
......
THE CELLS OF THE BASTILLE WILL ANSWER FOR YOU.
I'M GONNA GET OUTTA HERE.
MONSIEUR D'EON!
I DON'T THINK THEY'LL MISS ME.
DASH
TOK
SHE STARTS SINGING IN THE AFTER-NOON AND EVENINGS...
THOSE ARE SHOWTIMES FOR OPERAS AND SUCH.
TOK

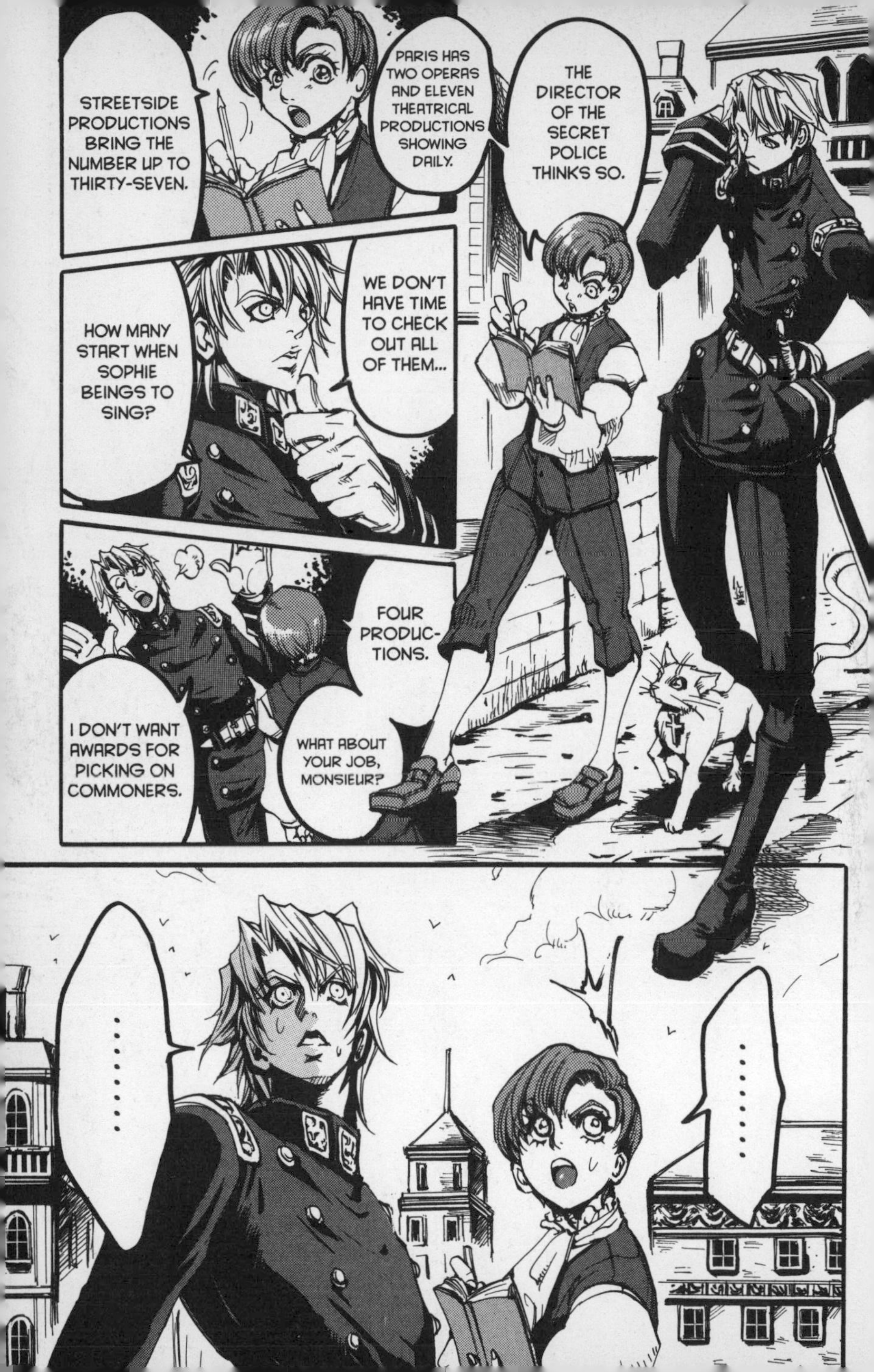
THE DIRECTOR OF THE SECRET POLICE THINKS SO.
PARIS HAS TWO OPERAS AND ELEVEN THEATRICAL PRODUCTIONS SHOWING DAILY.
STREETSIDE PRODUCTIONS BRING THE NUMBER UP TO THIRTY-SEVEN.
WE DON'T HAVE TIME TO CHECK OUT ALL OF THEM...
HOW MANY START WHEN SOPHIE BEINGS TO SING?
FOUR PRODUC-TIONS.
WHAT ABOUT YOUR JOB, MONSIEUR?
I DON'T WANT AWARDS FOR PICKING ON COMMONERS.
......
......

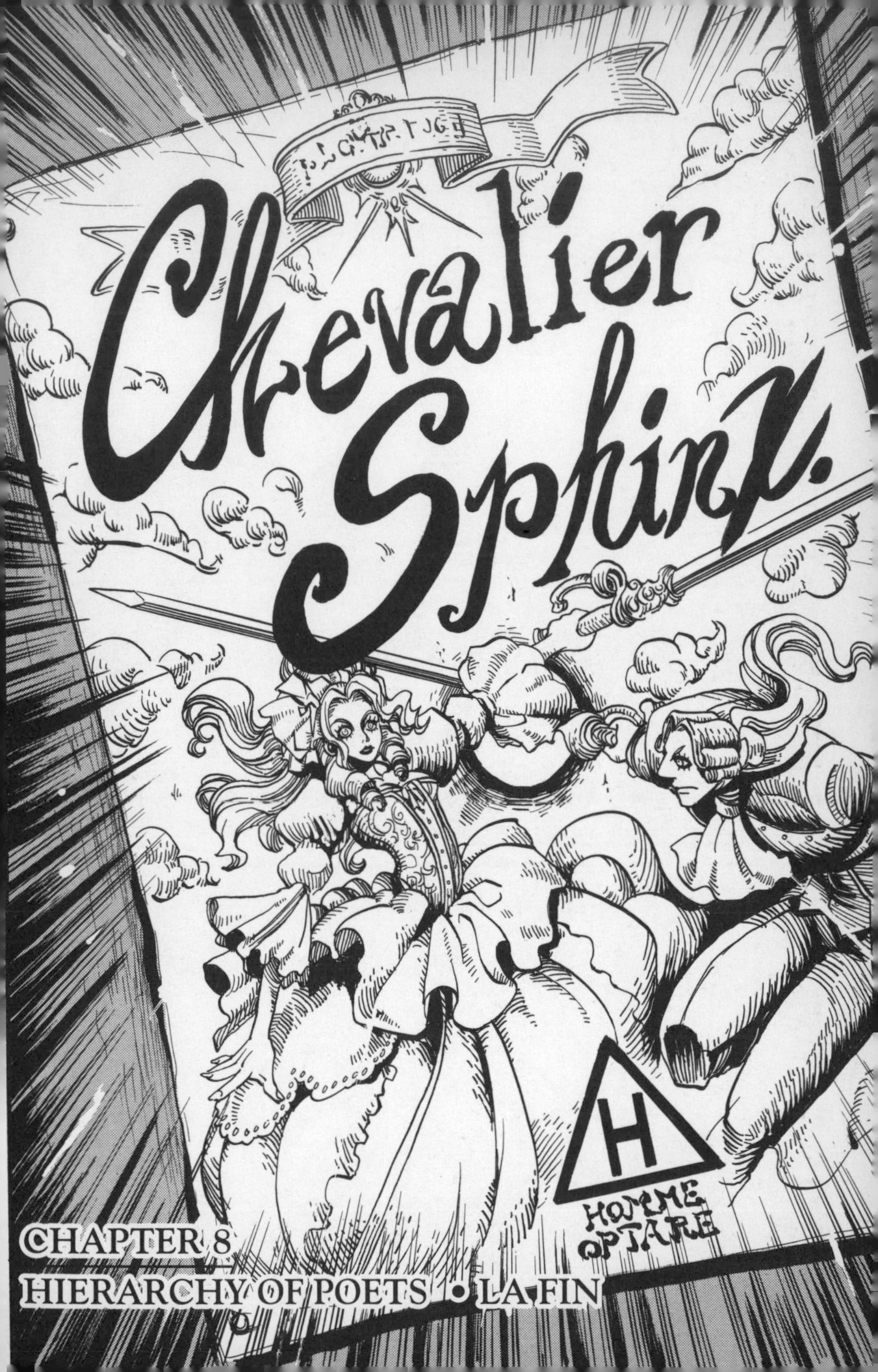
Chevalier Sphinx.
HOMME OPTARE
CHAPTER 8
HIERARCHY OF POETS • LA FIN

CHAPTER 9 • DEVOTEE

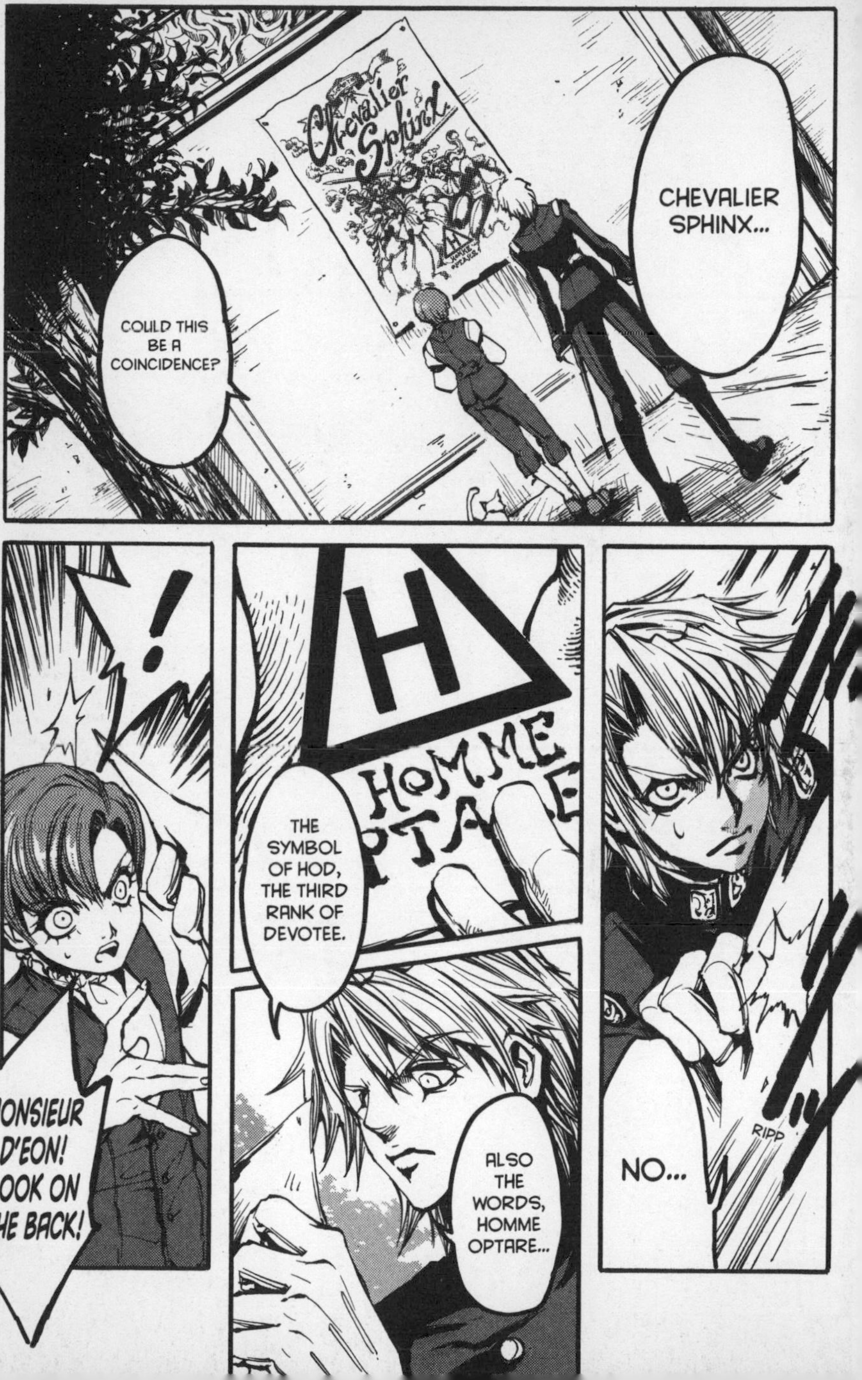
CHEVALIER SPHINX...
Chevalier Sphinx
COULD THIS BE A COINCIDENCE?
RIPP
NO...
HOMME
THE SYMBOL OF HOD, THE THIRD RANK OF DEVOTEE.
ALSO THE WORDS, HOMME OPTARE...
!
MONSIEUR D'EON! LOOK ON THE BACK!

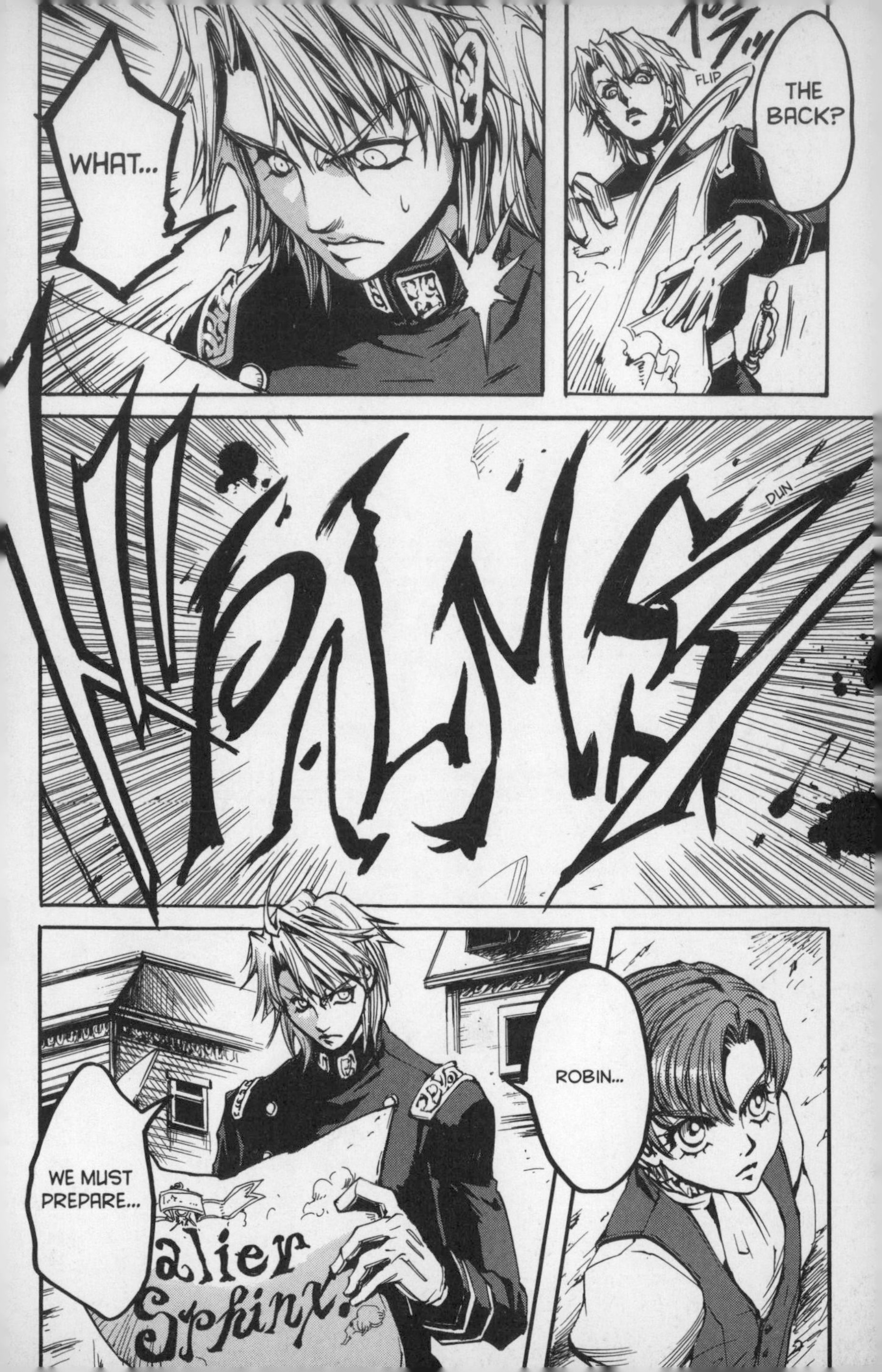
FLIP
THE BACK?
WHAT...
DUN
ROBIN...
WE MUST PREPARE...
alier Sphinx

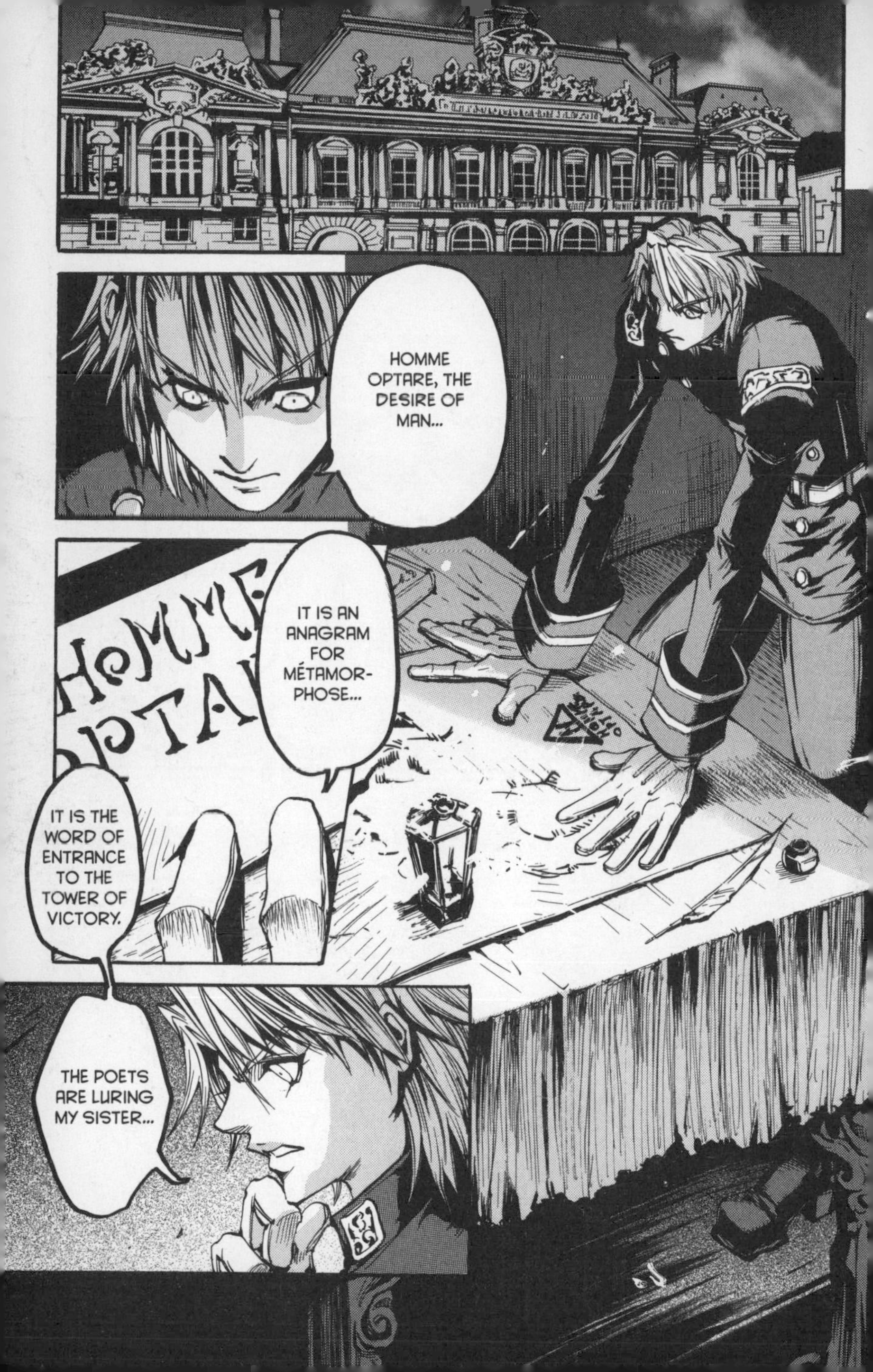
HOMME OPTARE, THE DESIRE OF MAN...
IT IS AN ANAGRAM FOR MÉTAMORPHOSE...
IT IS THE WORD OF ENTRANCE TO THE TOWER OF VICTORY.
THE POETS ARE LURING MY SISTER...

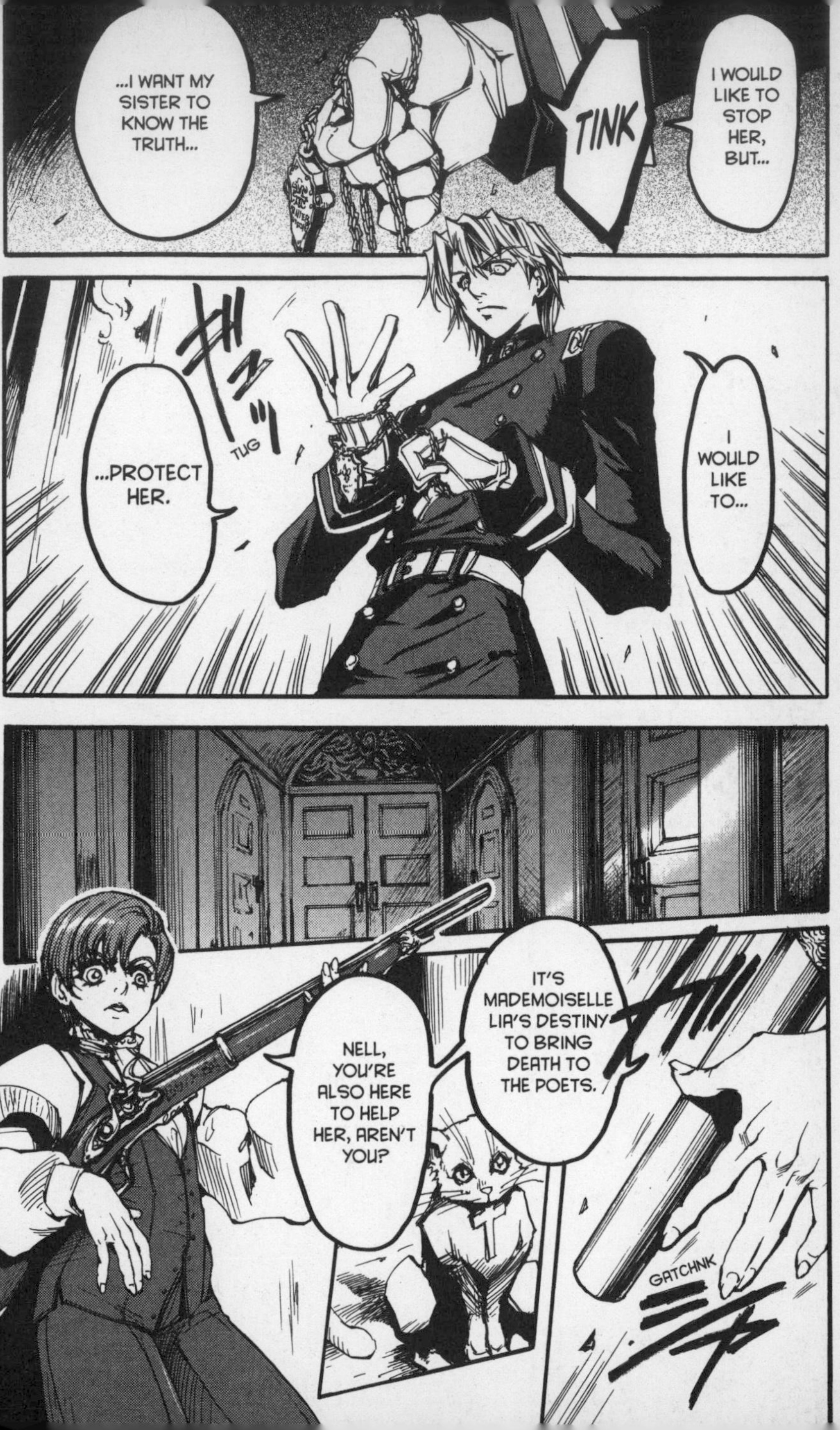
I WOULD LIKE TO STOP HER, BUT...
TINK
...I WANT MY SISTER TO KNOW THE TRUTH...
I WOULD LIKE TO...
TUG
...PROTECT HER.
IT'S MADEMOISELLE LIA'S DESTINY TO BRING DEATH TO THE POETS.
NELL, YOU'RE ALSO HERE TO HELP HER, AREN'T YOU?
GATCHNK

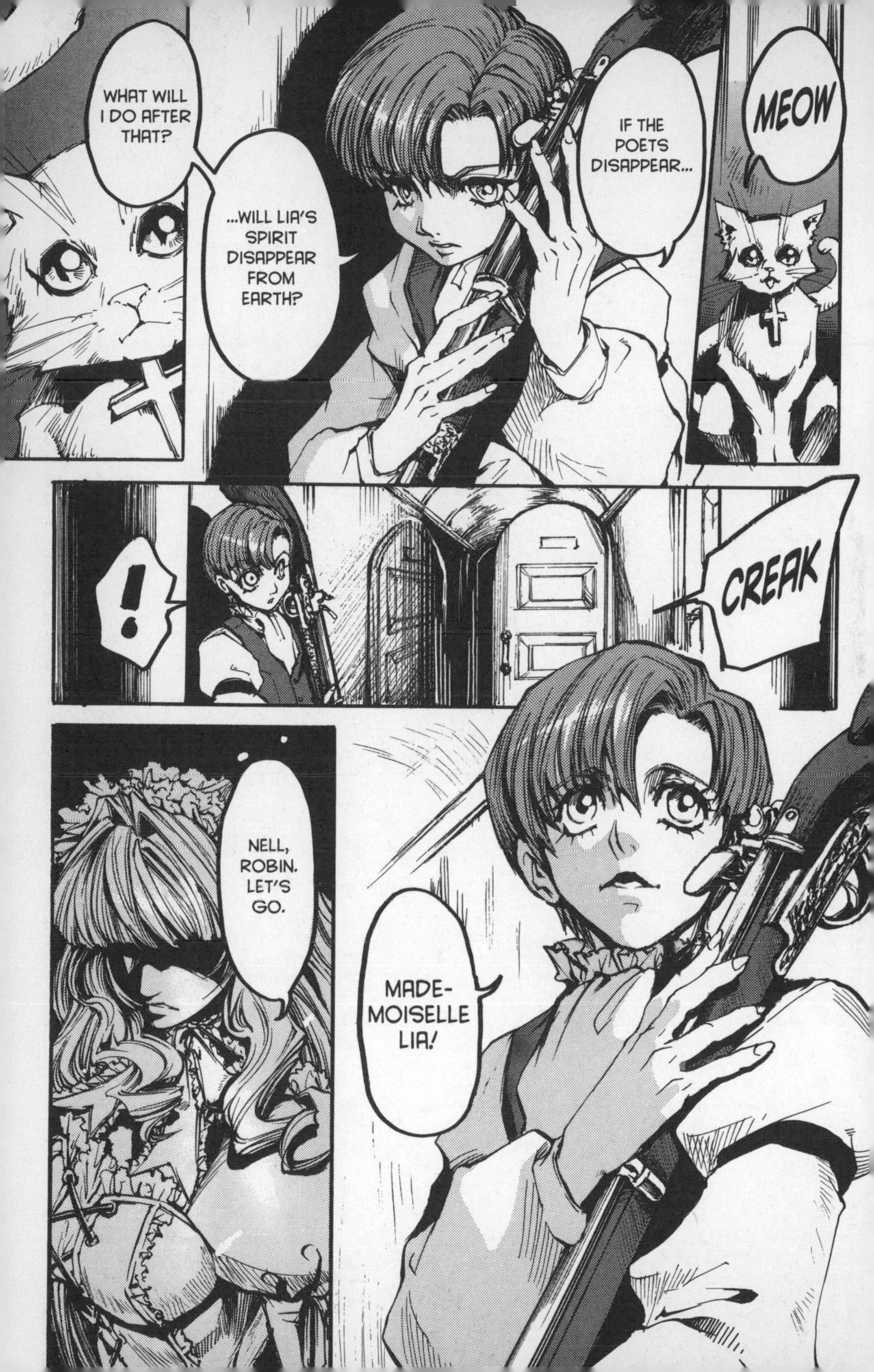
MEOW
IF THE POETS DISAPPEAR...
...WILL LIA'S SPIRIT DISAPPEAR FROM EARTH?
WHAT WILL I DO AFTER THAT?
CREAK
!
MADE-MOISELLE LIA!
NELL, ROBIN. LET'S GO.

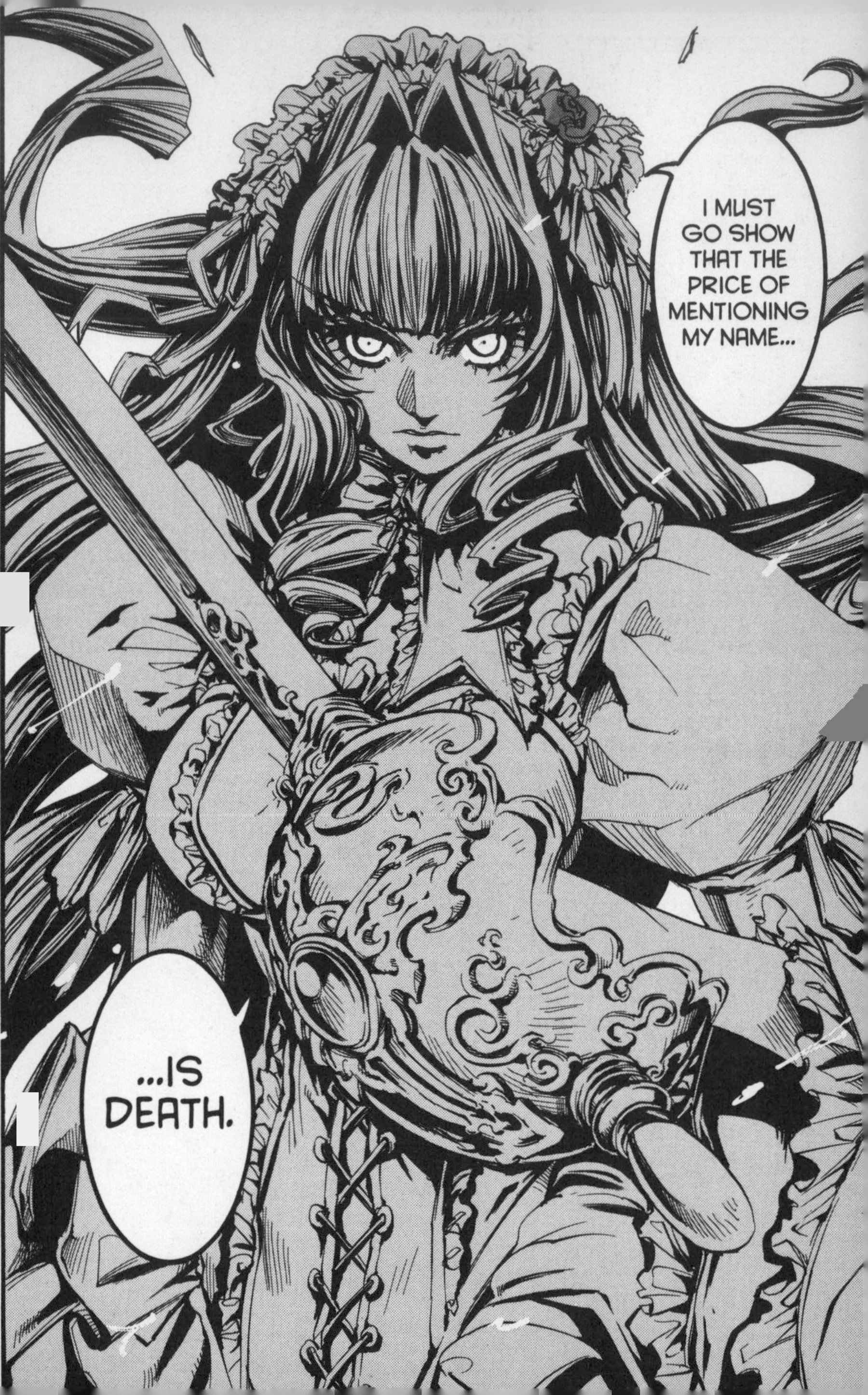
I MUST GO SHOW THAT THE PRICE OF MENTIONING MY NAME...
...IS DEATH.

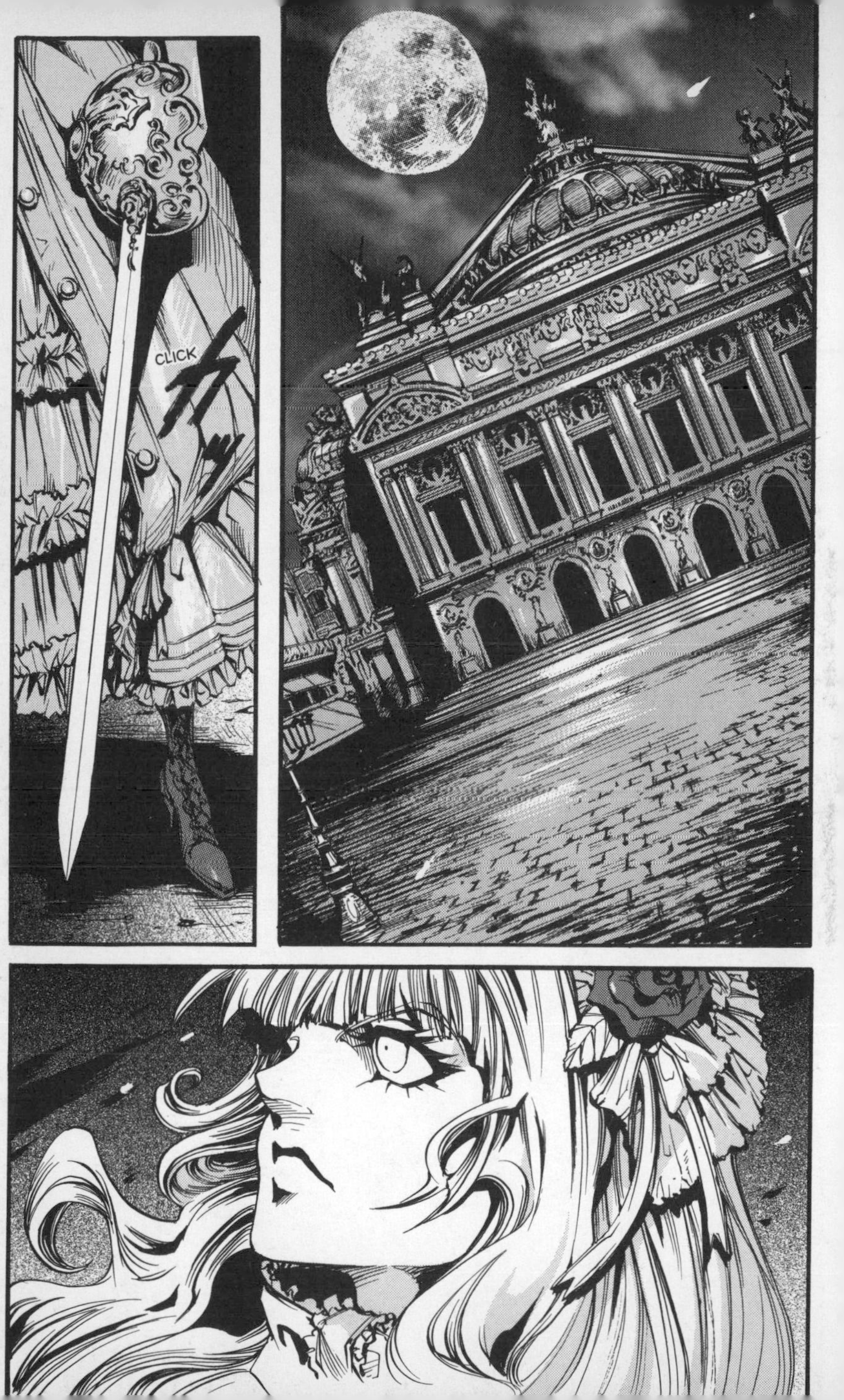
CLICK

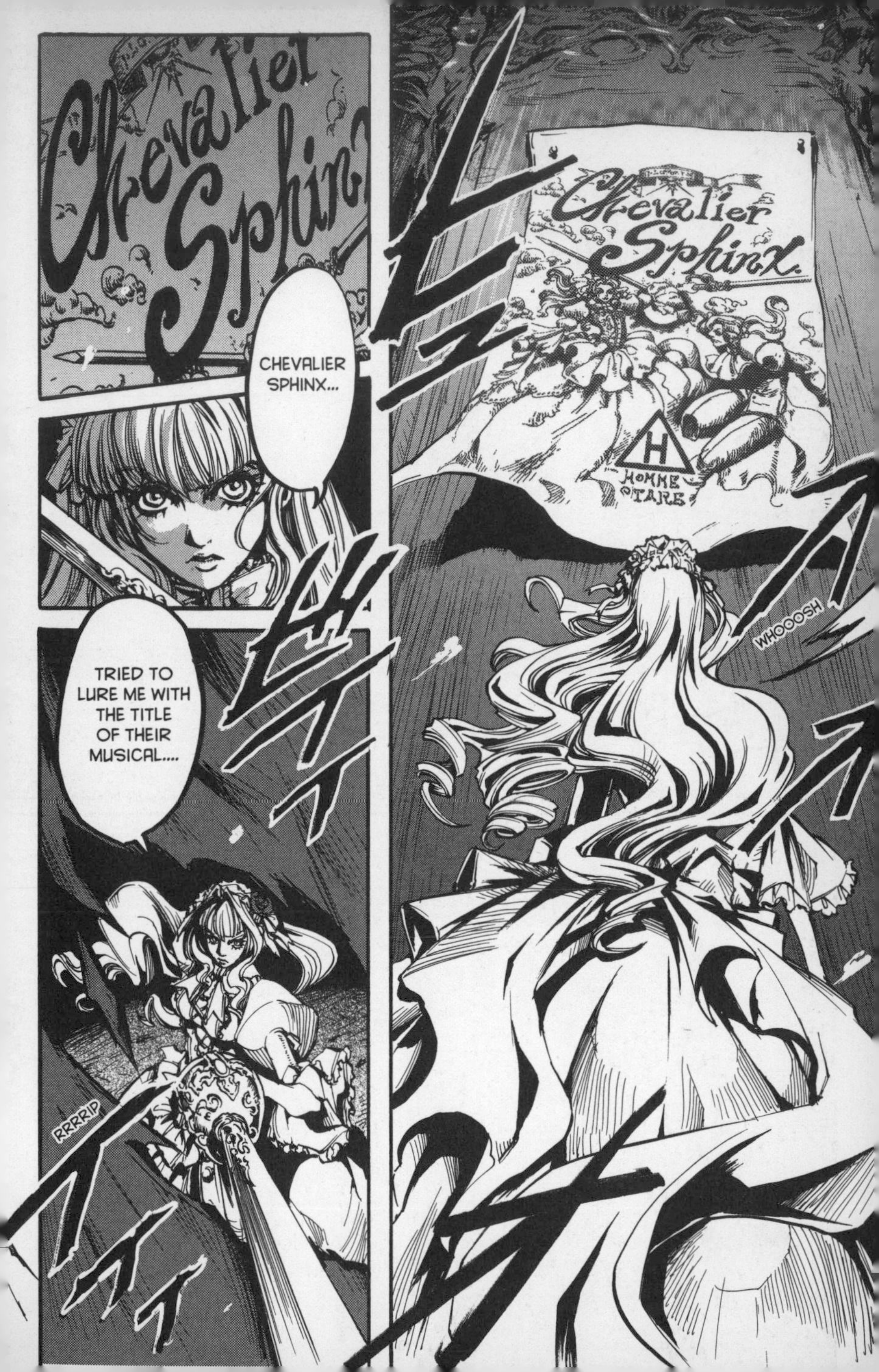
Chevalier Sphinx.
WHOOOSH
Chevalier Sphinx
CHEVALIER SPHINX...
TRIED TO LURE ME WITH THE TITLE OF THEIR MUSICAL....
RRRRIP

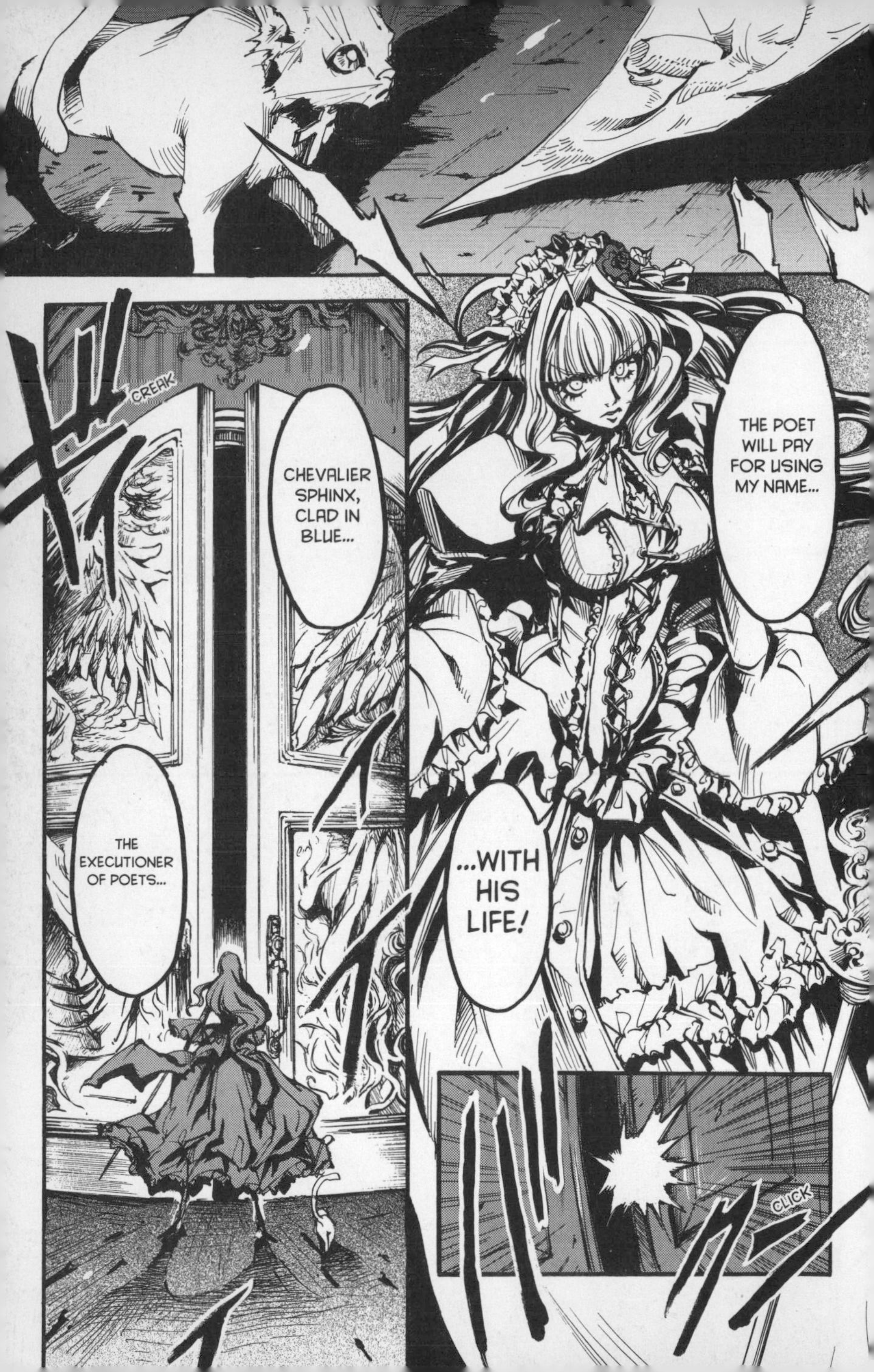
THE POET WILL PAY FOR USING MY NAME...
...WITH HIS LIFE!
CLICK
CREAK
CHEVALIER SPHINX, CLAD IN BLUE...
THE EXECUTIONER OF POETS...

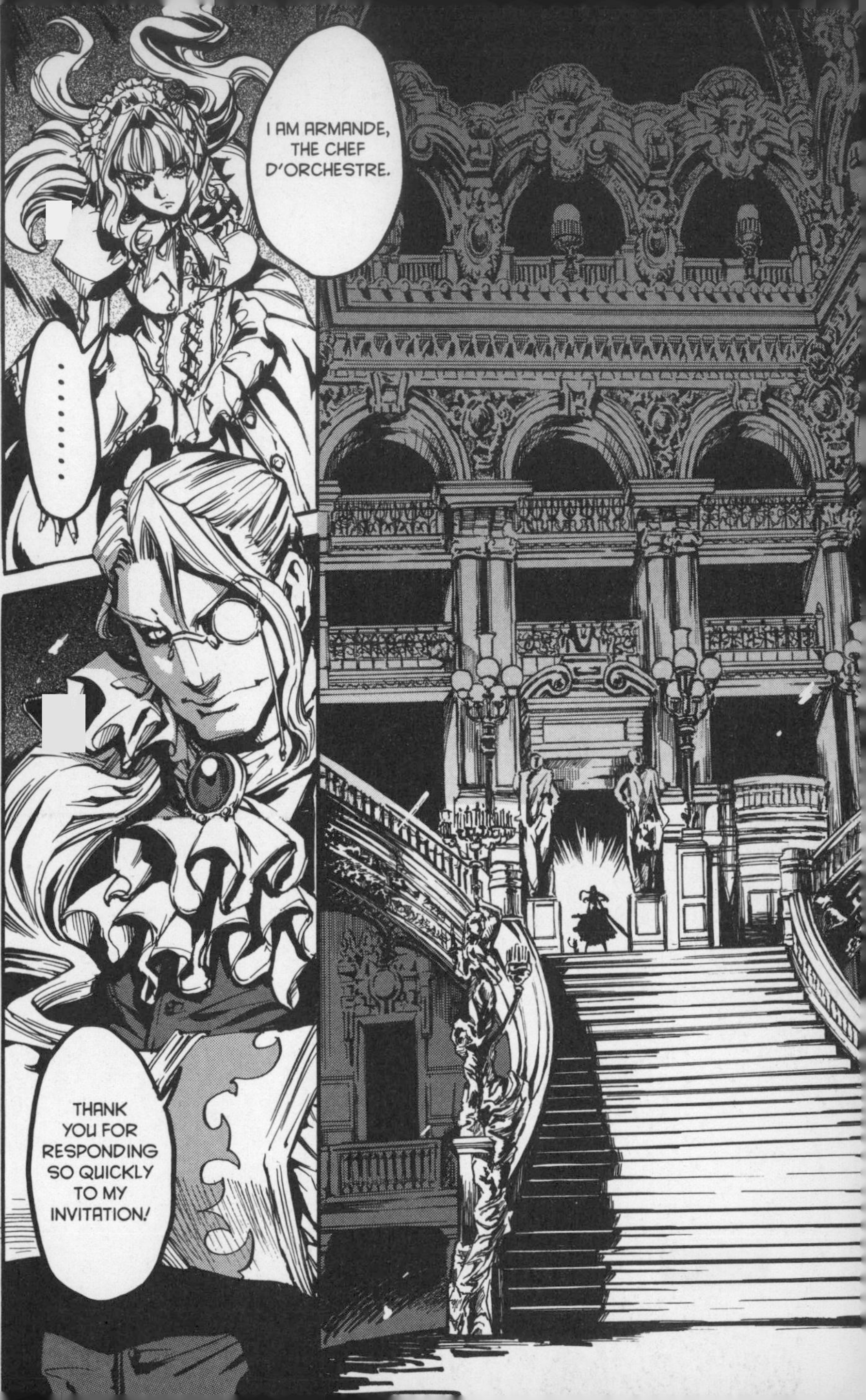
I AM ARMANDE, THE CHEF D'ORCHESTRE.
......
THANK YOU FOR RESPONDING SO QUICKLY TO MY INVITATION!

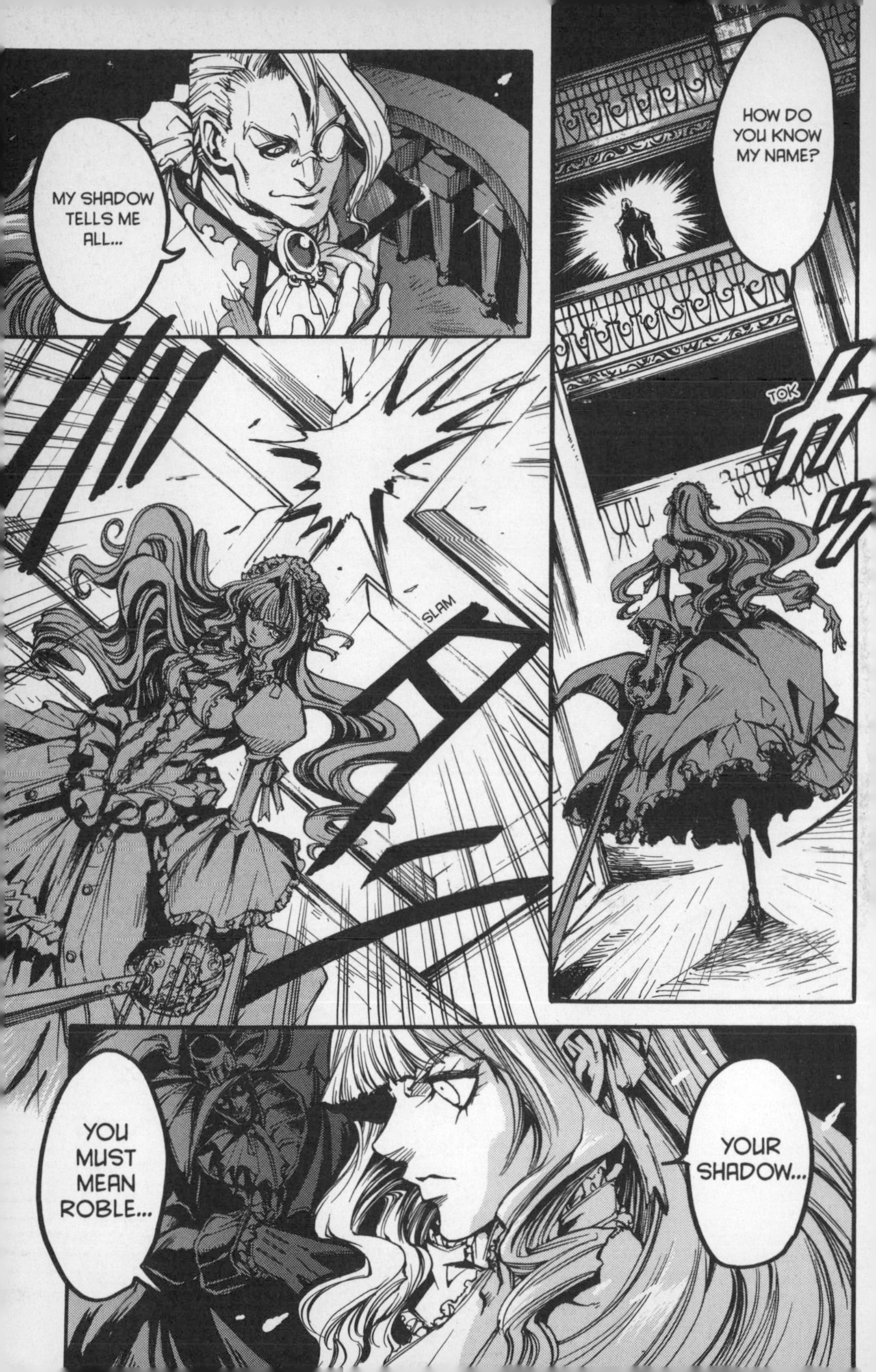
HOW DO YOU KNOW MY NAME?
TOK
MY SHADOW TELLS ME ALL...
SLAM
YOUR SHADOW...
YOU MUST MEAN ROBLE...

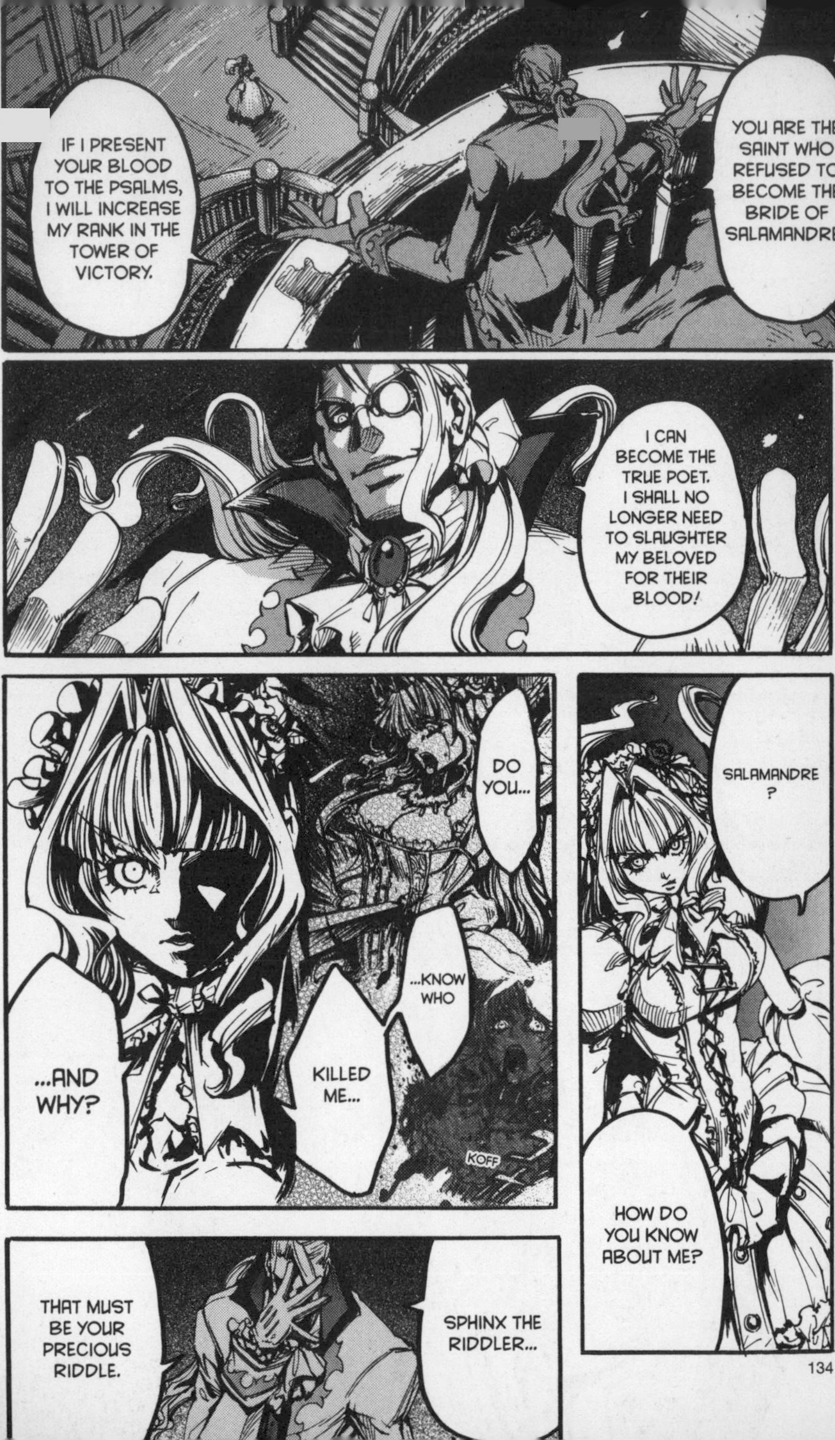
YOU ARE THE SAINT WHO REFUSED TO BECOME THE BRIDE OF SALAMANDRE!
IF I PRESENT YOUR BLOOD TO THE PSALMS, I WILL INCREASE MY RANK IN THE TOWER OF VICTORY.
I CAN BECOME THE TRUE POET. I SHALL NO LONGER NEED TO SLAUGHTER MY BELOVED FOR THEIR BLOOD!
SALAMANDRE ?
HOW DO YOU KNOW ABOUT ME?
DO YOU...
...KNOW WHO
KILLED ME...
KOFF
...AND WHY?
SPHINX THE RIDDLER...
THAT MUST BE YOUR PRECIOUS RIDDLE.

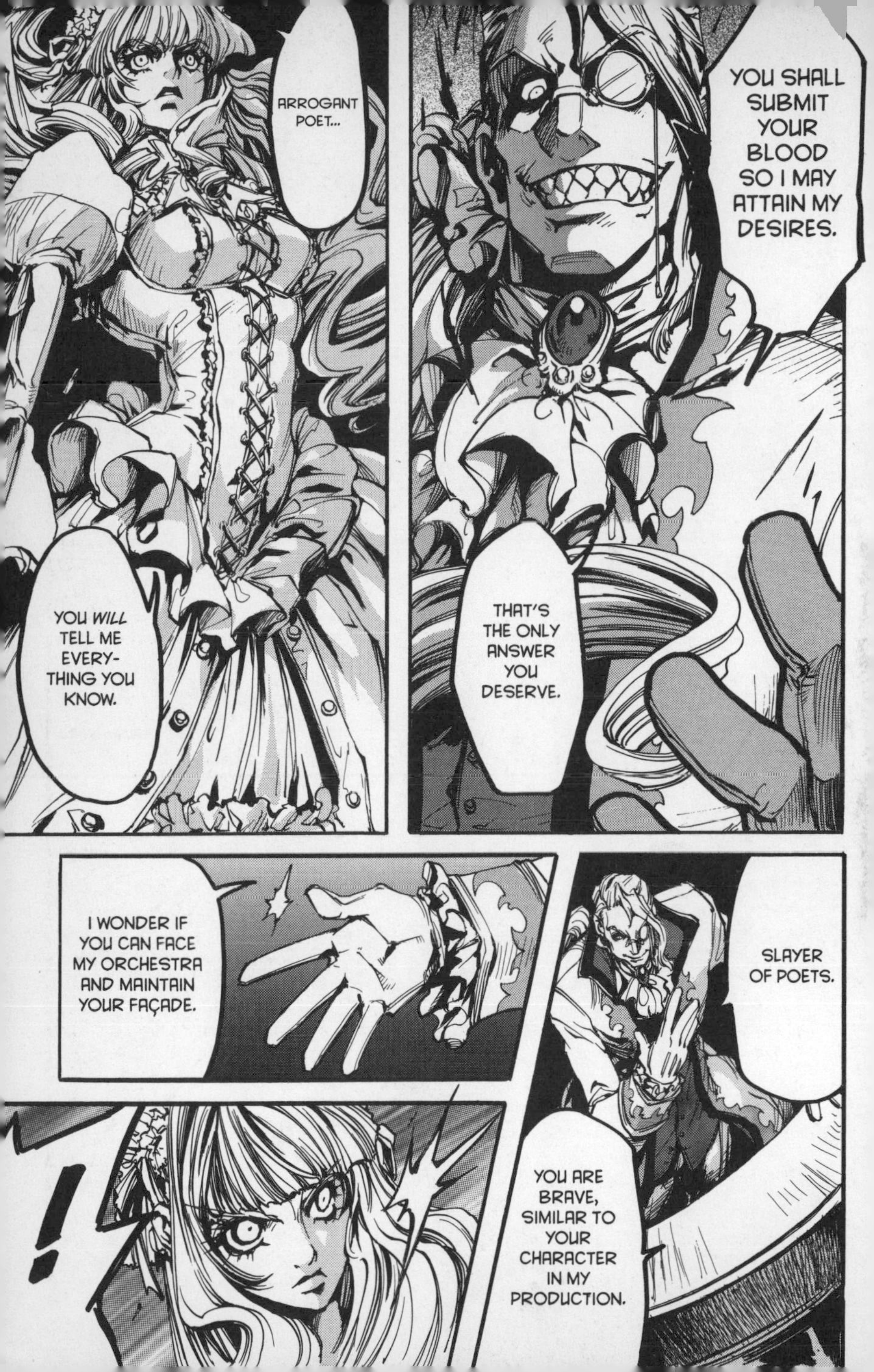
YOU SHALL SUBMIT YOUR BLOOD SO I MAY ATTAIN MY DESIRES.
THAT'S THE ONLY ANSWER YOU DESERVE.
ARROGANT POET...
YOU *WILL* TELL ME EVERY-THING YOU KNOW.
SLAYER OF POETS.
YOU ARE BRAVE, SIMILAR TO YOUR CHARACTER IN MY PRODUCTION.
I WONDER IF YOU CAN FACE MY ORCHESTRA AND MAINTAIN YOUR FAÇADE.
!

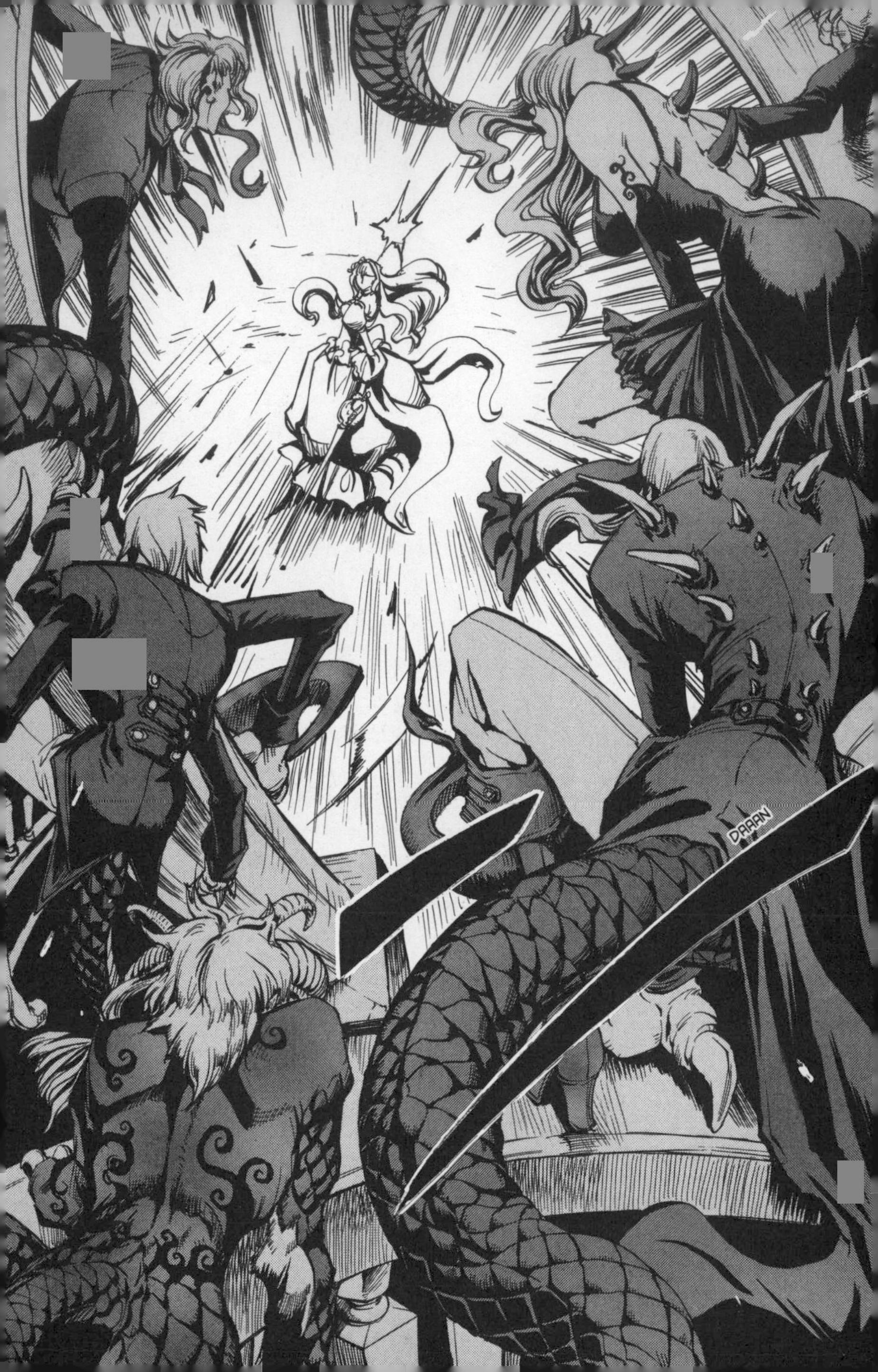
DAAAN

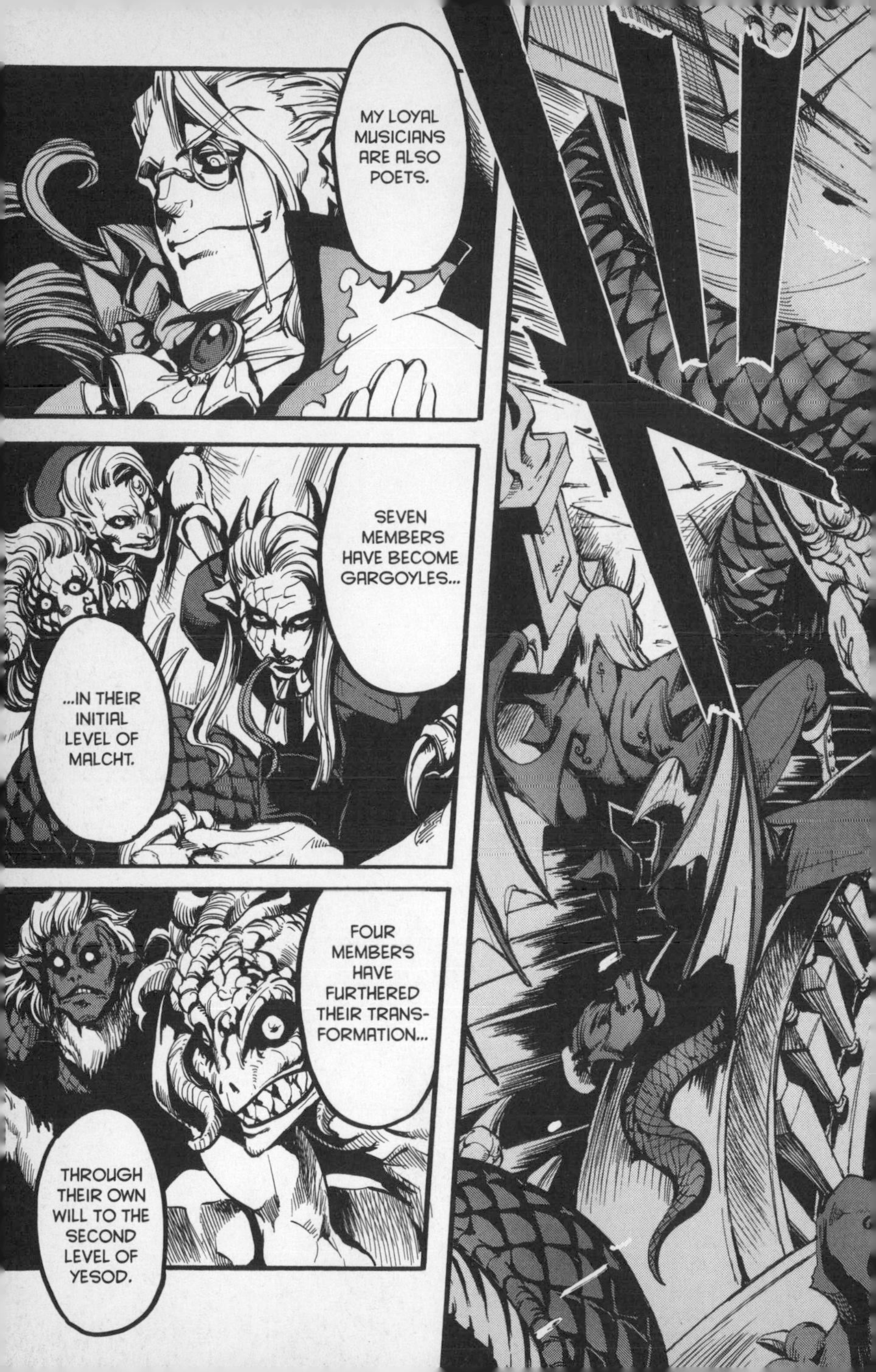
MY LOYAL MUSICIANS ARE ALSO POETS.
SEVEN MEMBERS HAVE BECOME GARGOYLES...
...IN THEIR INITIAL LEVEL OF MALCHT.
FOUR MEMBERS HAVE FURTHERED THEIR TRANS-FORMATION...
THROUGH THEIR OWN WILL TO THE SECOND LEVEL OF YESOD.

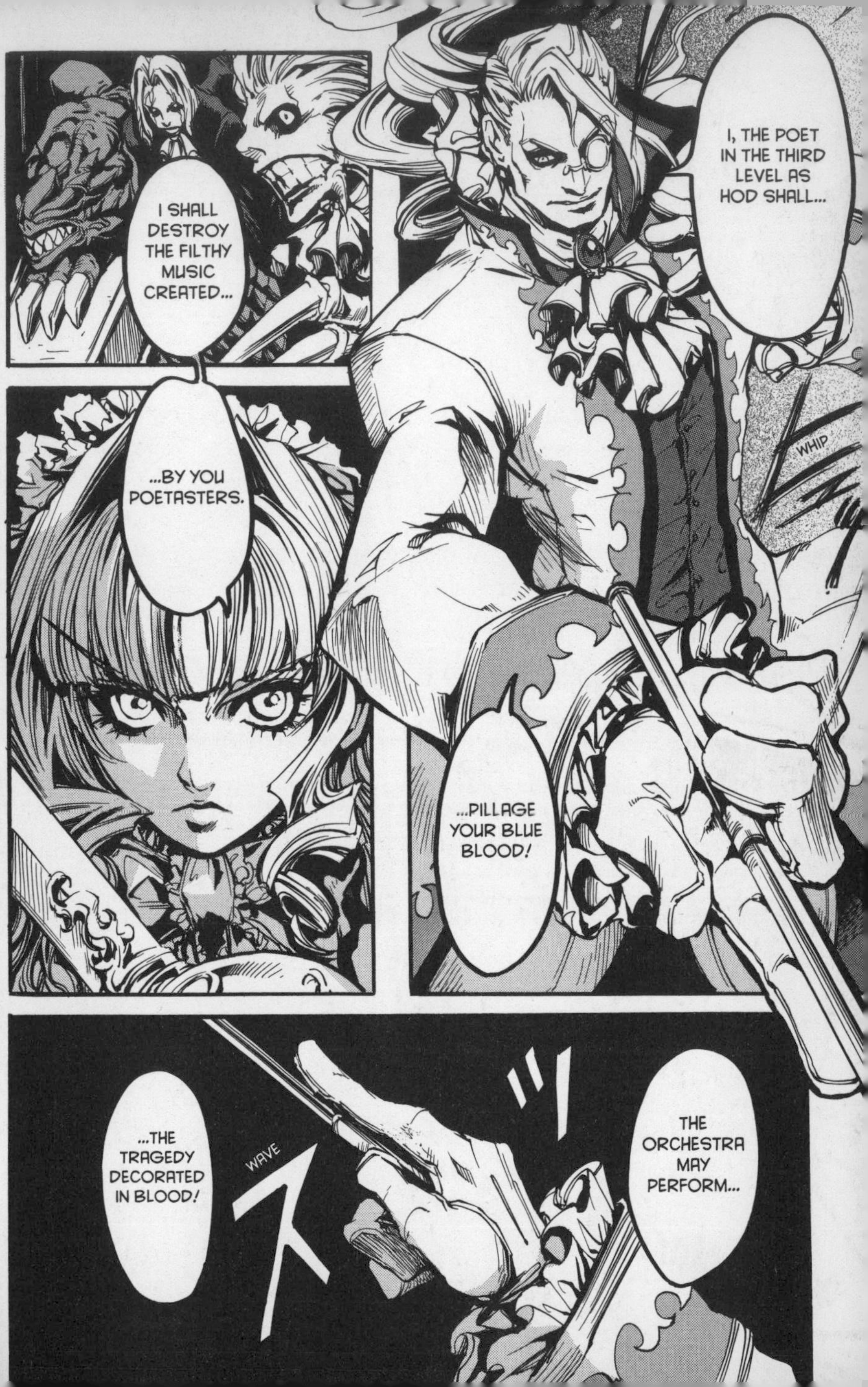
I, THE POET IN THE THIRD LEVEL AS HOD SHALL...
WHIP
...PILLAGE YOUR BLUE BLOOD!
I SHALL DESTROY THE FILTHY MUSIC CREATED...
...BY YOU POETASTERS.
THE ORCHESTRA MAY PERFORM...
WAVE
...THE TRAGEDY DECORATED IN BLOOD!

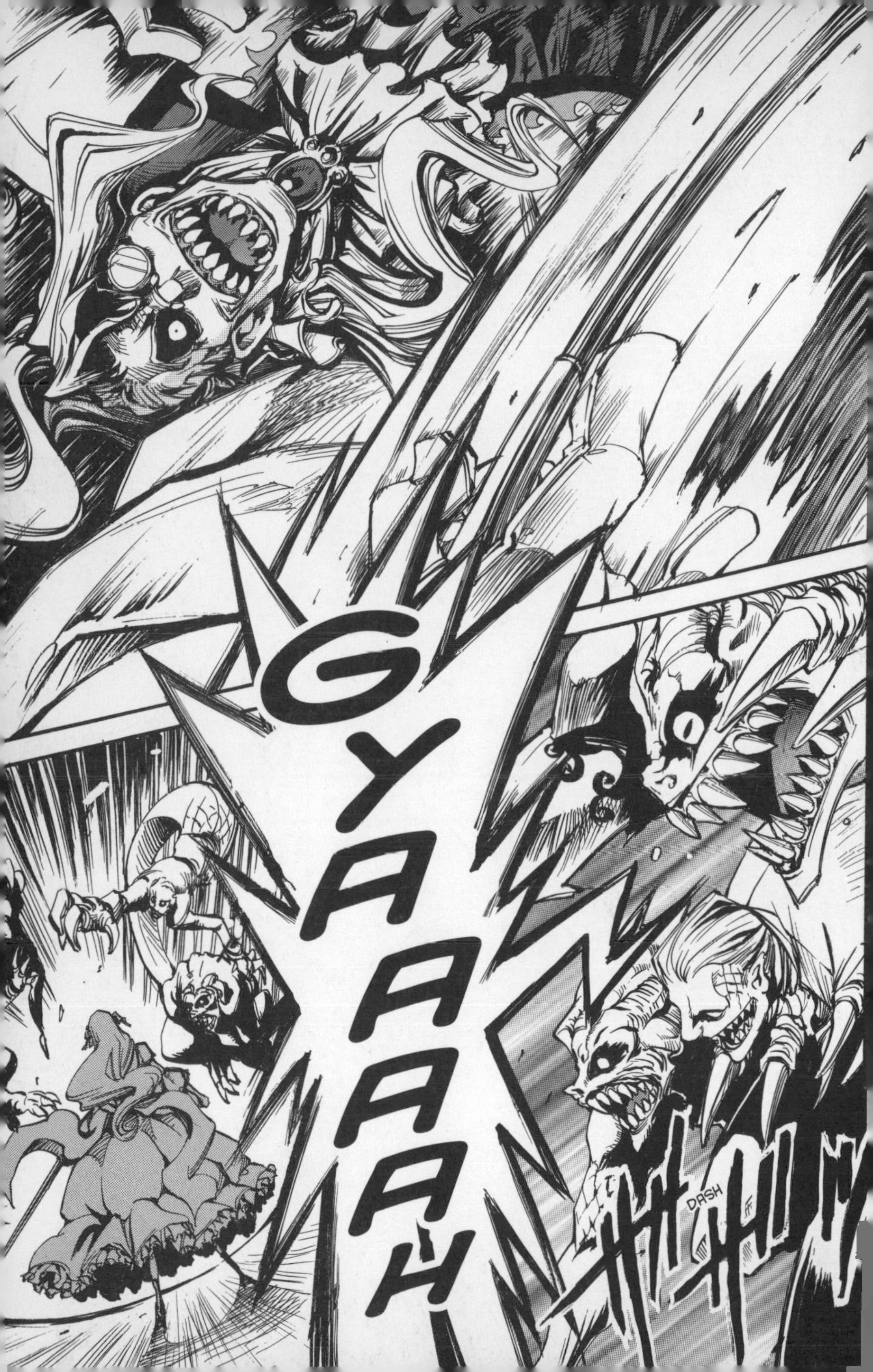
GYAAAAH
DASH

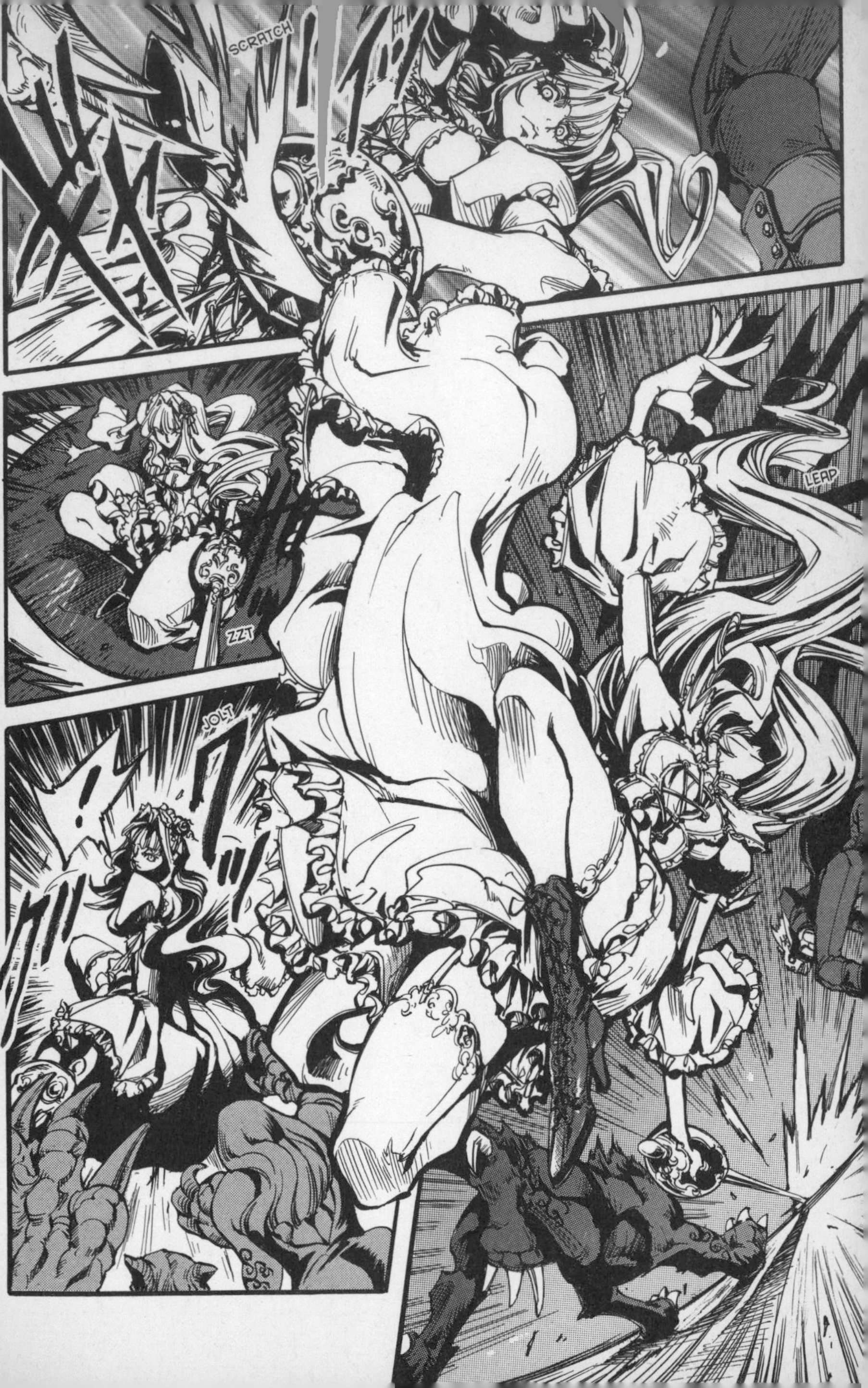
SCRATCH
LEAP
ZZT
JOLT

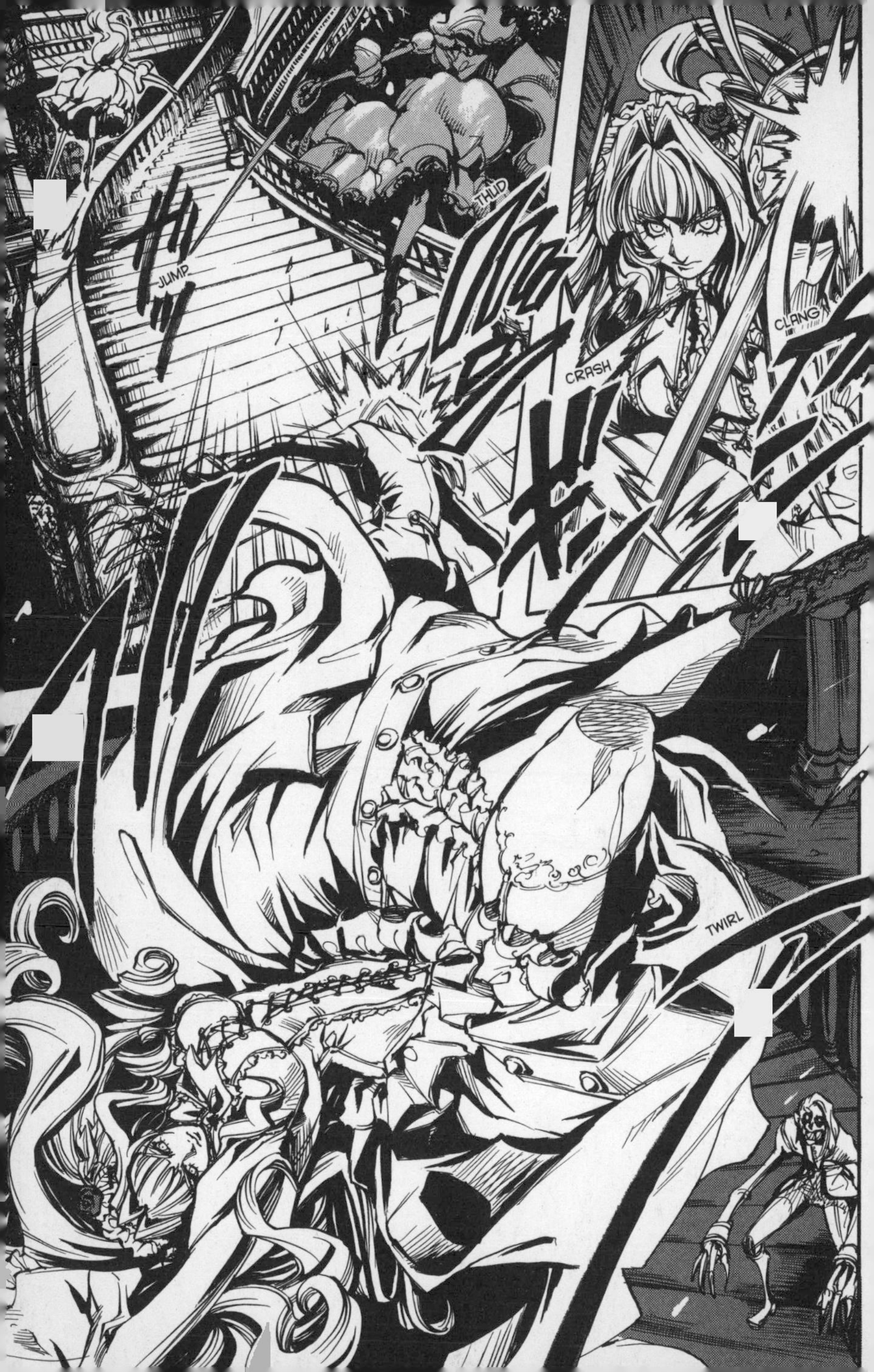
CLANG
CRASH
THUD
JUMP
TWIRL

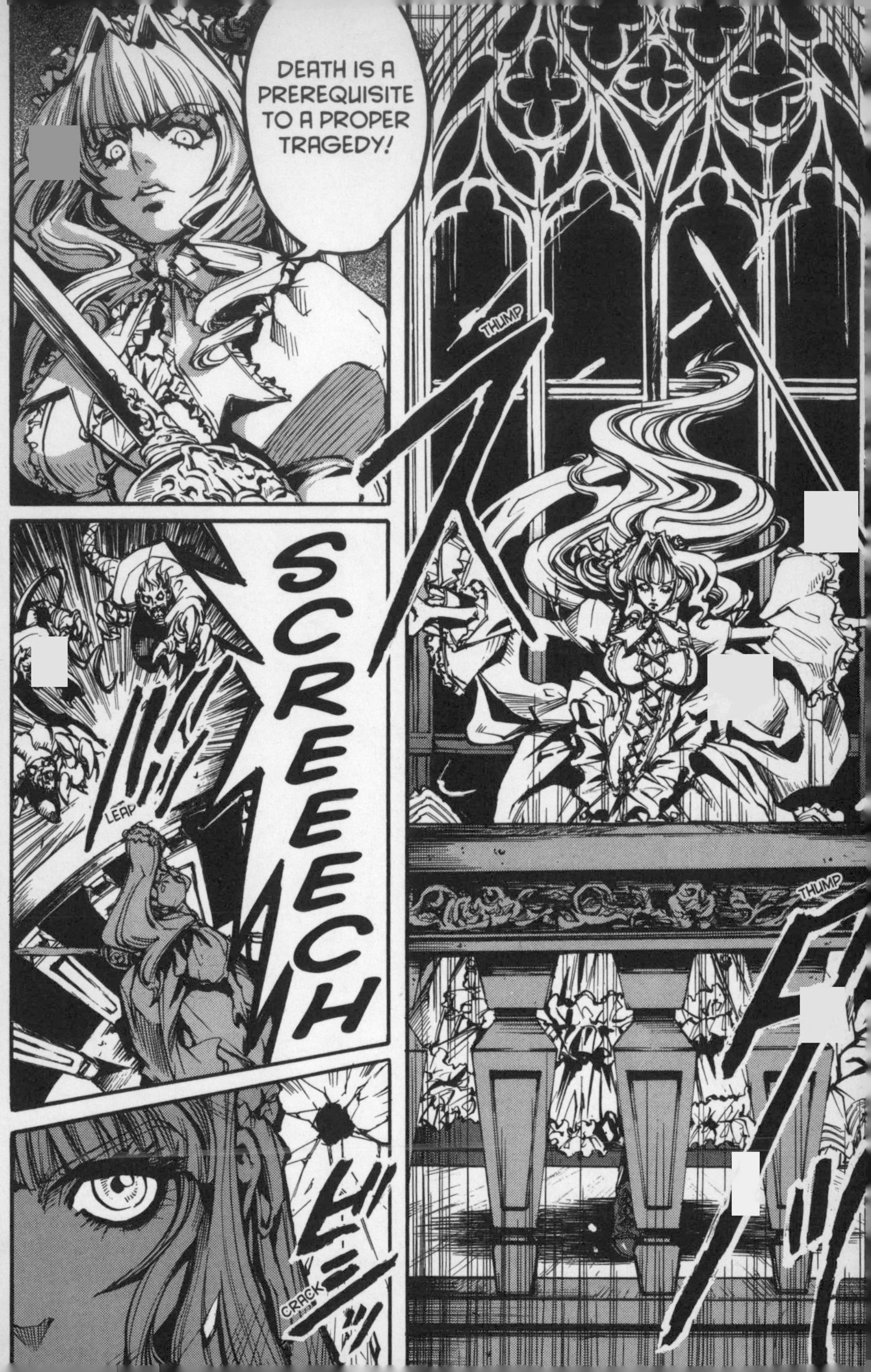
THUMP
THUMP
DEATH IS A PREREQUISITE TO A PROPER TRAGEDY!
SCREEECH
LEAP
CRACK

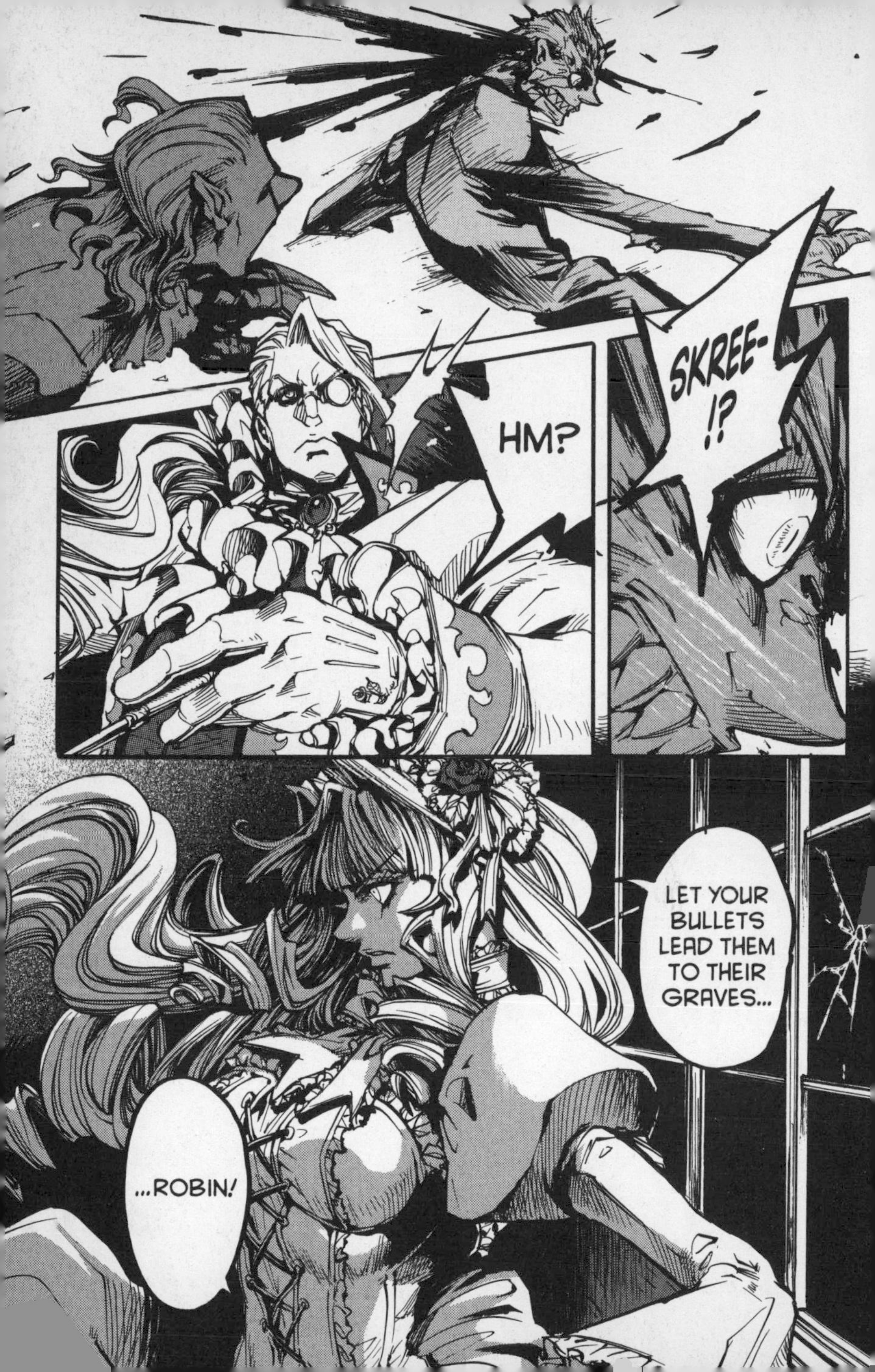
SKREE-
!?
HM?
LET YOUR BULLETS LEAD THEM TO THEIR GRAVES...
...ROBIN!

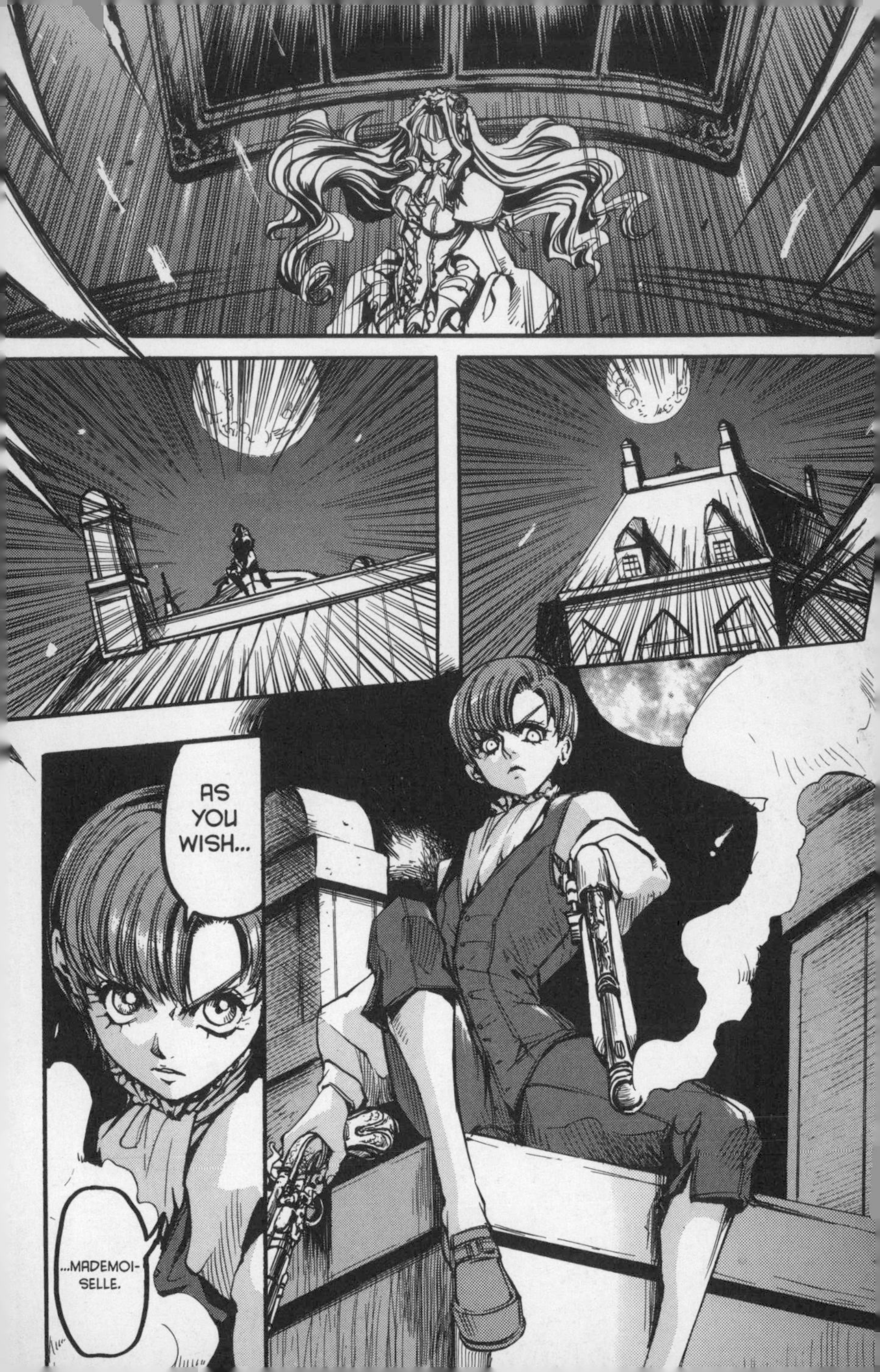
AS YOU WISH...
...MADEMOI-SELLE.

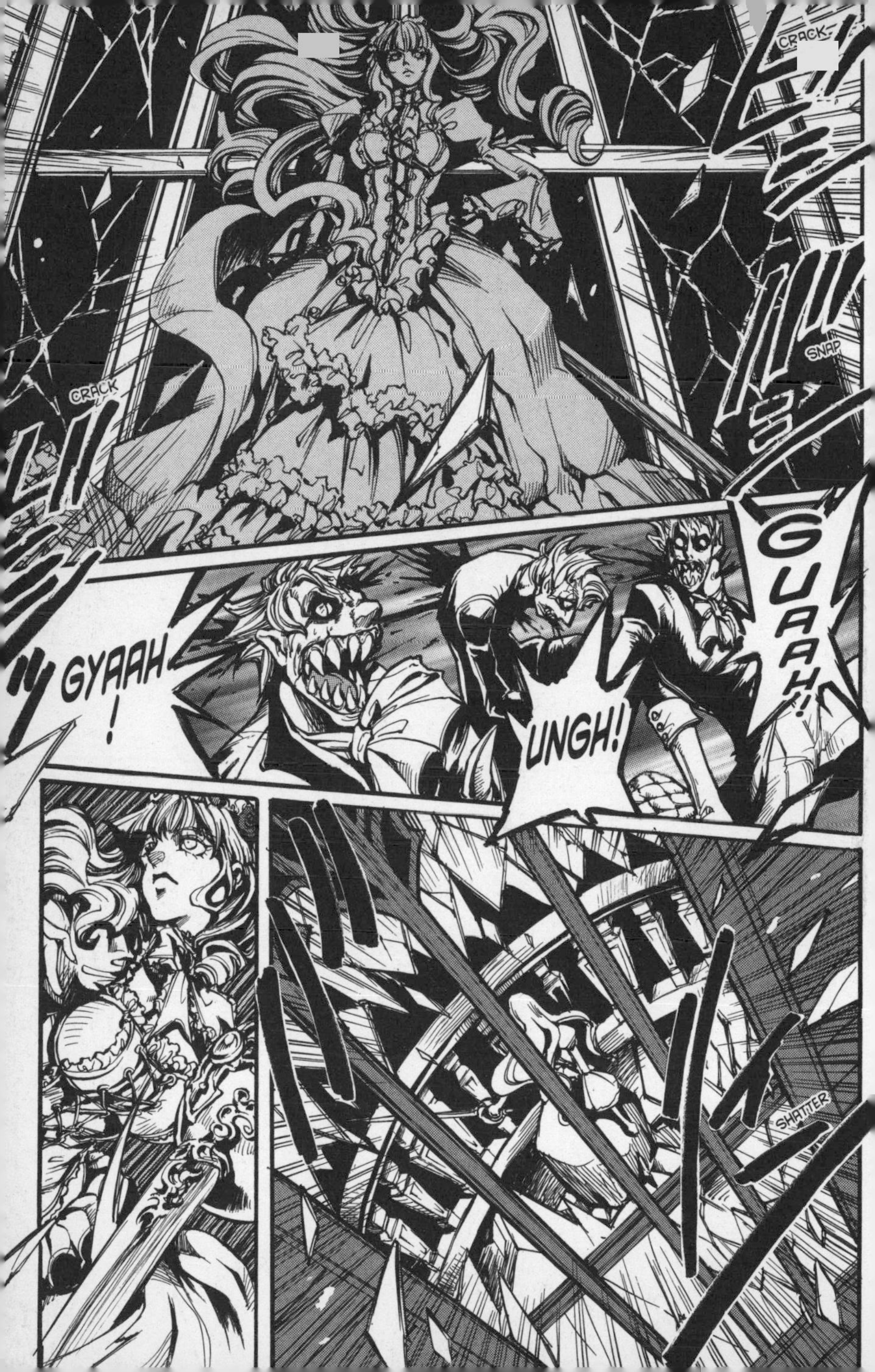
CRACK
SNAP
CRACK
GUAAAH!!
UNGH!
GYAAH!
SHATTER

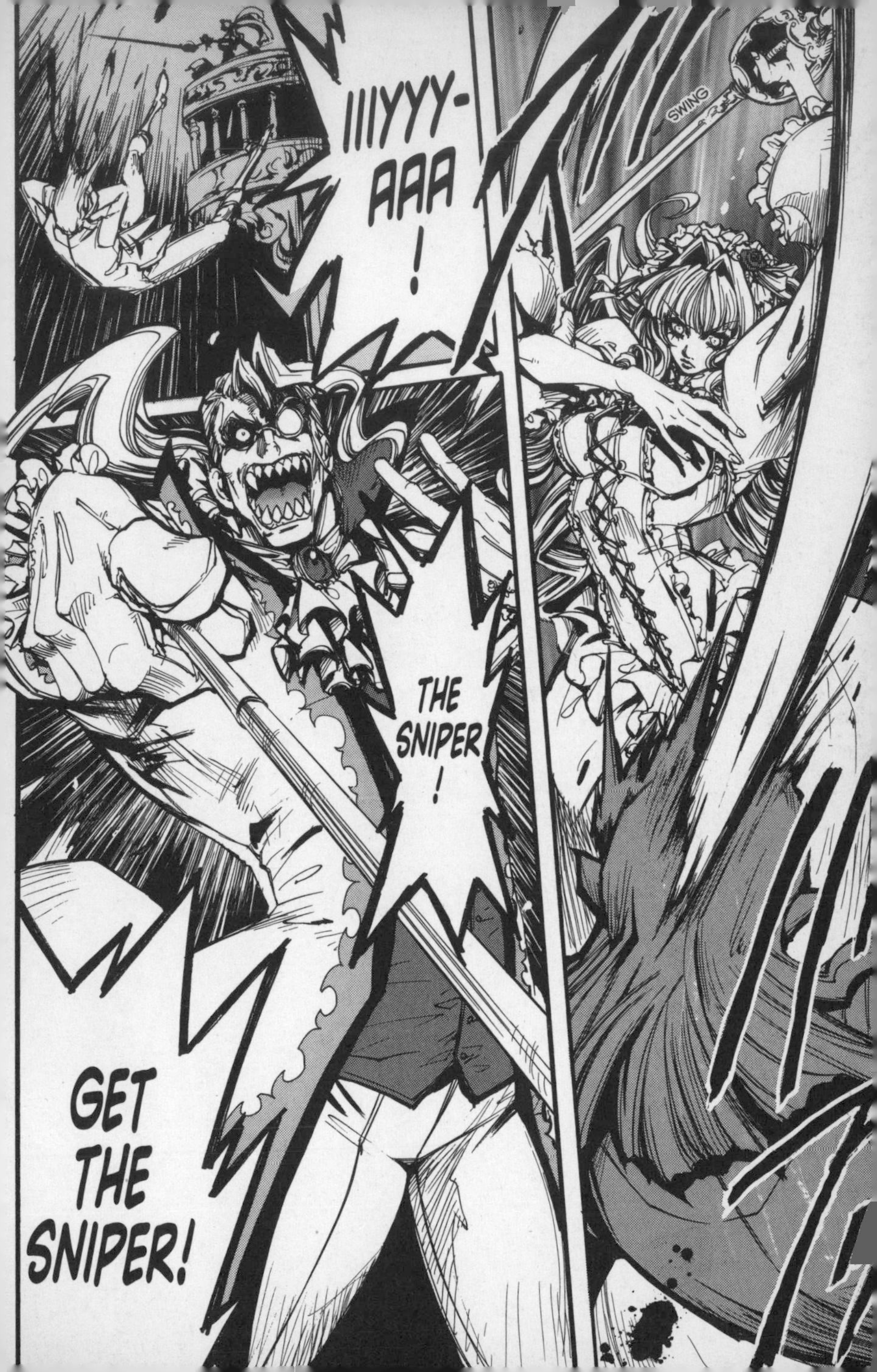
SWING
IIIYYY-AAA!
THE SNIPER!
GET THE SNIPER!

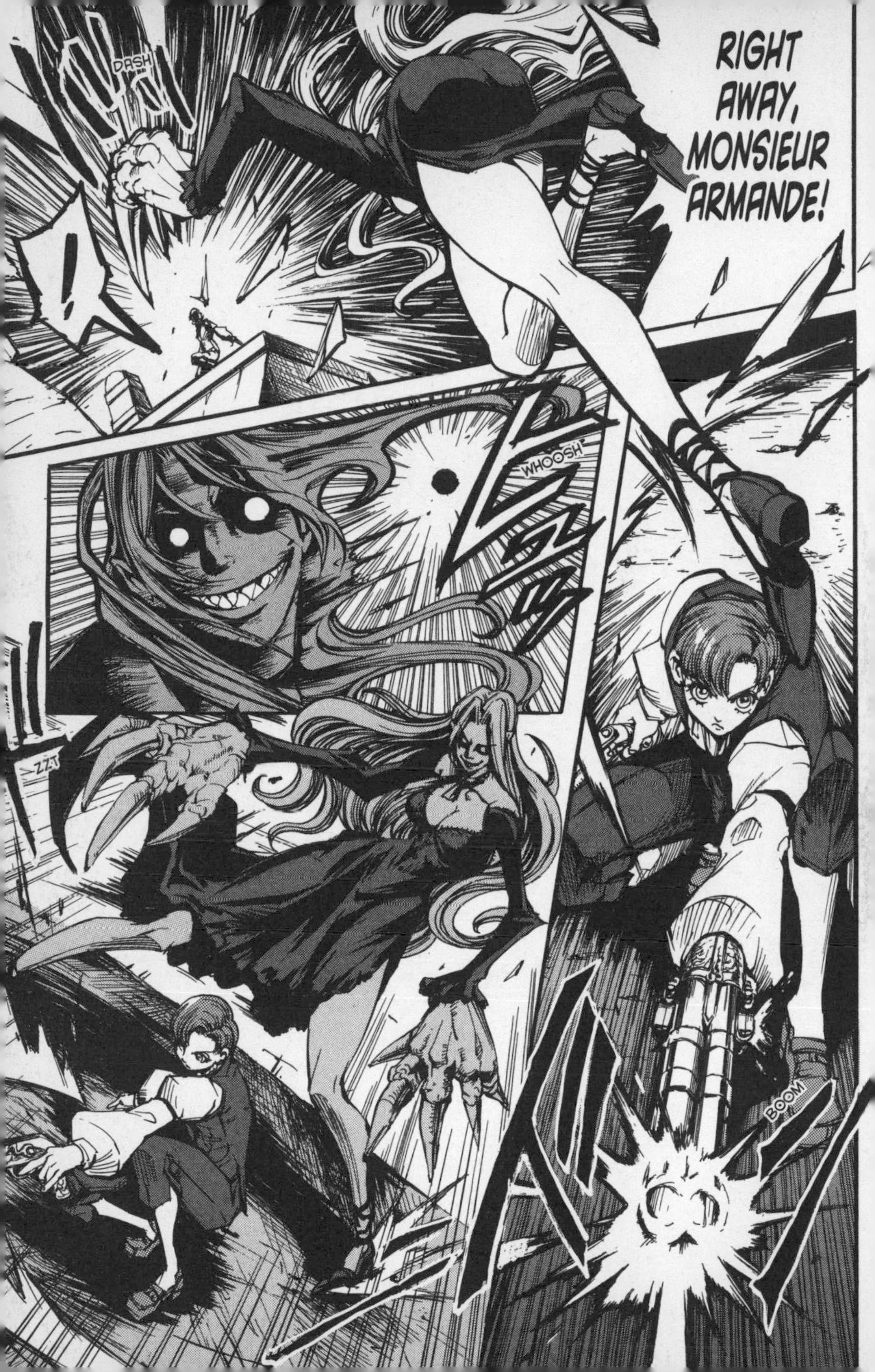
RIGHT AWAY, MONSIEUR ARMANDE!
DASH
WHOOSH
ZZAT
BOOM

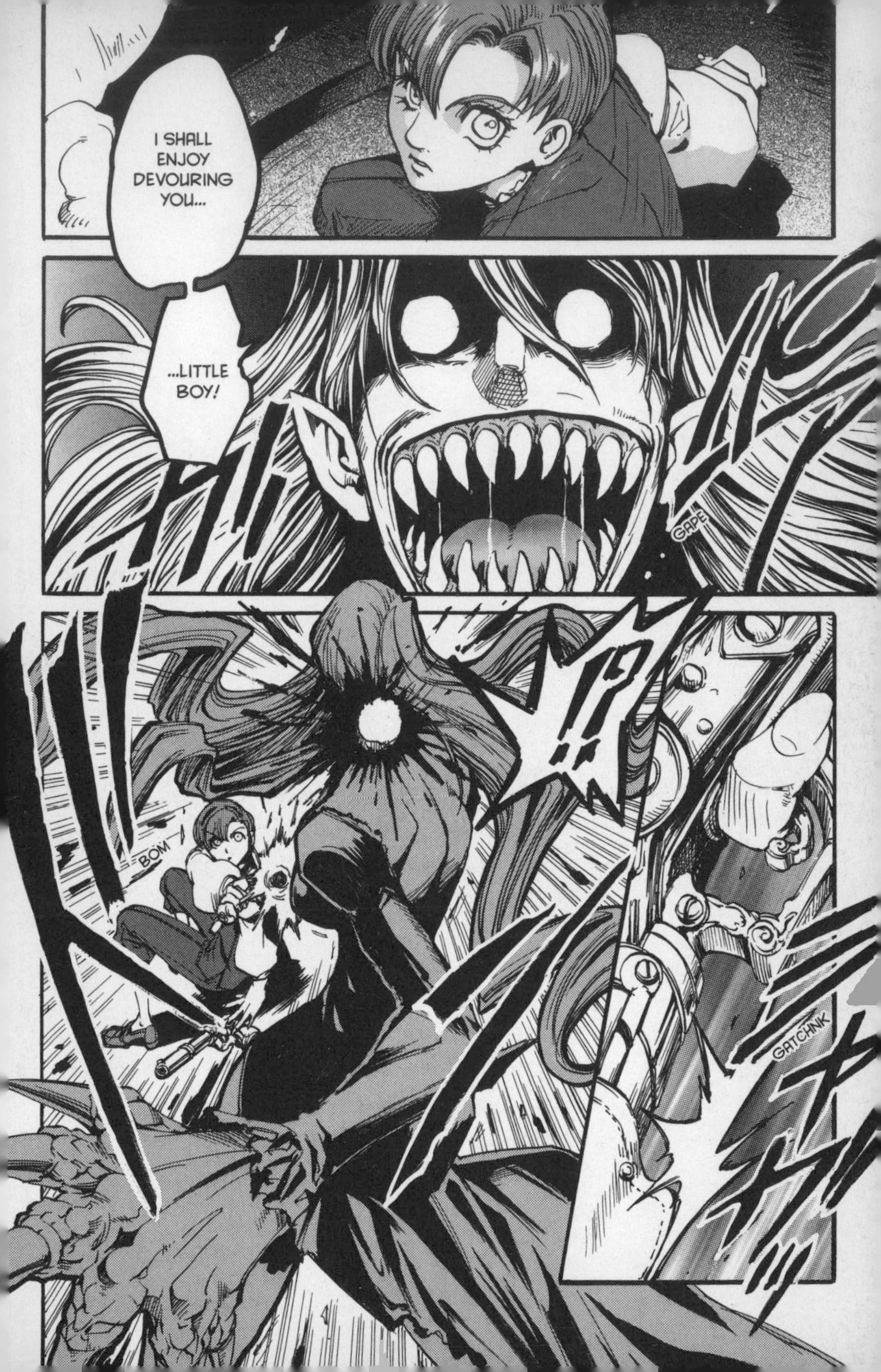
I SHALL ENJOY DEVOURING YOU...
...LITTLE BOY!
GAPE
GATCHNK
BOM

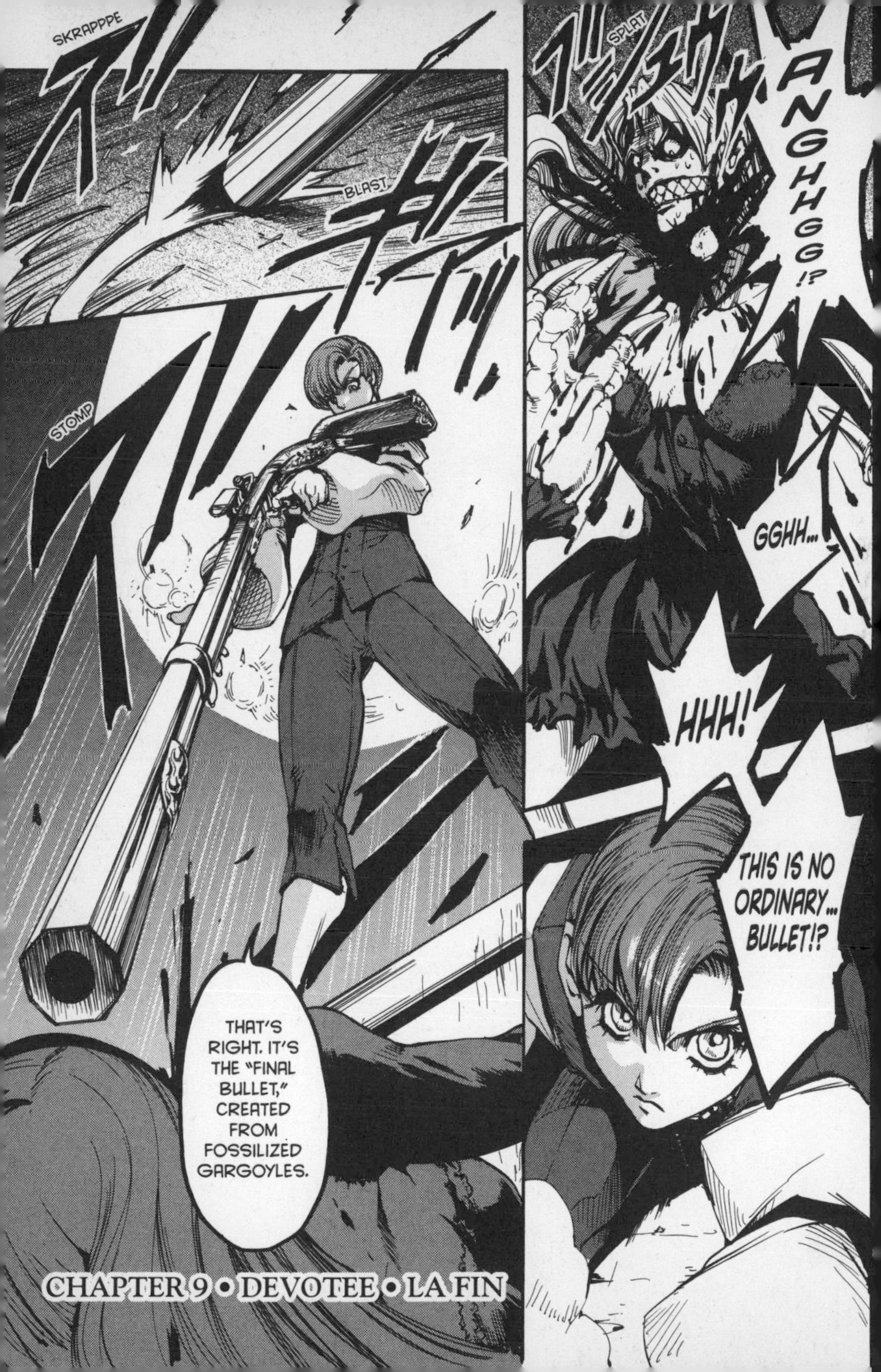
SPLAT
ANGHHGG!?
GGHH...
HHH!
THIS IS NO ORDINARY... BULLET!?
SKRAPPPE
BLAST
STOMP
THAT'S RIGHT. IT'S THE "FINAL BULLET," CREATED FROM FOSSILIZED GARGOYLES.
CHAPTER 9 • DEVOTEE • LA FIN

CHEVALIER

CHAPTER 10
THE MANIFESTATION OF THE "S"

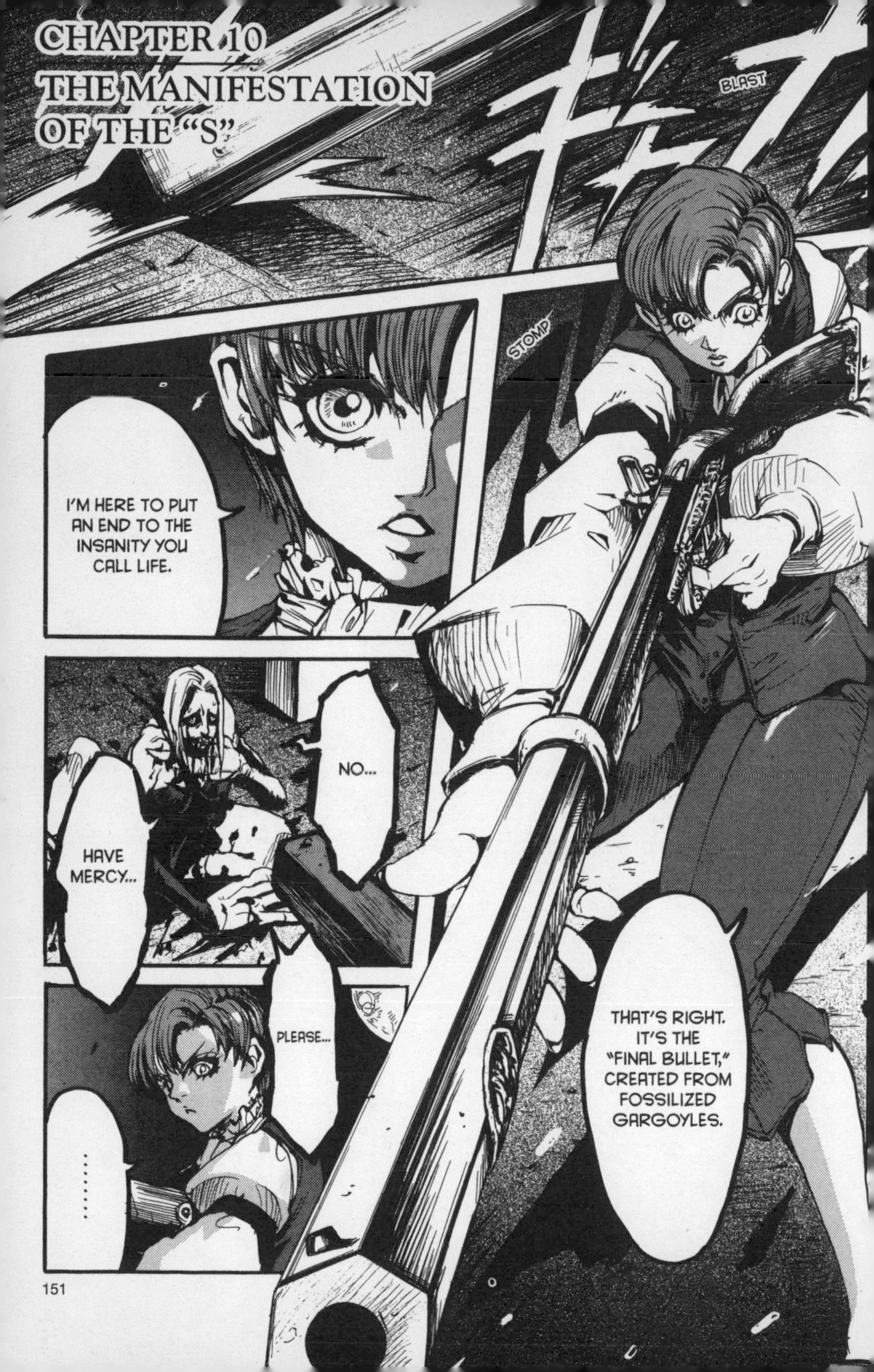
BLAST
STOMP
THAT'S RIGHT. IT'S THE "FINAL BULLET," CREATED FROM FOSSILIZED GARGOYLES.
I'M HERE TO PUT AN END TO THE INSANITY YOU CALL LIFE.
NO...
HAVE MERCY...
PLEASE...
......

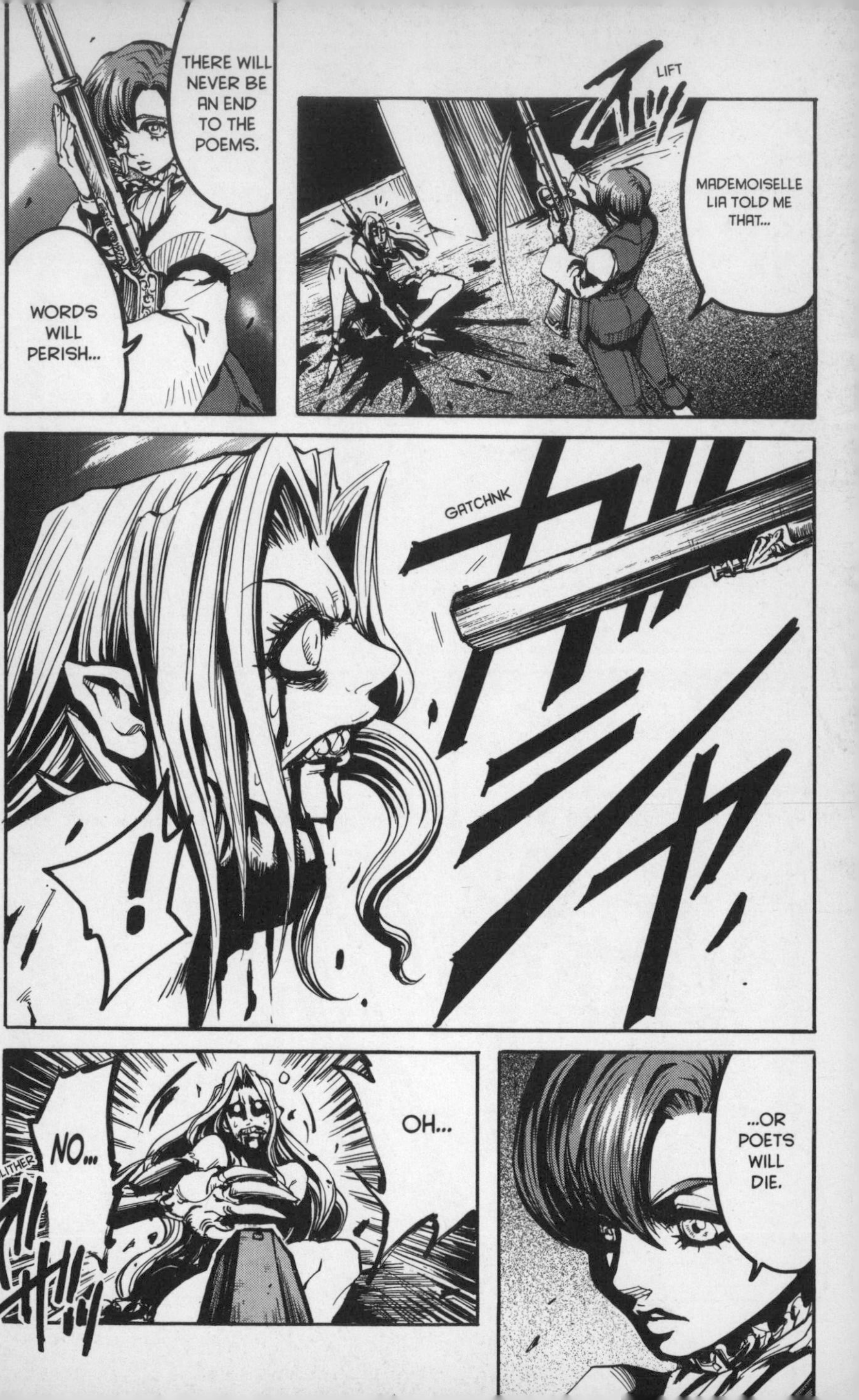
LIFT
MADEMOISELLE LIA TOLD ME THAT...
THERE WILL NEVER BE AN END TO THE POEMS.
WORDS WILL PERISH...
GATCHNK
...OR POETS WILL DIE.
OH...
NO...
SLITHER

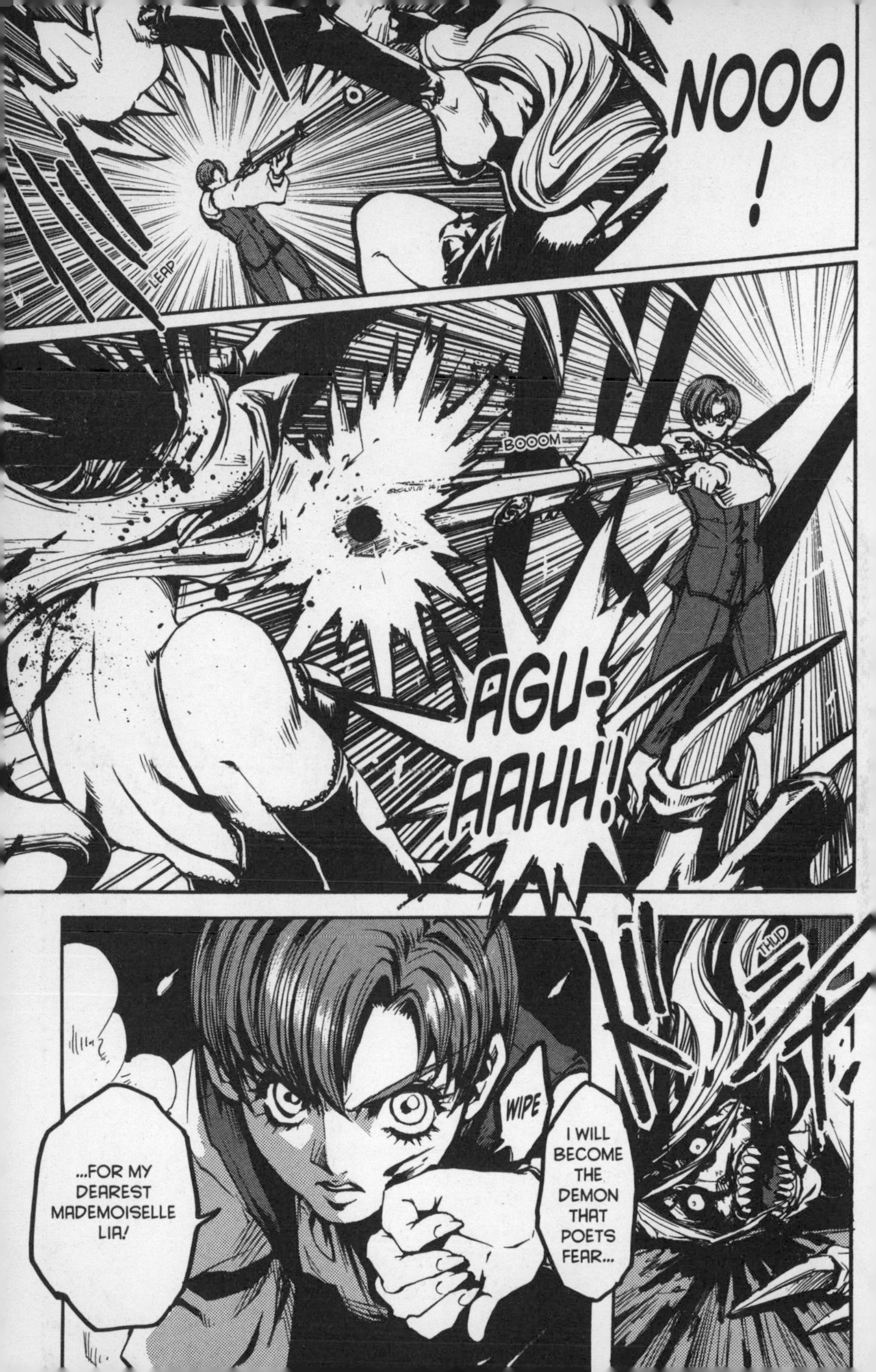
NOOO!
LEAP
BOOOM
AGU-AAHH!
THUD
WIPE
I WILL BECOME THE DEMON THAT POETS FEAR...
...FOR MY DEAREST MADEMOISELLE LIA!

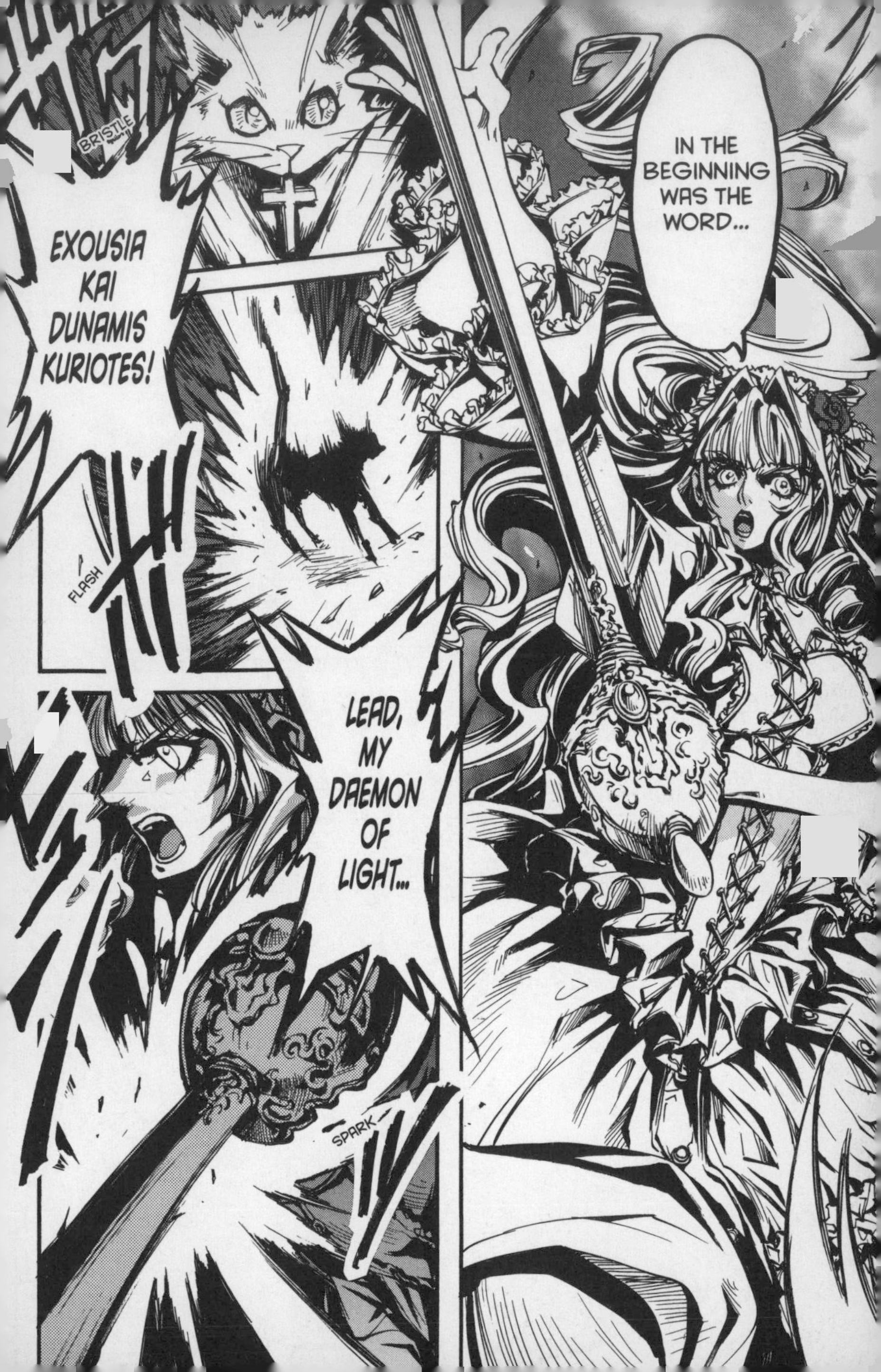
IN THE BEGINNING WAS THE WORD...
BRISTLE
EXOUSIA KAI DUNAMIS KURIOTES!
FLASH
LEAD, MY DAEMON OF LIGHT...
SPARK

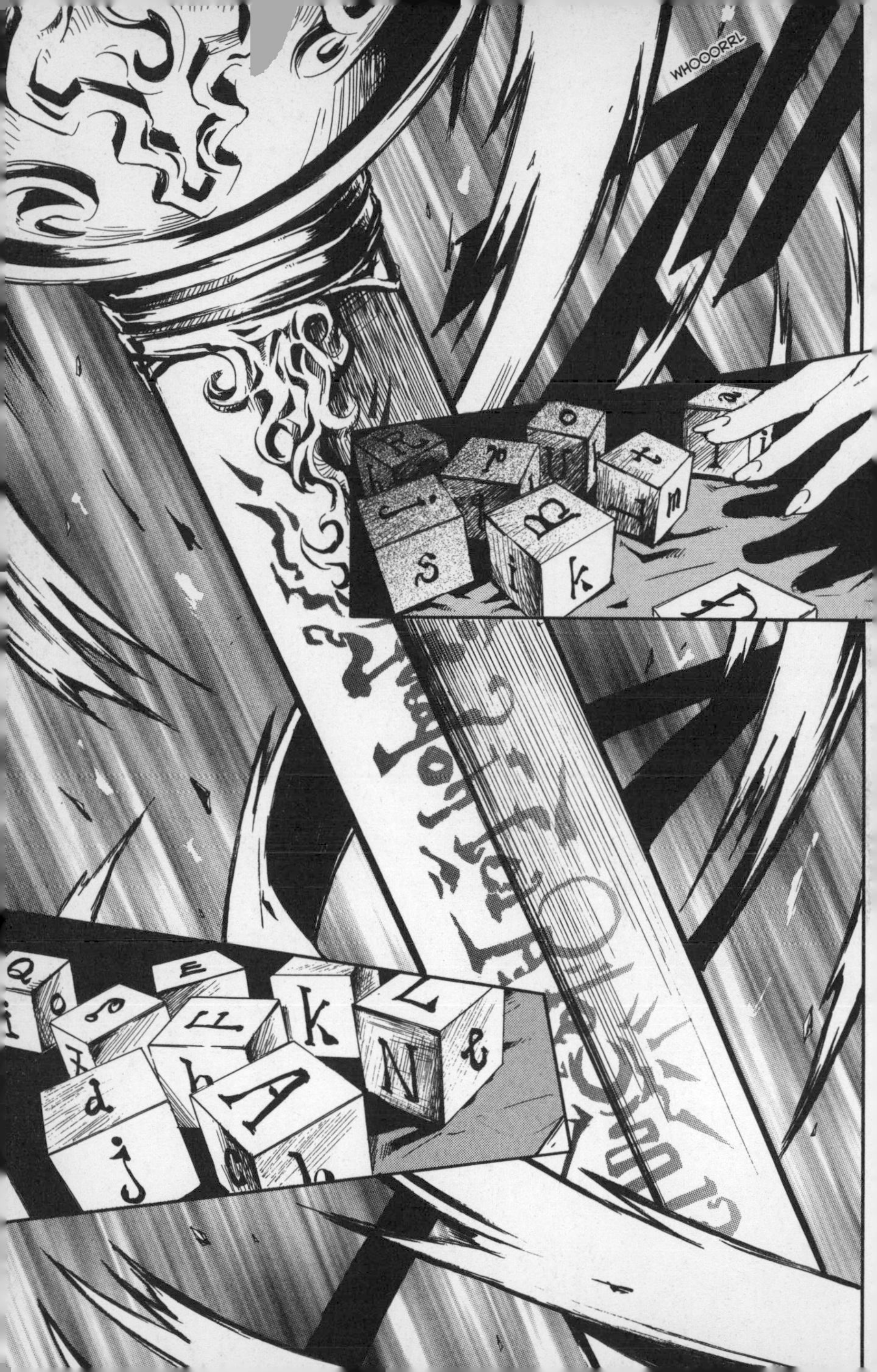
WHOOORRL

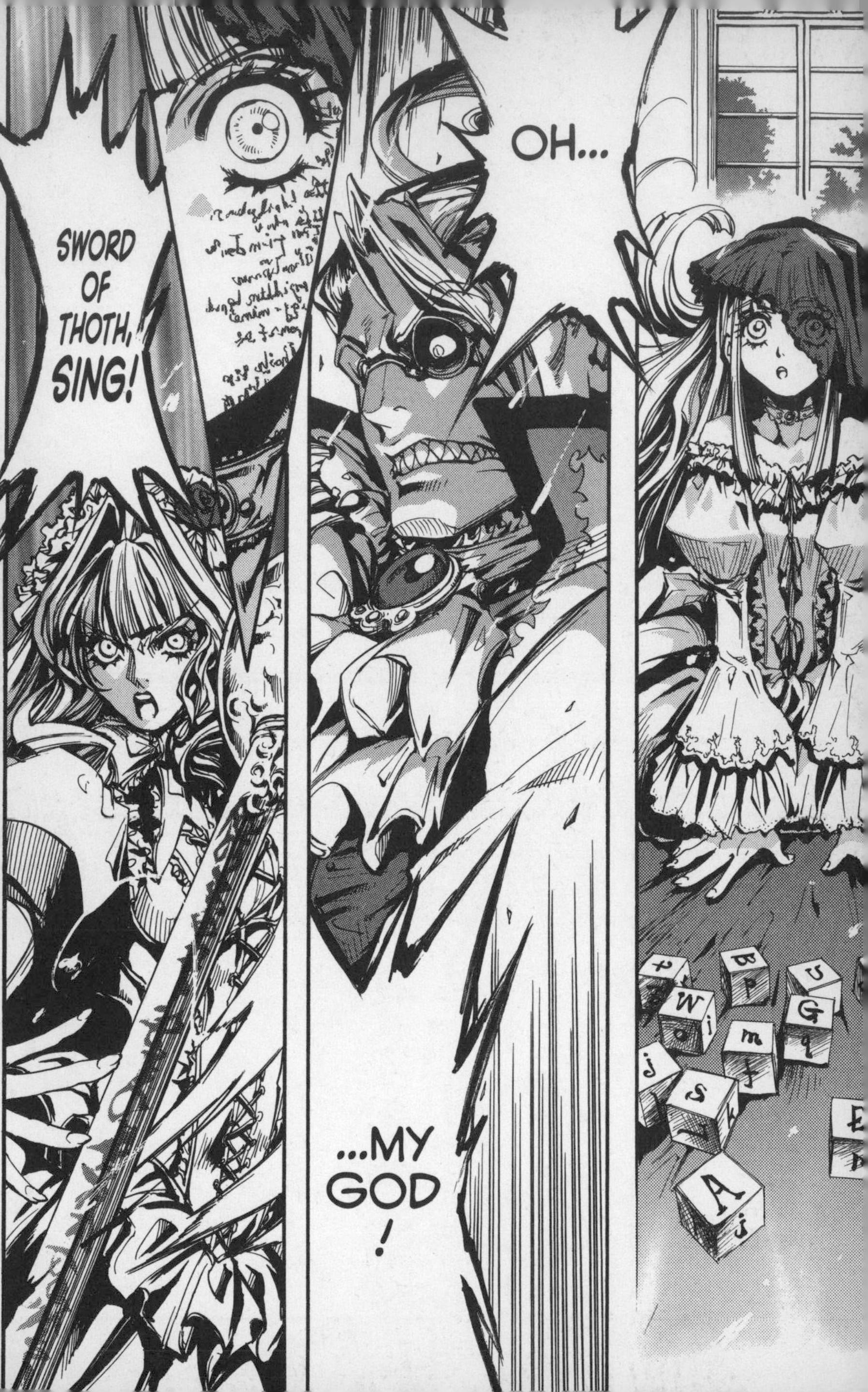
OH...
...MY GOD!
SWORD OF THOTH, SING!

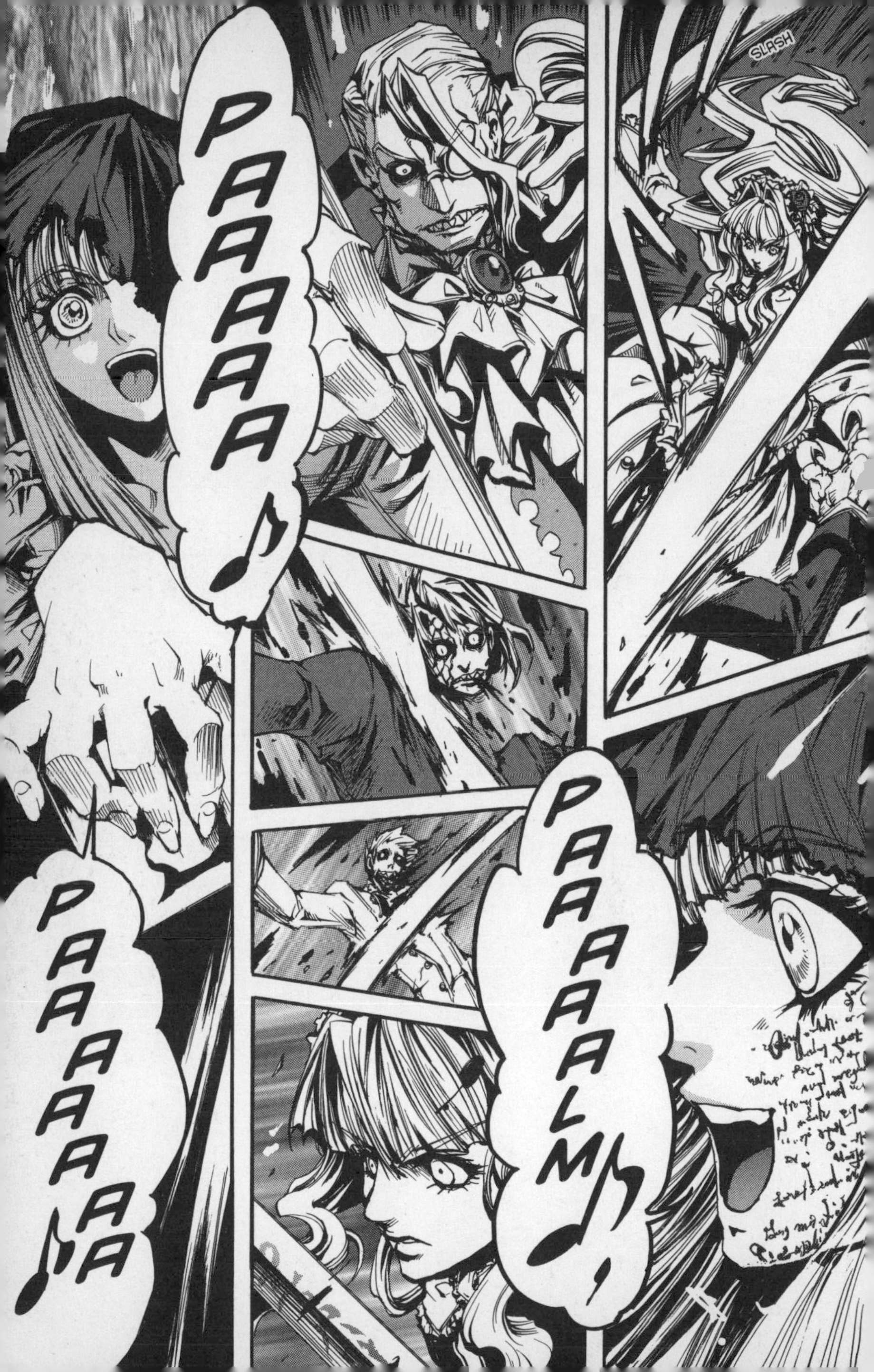
SLASH
PAAAAA♪
PAAAAALM♪
PAAAAAAA♪

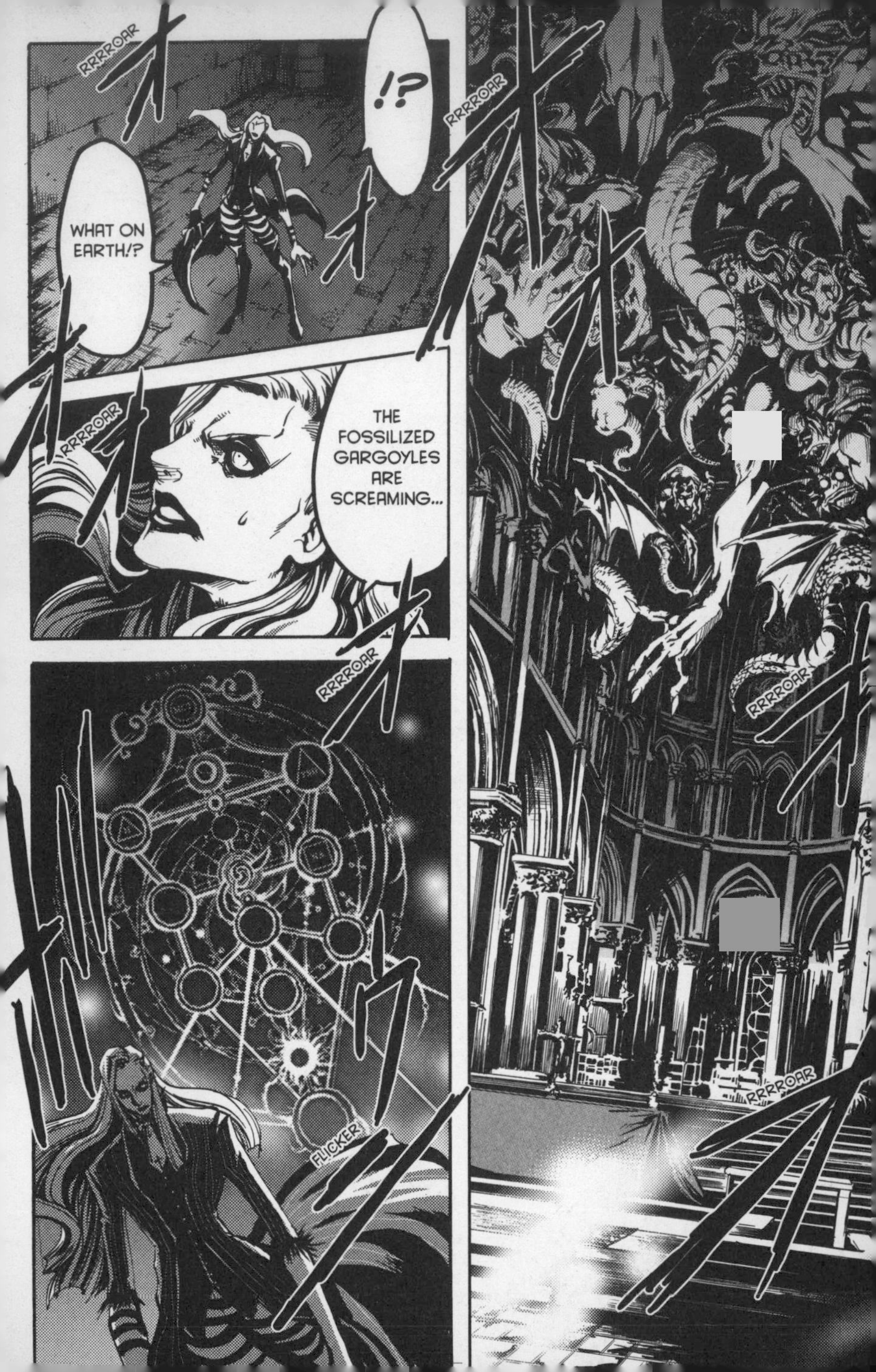
RRRROAR
RRRROAR
RRRROAR
RRRROAR
!?
WHAT ON EARTH!?
RRRROAR
THE FOSSILIZED GARGOYLES ARE SCREAMING...
RRRROAR
FLICKER

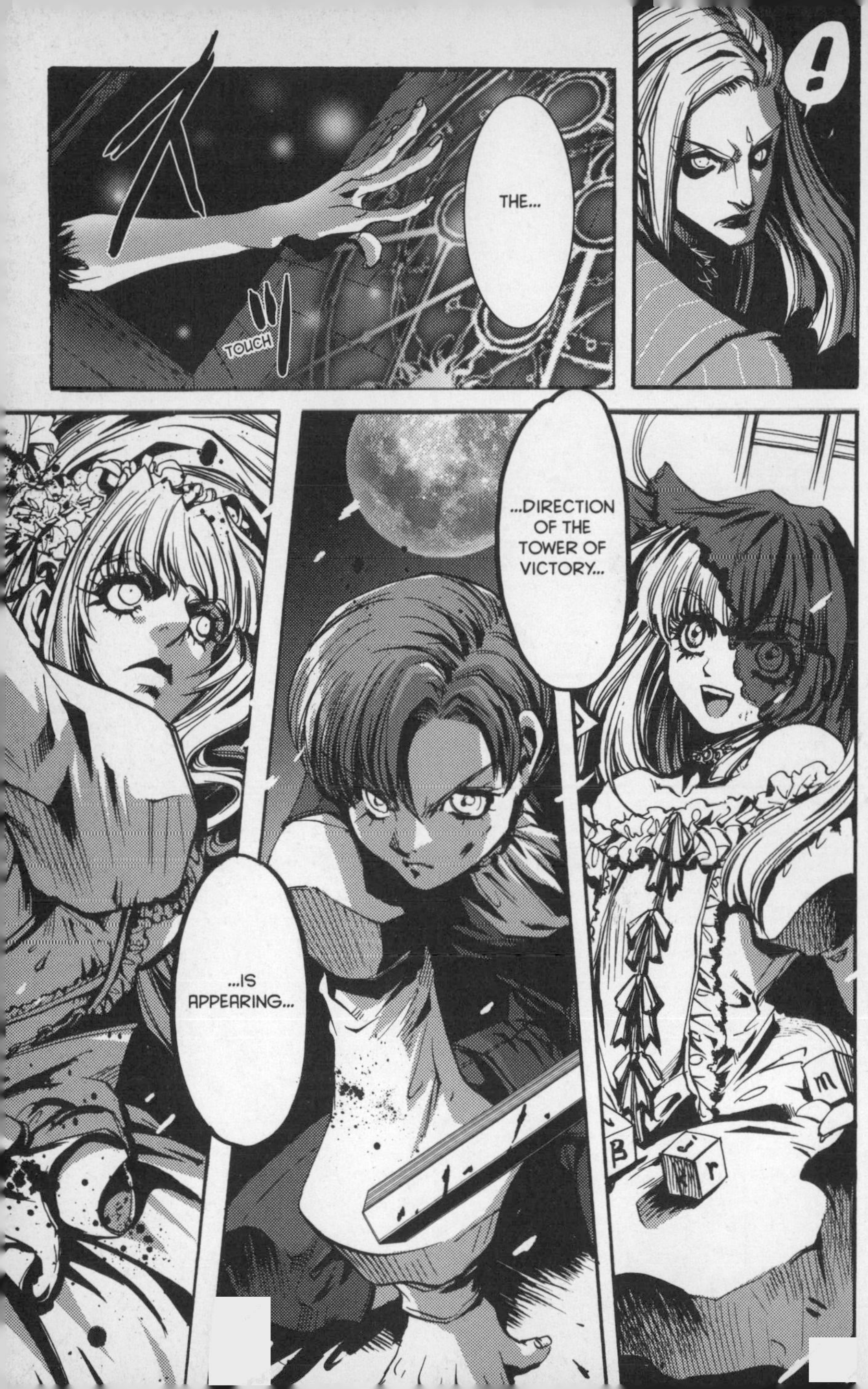
!
THE...
TOUCH
...DIRECTION OF THE TOWER OF VICTORY...
...IS APPEARING...

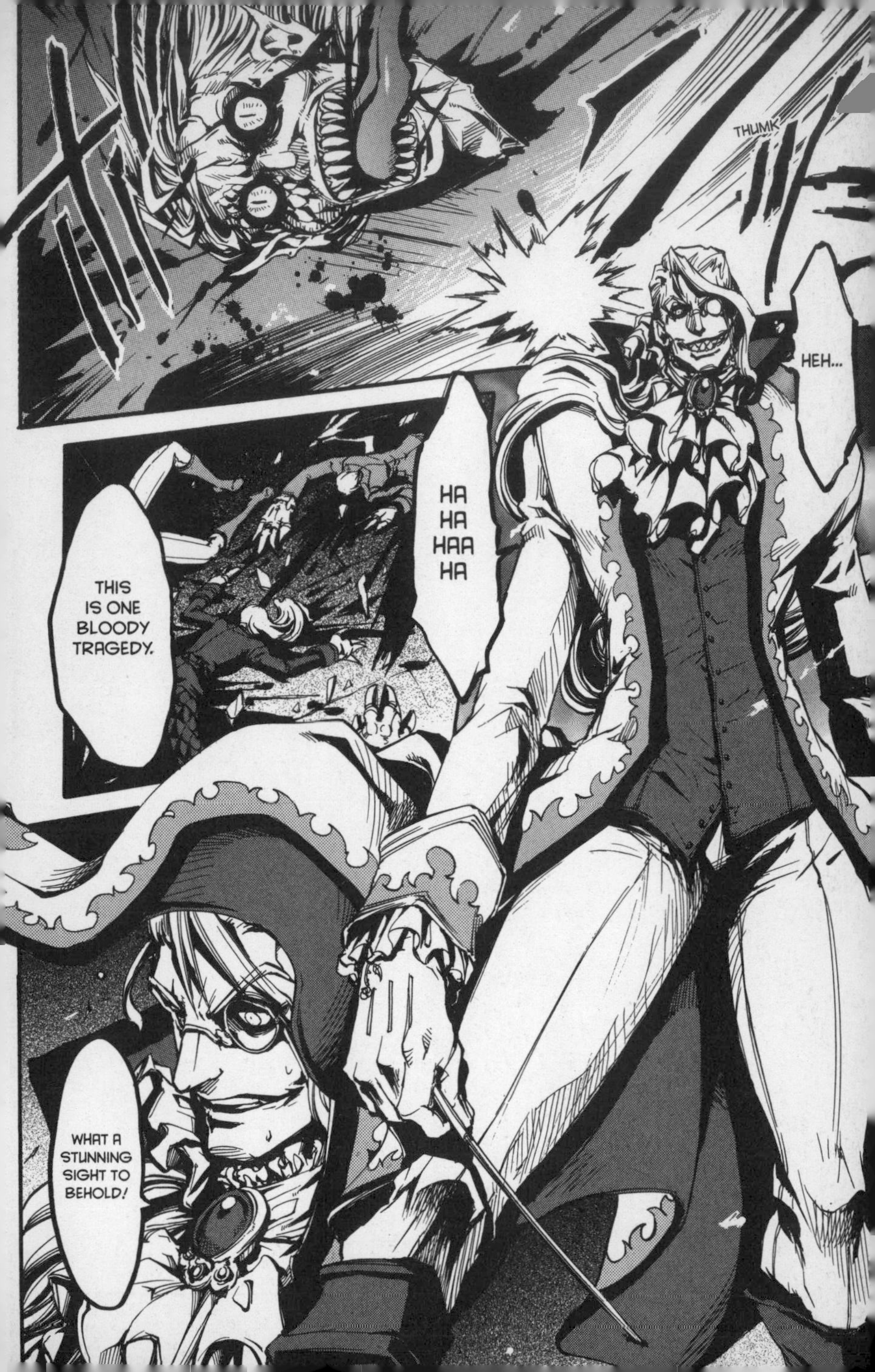
THUMK
HEH...
HA HA HAA HA
THIS IS ONE BLOODY TRAGEDY.
WHAT A STUNNING SIGHT TO BEHOLD!

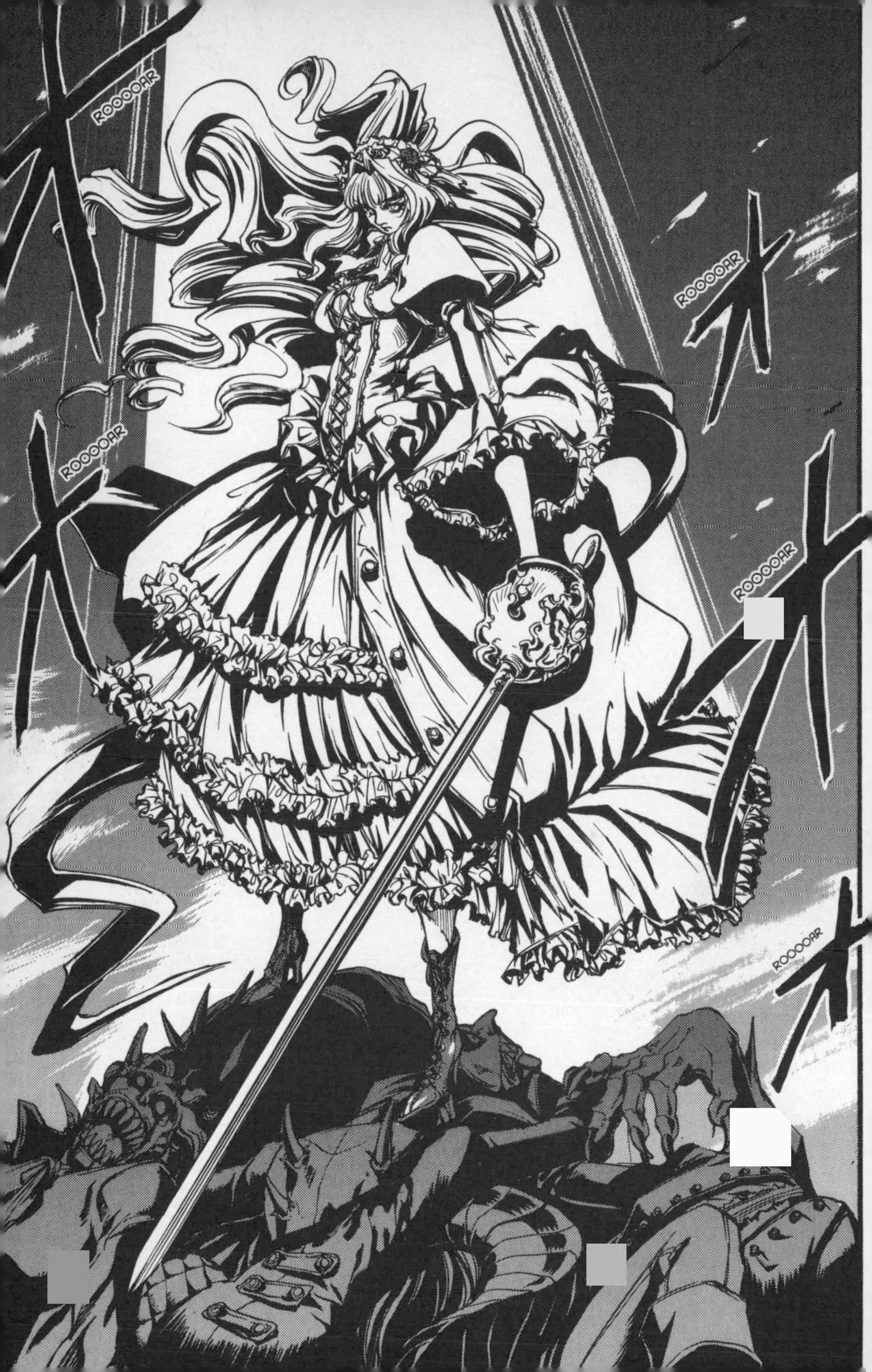
ROOOOAR
ROOOOAR
ROOOOAR
ROOOOAR
ROOOOAR

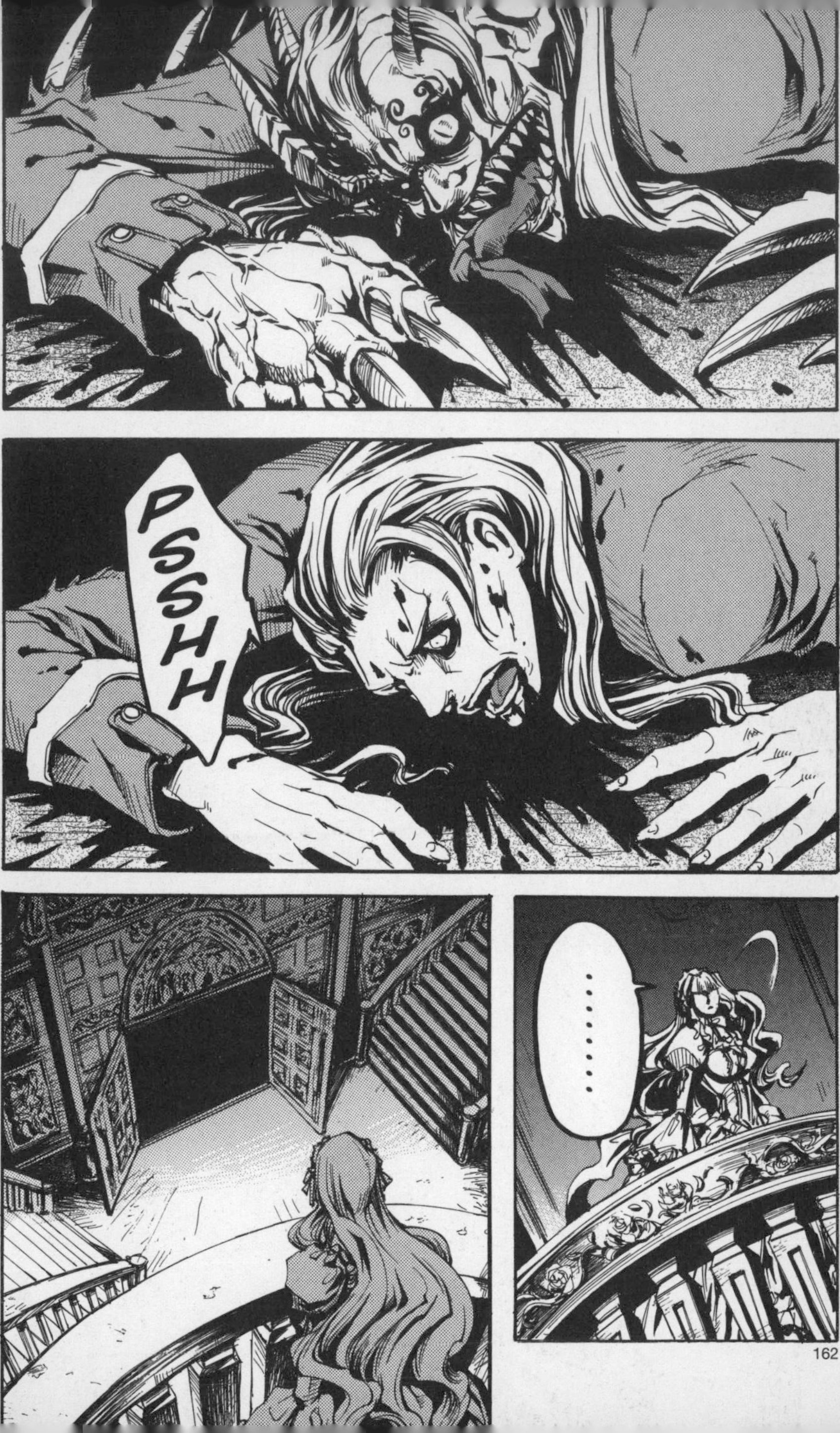
PSSHH
....

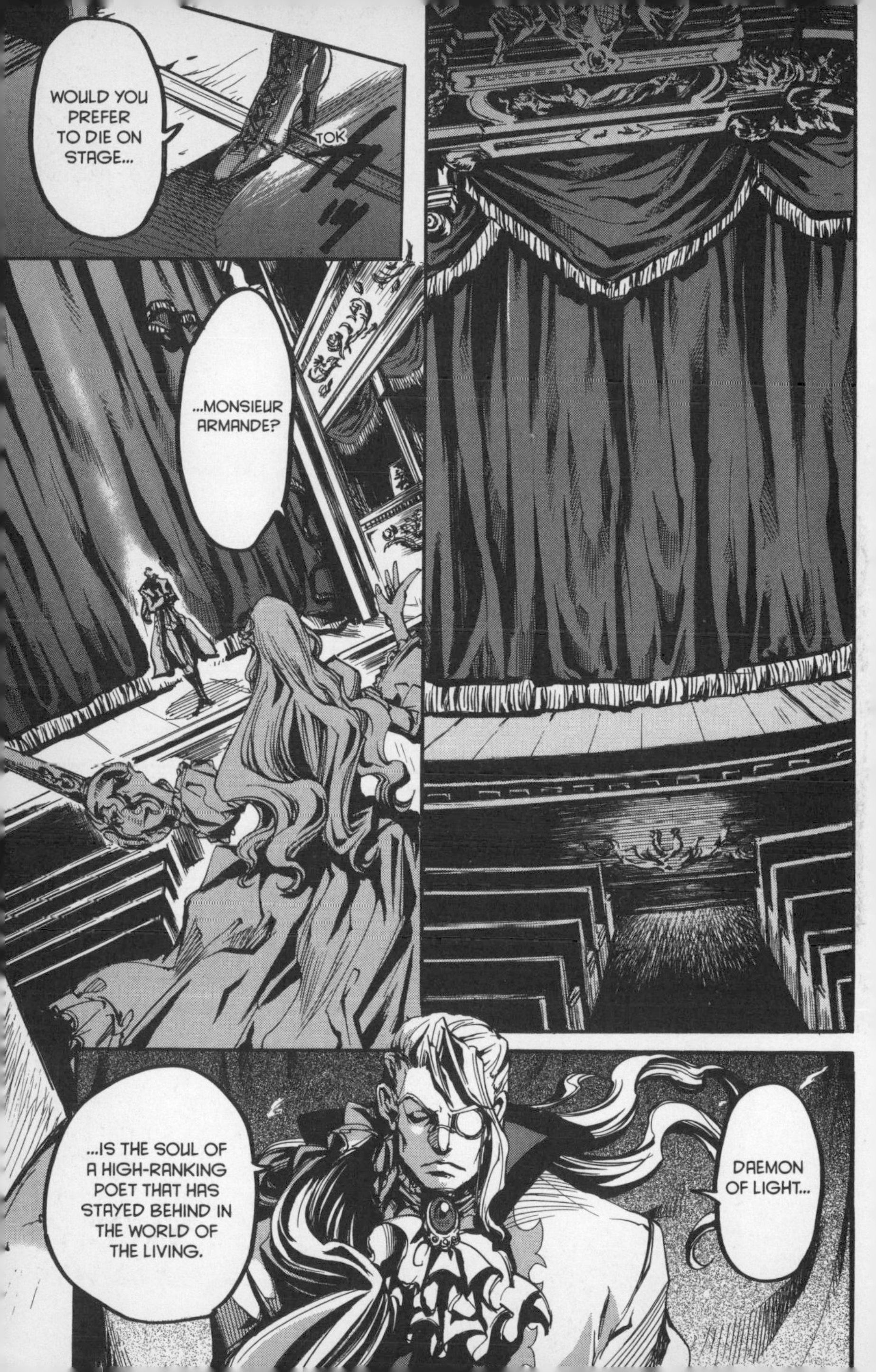
WOULD YOU PREFER TO DIE ON STAGE...
TOK
...MONSIEUR ARMANDE?
DAEMON OF LIGHT...
...IS THE SOUL OF A HIGH-RANKING POET THAT HAS STAYED BEHIND IN THE WORLD OF THE LIVING.

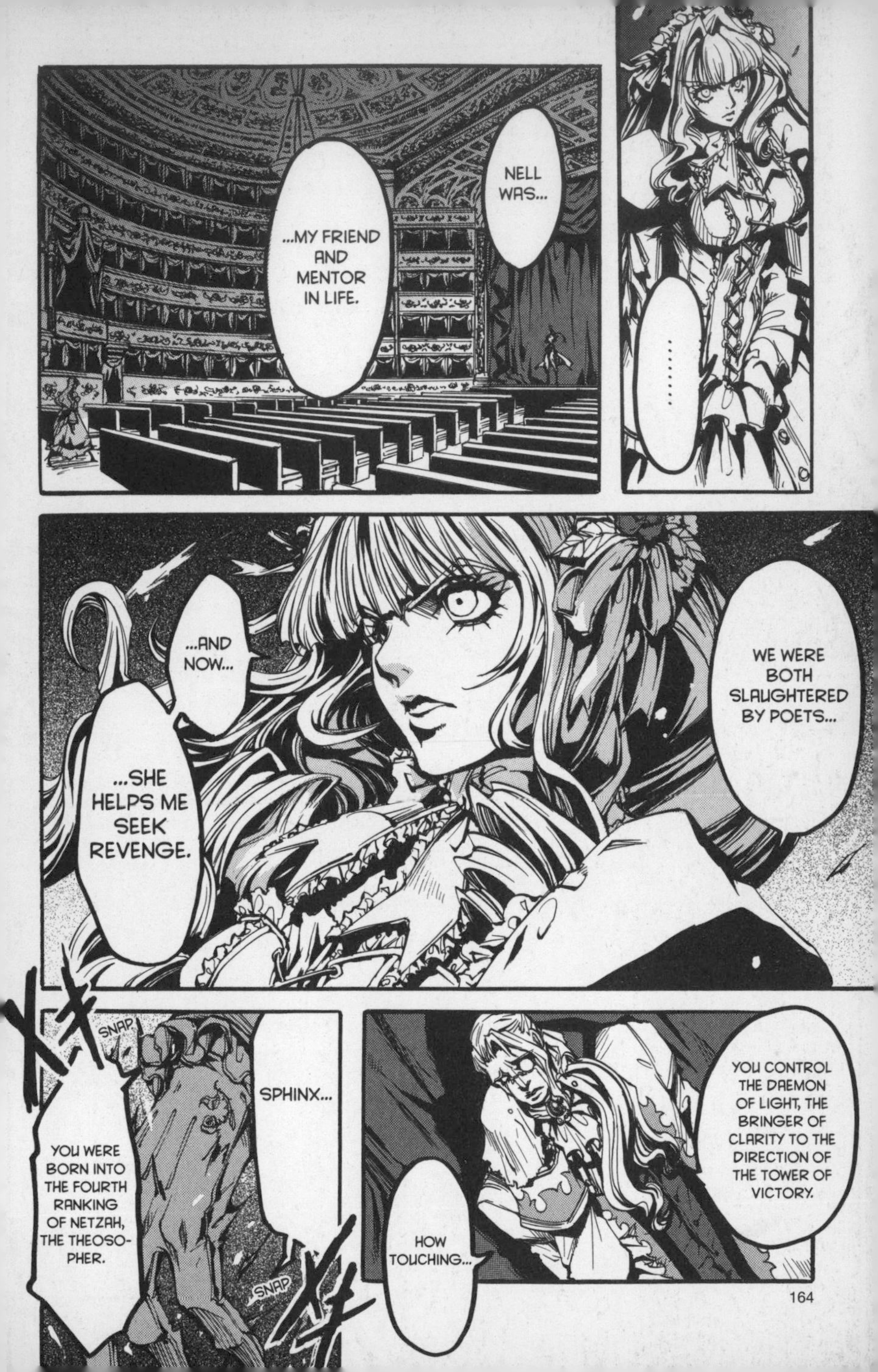
......
NELL WAS...
...MY FRIEND AND MENTOR IN LIFE.
WE WERE BOTH SLAUGHTERED BY POETS...
...AND NOW...
...SHE HELPS ME SEEK REVENGE.
YOU CONTROL THE DAEMON OF LIGHT, THE BRINGER OF CLARITY TO THE DIRECTION OF THE TOWER OF VICTORY.
HOW TOUCHING...
SNAP
SPHINX...
YOU WERE BORN INTO THE FOURTH RANKING OF NETZAH, THE THEOSO-PHER.
SNAP

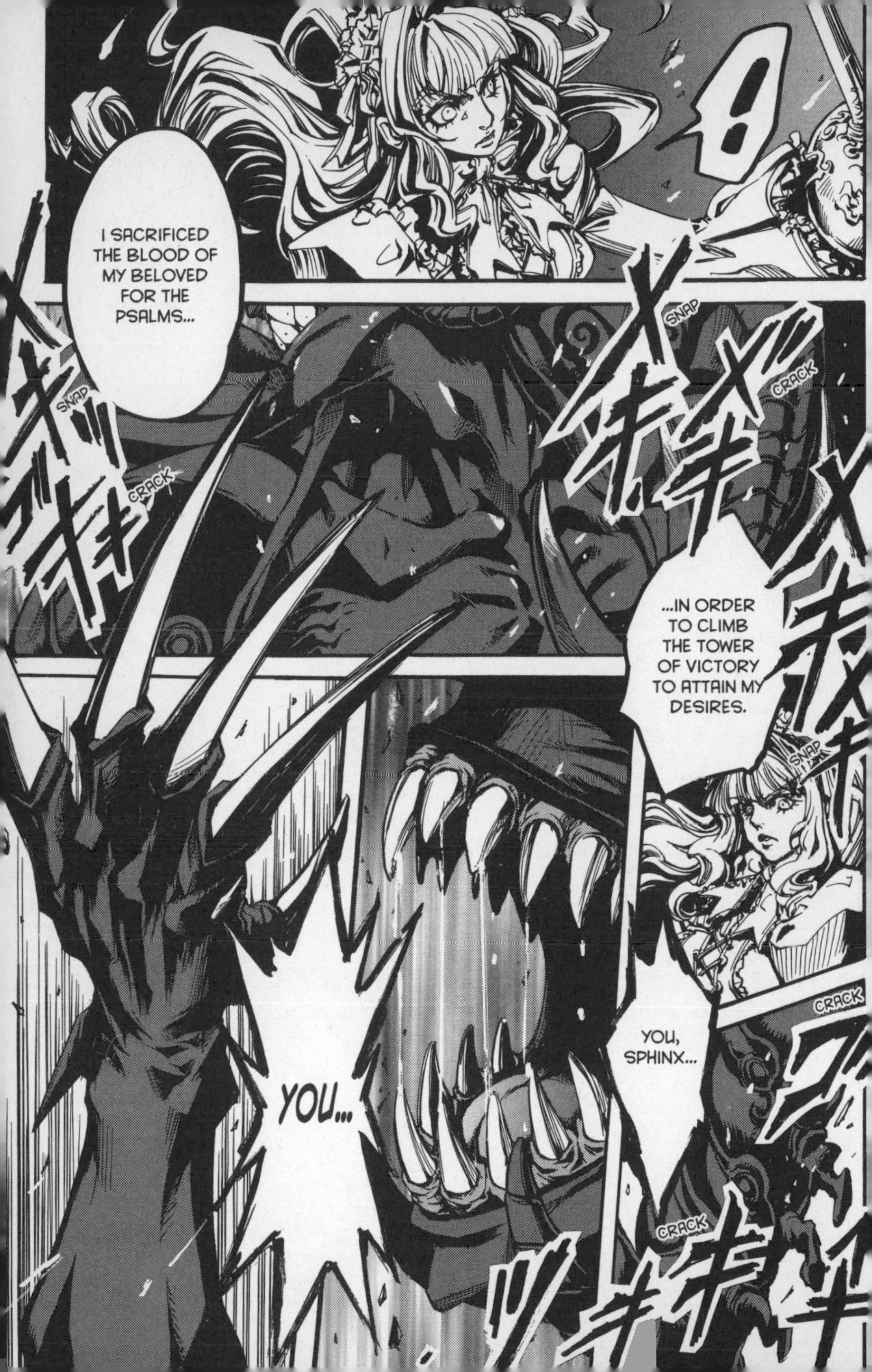
I SACRIFICED THE BLOOD OF MY BELOVED FOR THE PSALMS...
SNAP
CRACK
SNAP
CRACK
...IN ORDER TO CLIMB THE TOWER OF VICTORY TO ATTAIN MY DESIRES.
SNAP
CRACK
YOU, SPHINX...
YOU...
CRACK

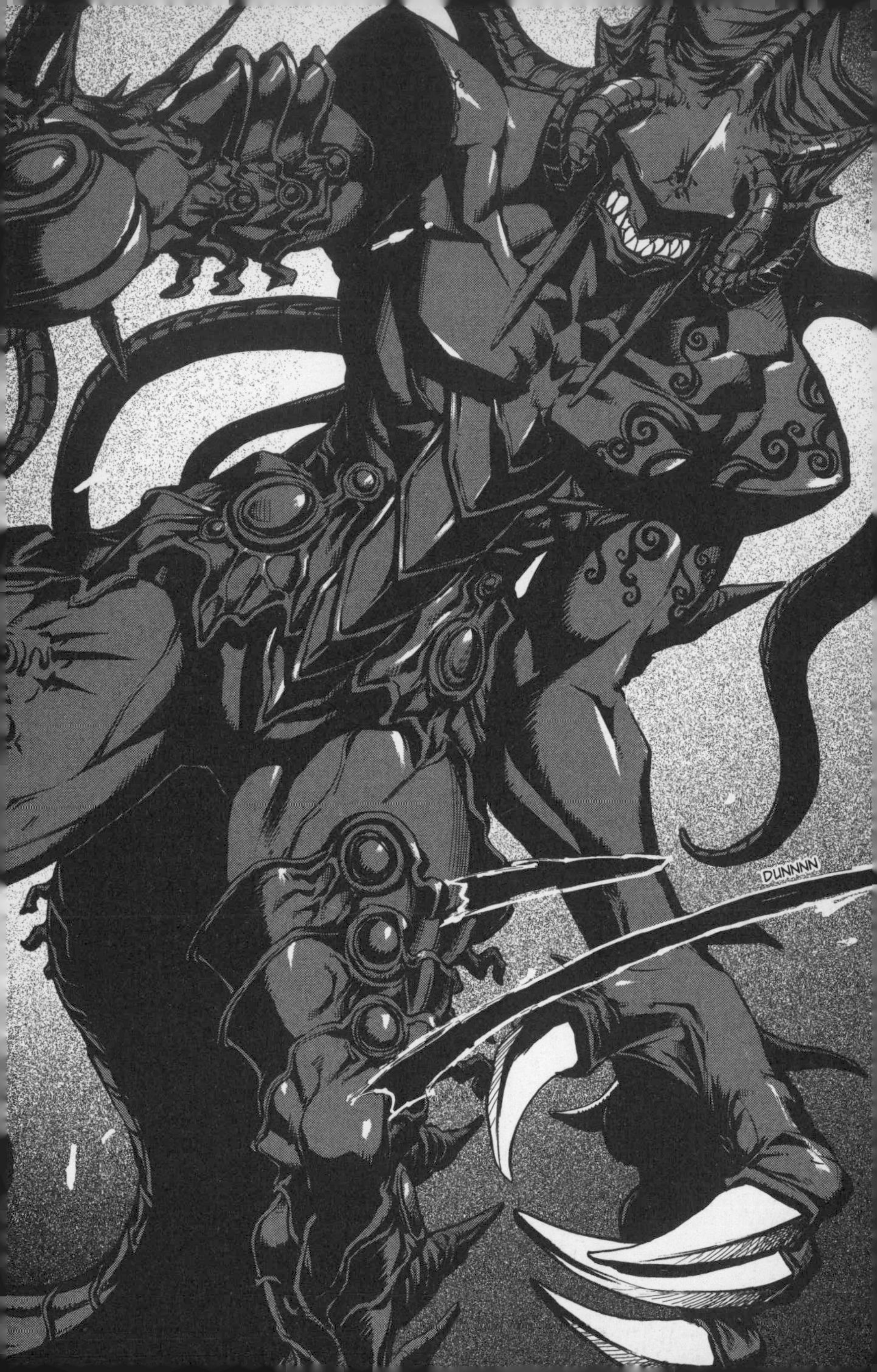
DUNNNN

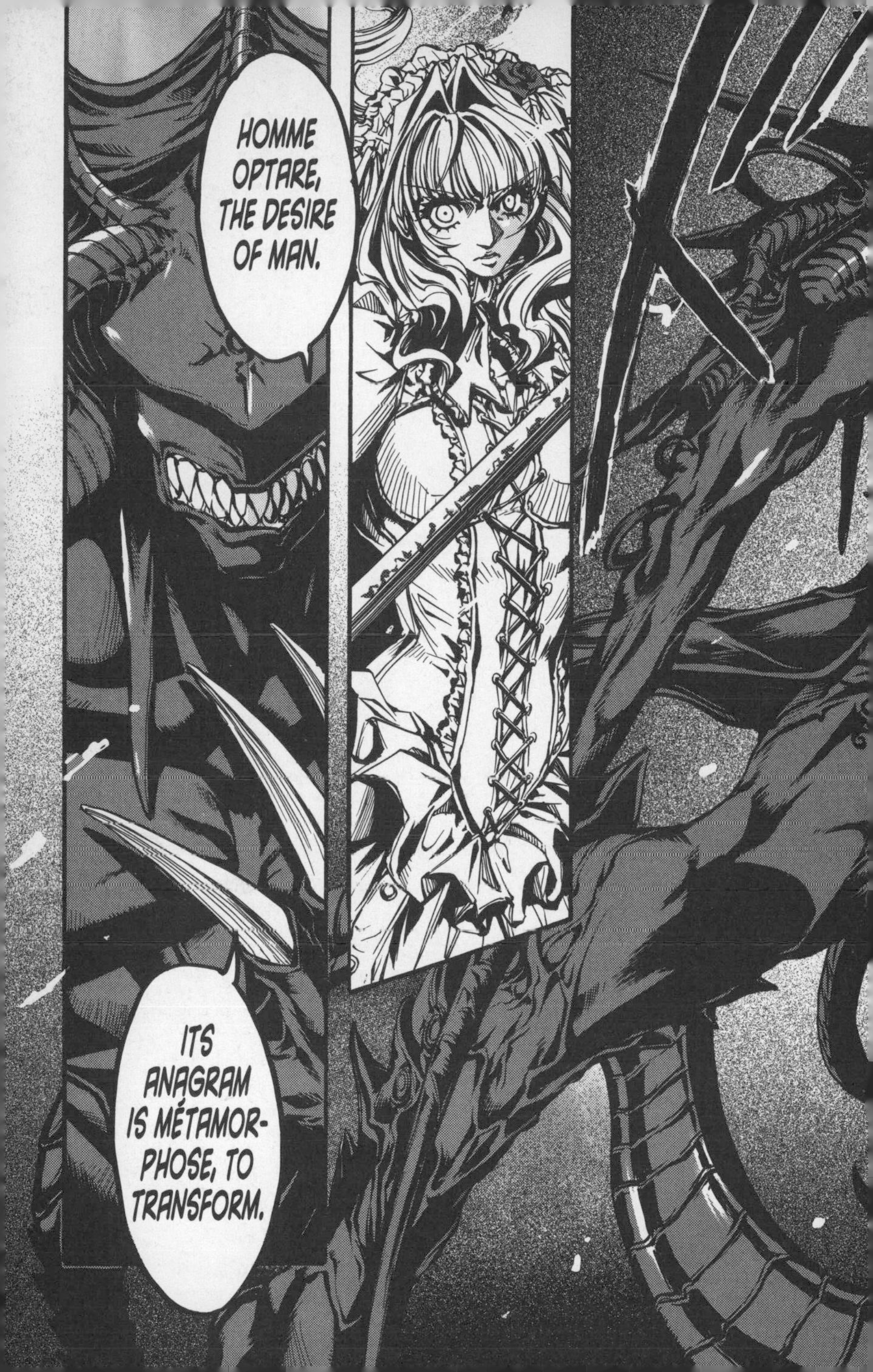
HOMME OPTARE, THE DESIRE OF MAN.
ITS ANAGRAM IS MÉTAMOR-PHOSE, TO TRANSFORM.

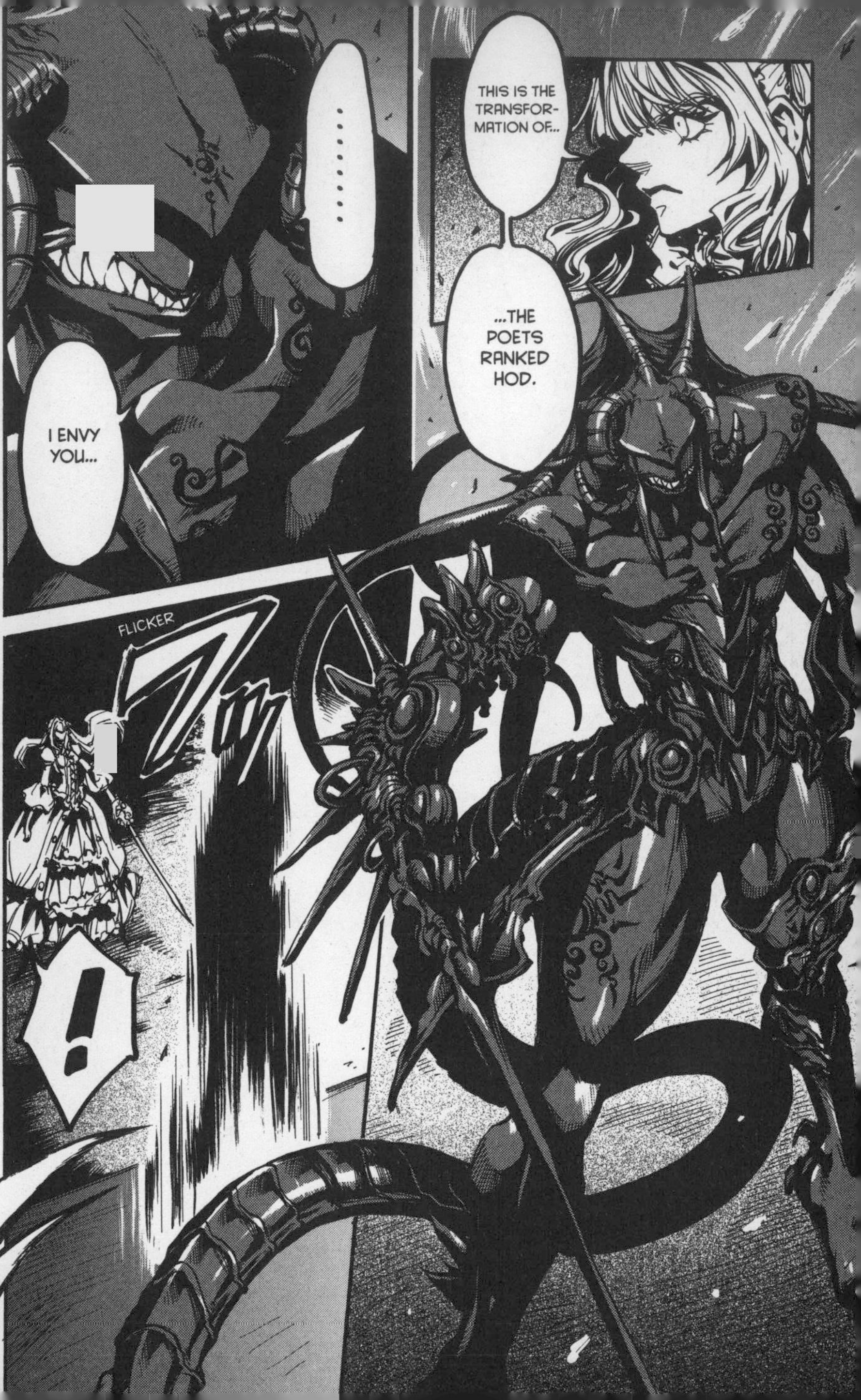
THIS IS THE TRANSFOR-MATION OF...
...THE POETS RANKED HOD.
......
I ENVY YOU...
FLICKER
!

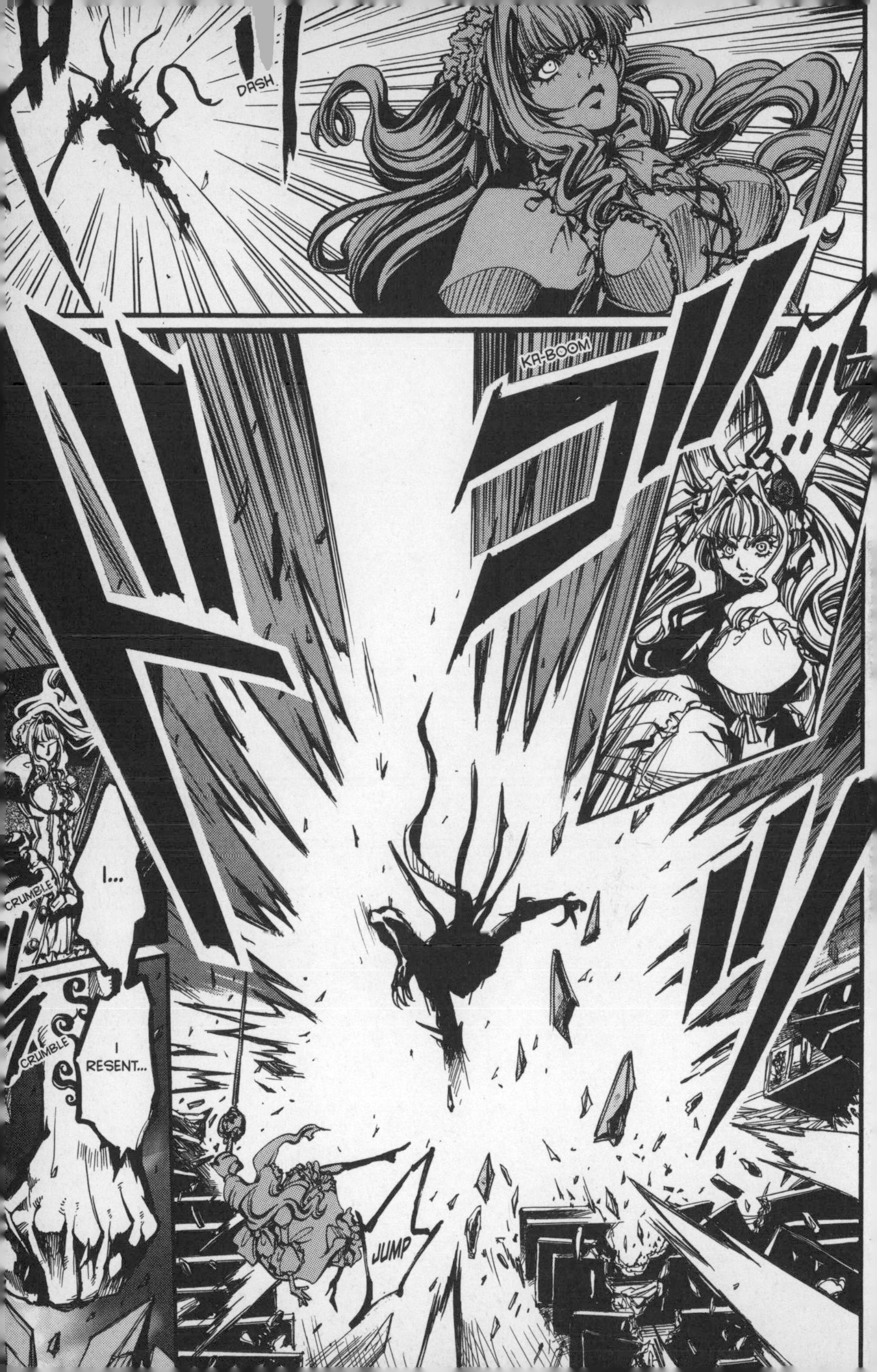
DASH
KA-BOOM
JUMP
I...
CRUMBLE
I RESENT...
CRUMBLE

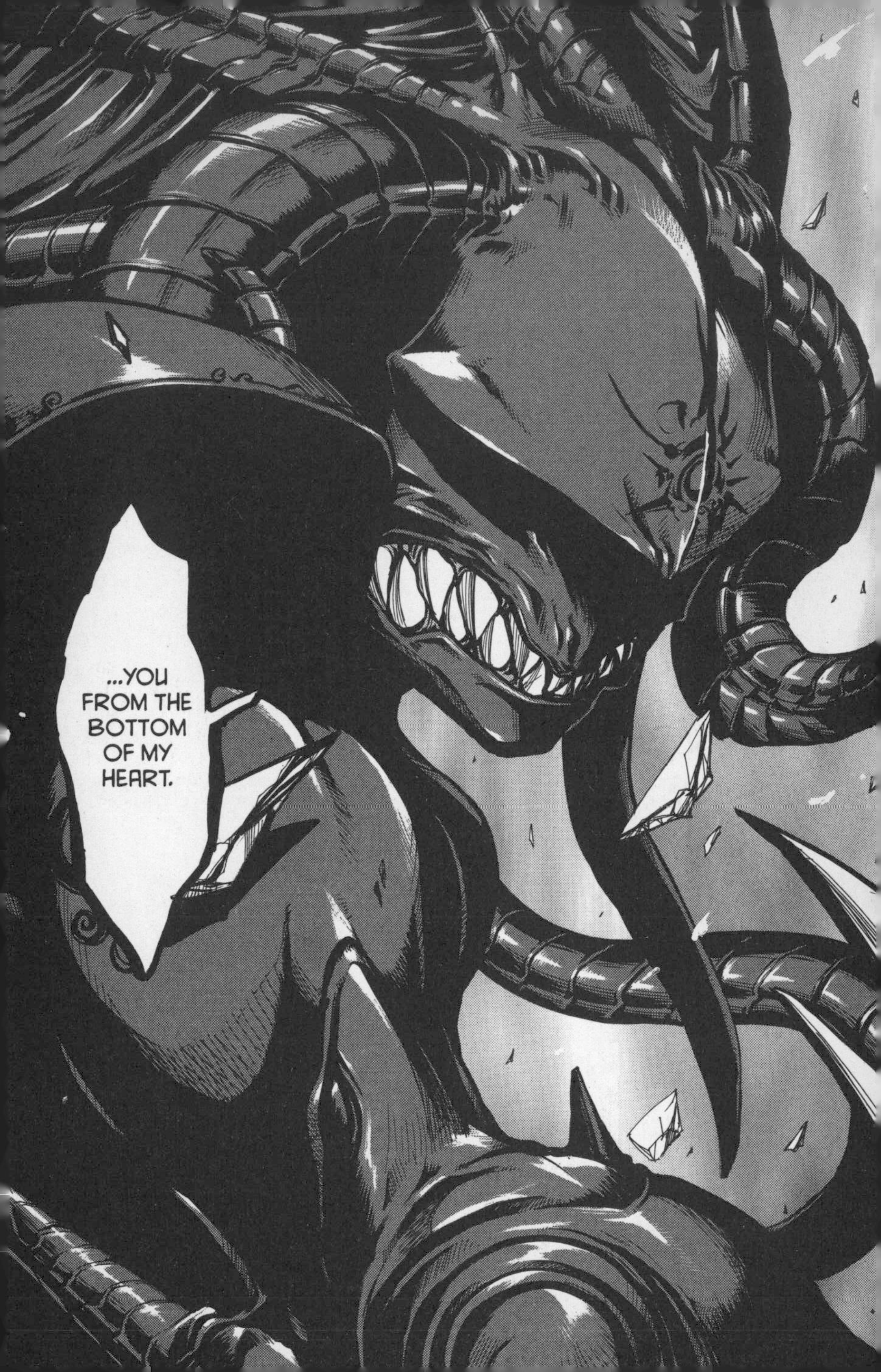
...YOU FROM THE BOTTOM OF MY HEART.

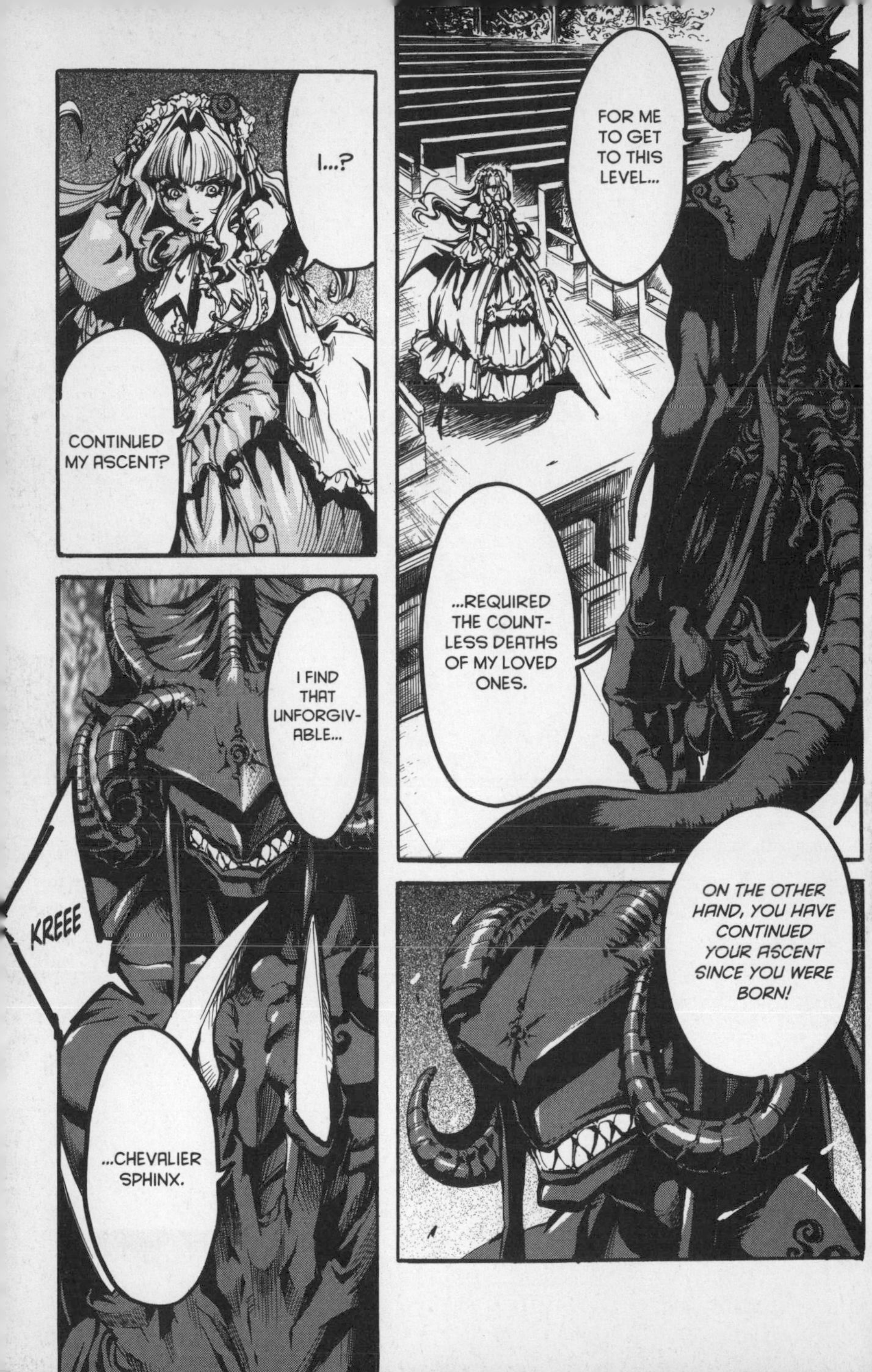
FOR ME TO GET TO THIS LEVEL...
...REQUIRED THE COUNT-LESS DEATHS OF MY LOVED ONES.
ON THE OTHER HAND, YOU HAVE CONTINUED YOUR ASCENT SINCE YOU WERE BORN!
I...?
CONTINUED MY ASCENT?
I FIND THAT UNFORGIV-ABLE...
KREEE
...CHEVALIER SPHINX.

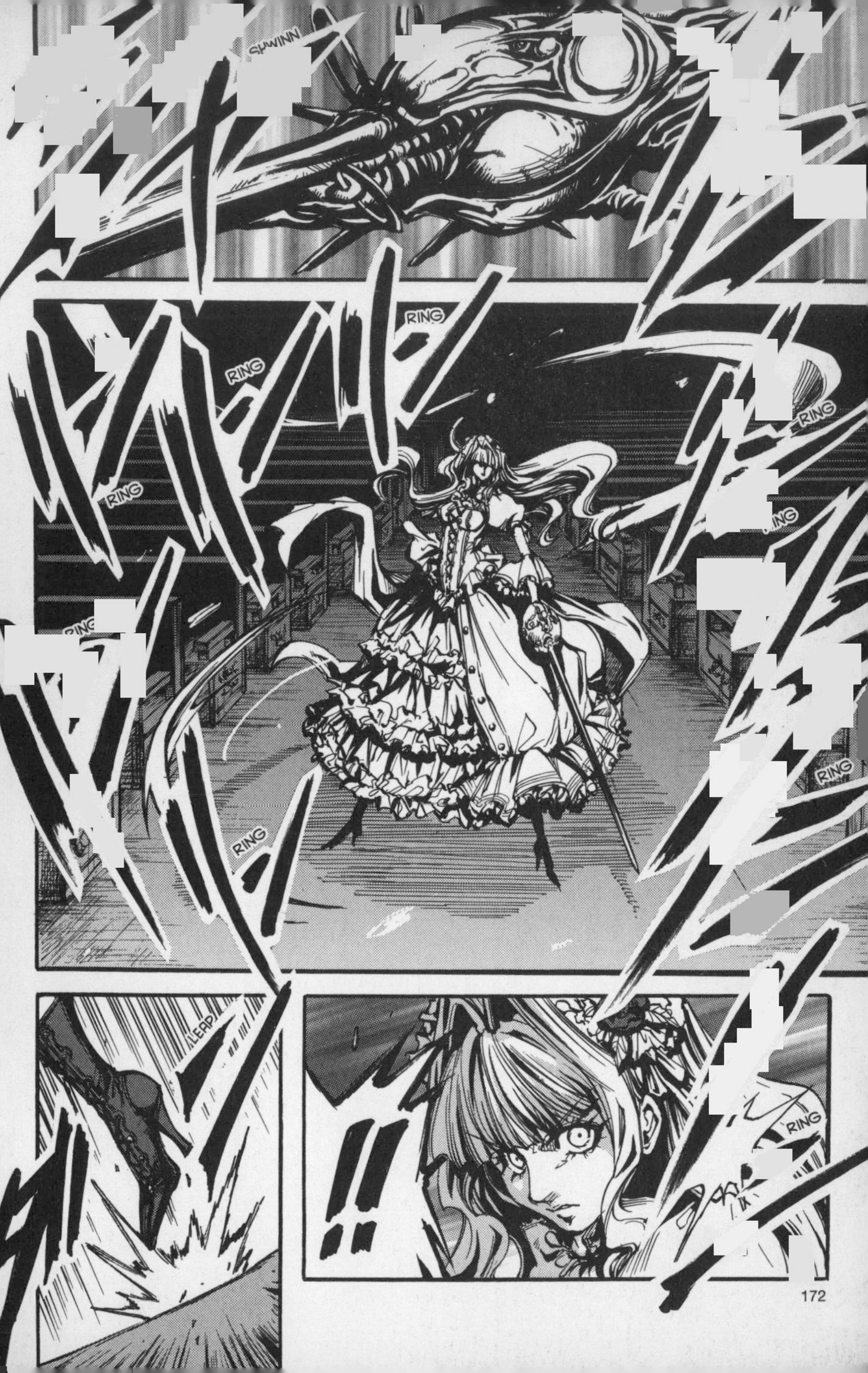

SHWINN
RING
RING
RING
RING
RING
RING
RING
RING
LEAP

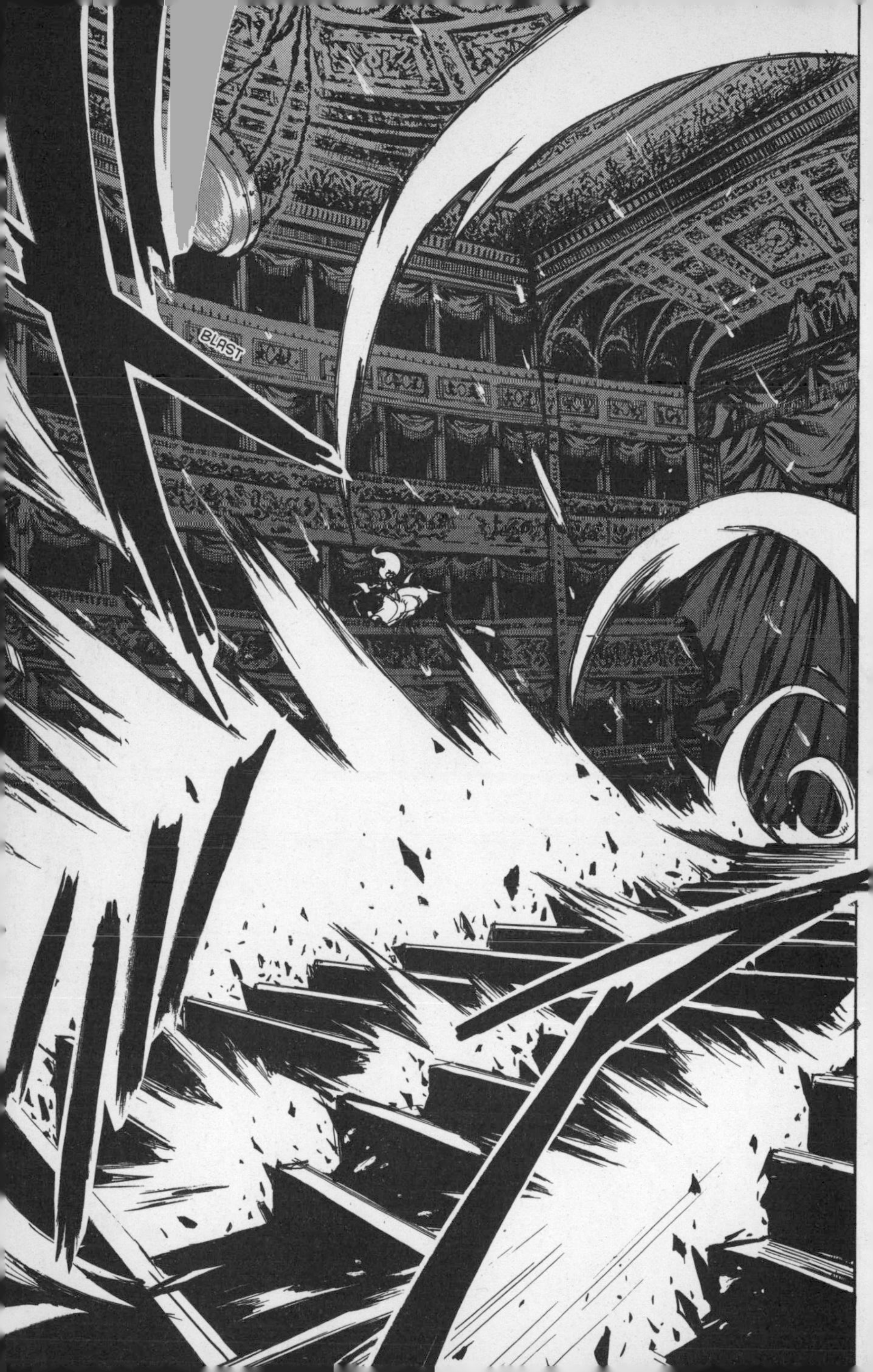
BLAST

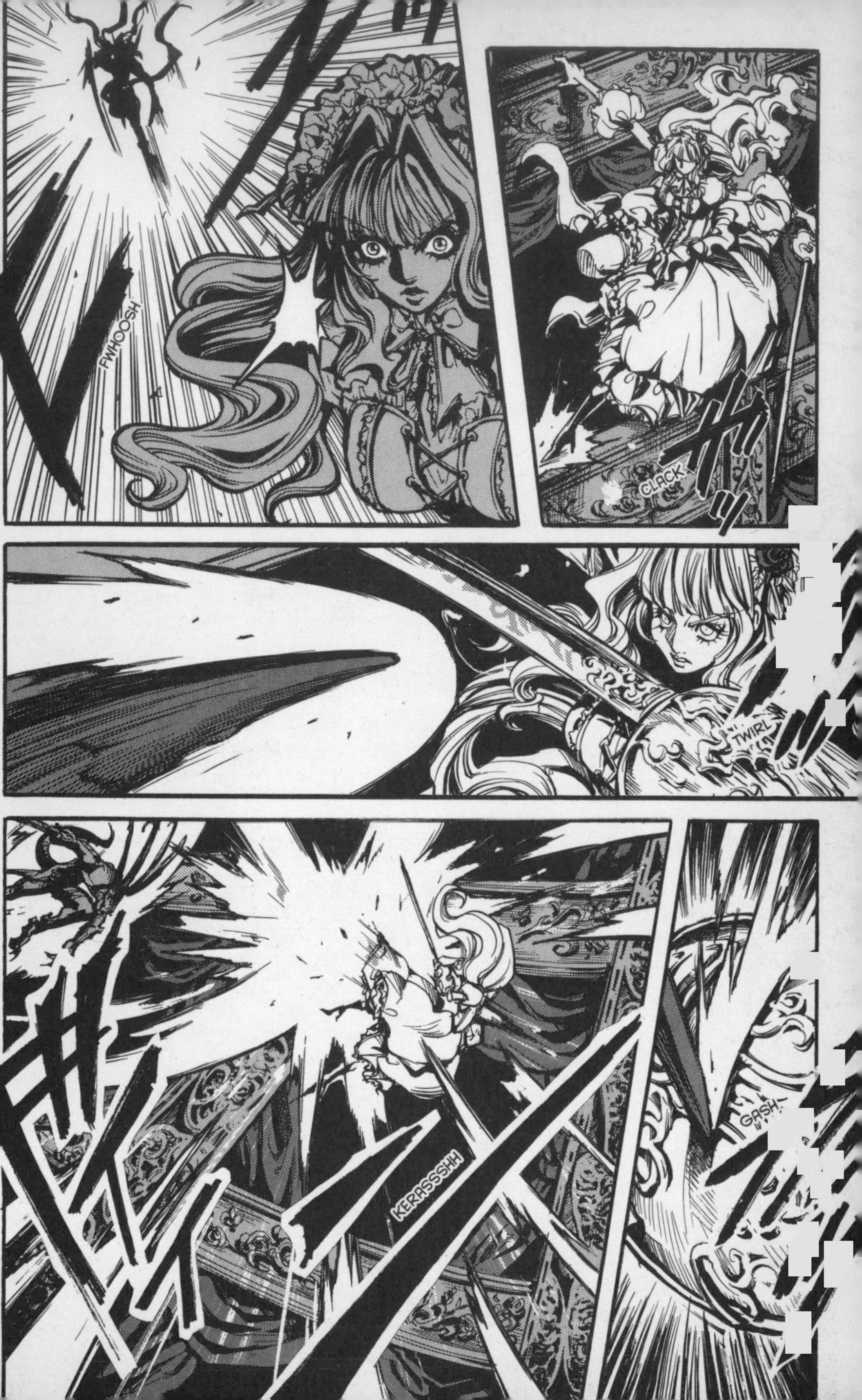
CLACK
FWHOOSH
TWIRL
GASH
KERASSSHH

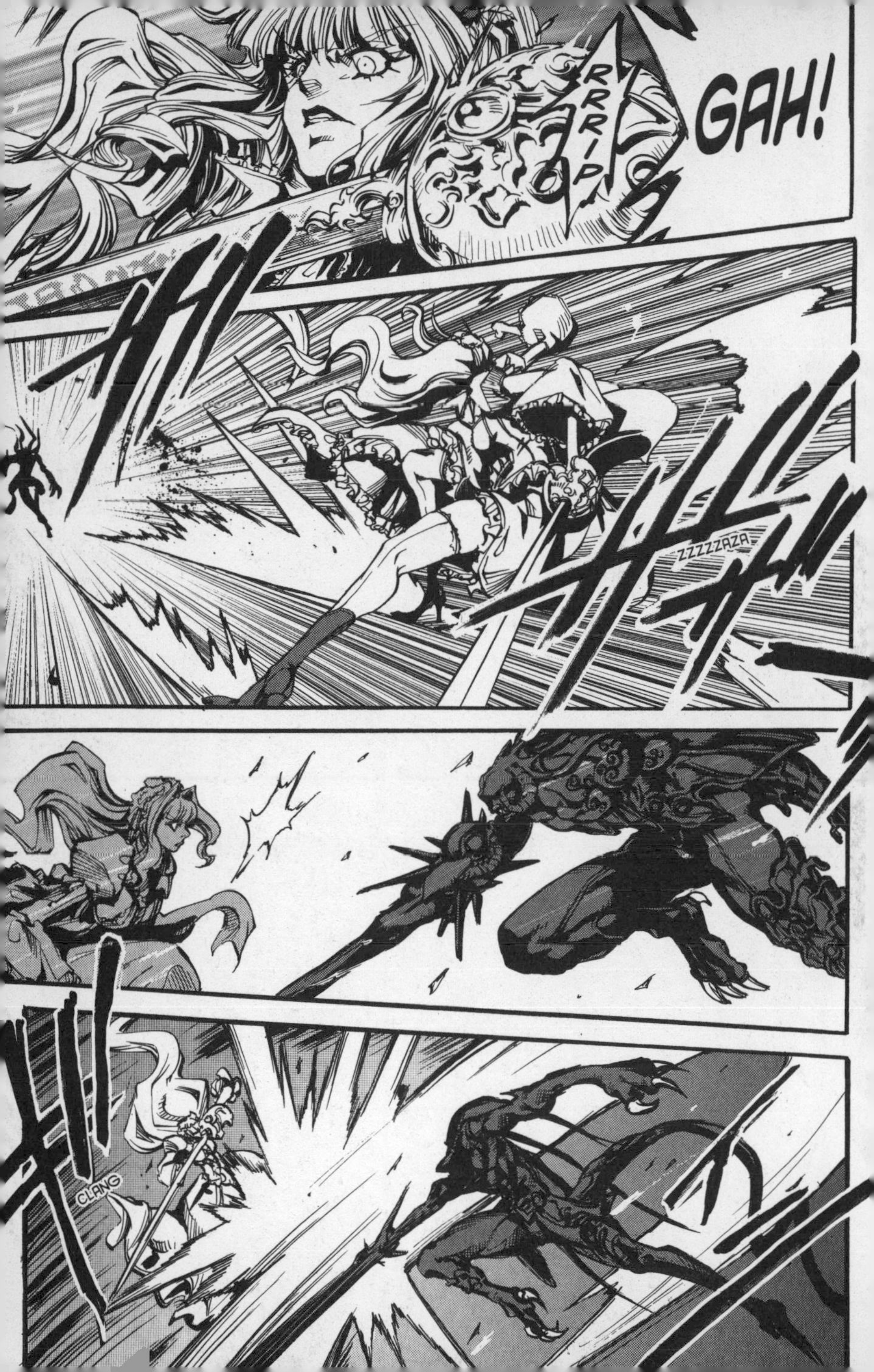
GAH!
RRRRIP
ZZZZZZAZA
CLANG

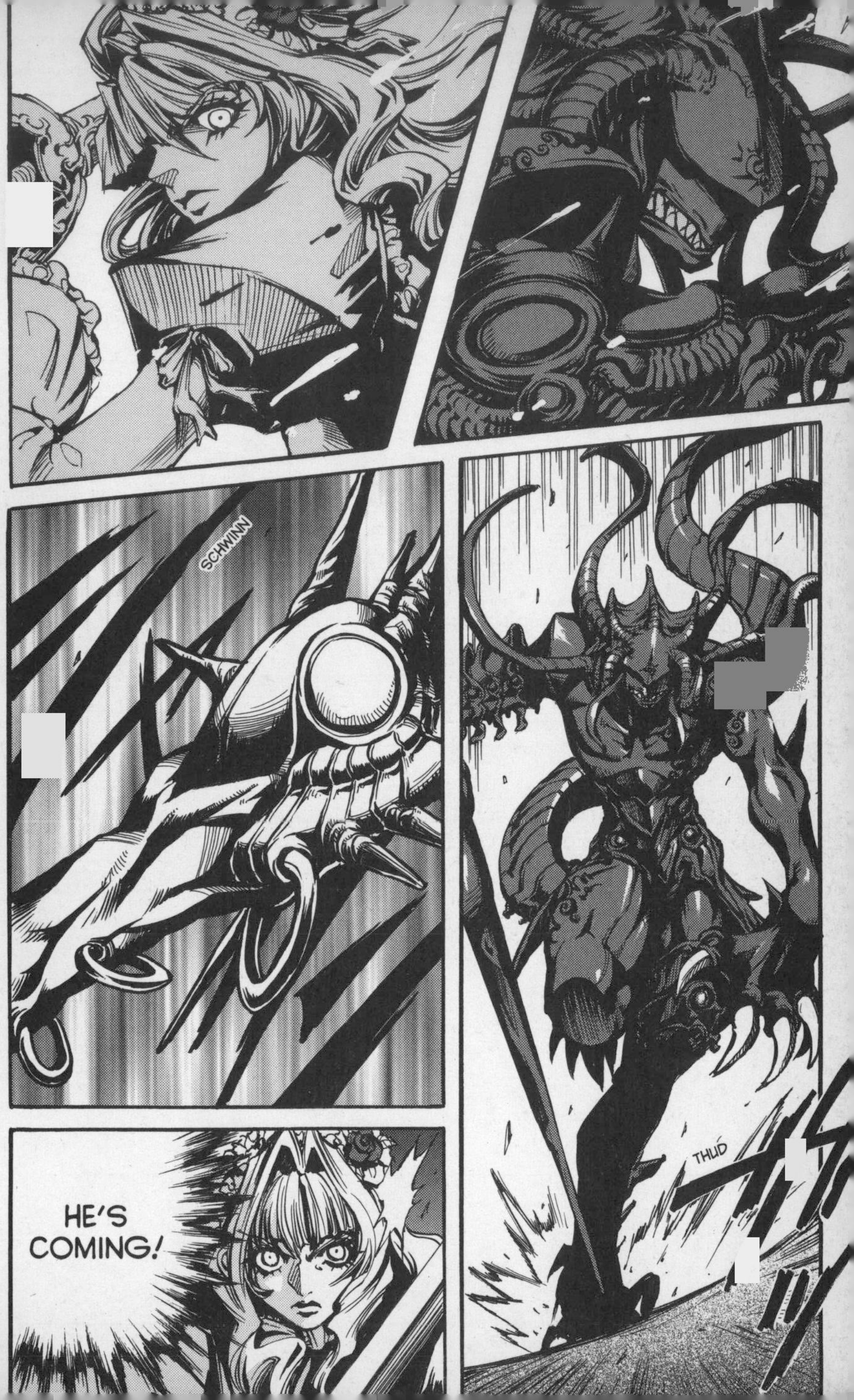
SCHWINN
THUD
HE'S COMING!

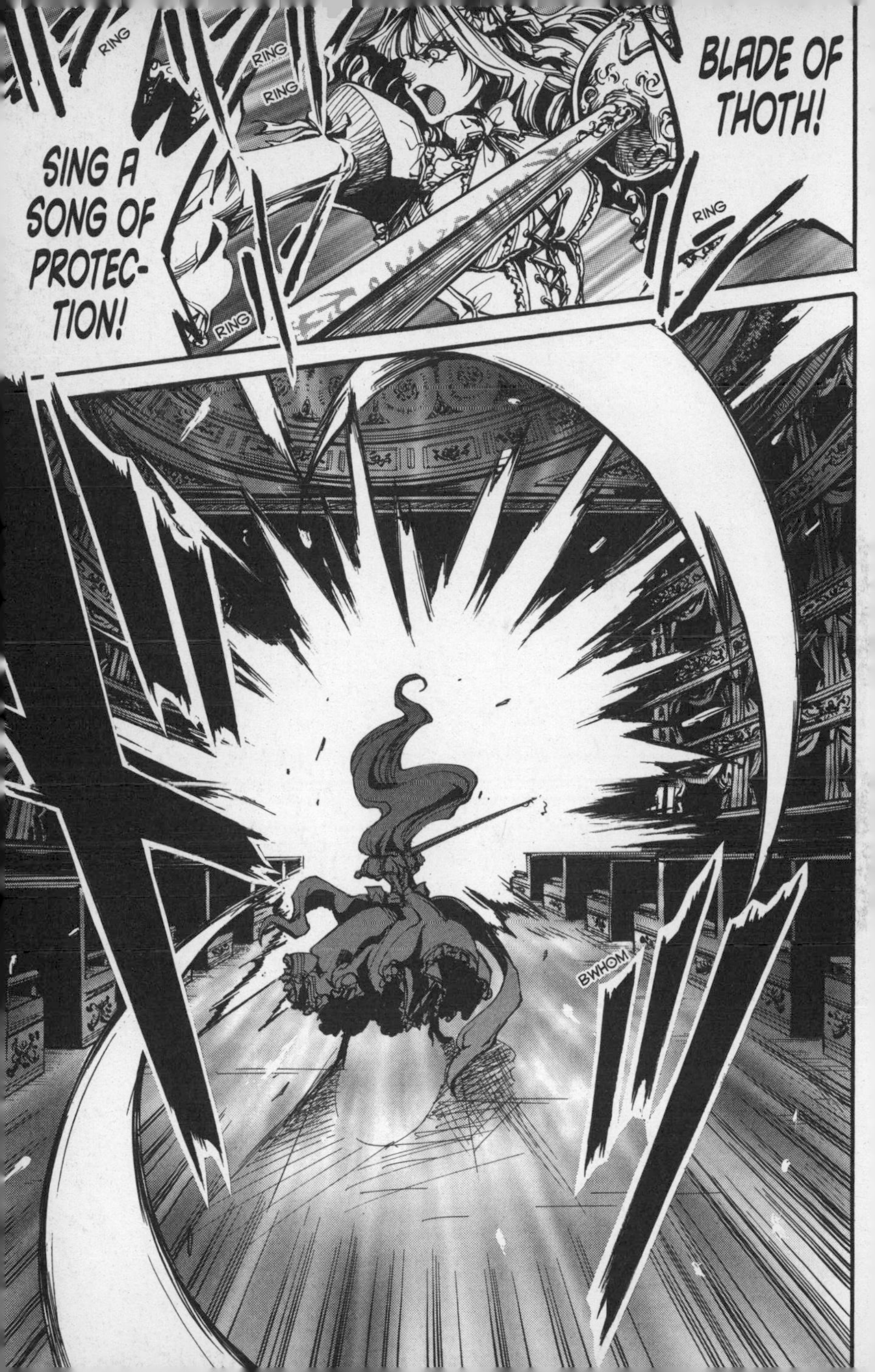
BLADE OF THOTH!
RING
RING
RING
RING
SING A SONG OF PROTECTION!
RING
BWHOM

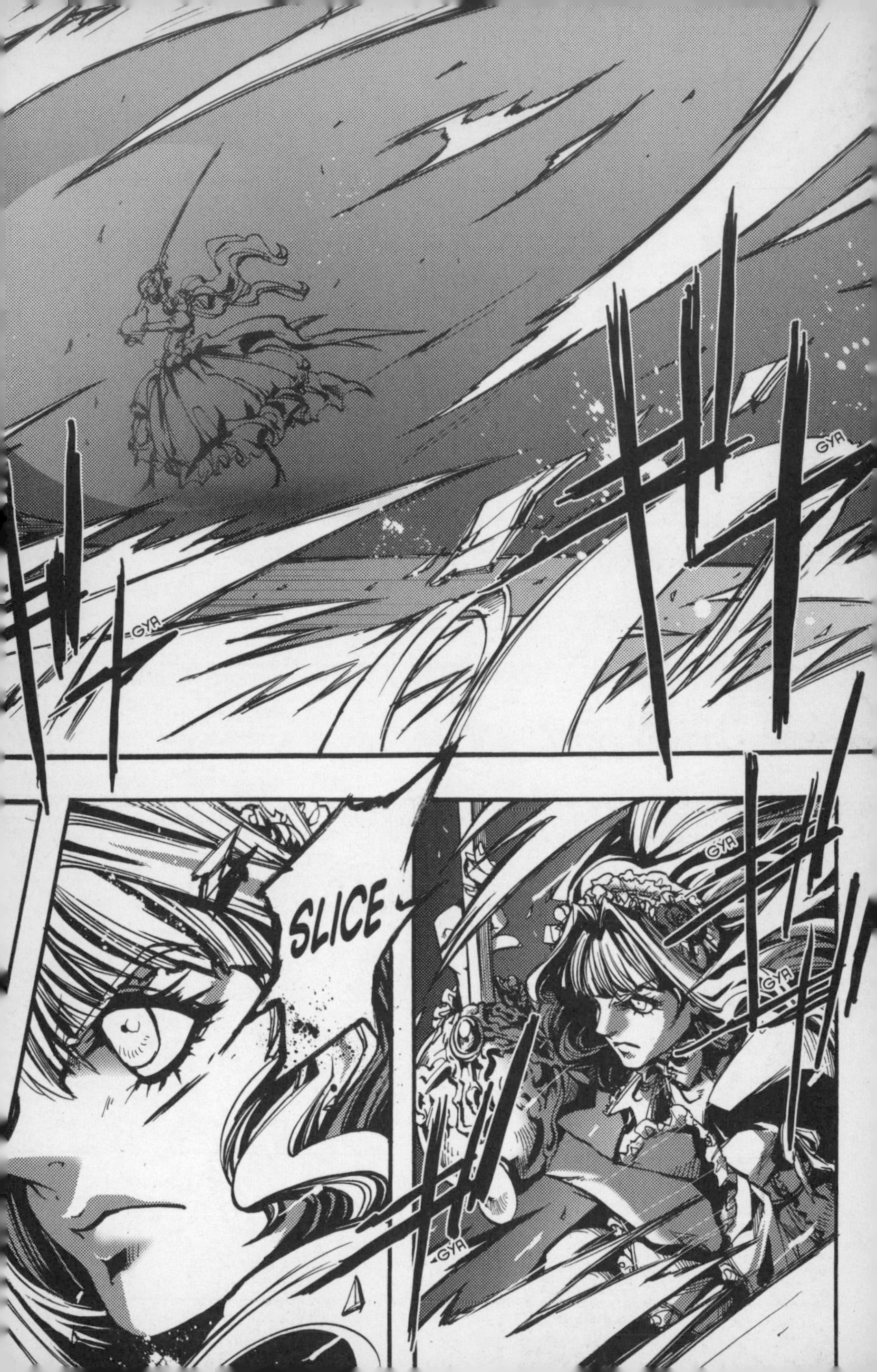
GYA
GYA
GYA
GYA
GYA
SLICE

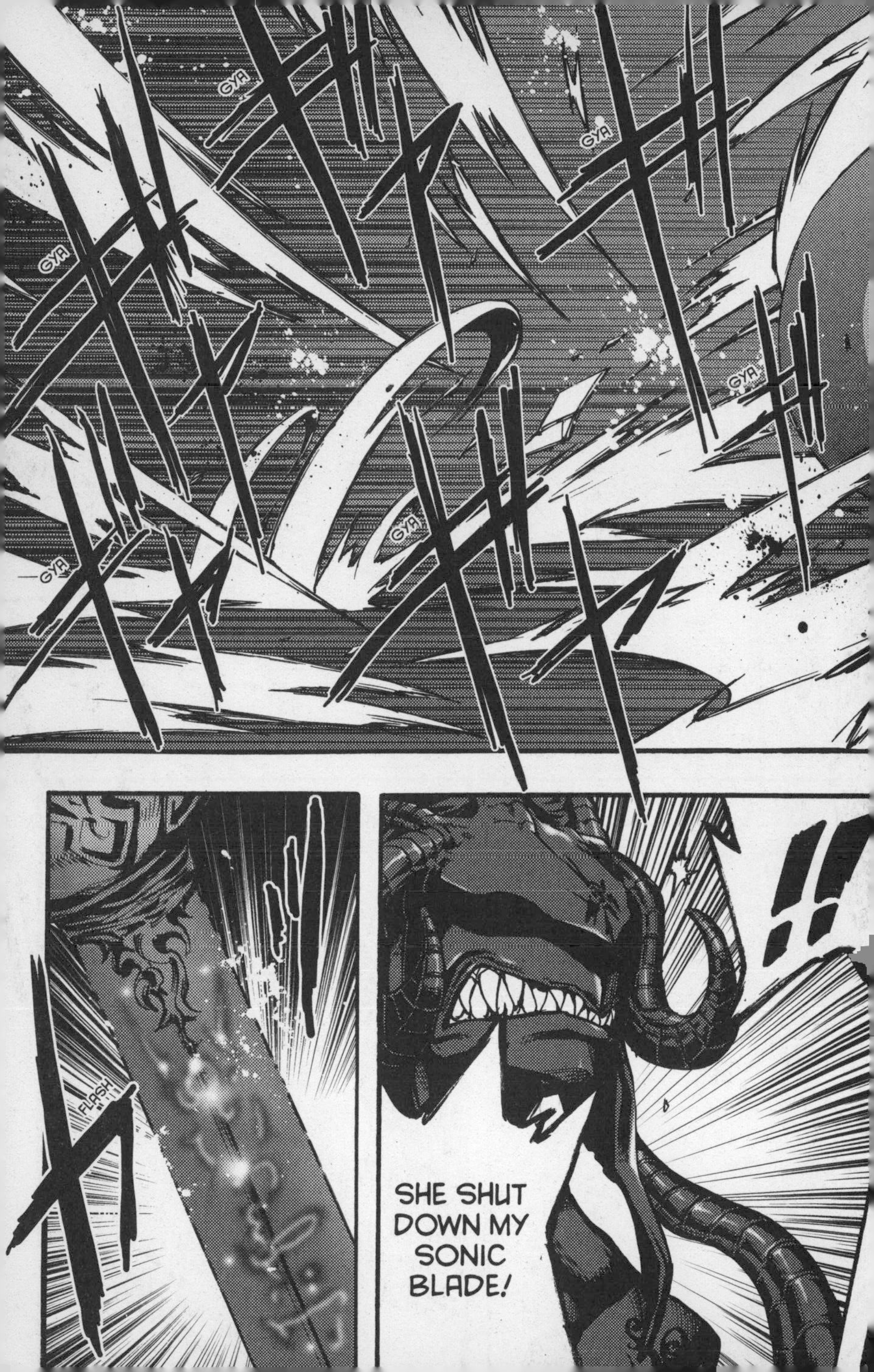
GYA
GYA
GYA
GYA
GYA
GYA
!!
SHE SHUT DOWN MY SONIC BLADE!
FLASH

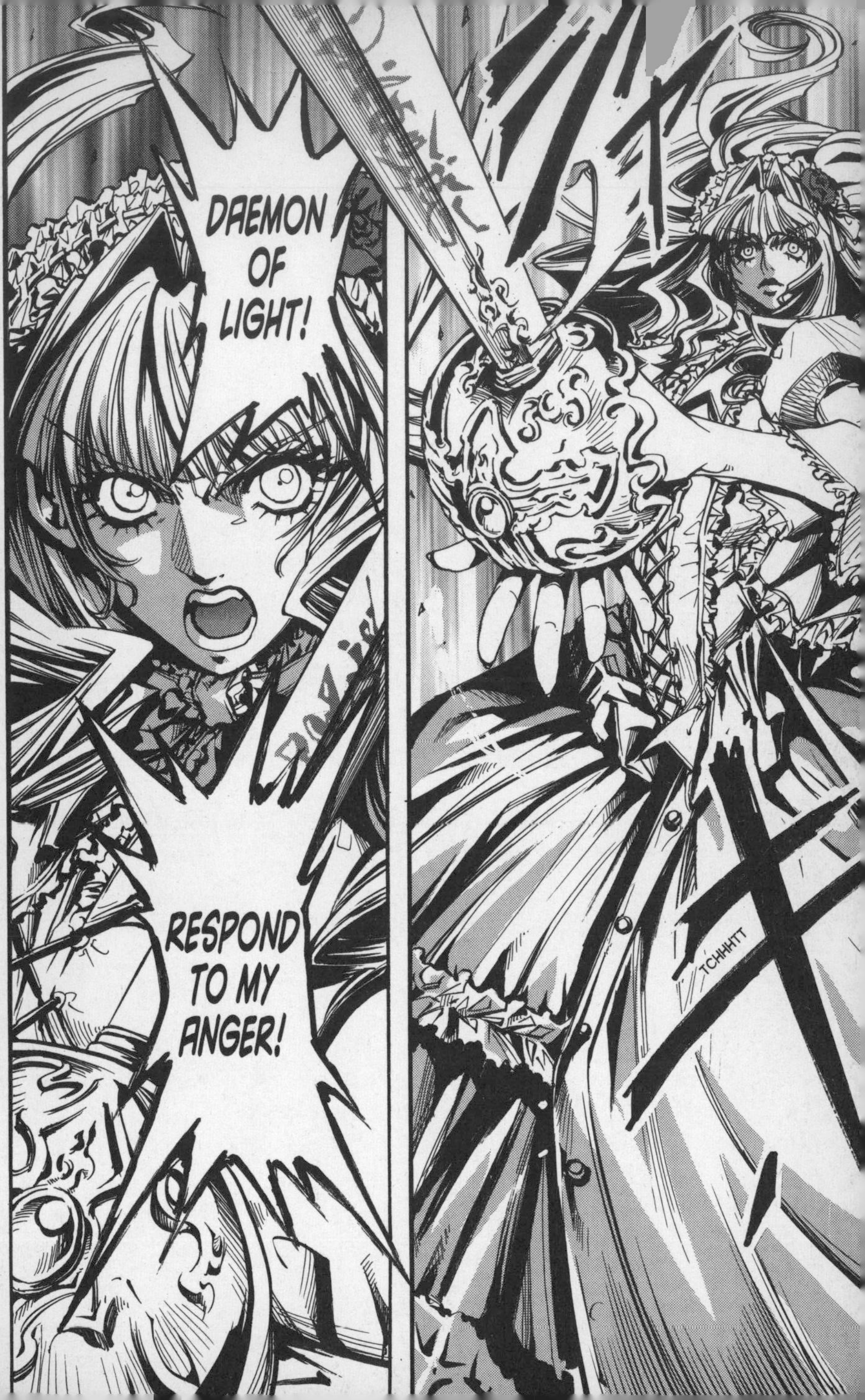
TCHHHTT
DAEMON OF LIGHT!
RESPOND TO MY ANGER!

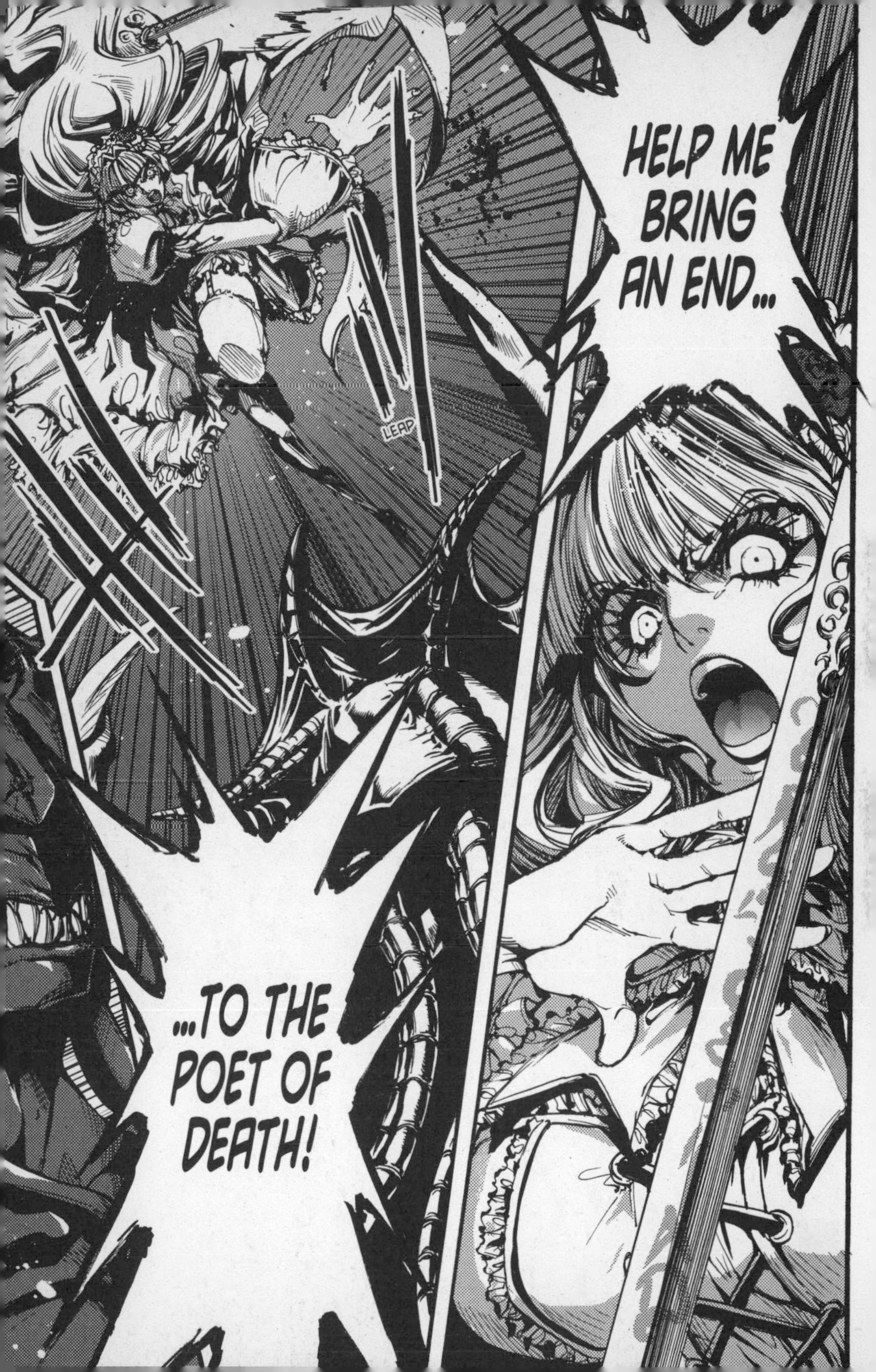
HELP ME BRING AN END...
LEAP
...TO THE POET OF DEATH!

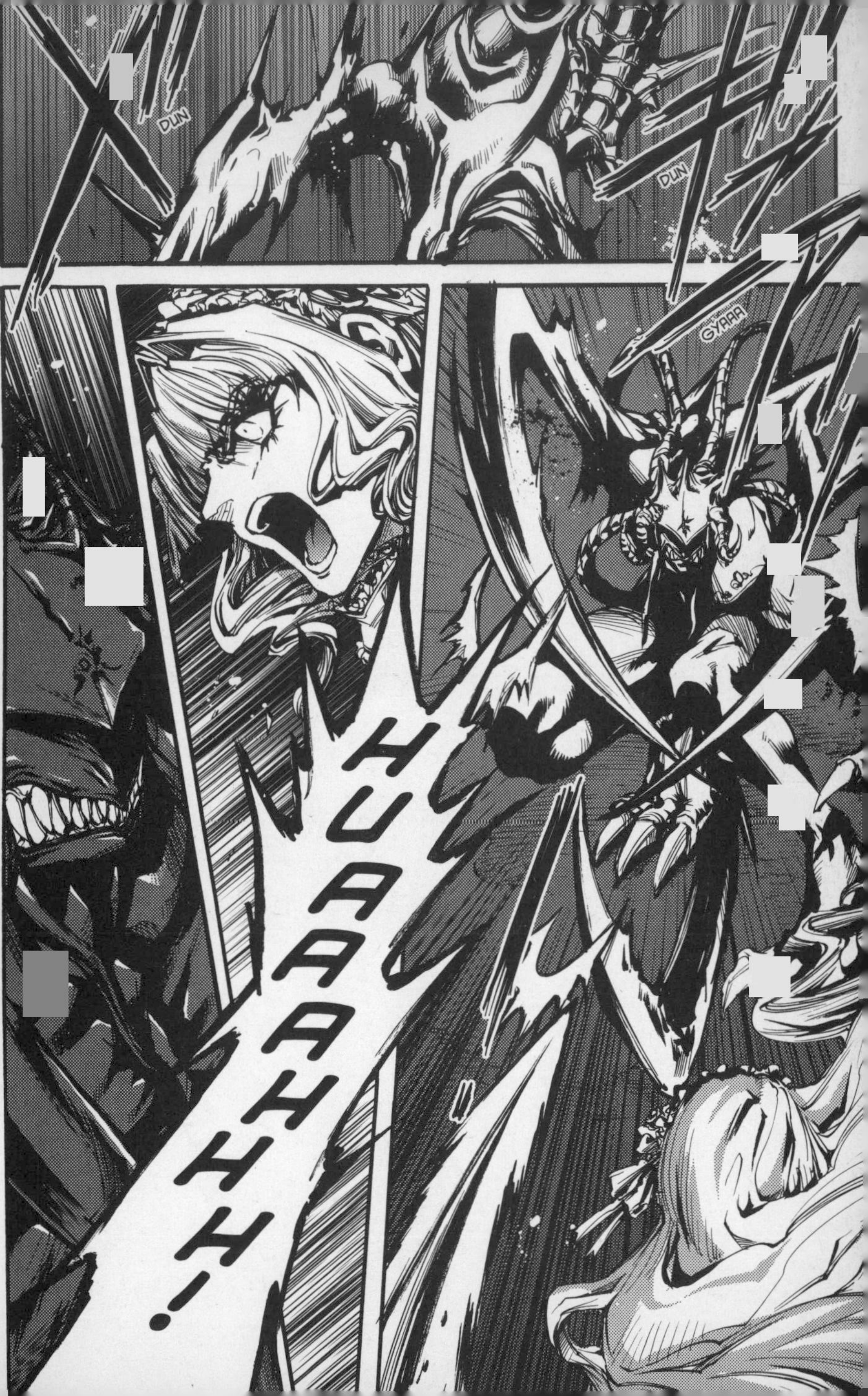
DUN
DUN
GYAAA
HUAAAHHH!

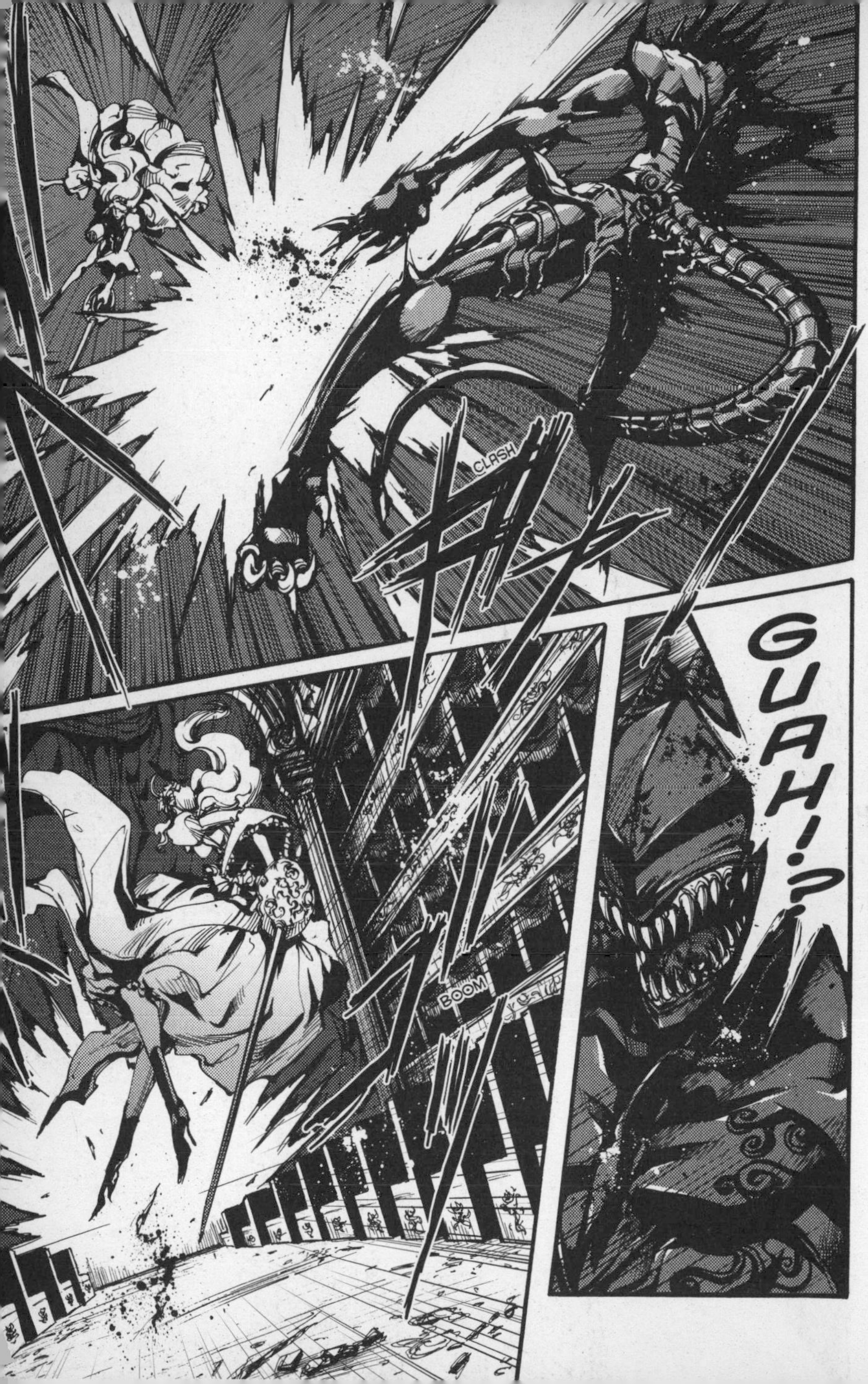
CLASH
GUAH!?
BOOM

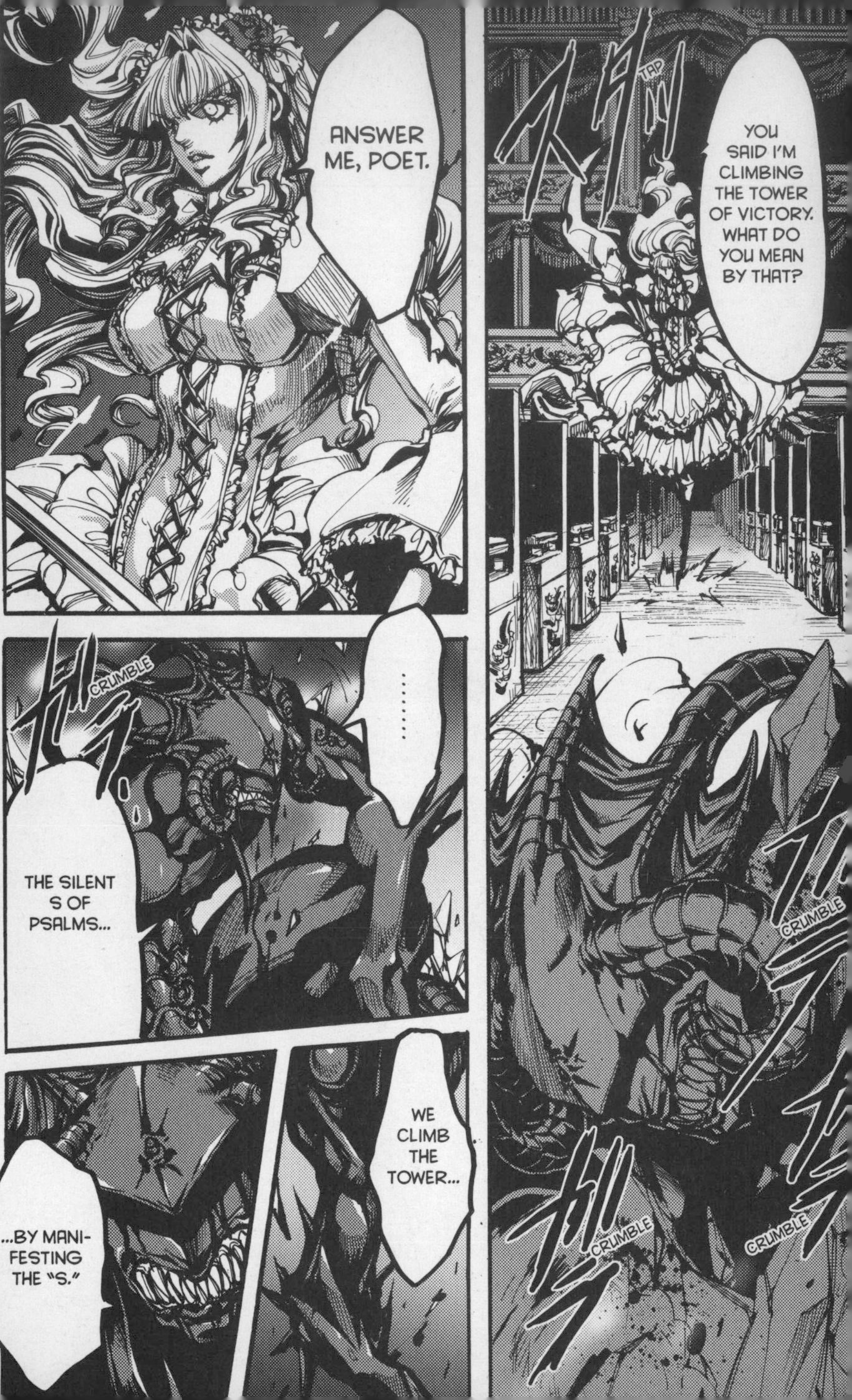
TAP
YOU SAID I'M CLIMBING THE TOWER OF VICTORY. WHAT DO YOU MEAN BY THAT?
CRUMBLE
CRUMBLE
CRUMBLE
ANSWER ME, POET.
CRUMBLE
......
THE SILENT S OF PSALMS...
WE CLIMB THE TOWER...
...BY MANI-FESTING THE "S."

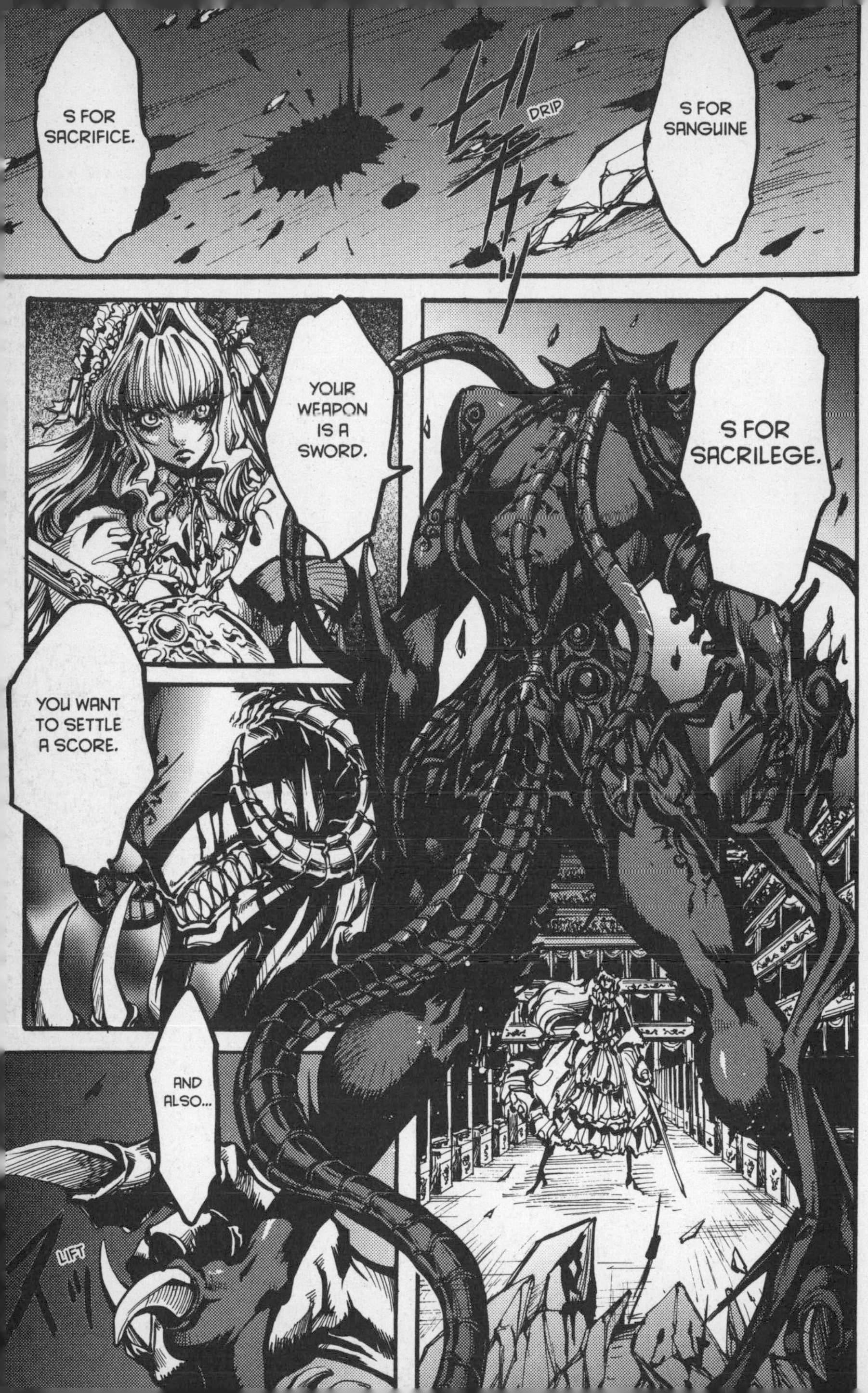
S FOR SANGUINE
DRIP
S FOR SACRIFICE.
S FOR SACRILEGE.
YOUR WEAPON IS A SWORD.
YOU WANT TO SETTLE A SCORE.
AND ALSO...
LIFT

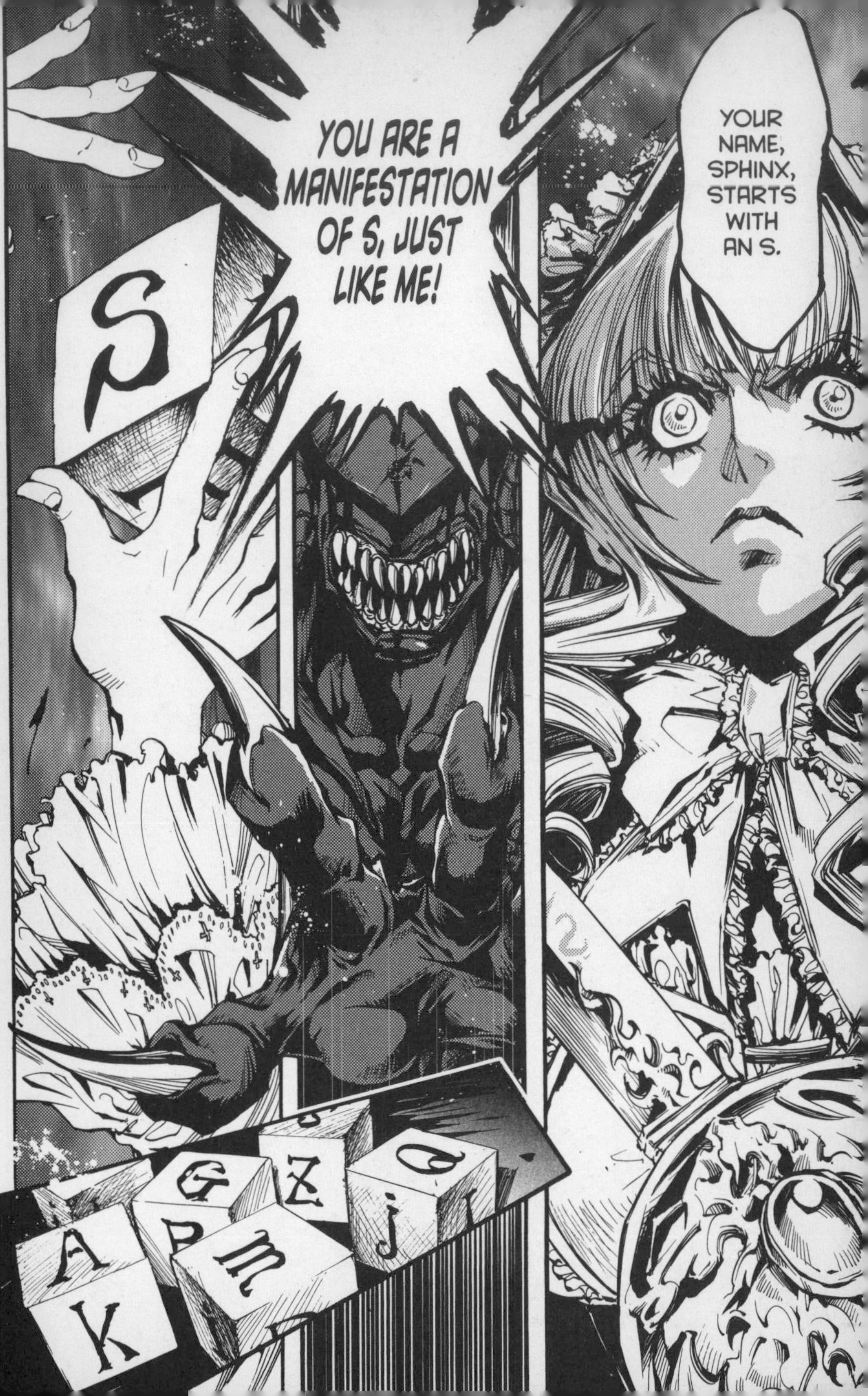
YOUR NAME, SPHINX, STARTS WITH AN S.
YOU ARE A MANIFESTATION OF S, JUST LIKE ME!

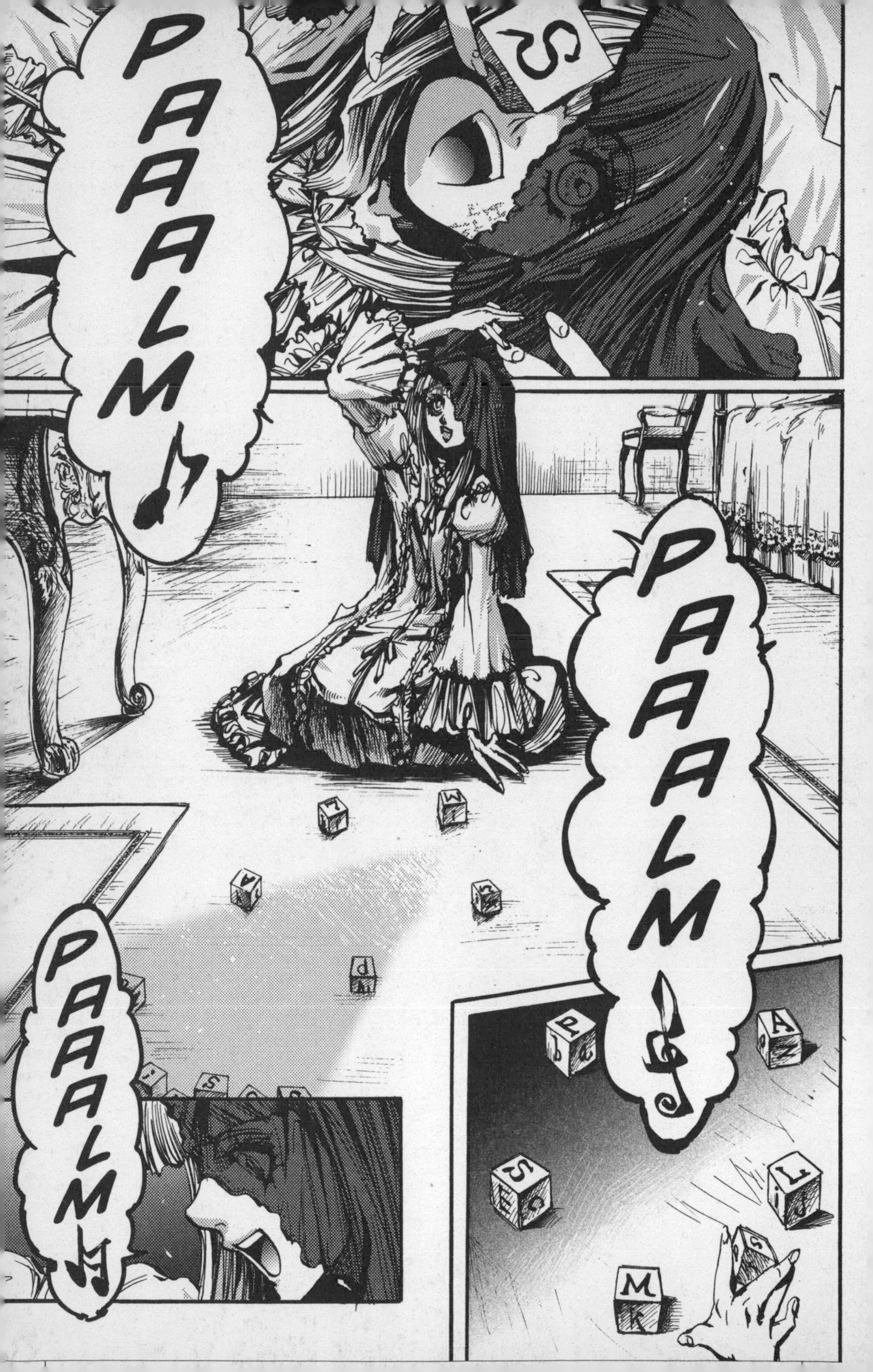
PAAALM♪
PAAALM♪
PAAALM♪

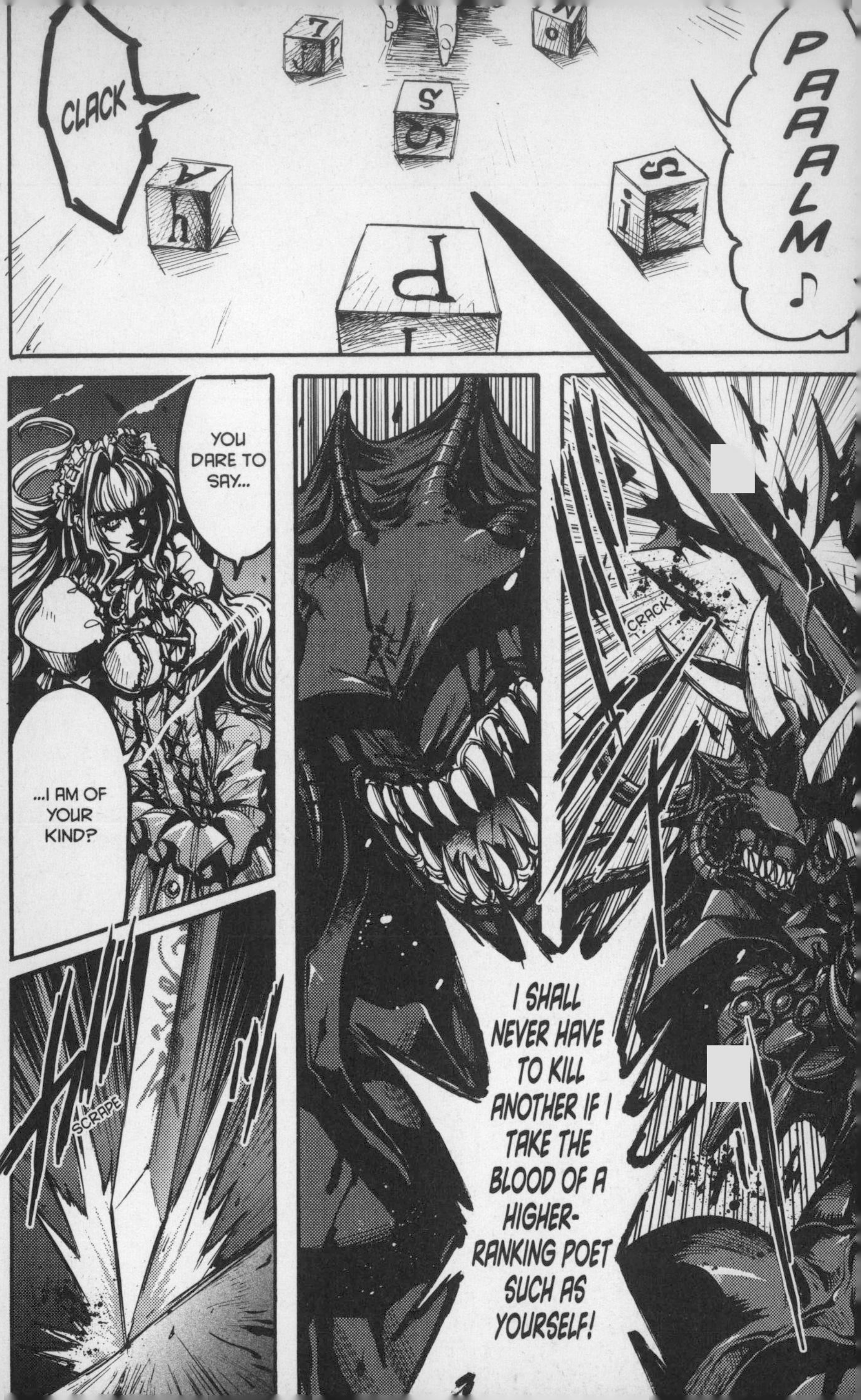
PAAALM♪
CLACK
CRACK
I SHALL NEVER HAVE TO KILL ANOTHER IF I TAKE THE BLOOD OF A HIGHER-RANKING POET SUCH AS YOURSELF!
YOU DARE TO SAY...
...I AM OF YOUR KIND?
SCRAPE

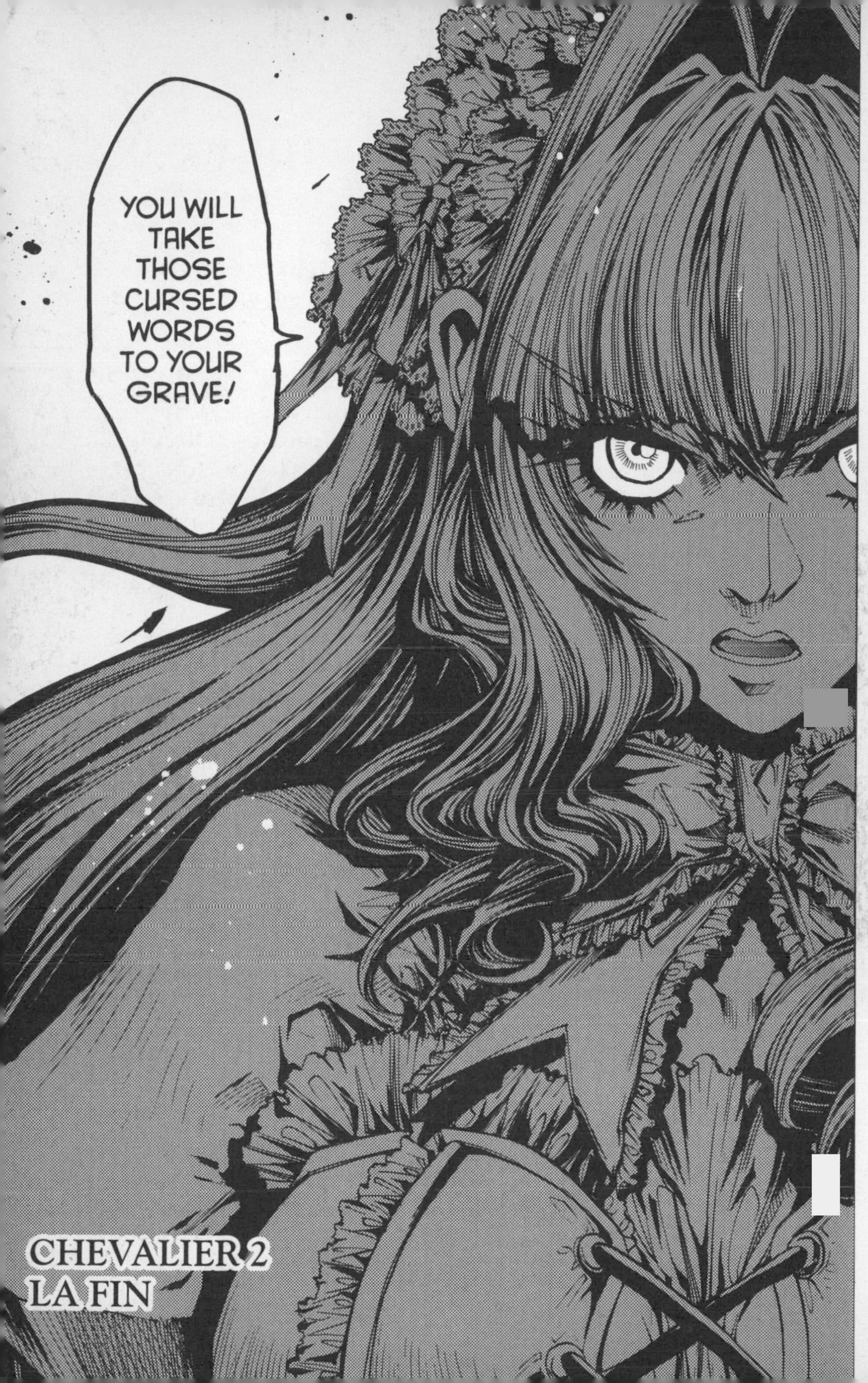
YOU WILL TAKE THOSE CURSED WORDS TO YOUR GRAVE!
CHEVALIER 2 LA FIN

IN THE BEGINNING WAS THE WORD...

Le Chevalier d'Eon has progressed to volume 2 thanks to your support! New characters are being introduced, and the mystery of the Psalms deepens.

D'Alembert's name remains in history books due to his role in writing and editing the world's first encyclopedia. It was an ambitious project that attempted to explain the natural world through the eyes of science. He questioned the Christian worldview that was dominant at the time. As a result, his work was criticized by the aristocracy and the church. He was a rebel and, to me, almost a heavy-metal type of character. As a result, I think Yumeji-san's decision to make d'Alembert resemble Marilyn Manson was appropriate.

On the other hand, Louis XV was an enigmatic character and was not well understood by his own court. The fact that he started his own secret police points to a very authoritarian and secretive nature. However, he apparently had a social side that relished balls and theater and found enjoyment in various hobbies. Why did he create Le Secret du Roi? When that question is answered, will the mystery behind the poets and Lia's death become clear?

D'Eon gives his flesh to help his sister find salvation.

The battles to come are only bound to become more difficult...

I hope you can't wait to read more!

Tou Ubukata

Thank you for your purchase!

夢路キリコ 2006

KIRIKO YUMEJI
2006

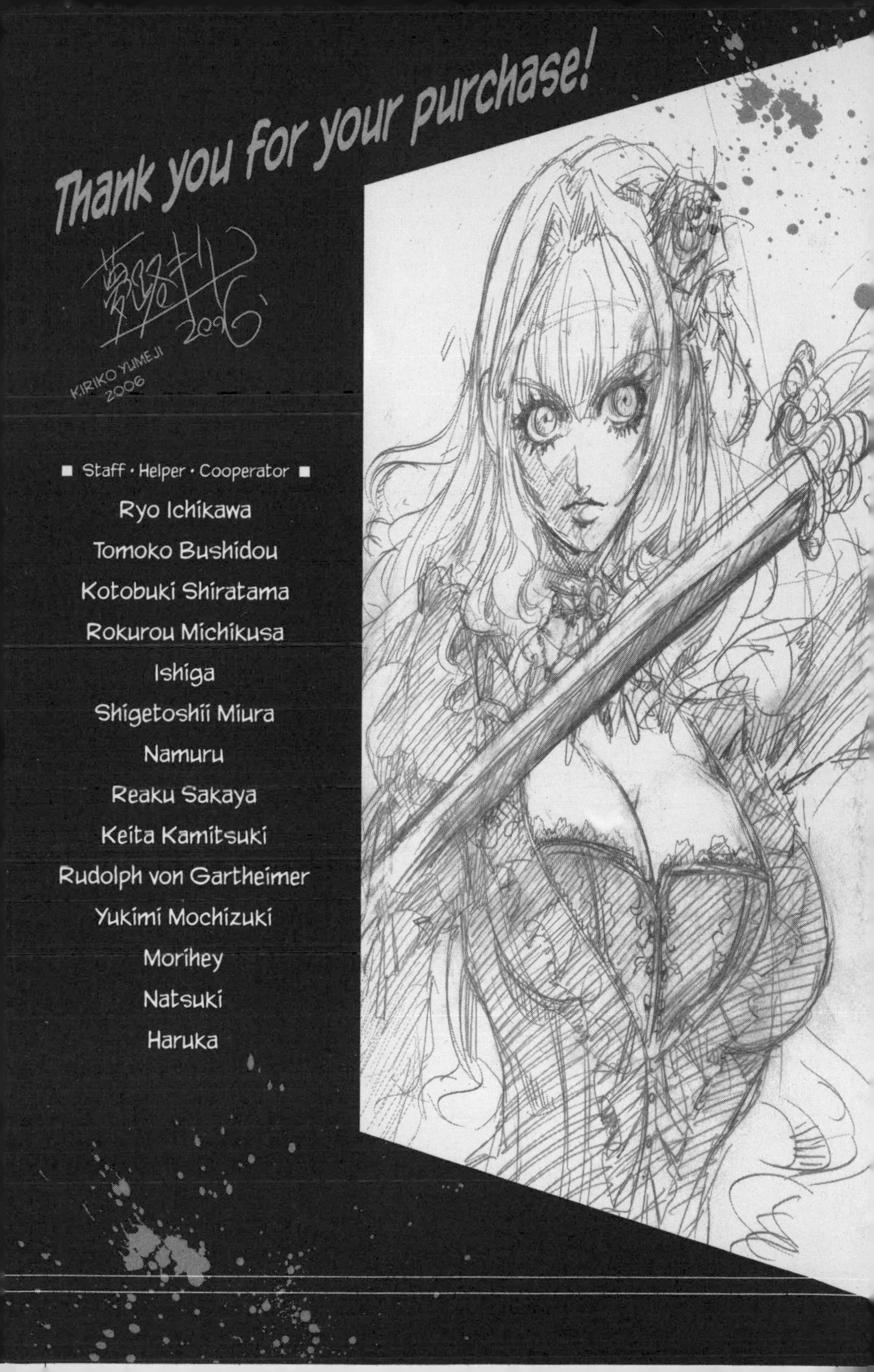

■ Staff · Helper · Cooperator ■

Ryo Ichikawa

Tomoko Bushidou

Kotobuki Shiratama

Rokurou Michikusa

Ishiga

Shigetoshii Miura

Namuru

Reaku Sakaya

Keita Kamitsuki

Rudolph von Gartheimer

Yukimi Mochizuki

Morihey

Natsuki

Haruka

Translation Notes

Though *Le Chevalier d'Eon* was created by a Japanese artist and writer, it is set in eighteenth-century France, and its unique mythology is made up of various elements of Western languages, history, philosophy, and theology. Understanding these references will enrich your reading experience. Here are notes on some of the allusions to Western culture you'll find in *Le Chavailier d'Eon*.

Le Secret du Roi, *page 3*

Le Secret du Roi, or the King's Secret, really did exist. It was the king's personal secret-service agency and a personal creation of King Louis XV. It was also known as the Black Cabinet. In addition to standard spy work like intelligence-gathering, Louis also used Le Secret du Roi to keep an eye on his ministers and advance French interests in the Far East. Despite being the subject of many rumors, Le Secret du Roi's existence was only officially confirmed just a few days before Louis XV's death.

Je te prie de m'excuser, *page 4*

In volume 1, a dead young woman was discovered on the riverbank with this phrase inscribed on her face. It is French for "Please forgive me."

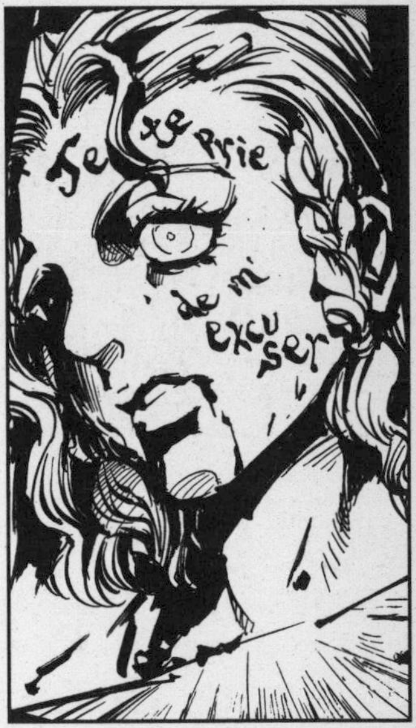
Je te prie
de m'
excuser

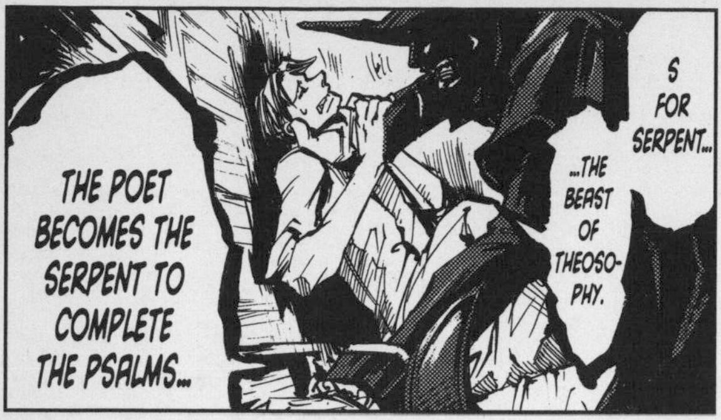
S FOR SERPENT...
...THE BEAST OF THEOSOPHY.
THE POET BECOMES THE SERPENT TO COMPLETE THE PSALMS...

Theosophy, *page 8*

Le Chevalier d'Eon draws on—and then transforms—numerous historical, religious, and Western cultural allusions in creating its unique mythology. So it's difficult to determine exactly what's intended by this reference to theosophy, which names not a single, coherent body of philosophical thought, but a body of vaguely related philosophical systems. Nearly any philosophy that promises knowledge of God through spiritual ecstasy, intuition, or personal revelation can be called theosophy (a word derived from the Greek for "wisdom of the divine")—which fits, in a twisted way, with the ambitions of the evil poets.

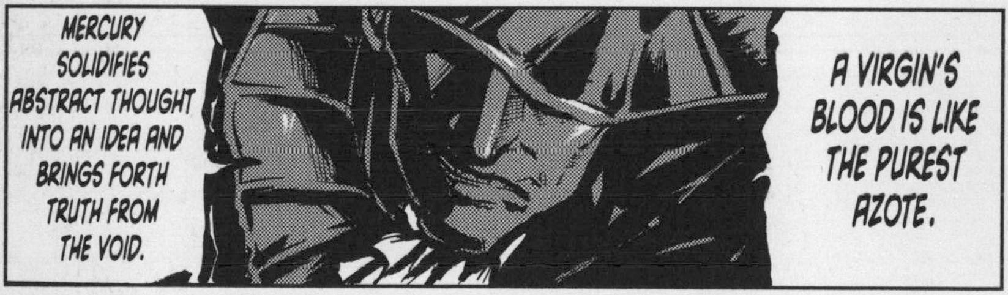
A VIRGIN'S BLOOD IS LIKE THE PUREST AZOTE.
MERCURY SOLIDIFIES ABSTRACT THOUGHT INTO AN IDEA AND BRINGS FORTH TRUTH FROM THE VOID.

Azote, *page 9*

Azote is French for nitrogen, though the Latin-derived name *nitrogène* was also later used. In 1789, the French chemist Antoine Lavoisier was the first to treat this substance as a separate element, which, since it doesn't contain oxygen and cannot support life, he named *azote* from two Greek roots that together mean "lifeless" or "without life."

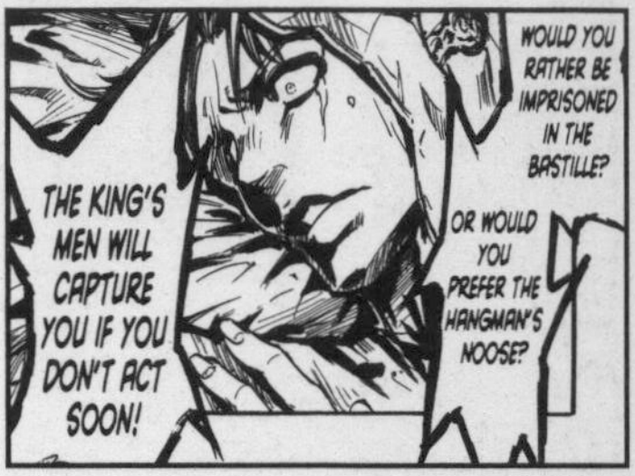
WOULD YOU RATHER BE IMPRISONED IN THE BASTILLE?
OR WOULD YOU PREFER THE HANGMAN'S NOOSE?
THE KING'S MEN WILL CAPTURE YOU IF YOU DON'T ACT SOON!

Bastille, *page 10*

Originally constructed as a fortress, then used as a castle, the Bastille was converted into a prison in the seventeenth century. But it is now perhaps most notorious for the events of July 14, 1789. On that day, a horde of commoners stormed the Bastille—an event that many historians believe marked the beginning of the French Revolution.

Gladiolus, *page 17*

By the early 1800s, the idea of using flowers to communicate secret messages, especially between lovers, was widespread throughout Europe. This was called "the language of flowers." However, though there have been many "authoritative" books on the subject, there is no general agreement on the meaning of each kind of flower. Here, the gladiolus means "secret rendezvous," but historically it has also meant "strength of character" and "remembrance."

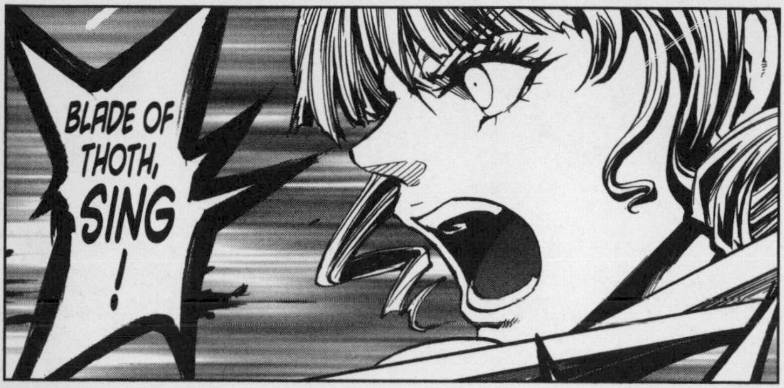
BLADE OF THOTH, SING!

Thoth, *page 24*

Thoth is in many ways an appropriate namesake for the Sphinx's sword. A god of the Egyptian pantheon, he was the creator of magic and the inventor of writing, as well as a divine messenger, recordkeeper, and mediator. Thoth was usually depicted in Egyptian sacred art as a man with the head of an ibis, holding a stylus and a scribe's plate.

Crucifixion, *page 53*

Le Chevalier d'Eon borrows heavily from Catholic iconography, appropriating some of its most potent images and ideas and incorporating them into its own imaginary mythology. In this dream sequence, the Chevalier Sphinx is crucified, recalling the crucifixion of Jesus Christ. Representations of crucifixion in Western culture usually carry tremendous symbolic and religious significance. When the image is used in a nonreligious context, the gesture can be interpreted as sacrilegious or, at the very least, iconoclastic. While this image may be shocking to many Western readers, it is considered to be much less so in Japan. In order to preserve the story's authenticity, and in deference to the creators' vision, we have chosen not to alter this image.

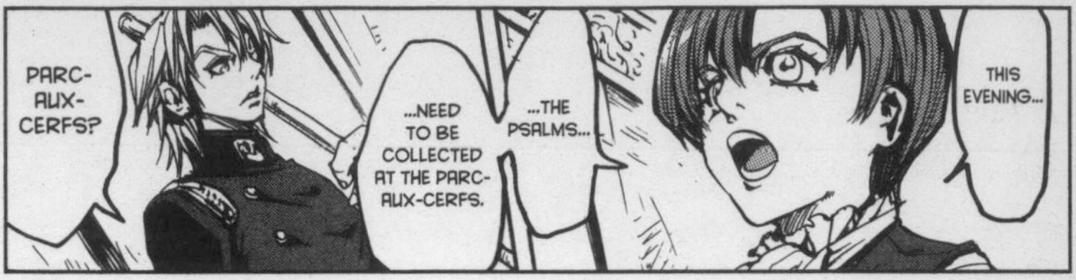
THIS EVENING...
...THE PSALMS...
...NEED TO BE COLLECTED AT THE PARC-AUX-CERFS.
PARC-AUX-CERFS?

Parc-aux-Cerfs, *page 66*

The name Parc-aux-Cerfs literally means "deer park" in French. Any clearing used as a hunting ground by the pre-Revolution aristocracy was given this generic name. And d'Eon is correct: Louis XV was known to hide his mistresses away in one particular Parc-aux-Cerfs.

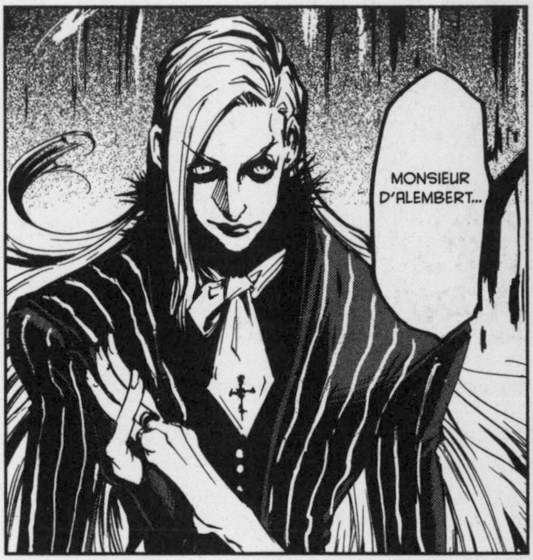
MONSIEUR D'ALEMBERT...

Jean Le Rond d'Alembert, *page 78*

D'Alembert is another figure taken from French history. The d'Alembert of our story espouses opinions that would almost be appropriate for the real d'Alembert. D'Alembert was one of the editors and writers of the famous *Dictionnaire raisonné des sciences, des arts, and des métiers*, the twenty-eight-volume encyclopedia he references on the next page. As a mathematician and philosopher, he was one of the great figures of the Enlightenment—and therefore an enemy of the church. But d'Alembert and his cohorts had many powerful supporters—including Madame de Pompadour (see notes for volume 1).

Adipocere, *page 86*

This is neither an anachronism or entirely a fantasy. This substance, also known as mortuary wax, was discovered by a French scientist in the eighteenth century. A residue from decomposing organic material, it can actually preserve a corpse for centuries, especially if the body is stored in a humid place.

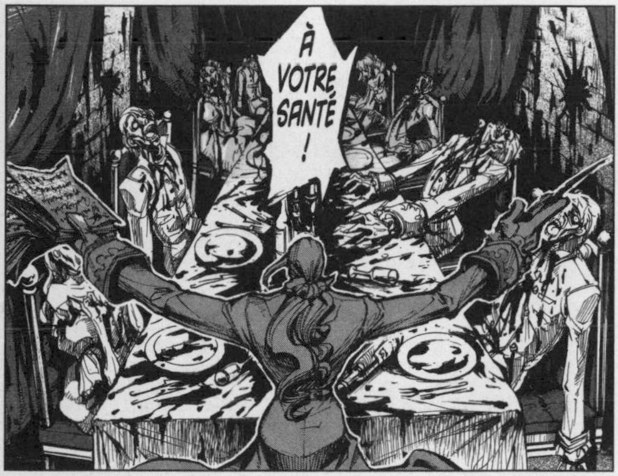
À VOTRE SANTÉ !

À votre santé, *page 99*

This French toast literally means "to your health."

Malcht, Yesod, Hod..., *page 108*

The poets' hierarchy is a perversion of the concept of the ten Sephirot (also Sephiroth or Sefirot) of the Jewish mystical system of Kabbalah. The Sephirot are the ten attributes of God through which he can manifest himself both physically and metaphysically. Though the poets' ranking borrows its names from Kabbalah, the attributes differ. For example, Hod traditionally stands for surrender, and Yesod for foundation.

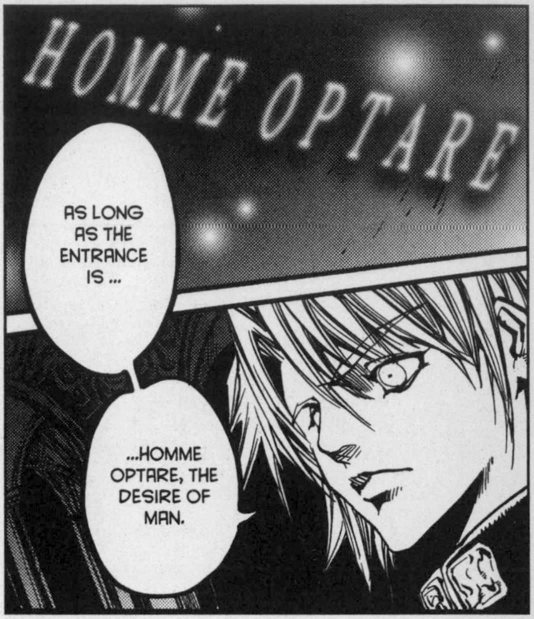
HOMME OPTARE
AS LONG AS THE ENTRANCE IS ...
...HOMME OPTARE, THE DESIRE OF MAN.

Homme optare, *page 110*

Homme is French for "man," and *optare* is Latin for "to wish." An approximate translation of this phrase, then, is "Desire of Man."

François de Robespierre, *page 113*

Though its significance is not yet explicit, Robin's real name is undeniably ominous. It immediately recalls Maximilien de Robespierre—the most notorious leader of the French Revolution. De Robespierre's unyielding purity of belief in the cause led to his playing a major role in the Reign of Terror, a period of revolutionary fervor during which thousands of people were executed by guillotine. Maximilien's father was named François de Robespierre.

PREVIEW OF VOLUME 3 OF

Le Chevalier d'Eon

We are pleased to present you with a preview
of volume 3. Please check our website
(www.delreymanga.com) to see when this
volume will be available in English. For now
you'll have to make do with the Japanese!

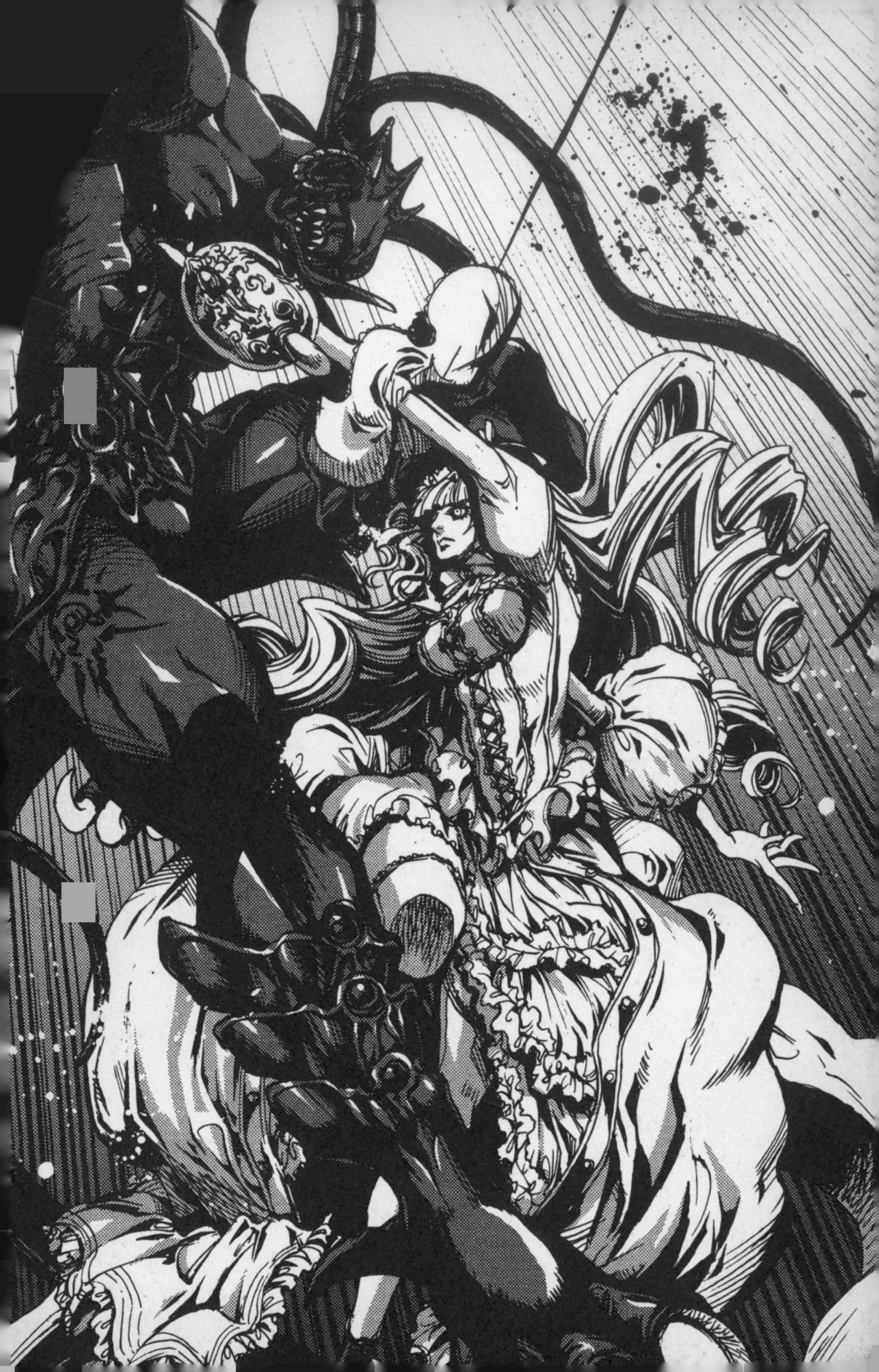

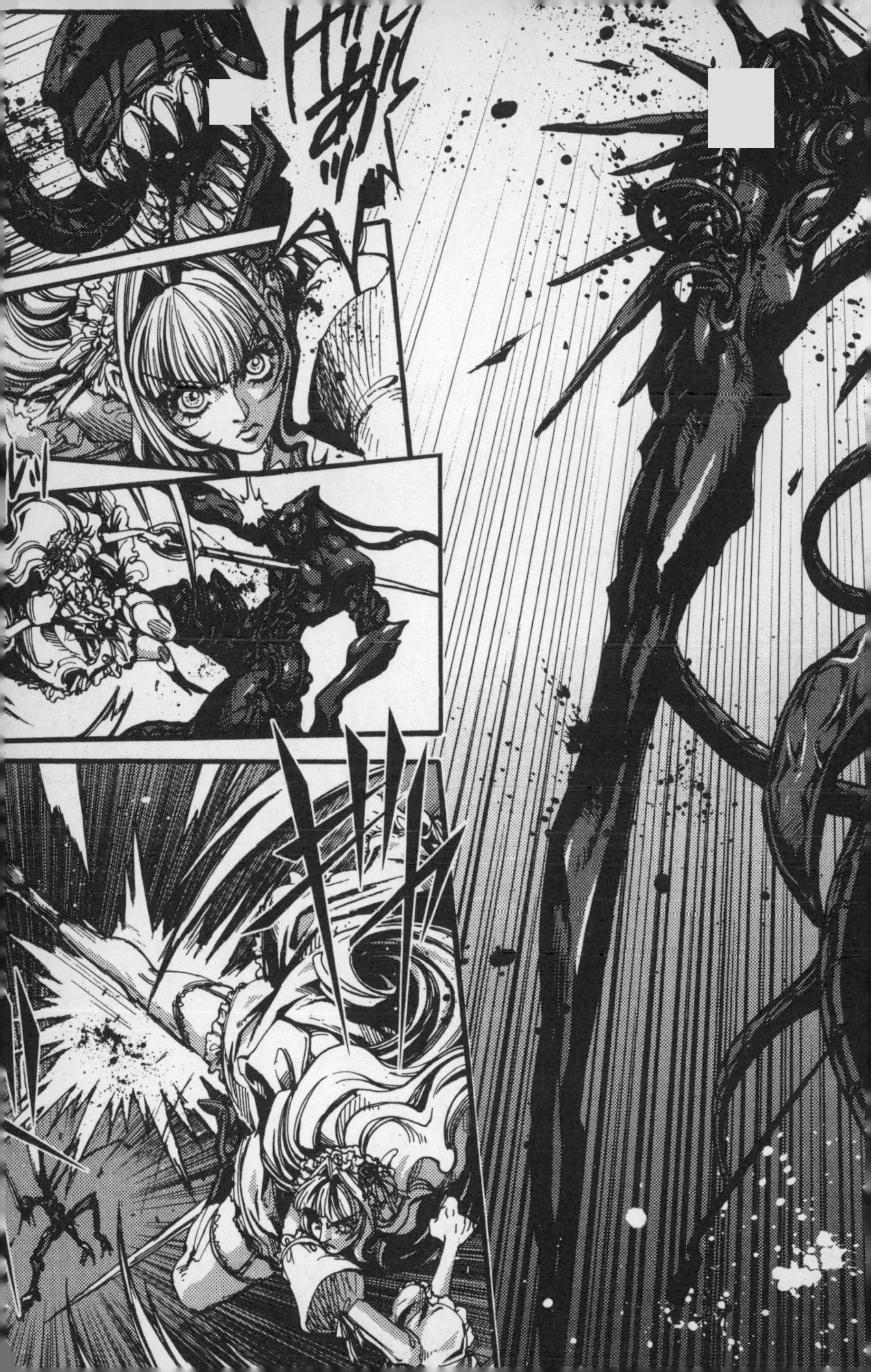

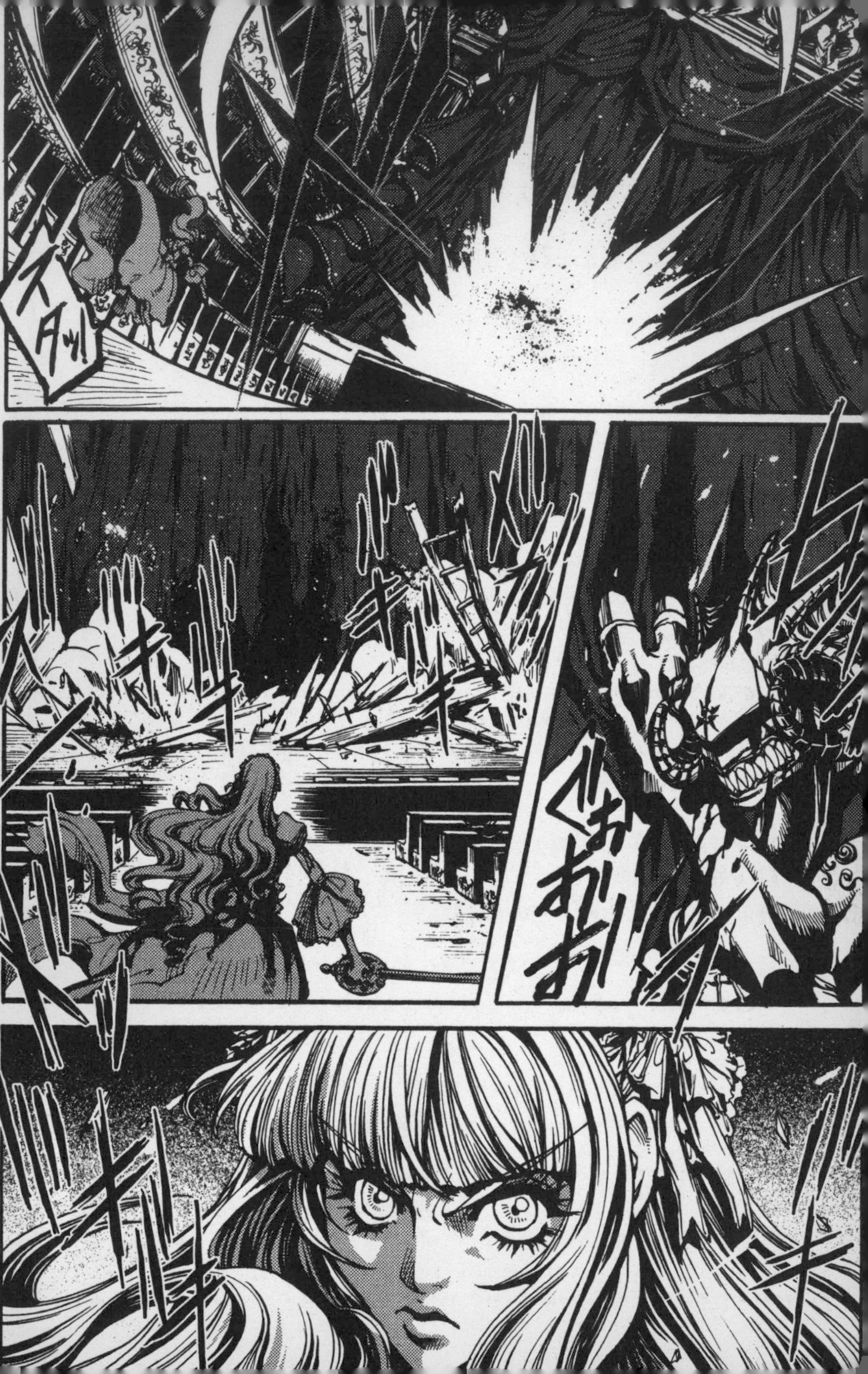
ズダッ!
くおおお

Tomare

YOU'RE GOING THE WRONG WAY!

MANGA IS A COMPLETELY DIFFERENT TYPE OF READING EXPERIENCE.

TO START AT THE BEGINNING, GO TO THE END!

That's Right!

AUTHENTIC MANGA IS READ THE TRADITIONAL JAPANESE WAY—FROM RIGHT TO LEFT, EXACTLY THE OPPOSITE OF HOW AMERICAN BOOKS ARE READ. IT'S EASY TO FOLLOW: JUST GO TO THE OTHER END OF THE BOOK, AND READ EACH PAGE —AND EACH PANEL—FROM RIGHT SIDE TO LEFT SIDE, STARTING AT THE TOP RIGHT. NOW YOU'RE EXPERIENCING MANGA AS IT WAS MEANT TO BE.